Ishi in Three Centuries

Ishi

in Three Centuries

EDITED BY KARL KROEBER
AND CLIFTON KROEBER

University of Nebraska Press Lincoln and London

Chapter 19, "Mister Ishi: Analogies of Exile,
Deliverance, and Liberty," © 2003 by Gerald
Vizenor.
Chapter 20, "Native Sovereignty and the Tricky
Mirror: Gerald Vizenor's 'Ishi and the Wood
Ducks,'" © 2003 by Louis Owens.
Chapter 21, "The Healer: Maidu Artist Frank
Day's Vision of Ishi," © 2003 by Rebecca
Dobkins.
Chapter 22, "What Wild Indian?" © 2003
by Frank Tuttle.
Acknowledgments for the use of previously
published material appear on pages 88
(Brandes), 193 (Shackley), and 300
(Luthin and Hinton).
Manufactured in the United States of America
∞
Library of Congress
Cataloging-in-Publication Data
Ishi in three centuries / edited by Karl Kroeber
and Clifton Kroeber.
p.   cm.
Includes bibliographical references and index.
ISBN-10: 0-8032-2725-4 (cl: alk. paper)
ISBN-13: 978-0-8032-2250-2 (pa: alk. paper)
1. Ishi, d. 1916. 2. Yana Indians—Social life
and customs. 3. Indians in popular culture—
United States. 4. Kroeber, A. L. (Alfred Louis),
1876–1960—Relations with Yana Indians.
5. Human remains (Archaeology)—Moral and
ethical aspects—United States. 6. Museum
exhibits—moral and ethical aspects—United
States. 7. Cultural property—Repatriation—
United States. I. Kroeber, Karl, 1926– II.
Kroeber, Clifton B.
E99.Y23 .1784 2003
979.4004'9757—dc21
2002035653

Frontispiece: Ishi during a trip to San Jose.
Reproduced from the *San Jose Daily Mercury*,
November 11, 1911.
Photos of Ishi on the part-opening pages are
courtesy of Phoebe Apperson Hearst Museum
of Anthropology and the Regents of the
University of California.

Contents

Acknowledgments

We wish to thank Therese Babineau, Curator of Photography Phoebe A. Hearst Museum, University of California, Berkeley; Lisa Miller, Archivist, National Archives and Records Administration (Pacific Region), San Bruno, California; Mary Frances Morrow, Reference Archivist, National Archives and Records Administration, Washington, DC; David Farrell and Lori Hines, Curators, Bancroft Library, University of California, Berkeley; Brea Black, Library Intern, California Historical Society, San Francisco, California; John de la Fontaine and Andrea Phillips, Reference Librarians, Occidental College Library, Los Angeles, California, for their generous help, without which we would have been unable to recover much of the new knowledge about Ishi's life and circumstances contained in this volume. We are also grateful, for their help on a variety of details, to Alan and Paul Kroeber; to Don Blades of Rutland, Vermont, for assistance with photographs; and to Katharine Wiley, for drawing the sketch map of San Francisco when Ishi lived there.

Editors' Introduction

The Yahi Indian known as Ishi, born about 1860, lived from 1870 to 1911 in the foothills of Mount Lassen with a few fellow tribe members, concealing themselves from surrounding whites. These Indians, who conducted their lives much as their ancestors had for thousands of years, hid themselves because white settlers and gold miners during the 1860s had systematically murdered all the Yahi they could find. After all the other members of these secret survivors had died, Ishi emerged from his long concealment in 1911 and was given refuge in the Anthropological Museum of the University of California in San Francisco, of which Alfred Kroeber was the director. There Ishi lived until his death from tuberculosis in 1916. In 1961 Theodora Kroeber, Alfred Kroeber's widow, published Ishi's forgotten history in *Ishi in Two Worlds,* an enormously popular book that has since been translated into more than a dozen languages.

The book helped California Indians to demand that public officials allow repatriation of Ishi's remains in his native land. This movement intensified in the late 1990s with the discovery that Ishi's brain had not been cremated in 1916 with the rest of his body but was preserved in the Smithsonian Institution in Washington DC. Responding to pressure from California Indians, the state government finally took legal steps to allow the Pit River Rancheria to receive for interment Ishi's ashes and brain, which the Smithsonian offered to this tribal group in 1999. This interment was carried out in August 2000 in an unpublicized place so as to forestall invasions by curiosity seekers and tourists.

In the spring of 1999 Karl Kroeber had written to Stanley Brandes, the chair of the Anthropology Department of the University of California at Berkeley, offering to testify at any appropriate venue that his parents, Alfred and Theodora Kroeber, would certainly have favored the repatriation of all remains of Ishi. Only with the reply of Professor Brandes did any member of our family learn that the Berkeley Anthropology Department, which Alfred Kroeber helped to found in 1901 and in which he served until his retirement in 1947, was debating the demand of a faction led by Professor Nancy Scheper-Hughes that the department ask the University of California to issue a public apology for the treatment of Ishi by Alfred Kroeber and other anthropologists during Ishi's years at the museum – first suggesting that the name of the building in which the department is housed, Kroeber Hall, might be changed, since, as one draft of the resolution asserted, "Kroeber's behavior to Ishi was indefensible." (See the contribution of Professor Scheper-Hughes to this volume, Chapter 8.) After several departmental meetings a much revised resolution was passed and published in the *Anthropological Newsletter* (Chapter 6, this volume). Some departmental members, however, although regretting that Ishi's brain had been sent to the Smithsonian, and favoring repatriation of Ishi's remains (we know of no academic anywhere who at any time has opposed Ishi's repatriation), felt that condemnation of anthropologists at the Museum was unjustified by the historical facts.

The account by Professor Emeritus George Foster, a former chair of the Berkeley anthropology department (Chapter 7), tells the story of the departmental controversy, which dramatizes the continuing power of Ishi's history to evoke passionate feelings and complex moral questionings.

This volume brings together the most important facts that have been learned about Ishi's experiences since the publication of Theodora Kroeber's book, which has remained the primary information source for commentators popular and professional. The essays collected also suggest what kinds of further historical research are needed to reach as comprehensive an understanding as possible of Ishi the man and his significance today for all of us, not just Indians. This seems especially important because claims that Ishi was treated with callous insensitivity by anthropologists have encouraged sensational media stories implying a sinister cabal of scientists dedicated (for unexplained reasons) to concealing some (mysterious and unspecified) facts about Ishi. We hope to forestall further such exploitations of Ishi by demonstrating that depicting him as mere victim does an injustice to the moral courage and spiritual vitality which makes him – both as an individual and as a representative of his wantonly destroyed culture – so admirable and exemplary a figure to so many people almost a century after his death. Descriptions of how he behaved under conditions of almost unbelievable psychic stress, along with records of stories he told, enable us to understand what Ishi does and might mean, not just for Native Americans, but for all of us in the twenty-first century.

We therefore begin this collection with the longest extant report of anyone who personally knew Ishi, Fred H. Zumwalt Jr.'s heretofore unpublished account of his childhood friendship with Ishi in San Francisco (Chapter 1). The memoir was evoked by the publication of *Ishi in Two Worlds* in 1961, which is referred to in almost every essay in this volume, not only because it has been the principal source of knowledge about Ishi for forty years but also because it anticipates central features of "Sixties culture" by illuminating the changes taking place in the late 1950s in the circumstances of Native Americans and in American anthropology. At that time American Indians were beginning to recover, economically, educationally, politically, and culturally, from the devastations wrought by the savage white conquest of their continent. This Indian Renaissance coincided with the petering out of traditional Boasian "salvage" anthropology, which had emerged sixty years earlier through the inspiration of Franz Boas as a reaction against the extermination of Native peoples. By 1890 most of the more than 400 distinct cultures that had flourished in North America before the arrival of Columbus had been annihilated or pushed to the edge of extinction. Boasians, developing the anti-Enlightenment conception of the eighteenth-century German Johann Herder, insisted that *every* human culture was precious because unique. The traditional history and language of each distinct Indian culture, however small its population and materially unimpressive, deserved respectful attention as a singular achievement of the human spirit. "Salvage anthropology" directly challenged modernist celebrations of abstract "primitivism," Freudian claims for metacultural psychological universals, and the United States' self-justification as the "American melting pot."

When the few dozen Boasians a century ago began to save as much as possible of the multitude of Indian languages and traditional cultures, many Indians also believed their heritages were doomed to extinction. They welcomed attempts to save records of their life ways and languages. This attitude, understandably, Ishi shared. By the late 1950s, however, attitudes of both Indians and anthropologists had changed. Boasians like Robert Heizer began to add to concern for the past new concern for current Indian conditions. Indian populations and self-respect, if not their economic well-being, were on the rise, and they began to gain legal redress for past injustices. Illustrative of these improvements were the California Indian Land Claims Commission hearings in the mid-1950s. The Indians won this case, opening the way for subsequent land claims successfully prosecuted by Indians through American courts. More than fifty white anthropologists participated in the California hearings, many of them for the first time actively involving themselves in the Indians' current concerns. Alfred Kroeber, asked as the leading authority on traditional California Indian cultural history to appear as an expert witness for the Federal Government against the native claimants, chose instead to testify at length for the Indians.

His effectiveness as a witness for the Indians depended upon his extraordinary knowledge of Indians' *past* history, the principal focus of all his scholarship.[1] In writing *Ishi in Two Worlds,* analogously, his wife conceived her primary task as recovering some understanding of the cultural heritage that enabled Ishi not to be overwhelmed or humanly diminished by his terrible personal experience in the late nineteenth and early twentieth centuries. As she wrote her first book at the age of sixty, she became progressively more absorbed in trying to recover something of the uniqueness of Ishi's personality as expressive of a cruelly destroyed culture. That concentration explains both her book's limitations and its emotional power.

When she wrote, there were few popular accounts of the extermination of Native peoples, and her story of the killing of the Yahi remains one of the most damning histories of these slaughters – in part because, avoiding abstract words such as "genocide," she keeps the story agonizingly particularized. She never lets readers conceal from themselves the primary horror of such events, that is, the maiming and murdering and enslaving of individuals. This links her book to the emergence at the beginning of the 1960s of antipathy toward ethnic injustices, a revulsion that helped to energize the Civil Rights movement.

Ishi in Two Worlds, however, is free from ideological didacticism. It concentrates on Ishi's personality. It sensitively evokes his intimate connection to the land his people inhabited. Theodora Kroeber knew the country at first hand, and she came from a family that, through its miners, ranchers, farmers, and shopkeepers, as well as their wives, in one fashion or another had lived in close contact with the lands of the western United States. Her reconstruction of Ishi's life of concealment carries conviction because her experience included long acquaintance with a natural world that is no refuge from urbanization, not a place to be visited briefly to watch exotic Indian activities, but a living environment that determines how daily one works and feels and imagines.

She also understood the exterminators. Her family background made her familiar with the cattlemen, farmhands, lawmen, bounty hunters, miners, drifters, and the rest, who conducted the massacres and private killings. The ghastliness of these events is that they are carried out not by alien monsters but by people shockingly like you and me. This is why their actions are so fearful. As long as we can think impersonally of crimes of Nazis, or Turks, or Stalinists, or Mongol hordes, we shield ourselves from confronting the hideous fact that particular men do these murders, men who may well be hard-working and keep their promises, love their wives, and are conscientious in rearing their children.

Because Theodora Kroeber knew how easy it is to oversimplify the inner life of any human being, her account of Ishi consistently reminds us of his ultimate core of personality we can never know. She makes readers feel the enigmaticness of Ishi's peculiarly terrible personal experience (including what she describes as his sexual starvation), but his special experience and his belonging to an alien culture, the sensational aspects of his history, never obscure his mysteriousness simply as a complex human being. But Boasian anthropology encouraged Theodora Kroeber to contextualize the darkening history of the Yahi and Ishi with the bright if distant glow of the long, long prehistory of all California Indians, "copper colored people on a golden land." Awareness of this long success of his tiny culture deepens the sadness of Ishi's story: we feel in the death of the man the disappearance of thousands of years of Yahi family life and society. Simultaneously, however, the evocation of ancient culture helps to explain how Ishi could with such swiftness adapt to the modern urban world, and how he could resist being made into a mere marginalized person, or being driven into self-pity or resentment. He was an irrefragably civilized man. At his first formal dinner in San Francisco, just days away from the Oroville jail, he made no mistakes in etiquette. His culture put a high premium on mannerly behavior. Saxton Pope's daughter remembers from having meals with Ishi when she was a child how good his manners were, even as he behaved at table with energetic spontaneity – making no secret, for example, of his fondness for the jelly her mother served.

Ishi in Two Worlds dramatizes through Ishi's personal experience how radically different cultures may both conflict and reinforce one another. Thus in the Hearst Museum Ishi found himself among people who were congenial to a man whose culture was founded on the pleasure of familiar social tasks neatly and efficiently carried out, and where hand-wrought artifacts were highly valued and meticulously cared for. Ishi, however, was troubled at learning that the Museum contained human bones, and distressed by the preservation of dead bodies in the hospital morgue. Yet he was fascinated by what he saw when Pope invited him into the operating room to observe close-up his surgery. Unlike most of us today, Ishi was experienced at butchery and dissection – for example, to obtain sinew – and so could more knowledgeably than most of us appreciate the value of Pope's skill as a modern surgeon.

Theodora Kroeber's attention to Ishi as active participant, whether his particular experience involved revulsion, bafflement, curiosity, or quiet pleasure, doubtless led to her ignoring possibilities of discovering current insights into Ishi's culture that might have been gleaned in the 1950s from Northern California native peoples – not only from Yana descendants (by the time she wrote there were no longer any *speakers* of Yana) but also from neighboring tribes. Such findings would now be of particular interest, since Indian attitudes toward Ishi have changed over the past four decades. As the essay of Karen Biestman points out (Chapter 10), there would have been more to be learned about Ishi from living Native Northern Californians than Theodora Kroeber realized – and something of what she missed this volume attempts to supply, even while continuing her efforts to delineate, as clearly as the blurred and eroded evidence allows, a chiaroscuro portrait of a strong man of good will, generosity, and patience, yet volatile and characterized by what she aptly calls *élan* – a man who underwent an experience for most of us nearly unimaginable, but which her account makes almost too poignantly imaginable. This focus of *Ishi in Two Worlds* accounts for the extraordinary personal quality of the book's reception on publication (as well as its translation into so many languages). All kinds of people telephoned Theodora Kroeber, wrote her letters, or appeared at her front door to tell her how much the book had affected them. Most valuable today are reports of people who had as children known Ishi in San Francisco.

To appreciate fully Ishi's amazing ability to create such friendships as he did with the Zumwalt family as well as the Museum staff, however, one must understand the terrible condition of all California Indians at the beginning of the twentieth century. The 1906 report of Charles Kelsey (see the Appendix for extracts) is a comprehensive account of the terrible effects of anti-Indian prejudice that reveals the origins and development of a 150-year-long history of abuse and mistreatment of Native Californians by the state's white population and its political leaders. From the time when California became a state, treatment of Native peoples by white citizenry that was brutal, contemptuous, and unfair was encouraged by officials of the California State Government and local politicians. Native Americans have been very badly treated in every part of America, but it is not easy to find a state with a more appalling record than California's.

Ishi's history, therefore, can foster keener understanding of current circumstances and attitudes of Native Californians by increasing our knowledge of the atrocious mistreatment they have suffered for so long. Ishi's Yahi people were singled out for specially savage extermination because (along with their kin the Yana) they chose not to accept passively the massive white invasions of their ancestral land. Like the Sioux and the Apache, they fought the invaders. They defended their homeland with skill, persistence, and courage, even though they possessed no weapons – their small hunting bows were all they had to defend what Alfred Kroeber called "the last free nation in the world."

Their resistive spirit is evoked in the first popular dramatization of what was to become California's extended history of maltreating nonwhites, especially Indians and Mexicans. This is the first novel published by a Native American, *Joaquin Murietta* (1854), by John Rollin Ridge, a Cherokee who wrote copiously in San Francisco, often under the name of Yellowbird. The novel depicts the rapacious brutality of the Anglo-Americans of the new state, who with the connivance of state officials stole the property of Native Californians, and killed them under the pretense that they were "criminals" (see the contribution of Justice Gary Strankman, Chapter 18). The protagonist of Ridge's novel, Joaquin Murietta (who may or may not have been a real person), is a Native Californian driven to Robin Hood-like banditry by these abuses, and his adventurous life becomes the means for Ridge to display the brutal oppressions by Anglo whites of all California Native peoples.

Ridge's still impressive 150-year-old novel of protest suggests how profitable it might be for our society to recognize why individuals nurtured by American Indian cultures resist and reject many aspects of contemporary society – and so effectively demonstrate by their personal behavior the contrastive value of cultures of limited material strength but more supportive of the dignity of all individuals and of mutuality of respect in all interpersonal relations. For this purpose we believe there could be no better exemplar than Ishi. This is why the individuality of Ishi the man deserves to be rescued from every kind of ideological polemics. The story of his life is an inspiriting one, even though his life was terrible. Few if any of us can even faintly imagine enduring the long concealment and the gradual loss of one's entire family and people, knowing that with one's own death will come to an end a cherished culture, developed and refined and enjoyed over the course of thousands of years. We hope to increase appreciation of Ishi's ability to carry that special burden (which is a burden to a lesser degree borne by all American Indians) with grace and a generosity of spirit whose attractiveness can still be felt a century after his death. To that end we have gathered at least a partially representative sample of commentary on Ishi's life and its meaning by Native Americans, for whom he has during the past forty years become increasingly the sharpest focus for creating respect for all Indian ways of life.

We also include reproductions of paintings by Native California artists of Ishi that suggest his continuing inspirational effect in the new century. These accompany a reemergence of Ishi's own language and voice. Thanks to efforts of dedicated scholars such as Ira Jacknis (Chapter 14), accessible to us and those who come after are recordings of Ishi's voice, singing and telling stories. We present translations and analyses of some of these stories (Chapters 15, 16, and 17), believing that they will encourage more translations and wider readership for these fascinating revelations of Ishi's inner life. His songs and stories are not curiosities. They are more vital even than the photographs of him, for, besides their spiritual resonances, they are artistic performances. They convey to us themes and forms of Yahi singing and storytelling, not as abstractions, but as performed by a unique individual. If we give them the attention they deserve, the songs and stories will allow both essential forms of Yahi culture and the special vitality of Ishi the man to enter into and enrich our imaginative capacities.

NOTE

1. Omer C. Stewart ["Kroeber and the Land Claims Commission," *The Kroeber Anthropological Society Papers* 25 (1961), 181–190] describes how Kroeber (then nearing 80) spoke or submitted to cross-examination for three hours a day for

ten days: "It was a masterful performance by a gifted scientist and talented, energetic scholar. Because of timing and emphasis, change of pace, and dozens of other practices which kept the interest of the Commissioners and others in the court room, Kroeber was an exceptionally impressive witness." Stewart points out that Kroeber, with the aid of Robert Heizer and a team of graduate students, had prepared by reviewing and revising his earlier ethnographic studies. Stewart's account of these hearings (in which he participated) provides a cogent assessment of the case's importance as a turning point both for Indians and the anthropological profession.

Ishi in Three Centuries

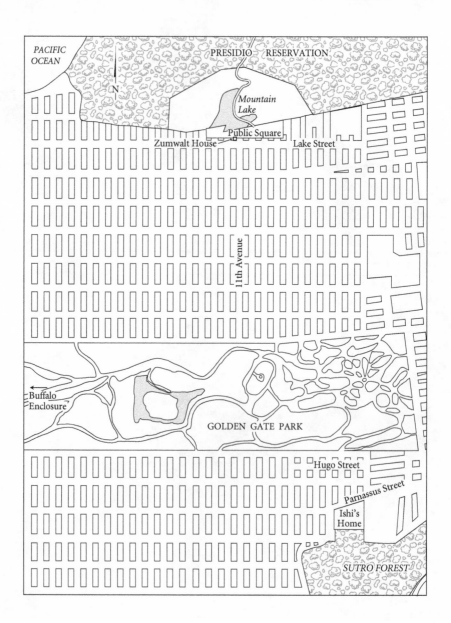

Map: The San Francisco of Ishi.

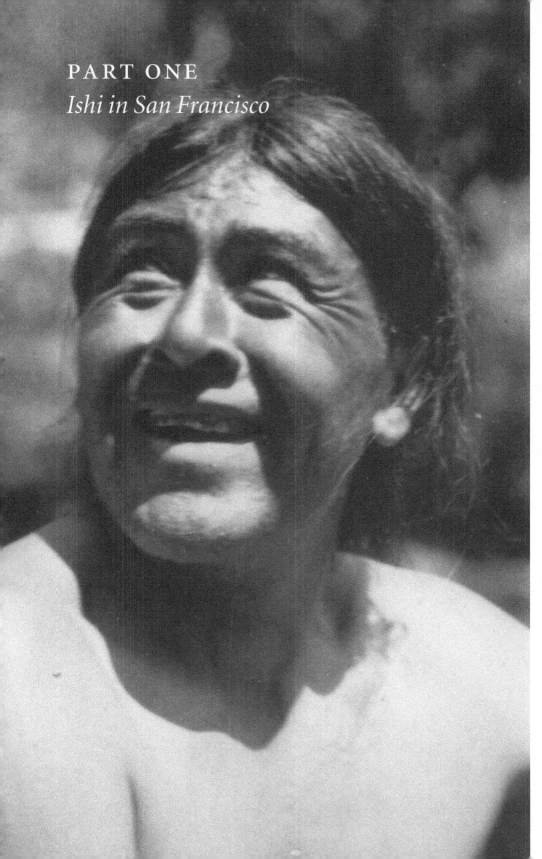

PART ONE
Ishi in San Francisco

Previous page. Ishi at Mill Creek, 1914.

Ishi at the University of California, Berkeley, 1911 [1912?].

Introduction to Part One

CLIFTON KROEBER

In September 1911 the Bureau of Indian Affairs sent Special Agent Charles Earl Kelsey to visit Ishi at the Anthropological Museum in San Francisco to make it clear to Ishi that he was free to return to his native country or to remove to a reservation if he so desired. Ishi rejected both options, saying, "I want to stay where I now am. I will grow old here, and die in this house." And, indeed, the remainder of Ishi's life was spent in San Francisco with the Museum as his home. The circumstances surrounding his emphatic choice need to be understood.

Although Kelsey met Ishi for the first time that September (and later entertained him at his home in San José, as well as visiting him subsequently at the Museum), he was well prepared for the encounter, since he had been planning to search for his people. In March 1911 Alfred Kroeber had written the Commissioner of Indian Affairs, reporting on the evidence of the survival of a remnant of a small group of Yana Indians who had hidden themselves for many years. He told of the Museum's sending T. T. Waterman with J. W. Hunt and Merle Apperson in October–November 1910 into Yana country to discover and open communications with these people. Kroeber urged the Bureau to continue this initiative (Kroeber 1911a).

In April the commissioner charged Kelsey to pursue the matter (Hauke 1911a), and Kelsey soon reported that promising preliminary inquiries led him to request authorization to spend $100 he believed would be necessary to "open negotiations" with the "wild" Indians in Tehama County (Kelsey 1911a). By the time the $100 in expenses was authorized, but before Kelsey set off, Ishi had revealed himself and had been brought to San Francisco.

In choosing Kelsey to search for the concealed Indian survivors, and then in authorizing him to offer Ishi freedom to live where he chose, the commissioner was relying on the official in the Bureau who had the deepest knowledge of the condition of California Indians at the time – a man who had unparalleled personal experience of the contemporary life of virtually every tribal group of Native Californians and had written extensively and eloquently on the practical and moral obligation of the government to redress the atrocious wrongs suffered by California Indians. Kelsey, by profession a lawyer practicing in San José, was a key figure in the Northern California Indian Association, an organization of white people that had come into being to improve the lot of Native Californians, for whom Kelsey had petitioned President Theodore Roosevelt in 1903 for aid in ameliorating Indian sufferings. Kelsey later played a role in obtaining from Congress an appropriation of $100,000 to benefit California Indians. He was appointed Special Agent for the Bureau of Indian Affairs and in 1906 conducted a study for the Bureau (demanded by Congress) on the condition of California's native people. After personally visiting every one of the fifty-five California counties in which Indians then lived, Kelsey wrote a report (from which we present a few extracts in Appendix 1 of this volume) that is the most complete, best informed, and cogently specific contemporary account of the miserable circumstances of California Indians at the time Ishi came out of hiding. This remarkable document is essential to understanding why Ishi chose to live the last years of his life in the Museum, even though anthropologists there were at first unsure it was the best home for him; later they made unusual efforts to accommodate his special needs (see Chapter 4 of this volume).

Reporting to the Bureau of Indian Affairs on September 6 on his meeting with Ishi, Kelsey conveyed Ishi's decision to remain at the Museum, and went on to observe that "it is rather a puzzle to know what to do with him," because he should not be returned "to the wilderness to live as he has done," yet he was totally "unacquainted with the ways of the white man." Kelsey speculated that it was conceivable that Ishi could be placed with "the few remaining Indians of Yana stock" near Redding, who might be willing, if paid a monthly stipend for the service, to let Ishi live among them (Kelsey 1911b). In his 1906 report, however, he had described the sanitary conditions of the Indian rancherias as bad and "the feeling of helplessness and despair is worse," while judging the California reservation system "an evil to be eliminated as fast as conditions warrant" (Kelsey 1906).

Kelsey's report on Ishi was supported by a thoughtful letter to the commissioner written by Charles L. Davis, who was a supervisor for farming for the Bureau and who, having read newspaper accounts of Ishi's arrival in San Francisco, took it upon himself to investigate Ishi's situation. Davis was impressed that at the Museum Ishi was being "cared for in the best manner possible" and was already demonstrating his "desire to remain with his new acquaintances"(Davis 1911).

In late October the commissioner's office responded to these letters by re-

questing Kelsey to ask Kroeber about the possibility of training Ishi "to conform, at least to a reasonable degree, to the customs of civilized life" (Hauke
1911c). Having received Kroeber's report on Ishi's life at the Museum, on December 16 (by which time Ishi had apparently also visited with him in San José)
Kelsey advised the commissioner:

> Ishi has been living at the museum since his capture. Living without effort is ap-
> parently satisfactory to him and he shows no apparent desire to get away or to re-
> turn to the wilds. The change from manzanita berries to three square meals a day
> has increased Ishi's avoirdupois by more than fifty pounds. . . . He was given care
> of the Egyptian room and has since helped the janitor in other parts of the build-
> ing. . . . The Indian has done a fair amount of work for his keep and does it fairly
> well. He seems intelligent and willing. But . . . I do not see that he is any nearer self-
> support than he was at the start. (Kelsey 1911c)

Kelsey concluded by observing that although Ishi was "welcome at the museum," the Museum might not indefinitely be financially able to "give him an
opportunity to earn his living," but that until such time (which of course never
came), Ishi's situation should not be unacceptable to the Bureau.[1]

The Commissioner accepted Kelsey's advice and made no further inquiries
about Ishi until May 1914. Then John W. Clark, the Executive Secretary of the
National Indian Association in New York, had written the Commissioner that a
friend had recently visited in San Francisco and feared that "no effort was being
made to teach him [Ishi] anything useful, or to Christianize him." Clark proposed that Ishi be relocated among the "advanced tribe" of the Kiowa at Saddle
Mountain, Oklahoma (Clark 1914). The Commissioner's Office asked Kroeber
to report on Ishi's situation. Kroeber (1914) replied in June:

> Ishi has taken readily to civilization and has been self-supporting for over a year,
> serving as assistant janitor and general helper about the Museum. His age appears
> to be between fifty and fifty-five; and he has learned English slowly, but frequently
> succeeds in making himself understood in a broken manner. Every month, how-
> ever, is adding slowly to his command of the language. His ignorance of civilized
> life was complete, but his mental development was in no sense stunted or sub-
> normal. He has picked up practical matters with the utmost quickness. He has
> been free to return to his old home and manner of living ever since being with us,
> but much prefers his present condition.

The Commissioner's Office then replied, rather dryly, to Clark and his friend
that, judging from Kroeber's report on Ishi, "there would appear to be doubts
as to the advisability of removing him, as suggested" (Commissioner of Indian

Affairs 1914). So far as I know, this was the last official notice taken of Ishi by the Bureau of Indian Affairs.

But there does exist a substantial body of information about his life at the Museum and in the San Francisco Bay area, although there is much that we do not know. One circumstance that should not be overlooked is that, although the Museum had been founded by Mrs. Hearst a decade earlier, and funded by her until 1908 (when it became a state-supported institution), it was opened to the general public only in October 1911, a scant month after Ishi's arrival. The earliest receptions he attended, in fact, were in celebration of the Museum's opening to the public, and although Ishi was a significant attraction for a while, it was the display of the collections from all over the world that made the Museum intensely popular with San Franciscans and tourists. During its first decade it attracted between ten and thirty thousand visitors annually.

Despite the assiduous research of Grace Buzaljko, among others, we will never be able to feel all that life was for Ishi, and what for him it was not, while he lived at the Museum. Some of Ishi's Yahi values and behaviors, talents, and interests were obvious enough to his friends there, as when he was working expertly at one of his handicrafts. Other Yahi life ways he did not continue; for example, he refused to wear Yahi clothing in San Francisco. He adopted some Anglo-American ways of doing, such as sitting up to the table in a chair and eating from plates with metal utensils. Other ways, however, such as shaking hands, he resisted to the end. He would not be cozened into acquiring facile, idiomatic English.

The chapters in this section offer suggestions about Ishi's inner life. It is well worth the effort to peer beneath and beyond Theodora Kroeber's sensitive portrayal of the man forty years ago, to get a little closer to how Ishi lived and may have thought during those four and a half years in San Francisco – even though we will never truly be able to enter his feelings or to agree about the evidence. Rachel Adams in her fine essay (Chapter 2) on Ishi's visit to the vaudeville, for instance, describes the photograph of him at the box in the Orpheum Theater along with Lily Lena as depicting Ishi's "visible discomfort as he grins nervously." Others, contrarily, have commented on how the picture shows surprisingly relaxed hands and a cheerful smile. There is no dispute, however, that Ishi was very intelligent, which shows in his constant vigilance, his close observation of all and everyone about him. Does this explain why he seems to have adjusted to his new life so rapidly, soon going out alone on streetcars, walking the streets crowded with people? These multitudes of human beings had at first appalled and frightened him, but surprisingly quickly the metropolitan overpopulation ceased to be of concern.

He had his reasons for wanting to abide in the Museum, as Waterman discovered when the scientists had suggested a visit to Ishi's homeland in 1914. Ishi, says Waterman (1918), "filed a number of objections. One was that in the hills there were no chairs. A second was, that there were no houses or beds. A third was, that there was very little to eat." He had been cold and gone empty so often, in the hills, that he had few illusions left. But once they did make the trip, "he proved to be a fine companion. He could swim and wash dishes and skylark with anybody, and outwalk everybody" (Waterman 1918). When the city people killed and skinned a rattlesnake and set out to cook it, however, he vigorously warned them not to risk ill fortune that could attend such conduct. Ishi was not indulging a quaint superstition. To Ishi, as to most Native Americans, humankind shares the world with other creatures. One does not gratuitously molest others, and relations with different creatures (deer and rattlesnakes, for instance) demand mutuality of respect, as among people. Is there a hint here of Ishi's skills in adapting to city life?

It is probably significant that, as Grace Buzaljko shows, Ishi became firm friends with the very different personalities among whom he lived at the Museum, yet he did not warm up to people of other tribes who visited. He was certainly not comfortable with the Yana, Sam Batwi (differences between the two are revealed in the contrast of stories offered by Hinton and Luthin in this volume, Chapter 17). Ishi seems truly to have been at ease with only one other Indian (Juan Dolores), although he met several at the Museum and elsewhere. The reason for this bias we will probably never know, although we can count on plenty of speculation.

As for his readiness to adopt many citified ways and talents and habits while rejecting some and passing others by, it is tempting to believe that Ishi at once picked up any talent or tool that would help him in what he saw worth doing. He quickly seized on any material or instrument that would do better or quicker practical work. He preferred glass to obsidian when flaking arrow points. He took up all the metal and wooden hand tools the Museum people used, if they simplified his handiwork. Furthermore, as demonstrated in Ira Jacknis' essay (Chapter 14), Ishi was willing to undergo long recording sessions, required by the primitive equipment of those days, in order to preserve Yahi songs and stories. From this perspective it is particularly interesting that he did not care to go far into English, not much beyond the five to six hundred words Sapir believed he commanded (with many more he understood but never used). Victor Golla, discussing Ishi's language (Chapter 13) notices that Ishi did not bother to learn to read English beyond simple signs and the numbers on streetcars he rode and on clock faces.

Ishi's practicality may explain why he seems to have become surprisingly confident and serene in his new world, and was able to take pleasure in companionship of various kinds. Waterman (1918) noticed that "he liked everybody and everybody liked him. I think that the closing years of his life were far the happiest of his life." That is difficult to know. Warburton's care for him during his long final illness suggests a companionship between two men, very different but equally skilled with their hands, who needed few words. Yet Jace Weaver (Chapter 3) speculates not unreasonably that Ishi must often have felt isolated and alone at the Museum. It appears, however, that Ishi experienced isolation and loneliness while hiding in his native country. Either way, there is a temptation toward romantic falsification. All that we can be sure of is that whatever he may have taken on from his new cultural world, and whatever of it he rejected, Ishi's going was a deep and irreparable loss to many white people whom he had so strongly affected during the final years of his life at the museum.

It is especially because Ishi was not confined within the Museum, either by the jobs for which he was paid or by his sessions with the anthropologists, that one wishes to know more about his daily life. He was encouraged to go out and around as much as he wished. He shopped along Seventh Street. He traveled out to Golden Gate Park to see the herd of bison there. He rode the trolley down to the Ferry Building, took the ferry across to Oakland, and then rode the trolley again to the end of the line, which left him a couple of blocks from the Berkeley campus. Matthew Stirling, who later became a professional anthropologist, recalled in the 1960s that as a high school student he had been a friend of Ishi, and how once, as they were riding together on a trolley, Ishi had coolly taken out a pair of wooden tweezers to pull hairs from his chin, the Yana mode of shaving (Stirling 1968:12). He visited frequently with students of the dental college, allowing repeated examinations and impressions to be taken of his mouth, apparently to please his hosts. He foregathered often with students of the medical school, sharing lunch and games with them and showing some how to use bow and arrow.

The richest evidence on Ishi's life in San Francisco is provided by those who became acquainted with him when they were children, as is demonstrated by Fred Zumwalt Jr.'s evocative memoir (Chapter 1). We know of these friendships only because Theodora Kroeber's *Ishi in Two Worlds* evoked responses from people who had known Ishi personally years before. He was in fact a playmate with a number of children who lived near the Museum. One young pair of girls, Marcella Healy and her "chum Bess," joined him frequently on his way down to Hugo Street, to do his shopping. The girls were not allowed to cross the street coming back toward the Museum, so Ishi would accompany them to their homes, up the hill across the way (T. Kroeber Papers). He also learned to play jacks with another little girl, ten years old when Ishi came to San Francisco. She lived nearby, visited the Museum often, and became one of Ishi's fast friends. "He did not treat me as a child, but as an adult," Dorothy Stevens wrote in 1977 (T. Kroeber Papers).

Mrs. Ralph Amendola, then eleven years old, recalled her school class visit to the Museum and how Ishi "shook hands with each and every one of us with a kind, sweet smile . . . our teacher told us he was noted for his gentleness" (T. Kroeber Papers).[2] She likewise remembered "his pleasant, kind, creased face" (T. Kroeber Papers). During a visit to the household of Charles Kelsey in San Jose, while awaiting lunch Ishi sat down on the floor with the very young Abbie Kelsey and was surprised, she remembered, to find the doll she lent to him could be dressed and undressed (T. Kroeber Papers).

One of Ishi's associations with a child provides an interesting parallel to Fred Zumwalt's experiences. Ishi formed a secret bonding with a very young girl who never told of the relation to her family, either then or later in life, but who gave the story to Theodora Kroeber in Berkeley in the early 1960s (Theodora Kroeber, personal communication). The lady, who at her request remains nameless, encountered Ishi first by a stream in the Sutro Forest, in the upland behind the Museum, where he often spent quiet hours by himself. They met frequently there afterward. According to Theodora Kroeber, the lady remembered padding around after Ishi through the woods, pretending they were on a hunt. Both were watchers and friends of the many little creatures in that urban wilderness. She learned to sit as long and as unmoving as he when they were waiting for a rabbit to come out of the brush, and quail would come to her hands as fearlessly as into Ishi's. So far as Theodora Kroeber knew, Ishi never mentioned this relation to others. She thought that he may have associated the white girl with his young sister, traces of whom as late as 1914 Alfred Kroeber was still trying to discover, as is revealed by a letter in that year to the head of the Round Valley Reservation.[3]

NOTES

1. Kroeber solved the financial problem that worried Kelsey by giving Ishi an official paid position beyond free housing at the Museum (see Chapter 4). After Ishi's death his savings in the Museum safe, amounting to a few hundred dollars, were sent to the Hospital as thanks for the many freely offered services to him during his several hospitalizations.

2. Mrs. Amendola's memory of Ishi shaking hands with everyone suggests his sensitivity to what the children would expect and appreciate, since usually with adults he was reluctant to initiate this white ritual of greeting and farewell.

3. Alfred Kroeber's letter of June 8, 1914, to the Superintendent of the Round Valley

Reservation, inquiring about the possibility of locating Ishi's sister, is in the collection of the National Archives and Records Administration, San Bruno, California, and is reproduced in Burrill (2001:102).

REFERENCES

FC: Files of the Commissioner of Indian Affairs, Department of the Interior, National Archives of the United States, Record Group 75, CCF 1907–1939, Washington DC.

Burrill, Richard. 2001. *Ishi rediscovered.* Sacramento CA: The Anthro Company.

Clark, John W. 1914. Letter to the Commissioner of Indian Affairs. May. FC.

Commissioner of Indian Affairs. 1914. Letter to Alfred L. Kroeber. FC.

Davis, Charles L. 1911. Letter to the Commissioner of Indian Affairs, September 5. FC.

Hauke, C. F. (Assistant Commissioner of Indian Affairs). 1911a. Letter to Charles Kelsey, April 7. FC.

———. 1911b. Letter to A. L. Kroeber, April 7. FC.

———. 1911c. Letter to Charles Kelsey, October 27. FC.

Kelsey, Charles. [1906] 1979. Report to the Commissioner of Indian Affairs. Reprinted in Heizer, Robert F., ed. *Federal concern about the conditions of California Indians, 1853 to 1913: eight documents.* Socorro NM: Ballena.

——— 1911a. Letter to the Commissioner of Indian Affairs, July 10. FC.

———. 1911b. Letter to the Commissioner of Indian Affairs, September 6. FC.

———. 1911c. Letter to the Commissioner of Indian Affairs, December 16. FC.

Kroeber, Alfred L. 1911a. Letter to the Commissioner of Indian Affairs, March 14. FC.

———. 1911b. Letter to Charles Kelsey, November 24. FC.

———. 1914. Letter to the Commissioner of Indian Affairs, June. FC.

Kroeber, Theodora. Papers. Bancroft Library, University of California at Berkeley.

Stirling, Matthew. 1968. Vanishing cultures mirror the yesterdays of man. In *Vanishing peoples of the earth.* Ed. Frederick C. Vosburgh. Washington DC: National Geographic Society, 12.

Waterman, Thomas T. 1918. The Yana Indians. *University of California Publications in American Archaeology and Ethnology* 13(2): 35–102.

1

A Personal Remembrance of Ishi

FRED H. ZUMWALT JR.

As recounted in the introduction to Part 1, after the publication of her book Ishi in
Two Worlds *in 1961, Theodora Kroeber received a number of visits, telephone calls,
and letters from readers who had as children known Ishi in San Francisco. Among
these the most fascinating was a letter from Fred H. Zumwalt Jr., on April 2, 1962.
To this Theodora Kroeber responded, saying how "delighted and excited" she was
by what Mr. Zumwalt had written, and asking him to send any further recollections of Ishi he might have that could be incorporated in a publication she envi-
sioned (but never realized) of personal memories of Ishi. This elicited Zumwalt's reply of April 24, 1962, which remains the longest and most detailed memoir extant
of actual meetings with Ishi as well as the most vividly evocative account of his personality yet discovered. Zumwalt's letters are preserved in the Theodora Kroeber
Papers, The Bancroft Library, University of California at Berkeley (Banc Mss 69/
145c).*

April 2, 1962
Mrs. Alfred Kroeber
c/o University of California
Berkeley 4, California

My dear Mrs. Kroeber,
    Perhaps few readers of your charming book about Ishi have the pleasant mem-
ories of him that I do. As a very small boy Ishi was not only something of a hero to
me but also a delightful playmate. He made a small bow and arrows with which he
taught me to shoot lizards, a willow seine for catching minnows and soft rabbit
skin moccasins with the fur on the inside. We spent hours calling quail and wild
ducks and stalking rabbits. I might mention that I then lived on Lake Street with
the lake directly in back of my parent's home, so that we had the lake and a then

somewhat wild area of the Presidio in which to wade and catch frogs and roam at will.

One memorable day in 1915 my mother took us both to the Fair and we were equally entranced by driving our own "bug." On that day the Indian Exhibit was closed to the public and we were the guests of those Indians who were here from other parts of the country. The movie of Ishi was shown and tribal dances were performed for our benefit. As I remember, we were the only two outsiders and during the showing of the movie Ishi and I sat alone in the auditorium. This must have been one of the last times that I saw Ishi, but I can recall how proud he was that day to receive some sort of honor from the other Indians and to be my host.

He was a kind, gentle, understanding and patient man, given over to laughter at my clumsy efforts to copy him; nevertheless, I can still walk silently in the woods and come within a few feet of deer. He could move so quietly that more than once he caught quail with his bare hands, after calling them to him. The usual way to catch them was by use of a net; this net was also used to catch ducks, small birds and an occasional rabbit. As I recall, he once went with my family on a picnic, near Lagunitas, and made some sort of a trap in the creek out of twigs set closely together that small fish could be driven into it and penned for a time. We caught two or three trout in the trap, which pleased him immensely.

May I thank you for several hours of delightful reading, which has evoked these nostalgic memories of the playmate of my childhood.

Sincerely,

Fred H. Zumwalt Jr.

April 24, 1962
Mrs. Theodora Kroeber
1325 Arch Street
Berkeley 8, California

Dear Mrs. Kroeber:

As promised, the following are the other things I can remember about Ishi that are not confused with things that I have read or heard about him. The possible confusion in my memory is due to my parents moving to Clay Street, in 1917, just around the corner from the Popes, and as you can well imagine, Ishi was not only a frequent topic of discussion but his teaching was followed by Dr. Pope on weekends when he busied himself making bows, arrows, arrow heads, quivers, bow string etc., as Ishi taught him to do.

Whether Dr. Pope told me, or Ishi, that the reason for there being three feathers on an arrow was to represent Man, Animal and Fish, I'm not sure. I do remember that the wild ducks and quail in the Presidio supplied certain feathers that Ishi wanted. Others came from pheasants and ducks during the hunting season but the best source of all was in Golden Gate Park around Stow Lake and the Old Aviary. Ishi had made friends with a keeper there and was permitted to gather fallen feathers which he cleaned and sorted for future use. Another source of feathers was from my mother and my aunt as they discarded hats, boas and hair ornaments. If I remember correctly, these latter were not for arrows but were to be used in ornamentation of some sort. Mud hen and seagull feathers were not good to use – the straighter a bird flew, the better the arrow would fly; the keener the sight of the bird, the more readily the arrow would "see" its mark; the faster the bird, the faster the arrow; even the arrow head was brushed with a dried duckwing to make it want to fly. The three elements of the arrow represented Earth in three ways – the Head, Underground; the Shaft, the Surface and the Feathers, the Air above.

My name was difficult for him so that he gave me the name of MUT – since I was a small child, I became so confused that when asked my name I would reply "Junior Mut." What Mut meant or why it was chosen for me I don't know, but he never called me by my real name – only Mut. His name for our Chinese laundry man was "Kite" after "Kite" brought me a dragon-kite, dried lichee nuts, ginger and brown sugar sticks on Chinese New Year in 1915. Ishi loved the sugar sticks and the Kite but not the lichee and ginger. Kite showed Ishi how to fly the kite and we must have been a sight to watch, the Chinese with black baggy pants, wearing a que, a black skull cap and felt slippers, Ishi in a scotch plaid wool shirt, but barefoot and I in a sailor suit. The scotch plaid wool shirt was the gift of John McLaren to Ishi and I seem to remember his wearing it frequently. I remember that he had a pair of army shoes that he wore on the street car but that he took off as soon as he arrived at my Parent's home. When I knew Ishi was coming to see me I would wait for him on the corner of 11th Avenue and Lake Streets so that I could look down 11th Avenue and see him get off the street car. Usually he would see me and start waving while still a block away – once across the street he would pick me up like a sack of potatoes and carry me into the garage where he would remove his shoes, casually give me a present, and greet Jerry, my King Charles Spaniel and Billy, my pet chipmunk. Billy would immediately run up his arm as soon as he opened the cage and dive into Ishi's shirt where he rode around all day – when it came time for Ishi to put him back in his cage Billy was usually sound asleep in a pocket somewhere. Jerry adored him too but was not permitted to go on our walks since he was too noisy and would frighten birds. Our walk would then begin by a trip to the kitchen for a handout of cookies, bar chocolate and jerky. I remember when my father brought home a freshly killed steer so that Ishi could show him how to make Jerky properly – This must have been in the fall of 1914. Ishi made a framework of peeled green willows over which the strips of meat were hung to dry after being sealed in boiling salted water. Each piece was cut up the middle so that it would hang in the shape of an inverted "V". The pieces were turned frequently so that the sun could dry all sizes [sides] and were taken in at night so that the fog would not dampen the meat and cause it to spoil. When finally dried it went into an old salt sack and was hung in the kitchen in back of an old wood and coal stove where it remained until eaten. We didn't allow it to remain very long. Our next point of call was the garden where Ishi examined the progress of slips that he brought from time to time. One of the gardeners in Golden Gate Park gave him slips of roses and fuchias which he brought to my mother and were planted. He was always pleased to see his gifts growing.

Our next regular stopping place was either the weeping willow tree on one side of the lake or the pine tree on the other side. If the pine tree side, then we would climb the tree where we could look into various small bird's nests and see how they were getting along; if the willow side we would investigate ducks['] nests in the pampas grass and then perhaps cross the roadway to call on patients in the Marine Hospital who might be out in the sunny garden with whom we would share our cookies and chocolate. Sometimes Billy would come out and beg for a piece of cookie or even take a bite from a piece held in Ishi's lips. Our walk led us along the Presidio Officers Club Golf Course at one point – Ishi thought very little of such a sport since it could be played by women and did not involve anything that could be put to much practical use. Ten pins, played indoors on rainy or cold days, was much more to his liking. Marbles were also a good game for a rainy day, played on the floor of our playroom in the attic but it was also a good time to work on sorting and matching feathers (the three for an arrow had to match perfectly as to color, texture and weight), turning and testing various pieces of wood that would eventually be made into bows and working on a couple of hides that my father had had tanned. If I remember correctly, Ishi appreciated the tanned hides for quiver making but regretted the loss of fat that a raw hide would have given him for working into sinews for strings. As nearly as I can recall, he twisted lengths of sinew or intestine to make bow strings and worked deer fat into them to keep them soft and pliable. It seems to me that bear fat was preferred for this purpose but that he had a pail of lard to use when no other acceptable fat was available.

My father often drove him back to the Affiliated Colleges in the evening under the pretense of having to make a call at the hospital since Ishi would not accept a ride unless he thought no one would be inconvenienced. He loved the fire-engine red 1911 Buick with all its brass and was not too pleased by the 1915 dark green car which superseded it although he enjoyed the two innovations of a self-starter and electric lights almost as much as my father. I know he thought the lighter for the old headlamps quite superior for making fire and I'm sure he would have enjoyed the modern cigarette lighter. A small magnifying glass which I gave him interested him more for its fire making ability than to look through. Don't think for a moment that Ishi was childish in this respect since he was anything but a child – it was only that Ishi's eyes were so good that he could see almost as well without the glass as with it. By the time I knew Ishi he had already accepted his new world and was interested in everything new whether it was a windup train or a telescope. An early day aviator named Beechey (killed in a crash in 1915) inspired Ishi to draw sketches of what he thought a plane looked like for me. I had a blackboard and chalk in my playroom and he covered it from time to time with sketches of things that he had seen or imagined that they must look like. As nearly as I can recall they were all "flat" pictures without perspective or depth.

Since I was ill a great deal as a child, I frequently could not go with him into the Presidio but from my bedroom could watch him moving about around the lake. From time to time he would stop, look up to the windows and wave so I would knew that he had not forgotten me. One day he returned with a few pieces of grass to which were attached butterfly cocoons. We put them in a glass jar in my room and over a short period of time watched them break open and the butterflies emerge. As soon as the sun had warmed and dried them, Ishi put them on the balcony to fly away to enjoy their freedom. In a way, Ishi did not approve of keeping anything wild in a cage[,] so eventually Billy, the chipmunk, was given his freedom too and would disappear into the Presidio for hours at a time returning at night to sleep in his cage. Finally, he didn't appear at home to sleep any longer but would come for handouts from the kitchen, for a time, and eventually became completely wild again.

I recall seeing a mountain lion on Dr. Pope's front lawn that had been shot with a bow and arrow but I'm not sure whether Dr. Pope or Ishi shot it. As nearly as I can remember I have the impression that Dr. Pope or someone else on the trip shot at it and that Ishi finally brought it down. About this same time Ishi took me to meet the beavers and bear in the park – At some time in the past he had killed both brown and black bear and had a healthy respect for them – The best time to kill them is just when they go into hibernation. The beavers were friends and should not be hurt. Of all the woods animals the porcupine was the best friend to man[.] He is the slow moving source of food that can be killed with a club by someone injured or old and therefor[e] never to be killed except in an emergency. The rabbit and deer however were made to provide food and shelter but nothing should be killed unless it was to be used.

Mushrooms grew in both the park and the Presidio but I cannot recall Ishi ever picking them although he did take home wild Iris roots from the Presidio and Marin County, whether to eat or for some other purpose, I don't know. Watercress and Nasturtium leaf sandwiches were among our favorites, also hard boiled eggs, and from Ishi I learned to suck the sweetness from the blossoms of the Nasturtium and to each [eat] the heart of the thistle blossom which closely resembled the artichoke. These we gathered while in the bud stage, boiled in a pot over an open fire by the lake and ate with butter and salt. The Presidio was full of wild blackberries and wild strawberries and these we stuff on as they ripened – I cannot now recall the name of another wild berry that grew in Marin County but it closely resembled a raspberry when picked but grew, on what seemed to me then, rather tall trees. Ishi picked them for me since they grew above my head. There was an old orchard on the slope of Tamalpais where we found apples, huckleberries and berry bushes gone wild. To get me out of the fog and into the sun we drove occasionally to Marin County for a picnic lunch which Ishi enjoyed since it involved the ferry trip to Sausalito and return. The minute we drove on to the ferry he would lead the way up on deck to watch the activity on the bay. If the fog horns were blowing we would try to imitate them but if it was clear we would toss bread to the sea gulls. I think Ishi had the idea that the noise of the fog horns was to make the fog go away. He was a quiet man and I cannot recall ever seeing him angry except once when I captured some baby frogs and squashed them for no purpose except to be cruel, as children often are; then he really thundered.

Since I was far too young to differentiate one Indian tribe from another, I insisted that I have a tepee which was put up by the lake by my father. In no time Ishi mastered the trick of putting it up by himself, and at my insistence we played at being indians to which he good naturedly gave in. It must have amused him to "play" at being an indian; particularly when he would submit to being scalped, burned at the stake etc. As I recall, he also was the pursuer at times and I too was scalped; tied to a stake etc. Usually this play ended by the cook calling us to lunch. In this connection I recall his liking for German pancakes with molasses which we called "Tarwater." I wish I could remember his names for other things but it is all so long ago that I'm afraid of confusing fact and fancy.

Dimly, I recall he had had a friend, another little boy, called "Gata" or "Gita" about whom I heard from time to time. Whether this one was real or was a projection of himself when small or was merely an imagined friend created for my benefit – I don't know but he served the purpose of imparting information to me about the outdoors, i.e., Gata's father told him never to step where he couldn't see where he placed his foot because he might step on a snake, break a twig or step on a loose stone; Gata's father showed him how to catch a fish with his hands by feeling among the rocks in an upstream motion; Gata was hungry and ate green manzanita berries and got sick; Gata was very cold, he was a long way from home and it was getting dark so he went down to the stream and drank a lot of water, took young pine needles to rub on his body and waited until the moon came out before he tried to find his way home again.

Just writing about Ishi makes me see him again, in my mind's eye, in a series of pictures with one thing in common to all – [h]is animated face, sparkling eyes and engaging grin. No matter what he was doing he would glance up from time to time and smile. Our communication was not only with words but by hand gestures, facial expressions and his sketches. With a stick he could draw in the signs to illustrate what he was saying. I can recall one afternoon when we both lay nose to the ground smelling the earth from different places around the lake so that I would learn how to tell one place from another by scent alone. Then Ishi drew an outline of the lake and marked from where each sample came.

I have no idea of when or where I first met Ishi – To me he was always there – nor have I any idea of the last time that I saw him – He just went away. To me, he will never be gone completely as long as I can still remember his great kindness, patience and understanding towards me. Through your book you have made him truly live again for which I cannot adequately express my thanks. I deeply regret that his gifts to me of material things are all lost but his gift of a love and some understanding of the outdoors I will continue to enjoy and treasure the rest of my life. It is said "no person is truly dead until no one left on earth has any recollection of that person" – so Ishi lives again brought back to life by your efforts.

I hope that these rather mixed-up pages of mine will in some way help to bring one side of his personality into focus – other vague remembrances are just too dim to try to record and are more just impressions than things remembered.

Sincerely yours,

Fred H. Zumwalt Jr.

2

Ishi's Two Bodies

Anthropology and Popular Culture

RACHEL ADAMS

In October 1911, the *San Francisco Sunday Call* ran a full-page story about Ishi's visit to a vaudeville show. That evening at the Orpheum Theater was surely one of the strangest of his life. A photograph depicts his visible discomfort as he grins nervously at the camera, surrounded by his companions, who pose with the conventional severity of the time (Figure 2.1). Indeed, the degree of composure Ishi exhibits is remarkable given that only a month earlier he had emerged from the wilderness of Mt. Lassen, driven by hunger and loneliness into the hands of the civilization responsible for the deaths of his family and friends. What could he have been thinking as he sat in the darkened theater box looking out at a house packed with more white people than he had ever seen before? What did the variety acts taking place onstage mean to him? We will never know, for Ishi left no record of his impressions of that night save the frightened smile captured by the newspaper image. What we do know is that these questions provoked considerable speculation among his contemporaries, the anthropologists and journalists who watched Ishi watch the evening's performance and came to very different conclusions about what they had seen. The disparities in these accounts have much to do with the assumptions about the relationship between native people and modernity that each author brought to the encounter. And although their reports, which were printed alongside one another in the newspaper, cannot be said to speak for Ishi, they tell a fascinating tale of their own about the dynamics that set the stage for his reception into the modern San Francisco of 1911. In what follows, I read the competing accounts of Ishi's night at the theater as the products of broader conflicts over cultural authority and aesthetic judgment. Whereas Ishi's story is about the meeting of two radically different cultures, the Yahi and the Anglo-American, it is also about struggles taking place within an increasingly diverse and hierarchical

Fig. 2.1. Ishi (*front left*) and others at the Orpheum Theatre in 1912. From the *San Francisco Call*, October 1911.

U.S. culture, between anthropology and popular ethnography, between professionals and the public, and between institutions of science and entertainment.[1]

The version of the evening's events provided by the reporter, Grant Wallace, is a representative example of Ishi's treatment within the popular press. While it is easy to dismiss the newspaper coverage for its sensationalism, it also must be understood as one of the primary organs for the wide dissemination of Ishi's story. Once fixed in print, these stories set the terms for how the papers' readers would interpret what they saw. However inaccurate, the details of Ishi's biography provided by the news were not simply journalistic fantasy; they combined a selective understanding of the anthropologists' official pronouncements with an available repertoire of popular beliefs about the Indian. Wallace's portrait of Ishi would have been recognizable to the paper's readers, for it draws on familiar, paradoxical stereotypes about the Indian as both an unredeemable savage and a tragically endangered natural resource. Ishi is at once a "barbarian," an "abysmal brute caveman," a "primordial savage of the stone age" and a man of "extraordinarily acute perceptive powers," with "long tapering fingers [that] might well have belonged to an artist and a thinker," who faces the confusing experience with "courage . . . fortitude and self control."[2] These are the well-worn characteristics of the Indians found in contemporary dime novels, storefront museums, and Wild West shows, which brought the excitement and drama of the frontier to American city-dwellers, who craved stories of the Western frontier.[3]

As they presented him to the public, the anthropologists charged with Ishi's care struggled to cordon off the showman's fabricated Indian from their own empirically derived knowledge about indigenous tribes. But popular culture provided a compelling and accessible lens through which the lovers of Western mythology who flocked to the University Museum could make the wild man meaningful. As Theodora Kroeber writes, Ishi fueled the imagination of a public seeking the "illusion and fantasy" promised by "the voice of the barker, falsetto and arresting, which entices the listeners to pay to see what waits behind drawn curtains – be it freak, belly dancer, hypnotist, or wild man from Borneo, or better yet, from Mount Lassen."[4] Often using the discourse of ethnography, contemporary popular culture challenged the anthropologists' exclusive claim to a professional language and specialized erudition on the subject of Native Americans. Indeed, at Chicago's Columbian Exposition in 1893, Buffalo Bill's Wild West was voted the most genuine ethnological exhibit for its "composition of so many races and nationalities."[5]

Wild West shows and popular ethnographic exhibits shared the perspective of European colonial anthropology, which drew a firm distinction between savagery and civilization.[6] From this viewpoint, the Indian was a more primitive ancestor in the great, unified narrative of human progress, which reached its pinnacle in the modern Anglo-American societies. However rudimentary and undeveloped, tribal life was interesting because it could tell white Americans about their own past, as well as emphasizing, by contrast, the accomplishments of Western civilization.[7] This developmental paradigm undergirds Wallace's account of the vaudeville excursion. According to the enterprising reporter, Ishi is the perfect subject for a journalistic "experiment" designed to study "the primordial savage of the stone age" during his first encounter with "the contaminating influences of civilization." Wallace describes the theater as a "temple of music and folly," the place where civilization reached its enlightened, even decadent heights. He explains that Ishi thought he was in heaven: "Poor, simple-minded wild man! He could not know that the heaven of white people is never likely to be so crowded as their vaudeville houses, nor that so far there never has been half the scramble to get through the pearly gates that there is every night to get a front seat at the Orpheum's top gallery." Ishi's unfamiliarity with the conventions of theatrical performance becomes an opportunity for the reporter to celebrate the sophistication of the modern audience. The Indian's primitive religious beliefs are the rude counterpart to those of urban San Franciscans, who worship the gods of commerce and luxury. Although many who met him would contemplate Ishi's apparently unspoiled condition with regret, holding up his perfection against the corrosive effects of city life, Wallace saw it as an occasion to promote the accomplishments of modernity.

The climactic moment of the evening is Ishi's introduction to "the silvery voiced and fascinating Orpheum headliner, Lily Lena of the London music halls." Modernity at its most decadent and pleasurable extreme is represented by a woman who enthralls and terrifies him with her charms. The importance of the meeting is illustrated by a large graphic that dominates the page, accompanied by a caption that reads: "Sketch of the Meeting of Ishi and Lily Lena. He is Shown in the Costume He Likes Best and She in the Costume the Audience Likes Best" (Figure 2.2). The sketch depicts Lena in high heels and a tight dress that barely comes down to the top of her thigh, shaking hands with a dark-skinned man wearing animal skins who looks nothing like Ishi but is a perfect rendition of the stereotypic wild Indian of contemporary sideshows and dime novels. As it is illustrated here, the encounter between Ishi and Lena mobilizes a predictable fantasy about the dark-skinned savage's innate attraction to white womanhood. However, instead of an irrepressible lust, the savage grows weak and docile when confronted by the white woman's allure. As Lena sang directly to Ishi, Wallace observed, "the cold sweat was standing out on Ishi's forehead. His face was drawn. His fingers, grasping the crimson hangings, trembled visibly and his first cigar, which he had been puffing with pretended sangfroid, now slowly grew cold and dropped from his teeth." Making a crude and obvious equation of Ishi's virility with the suddenly extinguished cigar, Wallace enjoys his discomfort at the sight of a white woman. The potential threat of the savage's untutored sexual desire is contained by his complete captivity to Lena's charms.

If Ishi was such a tragic figure, at once noble and gentle, why would Wallace want to contaminate him? Why take such apparent pleasure in his anxiety and fear? Whereas one obvious answer is the demand for sensationalism required by yellow journalism, there is also an element of class animosity at work among the participants in this story, one that had little to do with Ishi and everything to do with the reporter's attitude toward his companions, the anthropologists. In the midst of Wallace's exploded rhetoric are moments of sincere admiration for Ishi's bravery, but these are counteracted by his deep resentment toward the professional men who accompany him, whom he describes in overwhelmingly negative terms. Ultimately, it is clear that Wallace's goal is less to prove Ishi's

Fig. 2.2. Sketch of the meeting of Ishi and Lily Lena. From the *San Francisco Call*, October 1911.

inferiority than that of the anthropologists, a task he initiates by dismantling their claims to knowledge and professional expertise. As he describes their undertaking:

> The university professors, who have added Ishi to their museum of antiquities and curiosities and who are conducting this series of scientific experiments on him, justly regard him as a unique specimen of the genus homo, the like of which does not exist in all the world. They call him the 'uncontaminated man,' the one man who (possibly from lack of opportunity to talk) has never told a lie; the one man with no redeeming vices and no upsetting sins. This conclusion was decided doubtless from the fact that Ishi had never been brought into contact with the contaminating influences of civilization; therefore to permit the barbarian to mingle with our unsettled civilization is to expose him to contamination.[8]

Classifying the museum's contents as "antiquities and curiosities," Wallace equates the work of the University anthropologists with mass entertainment. He suggests the hypocrisy of their desire to preserve Ishi as an untainted man of nature by sealing him away in a museum where he will be protected from the contaminating effects of modernity only to be turned into a specimen for scientific examination. The reporter's scornful tone, use of the Latin phrase "genus homo," and dubious references to the pedants' disdain for "civilization" and its pleasures reveals his resentment toward the intellectual establishment the professors represent. Wallace conceives of his own social "experiment" as a counter to the experts' scientific methods, a way of demystifying the aura conferred on their objects and methods of study. His desire to blemish Ishi's innocence with a visit to the theater is motivated by his understanding of anthropology as a science devoted to the study of untainted human specimens, and anthropologists as haughty elites disdainful of the pleasures enjoyed by more ordinary folk. Having tainted Ishi, he will have compromised the primary document essential to their research.

Whereas Wallace was openly antagonistic toward the professors, many San Franciscans who flocked to the University Museum were simply confused by them. Charmed and delighted by the "wild Indian" himself, Ishi's visitors seemed unclear about the function of the anthropologists and the institution that sheltered him. Their misconception of the experts' professional status is reflected in letters sent to the museum offering assistance in deciphering Ishi's language and origins. These helpful hints are evidence that their authors did not understand or respect the firm boundary between the anthropologists' specialized knowledge, acquired through years of training and advanced degrees, and their own speculation. For example, one missive respectfully expressed doubts about Ishi's authenticity: "I understand very well how enthusiastic you can be if you have discovered a stone age man in the middle of civilization. But is he such?" The question is followed by the writer's own theory: "To me he looks like a Jewish student who wants to make a hit as [an] impersonator – the most striking point is his likeness with the notorious Dr. Cook the discoverer of Poles."[9] The purpose of this ruse, he concludes, is the anthropologists' desire to study the limits of public credulity. Another visitor who pondered over Ishi's ethnicity offered: "[I] am much interested in the aborigines of the continents. I believe in heredity and environment. Therefor [*sic*] I think the Japanese and Indian are the same. Many words alike etc."[10] Such were the voices of a public that, having seen Ishi described by one reporter as "a human document, with the key to most of the hieroglyphics lost," believed they had something to contribute to the task of interpretation.[11]

Other letters and newspaper stories echo the more resentful tone of the Wallace story. For example, an editorial in the *Call* commented acerbically, "scientific rejoicing over the capture of 'the only uncontaminated man' is complicated by the fact that the first thing his captors did was to put him in jail." Summing up the scientists' efforts, he writes, "apparently the cave man is placed in the same category as the chimpanzee and is held in captivity to make a scientific holiday regardless of the . . . fourteenth amendment of the constitution." The author's reference to the Fourteenth Amendment implies that Ishi deserves the rights of an ordinary American citizen. Denying his humanity as well as his constitutional rights, the anthropologists have treated him as an animal to suit the purposes of their own research. The author concludes with one last insult: "the pictures of the wild man are disappointing. He does not fulfill the ideal, and, in fact, he looks more intelligent than a professor of anthropology." As was the case with Wallace, the author's target is the experts and their methods rather than Ishi himself. The author's claim that the wild man does not live up to his expectations is an insult less to Ishi than to the professors' superior knowledge and authority.[12]

Hostility toward the anthropologists was most pronounced in print reactions to Ishi's death from tuberculosis four years after he moved to San Francisco. Popular accounts of his demise held the cold, inhumane methods of science, embodied by the University faculty, responsible for killing off its objects of study.[13] These articles charge the professors with sensationalism, while downplaying the reporters' own initial interest in the story. Reading them in isolation, it would be difficult to believe that journalists were responsible for planning Ishi's trip to the theater and dressing him in furs to look the part of an uncivilized wild man. Science was to blame for turning the Indian into a curious object and then examining him to death. "He furnished amusement and study to the savants at the University of California for a number of years, and doubtless much of Indian lore was learned from him," one reporter editorialized dubiously, "but we do not believe he was the marvel that the professors would have the public believe. He was just a starved-out Indian from the wilds of Deer Creek who, by hiding in its fastness, was able to long escape the white man's pursuit."[14] Exaggerating the significance of their find, the anthropologists were little more than mountebanks who used their status as experts to swindle a gullible public and exploit their object of study. "The white man with his food and clothing and shelter finally killed the Indian just as effectually as he would have killed him with the rifle," the obituary concluded. The impulse to preserve native cultures was little better than the quest to eradicate them; in the end, the Indian's death was the inevitable consequence of the march of progress. A second article reported, suspiciously, "an alleged Stone Age man said to have been adopted by the University of California as a valuable acquisition has just died. To be used by a high-brow institution as an anthropological acquisition is enough to kill any man."[15] Casting a dubious eye on Ishi's status as a survivor of the Stone Age, this piece accused the museum of hastening his death. No person could withstand the misery of being turned into a "valuable acquisition." Ishi's fatal illness was a consequence not of the innate frailty of his race, but of his treatment as a scientific specimen, an abuse to which anyone might succumb. By characterizing his death in this manner, these stories sought to debunk the anthropologists' professional mission and the institutions that promoted their activities. The popular press thus posthumously reconfigured Ishi from a stone-age relic to a person with common human desires and weaknesses.

Ishi's reception by the public who greeted him with respect and adoration, while often turning a cynical eye on the professional men who represented themselves as his guardians, is only one side of the story. His popularity forced the anthropologists, who seemed far more comfortable writing, teaching, or conducting research among their informants, to serve as intermediaries between Ishi and the crowds who loved him. That Kroeber found this an awkward position is evident in his response to the vaudeville excursion, which ran alongside Wallace's account of the evening. While Wallace drew on a series of predictable oppositions between savagery and civilization, innocence and corruption, primitivism and modernity, Kroeber underscored the utter difference of Ishi's cultural orientation, as well as his disdain for Wallace's reportorial enterprise. In a subsequent article he would comment sourly, "the reporter got his story. But he got it out of his imagination."[16] Merging his palpable distaste for Wallace's "experiment" with a genuine effort to imagine the effects of the spectacle on someone who had never seen more than fifty people together in one place, the anthropologist insisted that, while Ishi was indeed awed by the size of the audience, "the performance itself I am sure he did not appreciate." What Wallace took to be delight at the events on stage was, according to Kroeber, a reaction to those around him, "a pure automatic response or suggestion, for they might be laughing at a pun, a joke conveyed in words that were totally incomprehensible to him."[17] While Wallace believed that the delights of the vaudeville acts transcended cultural differences, Kroeber established Ishi's apparent pleasure as a polite imitation of his companions rather than a sign that he understood the performances. Expressions that appeared, from the reporter's developmental perspective, to confirm the universal language of Western theater, looked to the anthropologist like evidence of an alterity so extreme that it stretched the limits of the imagination.

One particular point of contention was the subject of Ishi's manhood. Recall that Wallace attempted to deflate the Indian's virility with the image of the damp, rapidly extinguished cigar. Kroeber appeared to concur when he explained that hysterical symptoms resulting from exposure to such a large crowd had caused Ishi to laugh like "a young girl." However, a few lines later he reconfirmed Ishi's manhood by asserting that "there is nothing undeveloped about him; he has the mind of a man and is a man in every sense. With the exception of the habits which he has acquired by his manner of living he is thoroughly normal."[18] *Normal* seems an odd word to describe anything about Ishi's situation, but Kroeber's insistence on his normality must be seen as a reaction against Wallace's representation of him as a primordial savage. Moreover, there is a matter of personal dignity at stake. In the face of stories that depicted the scientists as fussy, overcivilized pedants, Kroeber's comments about the Indian's manhood reinforce, by association, the manhood of the anthropologist who accompanied him.

The tone of defensiveness that colors Kroeber's response is certainly related to the challenge of making Ishi available to the public that clamored to see him, without exploiting his charge or compromising his understanding of the University Museum's function. As news of the discovery of an authentic wild man spread, the anthropologists were bombarded with requests from enterprising showmen eager to get their hands on "the last Stone Age man." According to Theodora Kroeber, the museum staff had to contend not only with reporters, but "motion picture companies, and entrepreneurs of carnival, circus, and vaudeville specialty acts"[19] who saw Ishi as a potential source of publicity and profit. One vaudeville impresario even proposed a two-man act featuring Ishi and Kroeber, which would play at the Orpheum, the very theater where Ishi would see his first variety program. His scheme attests to the currency of anthropologists and ethnographic discourse within early twentieth-century popular culture. During this period, it was common to find men who called themselves "professors" or "doctors" lecturing audiences at freak shows, vaudeville presentations, and ethnographic pageants where people from exotic lands were exhibited to the American public. Speaking with an authority and apparent erudition that was rarely confirmed by professional training, they delivered "educational" treatises about the human specimens on display.[20] While we do not have Kroeber's negative response to the vaudeville offer in print, evidence that he saw himself as a very different kind of professor, one whose dignity would be compromised by the world of show business, is to be found in a letter he wrote to the Board of Directors for the Pan-Pacific International Exposition regarding the content of the Fair's Native American village. Registering his objection to the type of living ethnographic exhibits typically mounted at World's Fairs, he described them as "amusement concessions . . . too often of the cheap show variety, thus being without educational significance."[21] Whereas Kroeber believed that the anthropologist's mission was to collect and disseminate knowledge about Native American cultures, those who requested his expertise sometimes desired only to profit from the respectability of his professional imprimatur.

As I have suggested, the anthropologist's position was complicated by the fact that ethnographic knowledge had a place in popular culture as well as in the academy. If the difference between the two was clear to the first generation of professional academics and curators, it was less so to the non-specialized public confronted by many different sources of information about Native Americans, all represented as true and accurate. In his history of the Smithsonian, Curtis Hinsley observes that the institutionalization of anthropology "presented an unusual opportunity for making a science, for drawing a clear line between speculative popularization or commercial humbuggery, and the sober search for truth."[22] It is instructive to interpret the anthropologists' treatment of Ishi and those who gathered around him as, in part, a product of their efforts to establish an emergent disciplinary discourse. In the United States, individual enthusiasts had been studying indigenous cultures for many decades, but anthropology acquired its institutional form only in the late nineteenth century, when a new system of training and accreditation was erected to separate the amateur from the professional. A Department of Anthropology had been created at the University of California just ten years before Ishi's appearance, and Kroeber was among the first generation of accredited university anthropologists.[23]

The task of situating American anthropology in museums and universities necessitated a break with popular modes of presenting indigenous people and artifacts. Before the era of institutionalization, museums reflected the idiosyncrasies of private collectors, who chose their contents based on an object's individual interest rather than its contribution to a larger portrait of a culture or people. P. T. Barnum transformed the exhibition of curiosities into mass entertainment with the establishment of his American Museum in 1841.[24] For the price of admission, visitors were presented with an array of unique artifacts, freaks, trained animals, performers, and informational lectures that promised to educate as well as entertain. At the American Museum, exotic exhibits such as the What Is It? – a black man supposed to be a missing link between human and animal species – were described in a jargon Robert Bogdan calls "anthropological humbug."[25] Touring the act in London during the 1860s, Barnum claimed that the creature was discovered in "the wilds of California," where "for the last 10 months it has been with a tribe of Indians."[26] The establishment of anthropology museums in "the wilds of California" required that their founders distinguish them from this tradition by emphasizing didacticism over sensation, replacing the jumble of the private collection with organizational logic, and demanding new standards of decorum and seriousness from the visitor. Nonetheless, as we have seen in responses to Ishi's arrival, the ability to discriminate between the curious and the representative, and the new understanding of institutional identity that accompanied these distinctions, did not necessarily register among the first generation of museum visitors.

Ishi appeared at a moment when the University museum itself was undergoing an institutional transition. Conceived under the auspices of wealthy regent Phoebe Apperson Hearst, the museum was intended to house her vast personal collection of antiquities gathered from around the world. As she made plans to donate her possessions to the University of California, Hearst was encouraged to take an interest in indigenous tribes, to balance her appreciation for European artifacts with a commitment to California's local history and cultures. When a location in Parnassus Heights, San Francisco, was established for cataloguing and exhibition, she concurred by making a place for Native American specimens alongside acquisitions from ancient Egypt, Peru, Greece, and Rome. This juxtaposition is indicative of the increasing importance of American anthropology, which for the first time found a place alongside the classical antiquities of acknowledged beauty and value. The new museum opened to the public two months after Ishi's arrival in 1911.[27] His presence at the opening reception, where he mingled shyly among benefactors, University regents, scientists and academics, attested to the contradictory relationship between the anthropology museum and the human subjects of ethnographic inquiry. Was he a guest or a living exhibit? How would his culture measure up to the great ancient civilizations already represented in the museum's collections?

In the face of fantastic newspaper accounts, eager crowds, and a deluge of requests to exhibit Ishi on vaudeville and in traveling shows, anthropologists encouraged him to assimilate by learning English and working for a living. Treating Ishi as if he were more a collaborator than a specimen was their strategy for resisting the popular belief in his irreconcilable difference, a barbarian survivor of the prehistoric past. If the popular conception of the Indian's absolute otherness is encapsulated in the sketch of Ishi and Lena, the anthropologist's intense personal bond with his subject is captured in a photograph of Ishi and Kroeber. A visual representation of the intimacy between the two, this image also illustrates Kroeber's attempt to prove Ishi's "normality" through sartorial means (Figure 2.3). But the differences between these men belie the more immediate parallelism, for the pale, bearded anthropologist who stands erect with his suit and tie neatly in place, clearly is not a double for the shorter, broader, and barefoot Ishi, who appears disheveled and uncomfortable in his civilized garb. Ishi was no more "normal" dressed in a suit and tie than he was swathed in a cave man's furs. Efforts to assimilate him often only further emphasized how alien he was in the modern environment. Instead of showing his equivalence with American men, the photograph suggests the limits of his adaptability to the new culture.

Attempting to debunk the evolutionary perspective of the news coverage, Kroeber went to considerable lengths to describe Ishi's situation by using analogies accessible to his readers. For example, he wrote, "it is as though we were to visit the moon. We would get used to the novelty of it in a short time and then when the surprise had worn off, while we understood nothing of what was going on about us we should learn to take it all for granted."[28] Throughout his writing about Ishi, Kroeber shows that he is familiar with popular misconceptions about indigenous people, and he works to dispel them through reason and evidence. At various points he deflates the "'missing link' of popular fantasy," the myth that fire is made by rubbing two sticks together, and the belief that nonwhite people were biologically inferior.[29] In a 1912 article Kroeber wrote: "Ishi himself is no nearer the 'missing link' or any antecedent form of human life than we are; but in what his environment, his associates, and his puny native civilization have made him, he represents a stage through which our ancestors passed thousands of years ago."[30] Asserting Ishi's fundamental equality with his Anglo-American contemporaries, Kroeber begins to articulate one of his most important contributions to the field of anthropology, the decoupling of culture from biology, by insisting that Ishi's differences were social and historical, not physiological.[31]

Rather than dispelling the myth that Ishi was a "Stone Age" relic, however, Kroeber's writing for mainstream publications often granted it legitimacy with the objective language of science. In enforcing Ishi's biological equality, Kroeber belittled his tribe as a "puny native civilization," giving voice to the same theory of cultural evolution as the newspapers and confirming that the Yahi represented a more primitive stage in the inevitable advance toward modernity. At times, when he recorded Ishi's story in newspapers and magazines, he employed

Fig. 2.3. Ishi and Kroeber. Courtesy of the Phoebe A. Hearst
Museum of Anthropology and the Regents of the University of
California.

a developmental rhetoric that included turns of phrase, such as "the progress of civilization,"[32] that undermined his Boasian conviction that cultures should not be measured against one another, or in relation to a unified standard of human achievement. In one instance, claiming that "in short [Ishi] has really lived in the stone age, as has so often been said," Kroeber equated cultural difference with temporal distance, appearing to position the native as a stranded outcast from history. Doubtless, the adjective "stone age" refers to the Yanas' rudimentary use of tools, but to most readers it would have evoked images of primitive barbarism. The flights of imagination inspired by Kroeber's choice of adjectives is evident in a newspaper headline that announced, "Stone Age Indian Hauled from Forests' Depths by Savants: Creature Found in the Wilds of Feather River a Link between Past and Present." Whereas the initial clause echoes Kroeber's own vocabulary, the description that follows figures Ishi as a "missing link" of the kind that was commonly found at freak shows of this period.[33] Despite his commitment to treating Ishi as an equal, Kroeber used the language of his time in a manner that could backfire by feeding directly into the popular fantasies he wished to contradict.

For anthropologists, reporters, and their audiences it was impossible not to read Ishi's story as a lesson about modernity, whether they believed it taught them about the desirable or tragic consequences of progress. How each described Ishi's response to the new culture is thus as much a barometer of how that group understood its place within its own culture as it is an assessment of Ishi himself. What was Ishi thinking that night in the darkened Orpheum theater? What did he make of his companions, the crowds dressed in evening wear, the antics onstage, the white woman who sang to him? My purpose has not been to resolve these questions, or to measure the accuracy of one version over another, but to explain why and how their answers were meaningful to Ishi's companions. Although Ishi's appearance was a surprising and unanticipated event, the responses to it were less so as they were forged in large part by the cultural location of their authors, which dictated a more familiar set of animosities and expectations. His sojourn in 1911 San Francisco forced unanticipated confrontations between the subjects of anthropology and the Indians of popular culture, an elite professional class, public institutions, and the audiences who frequented them. For Ishi not only occasioned an unprecedented and productive contact between Native American and Anglo-American cultures; he also brought the participants within separate spheres of a stratified U.S. culture into dialogue. If he could not transcend vast differences between his environment and theirs, his appeal crossed the lines of class and educational training. Ishi's own words are a fitting mode of closure here. His friends recalled that his favored way of saying goodbye was "you stay, I go."[34] After Ishi's death, the anthropologists, reporters, and public who loved him would be left behind to make sense of his life and, as they did so, their own place within an increasingly complex and hierarchical American culture.

NOTES

1. See Lawrence Levine, *Highbrow/Lowbrow: The Emergence of Cultural Hierarchy in America* (Cambridge: Harvard University, 1988) for a general description of this process, as it occurred in the American theater, museums, and public institutions.

2. Grant Wallace, "Ishi, the Last Aboriginal Savage in America, Finds Enchantment in a Vaudeville Show," *San Francisco Call,* 8 October 1911, reprinted in *Ishi the Last Yahi: A Documentary History,* ed. Robert F. Heizer and Theodora Kroeber (Berkeley: University of California, 1979), 108.

3. Ishi's life in San Francisco (1911–16) coincided with the period of the Wild West show's greatest popularity and commercial success. Encouraged by his friend and doctor Saxton Pope, he became a fan of these pageants, where he once was introduced to a Sioux Indian performer who pronounced him "a very high grade of Indian" [Theodora Kroeber, *Ishi in Two Worlds* (Berkeley: University of California, 1961), 228–229]. On Wild West pageants, see Richard Slotkin, "Buffalo Bill's 'Wild West' and the Mythologization of the American Empire," *Cultures of United States Imperialism,* ed. Donald Pease and Amy Kaplan (Durham: Duke University, 1993), 164–184.

4. *Ishi in Two Worlds*, 129.

5. Robert Rydell, *All the World's A Fair: Visions of Empire at American International Expositions, 1876–1916* (Chicago: University of Chicago, 1984), 97.

6. George Stocking, *Victorian Anthropology* (New York: Free Press, 1987). On significant, and often overlooked, differences between European and American anthropologies, see Karl Kroeber, *Artistry in Native American Myths* (Lincoln: University of Nebraska, 1998).

7. Of course, the same developmental paradigm could be put to opposite ends. For the critic of modernity, primitive people represented an idealized past when human society was more attuned to the natural world. On the "antimodern impulse," see T. J. Jackson Lears, *No Place of Grace: Antimodernism and the Transformation of American Cultures, 1880–1920* (New York: Pantheon, 1981).

8. Wallace, in *Ishi the Last Yahi: A Documentary History,* 108.

9. Letter to Thomas T. Waterman, Hearst Museum archives, University of California, Berkeley, 6 September 1911.

10. Quoted in *Ishi in Two Worlds*, 169.

11. Mary Ashe Miller, "Indian Enigma Is Study for Scientists," *San Francisco Call* 6 September 1911, in *Ishi the Last Yahi: A Documentary History,* 97.

12. "Scientific Fun with a Wild Man," Hearst Museum archives, nd.

13. By the time of his death, Ishi's public appeal had greatly diminished. After four

years in civilization, the wild man who lived at the University Museum was hardly a breaking story and the more he adapted to modern life, the less spectacular he became. In fact, within a few years of his appearance, newspapers were breaking stories that Ishi was *not* the last of his tribe, with headlines such as "Ishi Is Not The Last of Lost Tribe: Stockmen and Ranchers of Deer Creek Country Find Traces of Aborigines" and "Ishi's Squaw Seen Hunting for Mate: Parties Searching Underbrush Near Oroville for Wife of Lone Survivor" (Hearst Museum archives).

14. "Ishi's Death – A Chico Commentary," reprinted in *Ishi the Last Yahi: A Documentary History,* 242.

15. *Portland Oregon Telegram,* 30 March 1916, np, Hearst Museum archives.

16. Alfred Kroeber, "Ishi, the Last Aborigine," *Ishi the Last Yahi: A Documentary History,* 121.

17. "Ishi, the Last Aborigine," 121.

18. A. L. Kroeber, "It's All Too Much For Ishi, Says the Scientist," *San Francisco Call,* 8 October 1911, reprinted in *Ishi the Last Yahi: A Documentary History,* 111.

19. *Ishi in Two Worlds,* 129.

20. See Robert Bogdan, *Freak Show: Presenting Human Oddities for Amusement and Profit* (Chicago: University of Chicago, 1985) and Rydell, *All the World's a Fair.*

21. Unpublished letter, Alfred Kroeber to Board of Directors, Panama Pacific International Exposition, 23 June 1911. Kroeber Correspondence, Bancroft Library, University of California at Berkeley, Microfilm Reel 4.

22. Curtis Hinsley, *Savages and Scientists: The Smithsonian Institution and the Development of American Anthropology, 1846–1910* (Washington DC: Smithsonian Institution, 1981), 35.

23. *Ishi in Two Worlds,* 121.

24. Bluford Adams, *E Pluribus Barnum: The Great Showman and the Making of U.S. Popular Culture* (Minneapolis: University of Minnesota, 1997) and Neil Harris, *Humbug: The Art of P. T. Barnum* (Chicago: University of Chicago, 1973).

25. Bernth Lindfors, "P. T. Barnum and Africa," *Studies in Popular Culture* 7 (1984); James W. Cook, Jr., "Of Men, Missing Links, and Nondescripts: The Strange Career of P. T. Barnum's 'What Is It' Exhibition," *Freakery: Cultural Spectacles of the Extraordinary Body,* ed. Rosemarie Garland Thomson (New York: New York University, 1996), 139–157.

26. Quoted in Cook, "Of Men, Missing Links, and Nondescripts," 145.

27. *Ishi in Two Worlds,* 121–123.

28. Alfred Kroeber, "It's All Too Much for Ishi," in *Ishi the Last Yahi: A Documentary History,* 111.

29. Alfred Kroeber, "The Only Man in America Who Knows No Christmas: Ishi," in *Ishi the Last Yahi: A Documentary History,* 115.

30. A. L. Kroeber, "Ishi, the Last Aborigine," *The World's Work,* July 1912; reprinted in *Ishi the Last Yahi: A Documentary History,* 123.

31. For a discussion of Kroeber's influence on the anthropological study of human nature, see Carl Degler, "In the Wake of Boas," *In Search of Human Nature*, 84–104.

32. Alfred Kroeber, "The Only Man in America Who Knows No Christmas: Ishi," in *Ishi the Last Yahi: A Documentary History*, 114.

33. *San Francisco Evening Post*, 5 September 1911, front page.

34. *Ishi in Two Worlds*, 238.

3

When the Demons Come

(Retro)Spectacle among the Savages

JACE WEAVER

The exact contrary of what is generally
believed is often the truth.
Jean de la Bruyère

Myths are wonderful – you can do anything
with them you want.
Siegel Schuster

This is the West, sir. When the legend
becomes fact, print the legend.
The Man Who Shot Liberty Valance

When I was a child, my family moved for a few years from Oklahoma to Columbia, Missouri. On the edge of town was a restaurant called Pete's Steakhouse. While parents ate, children were entertained by an aged Indian. I say "entertained," but for the most part, he simply sat in full regalia outside a tepee down the hill from the parking lot, silent and stoic while kids played around him. His name was William Red Fox, a Lakota from Pine Ridge. Once a year he would come to my school, Thomas Hart Benton Elementary, and talk about his life and Plains history and culture.

After we moved back to Oklahoma, Red Fox, as he liked to be called (adamantly maintaining that "William" was simply an accommodation to whites) was "discovered" by Johnny Carson and began appearing on the *Tonight Show* – probably through the agency of Cash Asher, a writer who became his amanuensis. In 1971 Red Fox published his autobiography with Asher's assistance. *The Memoirs of Chief Red Fox* told a remarkable and emblematic story. Born in 1870, Red Fox heard the gunfire of the Battle of the Little Big Horn as a child. Sent to Carlisle, he eventually joined Buffalo Bill's Wild West Show, appearing with it at the Columbian Exposition in 1893. He fought in the Spanish-American War and met Thomas Edison, Alexander Graham Bell, Jack London, and Will Rogers. He performed with Pawnee Bill and the Miller 101 Ranch and appeared in movies from Thomas Ince through the 1930s. He campaigned in Indian dress for the daughter of William Jennings Bryan for Congress from Florida. In his sixties, and as interest in Indians waned, he somehow wound up at Pete's – a chapter of his life conveniently omitted from his autobiography – where he eventually sat with me. Ample photographs, surprisingly few of which actually showed Red Fox, documented his story.

There was only one problem with this account, called by one critic "dramatic and sensitive": In its key element, it was not true. Red Fox was apparently not an Indian.

Shortly after the book's publication, it was revealed that part of it was plagiarized from a previously published account. Gradually it came out that no one at Pine Ridge had ever heard of him. For McGraw-Hill, which had also published *Amelia Earhart Lives,* claiming that the lost aviator was alive and living in the United States incognita, the book was a public relations disaster. The media seized upon it with a vengeance. Art Buchwald had a field day, imagining the publisher trying to recoup its lost credibility by bringing out the reminiscences of a still living George Custer sitting in its reception area.

At the end of the day, the only question for measuring the worth of a life is "When you're alone at night in the dark and the demons come, what do you see?" Although, in some childlike way, I knew Bill Red Fox, I never knew – nor will I ever know – what he saw when he turned out the light in his modest home in central Missouri.

I have a better idea about the demons that lurked around Sarah Lockwood Winchester. The widow of William Winchester, heir to the firearms fortune, she had a séance with a medium in 1881 after her husband and infant daughter both died, leaving her alone. The psychic told her that the spirits of the many Indians killed by Winchester guns were stalking her. She was to build a home, and when it was finished, she would die, victim to the Natives' attempts upon her soul.

Determined to thwart the spirits, Winchester bought a small eight-room house in San José, California. For decades, workmen labored twenty-four hours a day. At night, Mrs. Winchester obsessively drew up plans for the next day's work. What today is known as the Winchester Mystery House has secret passages, doors that open on solid walls, lead nowhere, or reveal drop-offs to floors below. Indian statuary decorates the grounds. Clearly Mrs. Winchester wanted to confuse some spirits and appease others. She became a recluse, a self-confined prisoner, the only ghost who ever built its own haunted mansion. Construction halted only upon her death in 1922, when she was returned to be buried in New Haven, Connecticut. The restless Indian spirits warned of by the medium had their revenge.

Jacques Derrida states that "a traditional scholar doesn't believe in ghosts" (Smith 2000:39). Yet as Carlton Smith makes clear in his book *Coyote Kills John Wayne,* the West is a place both haunted and haunting. It is a place of ghost towns and restless spirits – Native, Anglo, Mexican, black, Chinese. It haunted William Red Fox and Sarah Winchester, and it continues to haunt the larger American psyche, bequeathing to us a mythology of frontier and uninhabited wilderness, of rough and ready justice and the Code of the West, of rugged individualism and a blithe belief that individuals can constantly reinvent themselves. D. H. Lawrence, however, averred that America itself is haunted. He wrote, "There are terrible spirits, ghosts, in the air of America" (Lawrence [1923] 1971:81).

As that mythical frontier closed, a ragged Indian emerged from it at an abattoir in Oroville, California. I wonder what demons Ishi saw in the privacy of the night – dubbed the "last wild Indian," moved to a museum, displayed, and, in the final indignity, dissected after death. He never revealed his real name, any more than Red Fox did. "Ishi," as he was called, means simply "man" in Yana, his language.

After Ishi wandered out of the "wilderness," the local sheriff locked him up in a cell for the insane to protect him from the curious already massing to catch a glimpse of the Wild Man of Oroville (Kroeber 1961:3). Though he was called the last wild Indian, he was not-whatever is meant by "last" or "wild." He was, however, the last Yahi. He had watched all others of his band be killed by whites or simply expire. How long he lived by himself is unknown, though it was probably not long. In all likelihood, he was found not long after his mother died and he was left alone. His hair was burned short in mourning. He was reportedly indifferent to whether he lived or died.

Less than a week later, Ishi saw his first demon of Western civilization up close. It was the locomotive, come to take him to his new home. According to Theodora Kroeber, "[T]wice a day Ishi heard it ever since he could remember, and he had watched the train hundreds of times as it snaked along below him, bellowing and belching. His mother had reassured him as a small boy when he was afraid of it, telling him that it was a Demon who followed white men wherever they went, but that Indians need have no fear of it; it never bothered them" (Kroeber 1961:118–119). Ishi stepped into the belly of the demon and waved goodbye. Very early the next day, he arrived in San Francisco at the anthropological museum of the University of California, not far from where Sarah Winchester continually built her life's mausoleum. He would remain there for four years and seven months until his death from consumption.

If Ishi thought he was leaving gawking masses behind when he entered the demon, he was mistaken. One autumn afternoon, more than 1000 visitors came to see him. Ishi, however, hated crowds. As Theodora Kroeber (1961:133) wrote:

> He was becoming fairly at ease with his friends in the museum, and concealing his sudden fears from them as best he could, but the crowding around of half a dozen people made his limbs become rigid; and his first closeup of a group of perhaps

eighty or a hundred people left his faculties paralyzed. With time, he came to realize that crowds were not intrinsically menacing, and his early terrible fear abated,
but not his dislike of people in numbers such that the individual becomes lost in
the faceless throng. He never liked strangers to come too close or to touch him. He
learned to suffer the handshake as a custom universal to the white man and of
friendly intent, and to acknowledge a preferred [sic] hand promptly and with
courtesy. He never himself initiated a handshake.

No dream, no wildest nightmare, prefigured for Ishi a city crowd, its clamor, its
endless hurrying past to be endlessly replaced by others of its kind, face indistin-
guishable from face. It was like a spring salmon run, one fish leaping sightlessly beyond or over another, and he disliked the smell of people in numbers. It suggested
to him the odor of old deer hide.

Ishi called white people "saltu." *Saltu* are beings of a different order altogether
from a *Yana*, a human being. *Saltu*. Ghosts. (Kroeber 1961:137)

Though Ishi may have often felt lonely and isolated in the museum, he was
not alone. Just as skeletal remains of Indians were stored and displayed with Native artifacts in museums throughout the United States, just as *El Negro*, a nameless African, was stuffed and mounted in a glass case in a museum in Banyoles,
Spain, in an exhibit described as "unique in the world," Ishi was, perhaps more
benignly, put on display at his museum home. (Swarns 2000:A4).[1] Just as the so-
called Venus Hottentot was paraded throughout Europe while alive and ware-
housed in a museum in death, Ishi, the last Yahi, was the last of a number of living archaeological specimens to be found in American museums in the late 19th
and early 20th centuries.

Theodora Kroeber (1961:129) wrote:

Ishi's arrival in San Francisco was quiet and private, coming as it did before the
days of klieg lights and microphones. But the newspapers announced that he was
come; reporters, motion picture companies, and entrepreneurs of carnival, circus,
and vaudeville specialty acts were as avid on the trail of novelty as they and their
radio and television brothers are today. The candid camera as an uncandid tool
waited upon the future. The reporters brought to the museum on Parnassus
Heights their clumsy box cameras and were followed by private persons, men,
women, and children with their Brownie and Graflex cameras. The wild man had
aroused a city's imagination.

Some fifteen years earlier, in September 1897, polar explorer Robert Peary's
ship *Hope* sailed into the Brooklyn shipyard in New York. On board, along with
more than 100 tons of meteorites, were six Greenlander Inuit. Within the first
two days that the *Hope* was in its berth, over 30,000 New Yorkers paid twenty-

five cents a head to view them. Peary had cabled ahead of his arrival with his guests (Thomas 2000:79).

Ur-anthropologist Franz Boas arranged for the Inuit to be housed at the American Museum of Natural History. Boas, however, had scant time for the Greenlanders. Instead, he turned over responsibility for them to his young student, Alfred Kroeber, who, later, with Thomas Waterman, would rescue Ishi from the Oroville jail and bring him to the University of California museum in San Francisco. Within a short time, however, all the Inuit became ill. Soon, four were dead from complications of tuberculosis, which would later claim Ishi as well. Kroeber would work with the Inuit until the end, collecting ethnographic data. His information about mortuary customs would be used to stage a funeral for the group's leader, Qisuk (Harper 2000:30–35). Franz Boas attended, standing alongside Minik, Qisuk's son. Unfortunately, Qisuk was not, at least corporally, in attendance. After his death at Bellevue Hospital, his body had been dissected at Columbia's College of Physicians and Surgeons; his bones had been macerated, bleached, and returned to the museum for addition to its collection. His brain was preserved in fluid and studied by noted physical anthropologist Aleš Hrdlička, who published an article about it, entitled "An Eskimo Brain," in 1901 (Harper 2000:85–92). By then, the Arctic explorer had washed his hands of those who had been called "Peary's people." Apparently no demons ever troubled the admiral's sleep, except perhaps the specter of Dr. Frederick Cook, who later challenged his claim to primacy over the North Pole (Herbert 1989:204–205).

Theodora Kroeber reported that Ishi, on his daily rounds, once entered the hospital next door to the museum, but seeing no one he recognized, he wandered down the hall, eventually coming upon the autopsy room, where he saw "several cadavers laid out on marble slabs, partly uncovered and in various stages of classroom dissection" (Kroeber 1961:176). The sight both horrified and appalled the Native, as did the presence in the museum of Egyptian and Peruvian mummies and the "bones of many, many Indians" (Kroeber 1961:177). Saxton Pope attempted to distract Ishi by focusing on the medical aspects of surgery.

Minik never experienced the terrifying confrontation that Ishi did. He was unaware of the subterfuge of the phony funeral until years later, when he read about it in a New York newspaper. This did not, however, stop a cartoonist for the *San Francisco Examiner* from imagining such a scene. An illustration for a 1909 article entitled "Why Arctic Explorer Peary's Neglected Eskimo Boy Wants to Shoot Him" showed a recoiling Minik discovering his father's skeleton in a museum case bearing the label, "Skeleton of Eskimo, presented by Robert E. Peary." Minik did make a futile and piteous attempt to get the museum to turn over his father's remains to him. A sensational headline in the January 6, 1907, *New York World* trumpeted, "Give Me My Father's Body" (Herbert 1989:205). Theodora Kroeber remarked on Ishi's "un-Indian volatility," "suggesting kinship with the Eskimos' expressive temperament" (Kroeber 1961:126).

"Mountebanks and showmen are part of the human condition," wrote Theodora Kroeber (1961:128). "The distance their message reaches and the tools of its transmittal change with time and place, but not their business which has always been to inform, to exaggerate, to advertise, to tell the world what it wants to hear. For the human condition is often drab, or disappointing, when it is not desperate." The San Francisco museum, she noted, was overrun by "mountebanks and plain and simple exploiters" (Kroeber 1961:128). Was William Red Fox among them? By his own description, he was working in movies at the time. It seems unlikely that he would have forgone an opportunity such as that presented by the Yahi's presence nearby. I would also like to imagine that, if they met, Ishi would have recognized the poseur as a *saltu*.

Of those who mobbed the San Francisco university museum, Kroeber (1961:129–130) wrote:

There were the impresarios of the large vaudeville circuits – Pantages and Orpheum – one of whom had the imagination to offer to "take over" both Kroeber and Ishi, to promote them as a two-man act under a billing of "educational" and "edifying." A cut below were those who wanted to "borrow" Ishi for a "showing," or as an "exhibit"; and below them, those who were ready to carry off Ishi to be part of a traveling carnival. And then there were the hard-bitten and unsavory tribe who operate narrow dives like peep shows on lower Market Street, calculated to catch the lonely sailor on liberty and the drifter with a nickel or a dime to pay to have a look at the well-illuminated painting of a nude woman, or at the highly realistic figure of a head hunter in the round and in the buff. For a few weeks at least, a live wild man might have been expected to be worth as much as two bits to see.

An indigenous person, whether in buckskin or buff, was easily worth twenty-five cents, whether it be Ishi, an Eskimo – or an African.

In central Africa, it was known that *muzungus* (whites) had something to do with the mass disappearances that had accompanied the slave trade. Natives in the Congo believed that they were "refugees from the land of the dead," explaining that "the white men are dead people who have once lived in our villages, but when they died, they came to the place where the dead are to be found, and there they shed their skins (just as some snakes), after which they had white bodies" (Bradford and Blume 1992:30). Sometimes, the Africans fled their approach, shouting, "Ghosts!"

In March 1903, as Red Fox rejoined Buffalo Bill's spectacle at New York's

Madison Square Garden, a young African male stood for sale in the slave market of Baschilele in the Congo Free State. Like Ishi, Ota Benga's family was dead. They had been killed by the *Force Publique* while he was away hunting. No mourning ritual was performed for them. Like Ishi, "Ota had lost his family, his world, and the world view that framed it" (Bradford and Blume 1992:106). A *muzungu* stepped forward and purchased him for a bolt of cloth and a pound of salt.

The *muzungu* was Samuel Phillips Verner, a slightly crazed missionary, adventurer, and would-be industrialist. He had been commissioned by anthropologist W J McGee to bring back pygmies for the 1904 World's Fair to be held in St. Louis (the Louisiana Purchase Exposition). For McGee the fair was an opportunity to elevate anthropology above the hobbyist level in the eyes of the public. Formerly of the Smithsonian, McGee once described the Seri Indians of Mexico as "zoocratic" in governance. His intent now was to assemble "representatives of all the world's races, ranging from the smallest pygmies to the most gigantic peoples, from the darkest blacks to the dominant whites," from the "'lowest known culture' to contrast with 'its highest culmination'" (Bradford and Blume 1992:94–95). Verner, perpetually strapped for cash, merely wanted his thousand-dollar fee. He pried apart Ota's lips to examine his teeth. Seeing that they had been filed to sharpened points, he was elated, knowing that this was one of those he had been sent to procure. He wrote McGee, "The first pygmy has been secured!" (Bradford and Blume 1992:103–106)

Just as Theodora Kroeber penned an account of Ishi and her husband, so Verner's grandson, Phillips Verner Bradford, authored the story of Ota in *Ota Benga: The Pygmy in the Zoo*. According to Bradford, Verner "saw himself as saving Ota. With salt and cloth he was buying him for freedom, Darwinism, and the West." For his part, Ota, like Ishi when he wandered into Oroville, was indifferent as to whether he lived or died. He had no reason to believe that this *muzungu* was anything other than a ghost, but he had nothing to lose by accompanying him when the alternative was a life of slavery in Africa (Bradford and Blume 1992:106).

Verner himself wrote accounts about Ota, beginning with *Harper's Weekly* while the Louisiana Purchase Exposition was in full swing. According to Bradford, however, he rewrote the encounter, "humanizing it, simplifying it, making it more comprehensible to himself and his readers – making it play more like Friday's first encounter with Robinson Crusoe" (Bradford and Blume 1992:106–107). He imputed delight to Ota at his salvation. Similarly, Theodora Kroeber presents Ishi as happy and congenial (Kroeber 1961:125–126). One must read the interstices. Surely, like Ota, the often withdrawn and solitary Yahi must have been haunted.

In 1914, when Kroeber, Waterman, and Pope proposed an expedition to his old homeland, Ishi resisted. He called the trip "crazy." When the whites would brook no refusal, he surrendered. According to Theodora Kroeber (1961:205–206):

> Resigned to his friends' madness he was, but very, very unhappy. . . . It would be like going to visit the Land of the Dead. The unquiet souls of his murdered people lingered there, some of them. To revisit *Wowunupo mu tetna* where the engineers had surprised him would be to relive the terrible fright, and his sister's flight in one direction and his own in another, never to find trace of her after that day. He would much have preferred not to go, but he made no further objection, merely protesting one gratuitous risk in getting ready for such a dubious expedition.

Though she states that he was happy on the trip and that it was therapeutic for him, her own evidence contradicts such a view. She notes that he "became suddenly eager to be back in the museum, to be *home*. The others of the party were reluctant to leave, to go back to 'civilization,' but Ishi eagerly forwarded the dismantling of the base camp and the loading of the pack animals. He even took with complaisance the horseback trip back," a prospect that normally terrified him (Kroeber 1961:205, 216).[2] Ishi was fleeing. At the train depot in Vina, as he stepped inside the demon for his return to San Francisco, he made his one and only public address, shouting to the assembled crowd, "Ladies and gentlemen! Goodbye!" (Kroeber 1961:216)

At the 1904 World's Fair, Indians were placed on the cultural continuum next to Africans, and thus the pygmies were encamped alongside the Natives. Ota got to know Geronimo, who was there under guard. The Apache warrior teased the Africans that whites were cannibals and that the pygmies had better keep a close eye on the crowd, because some of them looked hungry. Just as thousands of museum visitors watched Ishi chip arrowheads and make bows, so Geronimo made and sold bows and arrows to the fairgoers. He gave Ota an arrowhead as a gift (Bradford and Blume 1992:16).

For his part, Ota, who charged a nickel to display his sharpened teeth, was felt, poked, prodded, and jabbered at. He was seen by patrons as "pitiable" but also "to be feared and shuddered at." According to Bradford, the Africans "sensed the white man's hunger to see savages, wildmen, murderous flesh-eating terrors – to be titillated by demons, frightened by the apparition of their worst fears come to life." And, on at least one occasion, they obliged, lunging at the crowd, brandishing bows and arrows, and shouting war cries. The whites fled in terror (Bradford and Blume 1992:116, 119).

Following the St. Louis fair, Ota went back to Africa in the spring of 1905. A year later, however, he agreed to return to the United States with Verner, expecting only a brief stay. In August 1906, however, Verner, once again short of funds, unceremoniously dumped Ota, along with some chimps he had also collected in Africa, at the American Museum of Natural History. When the press spotted him, reporters pushed museum director Hermon Bumpus for comment, but he demurred. According to Bradford, "With dead Eskimos and negative press notices in recent memory, he wanted to steer Ota Benga away from publicity" (Bradford and Blume 1992:164).

At first, the museum fascinated Ota. He roamed its halls looking at the animal skeletons and chanting his hunting songs. He loved to climb Ahnighito, the giant meteorite that Peary had brought back with Minik and the other Inuits. But shortly, he grew haunted. "What had at first held his attention now made him want to flee. It was maddening to be inside – to be swallowed whole – so long. He had an image of himself stuffed, behind glass, but still somehow alive, crouching over a fake campfire, feeding meat to a lifeless child. Museum silence became a source of torment, a kind of noise; he needed birdsong, breezes, trees" (Bradford and Blume 1992:166). He tried to smuggle himself out by mingling with an exiting crowd. On another occasion, Bumpus showed him off to wealthy patrons. When he told Ota to get Florence Guggenheim a chair, the African hurled the seat, narrowly missing her head. Bumpus found him sitting on Ahnighito, and he refused to dismount. The museum director wrote Verner, "Ota Benga restless. Chimpanzees need attention. When can you reach New York?" (Bradford and Blume 1992:167)

Verner solved Bumpus's problem in late August 1906, when William Temple Hornaday, director of the Bronx Zoological Gardens, agreed to buy Verner's horned viper, the chimpanzees, and Ota Benga. Though Ota was not particularly unhappy at the zoo, he still expected to return home to Africa. On September 8, Hornaday, in a bold deployment of Social Darwinism that eluded even W J McGee, put Ota Benga on display in the Monkey House. The following day, the *New York Times* headlined, "Bushman Shares a Cage with Bronx Park Apes," and thousands of gawkers descended upon the zoo. A sign on the enclosure read, "The African Pygmy, 'Ota Benga.' Age, 28 years. Height, 4 feet 11 inches. Weight 103 pounds. Brought from the Kasai River, Congo Free State, South Central Africa, by Dr. Samuel P. Verner, Exhibited each afternoon during September" (Bradford and Blume 1992:178–181). On September 16 an estimated 40,000 visitors came to witness the spectacle. The *Times* wrote, "Nearly every man, woman, and child of this crowd made for the monkey house to see the star attraction in the park – the wild man from Africa. They chased him about the grounds all day, howling, jeering and yelling. Some of them poked him in the ribs, others tripped him up, all laughed at him" (quoted in Bradford and Blume 1992:185).

Protests by black clergy and Ota's increasing lack of cooperation in his exploitation quickly closed the macabre exhibit. On September 27 Ota left the zoo for the Howard Colored Orphan Asylum. He gradually faded from public view. His filed teeth were capped to present a more "normal" visage. In January 1910, he left the orphanage for Lynchburg Baptist Seminary in Virginia. Though there he met luminaries like Booker T. Washington and W. E. B. DuBois, he kept largely to himself, walking in the woods. He was plagued by nightmares of the museum and his inability to afford passage back to the Congo. In one dream, according to Bradford, Ota saw himself back at the museum, walking through the exhibits with Verner. Verner explained how wealthy men donated objects for display. Bradford writes, "This gave Ota a surprising idea. He too would make a donation: He would donate himself. Would he not then be a rich man? No one else had yet donated a pygmy to the museum. Besides, he had nothing else to donate. He would give himself to Bumpus. Bumpus would put him to sleep behind the panels of his own glass case like a stuffed animal" (Bradford and Blume 1992:215–216).

March 1916 proved the pivotal month for all three living fossils, these museum-dwelling tributes to the dark birth pangs of anthropology. The previous summer, the three-masted schooner *George B. Cluett,* under charter to the American Museum of Natural History, arrived in Greenland, only to be subsequently frozen in for the winter. By March, Minik, who had gone back to the Arctic in 1909, was calculating his return to New York aboard the stranded vessel (Harper 2000:200–203).

Thousands of miles away, Ishi's tuberculosis had worsened. He died at noon on March 25. In Virginia, on March 20, while Ishi lay on his deathbed in California, Ota Benga built a fire, broke the caps off his teeth, stripped to his loincloth, and began to dance and sing around the fire. He then took a stolen revolver, and still singing, put the gun to his heart and fired once. Ota Benga sent his soul back to Africa (Bradford and Blume 1992:216–218). When he heard the news, an unfazed Hornaday wrote, "Evidently, he felt that he would rather die than work for a living" (Bradford and Blume 1992:220).

On September 21, 1916, Minik disembarked in New York. He called a press conference, claiming to have information about the controversy between Peary and Cook that had raged when he departed some years earlier. No one much cared. Perhaps interest in the polar discovery issue had long since waned. Perhaps no one paid attention to him because he was no longer a cute Inuit boy. Or perhaps no one listened as Minik asserted his own desperate agency because people preferred their scientific specimens dumb. He took odd jobs, eventually working as a lumberjack in New Hampshire. He died in the influenza epidemic of 1918 and was buried in a small graveyard on the banks of Indian Stream. The era of the living fossils was over.

On March 24, 1916, Alfred Kroeber, away in New York, knowing Yahi beliefs about the dead, and remembering Ishi's horror at discovering the dissection room, wrote to his museum colleagues (Kroeber 1961:234):

> Please stand by our contingently made outline of action, and insist on it as my personal wish. . . . I do not . . . see that an autopsy would lead to anything of consequence, but would resolve itself into a general dissection. Please shut down on it. . . . If there is any talk about the interests of science, say for me that science can go to hell. We propose to stand by our friends. Besides, I cannot believe that any scientific value is materially involved. We have hundreds of Indian skeletons and nobody ever comes near to study. The prime interest in this case would be of a morbid romantic nature.

The letter arrived too late. Saxton Pope performed the autopsy.

As part of the autopsy, Pope removed Ishi's brain and preserved it. The rest of the Indian's remains were cremated, in accordance with what were understood to be his wishes. His ashes were placed in a small Santa Clara Pueblo jar and interred at Mount Olivet Cemetery. Seven months later, Kroeber wrote to Aleš Hrdlička, the physical anthropologist who had studied Qisuk's brain: "I find that at Ishi's death last spring his brain was removed and preserved. There is no one here who can put it to scientific use. If you wish it, I shall be glad to deposit it in the National Museum Collection." Hrdlička replied that he would "be very glad" to have the specimen. On January 5, 1917, Ishi's brain was shipped to the Smithsonian Institution (Thomas 2000:221).

In May 1997, California Indians announced their intention to rebury Ishi in his tribal homeland. They refused to proceed with their plans without the brain. After a two-year search, his brain was located at the Smithsonian's curation facility in Silver Spring, Maryland. The museum agreed to return the brain in accordance with the provisions of the National Museum of the American Indian Act. Until the Natives' inquiry, museum officials stated, they had not known that anyone was looking for it (Thomas 2000:220–221).

In an essay on James Fenimore Cooper, D. H. Lawrence ([1923] 1971:56) wrote:

> America hurts, because it has a powerful disintegrative influence upon the white psyche. It is full of grinning, unappeased aboriginal demons, too, ghosts, and it persecutes the white men, like some Eumenides, until the white men give up their absolute whiteness. America is tense with latent violence and resistance. . . .

Yet one day the demons of America must be placated, the ghosts must be appeased, the Spirit of Place atoned for. Then the true passionate love for American Soil will appear. As yet, there is too much menace in the landscape.

Minik and Ota Benga remain buried in that American Soil, that menacing landscape far from home. In August 1997, Qisuk and his companions were reburied, without Minik, at Qaanag, Greenland (Harper 2000:228). Ishi has finally gone home. Perhaps those restless spirits, those ghosts that haunted William Red Fox and Sarah Winchester and untold others, are finding appeasement at last.

> Doom! Doom! Doom! Something seems to whisper it in the very dark trees of America. Doom!
> Doom of what?
> Doom of our white day. We are doomed, doomed. And the doom is in America. The doom of our white day.
> Ah, well, if my day is doomed, and I am doomed with my day, it is something greater than I which dooms me, so I accept my doom as a sign of the greatness which is more than I am.
>
> D. H. Lawrence

NOTES

1. *El Negro* was first displayed in 1888 and was removed from exhibit and repatriated to Botswana only in 2000. As of this writing, South Africa still awaits the return of the so-called Venus Hottentot, whose skeleton and preserved genitals remain in France.

2. Emphasis original.

REFERENCES

Bradford, Philips Verner, and Harvey Blume. 1992. *Ota Benga: the pygmy in the zoo.* New York: St. Martin's.

Harper, Kenn. 2000. *Give me my father's body: the life of Minik, the New York Eskimo.* South Royalton VT: Steerforth.

Herbert, Wally. 1989. *The noose of laurels: the discovery of the North Pole.* London: Hodder & Stoughton.

Kroeber, Theodora. 1961. *Ishi in two worlds: a biography of the last wild Indian in North America.* Berkeley: University of California.

Lawrence, D. H. [1923] 1971. *Studies in classic American literature.* Reprint, London: Penguin.

Red Fox, William. 1971. *The memoirs of Chief Red Fox.* New York: McGraw-Hill.

Smith, Carlton. 2000. *Coyote kills John Wayne: postmodernism and contemporary fictions of the transcultural frontier.* Hanover NH: Dartmouth College/University Press of New England.

Swarns, Rachel L. 2000. Africa rejoices as a wandering soul finds rest. *The New York Times,* 6 October.

Thomas, David Hurst. 2000. *Skull wars.* New York: Basic Books.

4

Kroeber, Pope, and Ishi

GRACE WILSON BUZALJKO

This paper was written in reaction to the Berkeley Anthropology Department's
public statement in 1999, apologizing that its former chairman, Alfred L. Kroeber,
had in 1916 "failed in his efforts to honor Ishi's wishes not to be autopsied and he
inexplicably arranged for Ishi's brain to be shipped to and to be curated at the
Smithsonian" (Brandes 1999).

First of all, as one who has been studying the history of the Berkeley department since 1981 and has read all the extant correspondence about Ishi between
Kroeber, Thomas T. Waterman (Kroeber's colleague), Edward W. Gifford
(Kroeber's museum assistant), and Saxton T. Pope (Ishi's personal physician), I
think it highly unjust to blame Kroeber for failing to prevent Ishi's autopsy and
the removal of his brain. His later decision to send the brain to the Smithsonian
stemmed from the limited options that seemed open to him.

In the summer of 1915 Kroeber began the first sabbatical he had had in the fourteen years he had been with the department. Before leaving, he arranged for linguist Edward Sapir to come for the summer from Ottawa, where he was head of
the department of anthropology at the Canadian Geological Survey, to work
with Ishi. Sapir was to write down and translate Yahi myths and vocabulary
items dictated by Ishi, tasks that were highly demanding but possible because
Sapir had worked earlier with a few Northern and Central Yana people, who
were speakers of languages related to Yahi (see Sapir 1910:2–4). The plan was
that the interviews would take place in Berkeley and that Ishi would stay there
with Waterman; his wife, Grace (Godwin) Waterman; and their two-year-
old daughter, Helen, who was recovering from nephritis (inflammation of the
kidneys).

It was not until 1920 that Pope admitted "retrospectively" that Ishi's "active

48

tuberculosis start[ed]" in the winter of 1914–15, when he was in the University of California Hospital in San Francisco for two months and had positive reactions to tuberculin skin tests, though no tubercle bacilli were found in his sputum (Pope 1920:196). Fortunately, none of the Waterman family contracted the disease. Ishi slept on the outdoor sleeping porch, and Thomas Waterman shared it with him, as Gifford mentioned to Kroeber (Gifford-Kroeber Letters, Department and Museum of Anthropology Archives, Bancroft Library, August 10, 1915). Also, Ishi and Sapir probably did not work together at the fairly small Waterman house but in the Anthropology Building on the Berkeley campus, several blocks to the north.

Shortly after Sapir and Ishi began their work, Kroeber wrote Gifford from Zuni pueblo in New Mexico, requesting him to ask Waterman or Sapir to keep "fairly regular tab" on Ishi's afternoon temperatures and weight, "and if either shows unfavorable symptoms, shoot him over to Pope for examination. It's our responsibility and we ought to live up to it fully" (Gifford-Kroeber letters, July 7, 1915). Kroeber was spending the summer in Zuni to study its social organization, under the auspices of the American Museum of Natural History in New York. Having lost his wife, Henriette Rothschild Kroeber, to tuberculosis less than two years before, Kroeber was fully aware of the symptoms of the disease.

From Zuni Kroeber traveled to New York, where he made a seemingly abrupt decision to visit western Europe, which was then in the early throes of World War I. It was not difficult to book passage. In late August, about a week before he was to sail, Kroeber received two letters from Gifford, who reported that Ishi had been readmitted to the hospital for observation. This time two doctors had made a tentative diagnosis that fluids were collecting between his left lung and the membranes covering it. In the second note, written the same day (August 22), Gifford asked Kroeber for instructions on appointing either Waterman or himself as administrator in the event of Ishi's death (Gifford 1915, in A. L. Kroeber Papers, Bancroft Library).

On August 28, Kroeber wrote to Waterman about Ishi's prognosis (Kroeber 1915a):

> We have got to handle the case. The physicians go by the book and rule, and it's up to us to apply our knowledge of the individual and our judgment to their findings and advice. He undoubtedly has had tb since last winter, though for the last 6 months it has been only latent. He crowded it back that far once, and there is no reason why he should not do so again, if things break well. But it's damn serious.

Kroeber went on to describe Saxton Pope as "over optimistic," but nevertheless he expressed greater confidence in him than in the other doctors on the hospital staff. Kroeber emphasized to Waterman that "in any event the ultimate responsibility will rest with you" (Kroeber 1915b).

To Gifford the next day Kroeber replied (Gifford-Kroeber Letters, August 29, 1915):

I have written Waterman fully about Ishi. As to administratorship, there is nothing beyond the desirability that in case of his going off the matter should be decently attended to and the funds he has [from his salary as museum helper] be used to bury him like a gentleman instead of reverting to the state.

Long-standing attachment and academic status played a part in Kroeber's decision to write to these younger colleagues. Waterman had been Kroeber's graduate student at Berkeley starting in 1907, and an instructor by 1910. He had earned a doctorate in anthropology under Franz Boas at Columbia University in 1914. He was assistant professor and acting head of the Anthropology Department and its museum during Kroeber's absence. Gifford, whose formal education had ended at Alameda High School in Oakland, had held a nonacademic appointment as associate curator of the museum since 1912. Kroeber, perennially shorthanded and seeing a promising novice, had sent Gifford for two seasons of fieldwork among the Central Sierra Miwok. He had also assigned him to begin lecturing in the fall of 1915 in Anthropology's year-long introductory course with Waterman and Wilson D. Wallis, who was about to receive his doctorate from the University of Pennsylvania and would be substituting for Kroeber (Kroeber 1915a; University of California 1915:46).

On November 7, 1915, Waterman sent Kroeber a summarizing letter about Ishi, thinking that he might not have received mail while in Europe; this letter was awaiting him when he returned to New York on November 21. In it Waterman said that Ishi had been kept in the hospital until early October, when, as he put it, "they could not accomodate him further, then at Warburton's suggestion we rigged up the Pacific Islands room for an infirmary and put him in there. Warburton is taking fine care of him and Pope says he is better off than in the hospital" (Kroeber Papers).[1]

Arthur Warburton, a skillful former British seaman, was the museum's preparator. The unsung hero of the last five months of Ishi's life, he washed and cared for Ishi, cooked most of his meals, and saw to it that a new museum helper, Richard Kretschmer, was on hand when he went off duty to his own home and family. In addition, Frances McMahon, the clerk-stenographer at the museum, often prepared Ishi's lunches (Gifford-Kroeber Letters, September 30, 1915; Herman 1953, lists of museum helpers and assistants and of typists, clerks, etc.).

Comparing the amounts of information from his two assistants awaiting him in New York, Kroeber wrote Gifford, "Just a line to let you know that I am back after a trip I would not have missed for anything, and keen on getting to work. . . . Keep me posted on Ishi's condition: Waterman is less in touch with him and an irregular correspondent" (Gifford-Kroeber Letters, November 21, 1915). Waterman, teaching five days a week in Berkeley, could usually visit San Francisco only on Sundays (Waterman 1915b). Not incidentally, Gifford had told Kroeber on September 30 that the doctors had said that Ishi was "in no condition to move to the country." Thus Kroeber's earlier ruminations to Waterman (Kroeber 1915a) and to Gifford (Gifford-Kroeber Letters, August 29, 1915) about friends in rural places who might care for Ishi upon his discharge from the hospital were never pursued.

Kroeber had made arrangements to spend the winter and spring of 1915–16 in New York City, where he would have office space at the American Museum of Natural History and would continue work on a massive research and writing project, his *Handbook of the Indians of California* (Kroeber 1925). His major goal in California had always been to record the languages and cultures of its Indian people, and now he would have seven months of time, free from teaching and administering, to organize the materials that he and his colleagues, professional and nonprofessional, had collected over the years. It was, as he later described it to anthropologist and feminist Elsie Clews Parsons, his "first chance to work since kid days" (letter to Parsons, June 11, 1916, quoted in Rosemary Lévy Zumwalt 1992:172). To deflect him from this path would be difficult.

The next principal character in this drama, Pope, was born at an army post in Texas in 1875, the third of seven children of an army surgeon, and was reared at a series of other military posts, mainly in the West. He originally planned to become an engineer, but, according to one biographer, on the evening he was due to leave for Stanford, his father remarked that none of his six sons appeared likely to follow him in his profession. Saxton immediately changed his field of study, enrolling in the University of California's school of medicine in San Francisco (Berry 1929:133). Smaller in stature than his brothers, he may have always felt it necessary to compete with them. He graduated in 1899 with second highest honors. First honors went to Emma Wightman, who became his wife and partner in a medical practice the couple set up in Watsonville, about eighty miles south of San Francisco. As their family grew to include two sons and two daughters, Emma W. Pope gave up her profession to care for them (Berry 1929:135–137, 141; Eloesser 1973:846).

In 1912 Saxton Pope returned to the University's medical school as an instructor in surgery. A man of many talents, he was a musician and a maker of fine musical instruments; he entertained not only his own children but the young patients in the hospital with his sleight-of-hand magic. Indeed, Pope

(1920:181) wrote, it was these skills – to "vanish coins, change eggs into paper, swallow impossible objects at will" – that "convinced Ishi that I was a real doctor, much more than any medication or surgery at my command."[2]

That same year Pope and another doctor at the hospital, J. V. Cooke, "took up the practice of archery ... under Ishi's guidance, at first according to the Indian's own methods, though later we followed the English style," as Pope (1918:104) said in the first of three monographs he wrote on Ishi and archery in the Anthropology Department's series.[3] "What the writer knows of Ishi's archery is based upon three years' association with him. In this period many hours were spent in making bows and arrows, in talking about shooting, in target practice, and in hunting trips in the fields and woods." He and Ishi were unselfconscious in their linguistic efforts. "Together, they spoke a pidgin Yana-English all their own," Theodora Kroeber later wrote (1961:153).

Here is Pope's vivid description of Ishi preparing for a deer hunt, from his later book for general readers, *Hunting with the Bow and Arrow* (Pope [1923a] 1947:32–33):

> He would eat no fish the day before the hunt, and smoke no tobacco, for these odors are detected a great way off. He rose early, bathed in the creek, rubbed himself with the aromatic leaves of yerba buena, washed out his mouth, drank water, but ate no food. Dressed in a loin cloth, but without shirt, leggings or moccasins, he set out, bow and quiver at his side. He said that clothing made too much noise in the brush, and naturally one is more cautious in his movements when reminded by his sensitive hide that he is touching a sharp twig. . . . As he walked, he placed every footfall with precise care; the most stealthy step I ever saw; he was used to it; lived by it. . . .

Pope ([1923a] 1947:33–34) continued:

> Although Ishi took me on many deer hunts and we had several shots at deer, owing to the distance or the fall of the ground or obstructing trees, we registered nothing better than encouraging misses. He was undoubtedly hampered by the presence of a novice, and unduly hastened by the white man's lack of time. . . .
>
> That he had shot many deer, even since boyhood, there was no doubt. To prove that he could shoot through one with his arrows, I had him discharge several at a buck killed by our packer [with a gun]. Shooting at forty yards, one arrow went through the chest wall, half its length; another struck the spine and fractured it, both being mortal wounds.

Thus the 1914 Deer Creek photographs of Ishi pulling an arrow out of a dead deer were staged.

These were the happy times with Pope and the others in the woods and hills of northern California. But life for Ishi in the museum in San Francisco had its darker side, even before his final illness, as Pope (1920:180) wrote:

> The presence of all the bones of the dead, their belongings, and the mummies were ever a source of anxiety to him. He locked his bedroom door at night to keep out spirits. When [in 1914] we stored our camping provender temporarily in the Museum bone room, Ishi was not only disgusted [but] genuinely alarmed. It was only after the reassurance that the "bunch a mi si tee" could not enter through the tin of the cans that he was relieved.

Ishi was the only full-time resident of the museum. There were three regular museum guards in those years: Arthur Poyser, Llewellyn Loud, and Robert Gibson. Poyser and Loud also worked part-time as janitors, and there were a few substitute guards who could be called upon as needed (Herman 1953, list of museum guards and janitors). Two guards were on duty on any one night as protectors against fire, and others were on day duty, but none of them made their home at the museum. All (including Loud, who was unmarried) had living quarters in San Francisco, Oakland, or nearby towns.[4]

Loud, according to Pope (1920:132), was Ishi's roommate. He was a taciturn, intelligent man from rural Maine who had been an independent student at Berkeley. Like Ishi, he had arrived at the museum in 1911. Kroeber came to entrust Loud with solitary excavations at near and distant prehistoric Indian sites, as he did in 1913, when he sent him to the Humboldt Bay area of northwestern California to investigate a former Wiyot site (Heizer 1970; Kroeber 1947). Inevitably Ishi would have known about this other work of Loud's and also about Loud's work in the museum's bone room, so that his association with Loud may have been a somewhat uneasy one. For his part, Loud did not comment on Ishi in his letters or his published writings, which Kroeber edited. However, with his strong sense of social justice, Loud would have felt an affinity with him, as he did with the descendants of the Wiyot survivors of the white massacres and removals of 1860–63, whom he interviewed and whose earlier history he reprinted from accounts by sympathetic whites which had been sent to the San Francisco *Bulletin*, a city newspaper (Loud 1918:323–337).

While Loud was away at the Wiyot site in 1913, Kroeber arranged to have Juan Dolores, his Papago (or Tohono O'odham) friend, work as a substitute guard for four months and stay on for another month to resume his work on Papago grammar (see Dolores 1913, 1923; Kroeber 1921; Kroeber 1949). During that time Dolores shared Ishi's room, and the two men became good friends, although their life experiences were very different. Dolores had been reared on the Papago reservation in Arizona, had graduated from Hampton Institute in Virginia, and usually worked as a teamster, in the traditional meaning of that word, or as a skilled laborer at large construction sites in the West.[5]

Ishi himself was an employee of the University, at least from August 22, 1912, when the department's revolving fund statement showed that he was being paid $2.50 a week as a janitorial assistant (University of California, Department of Anthropology and Museum Accounts Files, statement for October 1–22, 1912). By the 1913–14 year Ishi's position was regularized and his yearly salary was being paid out of the general University account. As Kroeber (1913) commented to University of California President Benjamin Ide Wheeler and the other University administrators, "Ishi is now virtually a factotum, and his labor is worth far more than $200 annually. The difficult problem of his future has been solved with economic and moral advantage to himself and the University."

On December 16, 1915, on a readers' and helpers' roll, Waterman listed Ishi's salary at $25 a month for the next six months; by comparison, Loud was then earning $40 a month (Waterman 1915a). Ishi continued to receive his small salary even after he became seriously ill. Waterman had told Kroeber on November 7, 1915, "I have not brought up the matter of his salary [with the University administrators], as I chose to consider that we were entitled to detail him to stay in bed in the museum if we thought fit" (Kroeber Papers).

In his sickroom at the museum, Ishi had a brief respite from about mid-November to mid-December, with lower afternoon temperatures and a lessening of the hiccups that had racked him earlier (Warburton Notes to Gifford, November 23 to December 20, 1915; Waterman in Kroeber Papers, November 17 and December 4, 1915). After that, his decline was fairly steady. Gifford's letter to Kroeber on February 4, 1916, would have been the capstone if Kroeber had intended to see Ishi before he died: "Dr. Pope . . . says [Ishi's] condition is not at all reassuring. . . . Pope believes that the disease is spreading to the stomach and intestines, and furthermore, that Ishi is gradually failing" (Kroeber Papers).

On March 18, Gifford wrote to tell Kroeber that Ishi's death was impending:

Yesterday Doctors Summersgill and ——— visited Ishi. For the first time his sputum shows signs of tubercolosis [sic] germs. Pope came in this morning and removed Ishi to the isolation ward in the hospital. . . . Pope says he will probably not last over two weeks, or a month at the outside. He wants to make a cast of his face and hands after death; also to perform an autopsy. I told him that it is your order, and the Indian's wish, that he have a proper burial . . . .

Although Pope did not say so, I gathered . . . that the hospital would like to have the body. I am going to see Waterman immediately.

Upon receipt of this letter, if you have any further instructions, you had better telegraph them (Gifford-Kroeber Letters).

On March 24 Kroeber sent Gifford both a letter and a telegram (Gifford-Kroeber Letters). In the letter Kroeber objected strongly to an autopsy and the possible use of Ishi's body for anatomical study: "If there is any talk about the interests of science, say for me that science can go to hell. We propose to stand by our friends." The letter arrived too late. The telegram was received at Western Union in downtown San Francisco at 6:17 A.M. on March 25. Ishi died at noon that day. The wire read, "Urge complete adherence original plans. Pope will honor my wishes." If Gifford showed Pope the telegram, it did not deter him.

Meanwhile, a grief-stricken Waterman was writing to Kroeber, "As you have heard from Gifford, the poor old Indian is dying. The work last summer was too much for him. He was the best friend I had in the world, and I killed him by letting Sapir ride him too hard, and by letting him sneak out of lunches" (Kroeber Papers, March 25).

Waterman, distraught, blamed both himself and Sapir, and then sided with Pope against Gifford. On March 30 Gifford told Kroeber how events had transpired: " . . . an autopsy was performed and . . . the brain was preserved. However, the matter, as you well know, was not entirely in my hands, as I am not the acting head of the department" (Gifford-Kroeber Letters).

Pope was a combination of scientist and romantic, with the scientist having had the upper hand in this crisis. A resident physician, E. H. Falconer, prepared the clinical record of Ishi's last admission to the hospital, giving the diagnosis at death before the autopsy as pulmonary tuberculosis. Pope, who seemed unconvinced of this diagnosis because Ishi had not shown all the typical symptoms, insisted on the autopsy. It was conducted by Dr. J. V. Cooke of the hospital's pathology laboratory, who, like Pope, had been Ishi's archery student. Cooke noted that the brain was removed, thus giving some indication that this action was not standard procedure. From the autopsy report, Pope concluded, Ishi had died of bovine tuberculosis, derived through the intestinal tract. Ishi's brain was not studied after all. These two medical reports and Pope's conclusions were published in his *Medical History of Ishi* (Pope 1920:206–213).

Pope, having understood from Ishi that the Yahi customarily burned their dead, also changed Kroeber's earlier instructions from a burial for Ishi to a cremation. The ashes were put in a small black Pueblo jar and placed in a niche at Mount Olivet Cemetery (later called Olivet Memorial Park) in Colma, near San Francisco (Gifford-Kroeber Letters, March 30, 1916).

In New York in early June, shortly before Kroeber planned to leave for a return to Zuni and San Francisco, he received an invitation from Elsie Clews Parsons to visit her summer home in Lenox, Massachusetts. He had to decline her invitation but took the occasion to write a letter that reveals something of his interior life in these weeks after Ishi's death: "As I am forty today, I may still if fate wills it, and in spite of all the waste of the past, take and give a few blows before they roll me over into the ditch or I retire into the sheath of the old age class" (Kroeber, letter to Parsons, June 11, 1916, American Philosophical Society, quoted in Rosemary Lévy Zumwalt 1992:172).

After his summer in Zuni, Kroeber returned to the museum in San Francisco in late August 1916. There he found a macabre object awaiting him: a container holding Ishi's brain (Foster 1999). Why it had been delivered to him is a mystery, and Kroeber may have been too upset and angry to discuss the issue calmly with Pope. As we now know from the research of Rockafellar and Starn (1999), within two months Kroeber decided to offer the brain to a noted physical anthropologist, Aleš Hrdlička, of the Smithsonian's Museum of Natural History, with whom he had been corresponding on other matters (Kroeber 1916). To Kroeber, this decision must have seemed to be virtually the only one open to him. Hrdlička had visited him at the museum in San Francisco in January 1915 to view some of the ancient Egyptian skeletal remains that archaeologist George A. Reisner had unearthed under Phoebe A. Hearst's sponsorship. Kroeber knew that Hrdlička was even more interested in the origin and antiquity of the first humans in the Americas and that he had a collection of human and nonhuman primate brains. Hrdlička for his part accepted Kroeber's offer.[6]

The series of crises around Ishi's death, his autopsy, and Kroeber's discovery of the brain must have been factors in Kroeber's request for a leave of absence from Berkeley for the first six months of 1918. It may have been at this time that he underwent a brief psychoanalysis in New York City while again working at the American Museum (but see note 7). Another factor in his discouragement was a serious ear ailment, Ménière's disease, which troubled him for nearly ten years, periodically causing pain, nausea, and vertigo, and which medical doctors neither identified for him nor assuaged (Kroeber 1942; T. Kroeber 1970:86–87). Still another factor was the slowness of his promotion at Berkeley. He had been with the University since 1901 but was not made a full professor until 1919, although his peers in his profession had elected him president of the American Anthropological Association for two one-year terms, in 1917 and 1918. However, it is now known that 1918 was especially notable for Kroeber for the closeness that developed that year between him and Elsie Clews Parsons. (Recent biographies of Parsons by Rosemary Lévy Zumwalt [1992] and Desley Deacon [1997] draw upon previously unknown letters to her from Kroeber, now filed with the Parsons Papers, American Philosophical Society, Philadelphia.)

Kroeber spent a good part of his time between 1920 and 1923 as a lay analyst, at first at the Stanford neuropsychiatric clinic in San Francisco and later in private practice. At the clinic Pope and another medical doctor, Henry Harris, referred patients to him. At the end of his three-year experiment Kroeber returned to anthropology, although with "many new insights into the human mind" (Kroeber 1952:300; T. Kroeber 1970:104–107).[7]

Meanwhile Pope and Kroeber had experienced another difference of opinion, this one concerning the protection of Ishi's memory. In late 1918 and early 1919 Kroeber had edited Pope's *Medical History of Ishi* for the Anthropology Department's monograph series. Just before it was due to be published, Pope discovered that one photograph had been omitted. This was doubtless the one he had intended to accompany his description of Ishi's last days at the museum (Pope 1920:205):

> At this period, when he seemed to be failing so rapidly that the end must be near, I coaxed him to get out of bed and let me take his picture once more. He was always happy to be photographed, and accommodated me. It was only after the picture was developed that I recognized to what a pitiful condition he had been reduced. Had this been apparent before, I should not have asked this exertion of him.

Pope probably phoned the museum to find out what had happened to the missing illustration. Clerk A. Allison Simonds sent a crisp reply (Simonds 1920):

> I am sorry to tell you that at this stage nothing can be done about the additional plate which you wish inserted in your paper. Dr. Kroeber removed this plate before approving the paper. He naturally thought that if you had any objection you would register it early in the game. . . . Now that Dr. Kroeber is in New York and the paper is practically ready to come off the press nothing can be done. . . . I know he had strong objections to it. . . . I think for one that he considered the picture too mournful and unesthetic.

Thus Kroeber succeeded in censoring the photograph from a University-sponsored series. Pope's response was not recorded, but he did not use the picture in his subsequent publications on Ishi and archery. I can describe the photograph because naturalist Kurt Rademacher showed a print of it at the Oakland Museum symposium on Ishi in 1994; he had rephotographed it and several others from a Saxton Pope scrapbook in the possession of the Pope family (Rademacher 1993, 1994; personal communication, May 14, 2000). The picture shows Pope, posturing with uplifted bow and arrow over Ishi, who is gaunt, staring, and near collapse, seated on the floor of his sickroom, holding a bow. One can only say that it is a very callous depiction indeed.

*   *   *

Even after writing three monographs, Pope's passion for archery was still un-abated, and he went on to publish two books for general readers. *Hunting with the Bow and Arrow* opened with a tribute to Ishi (Pope [1923a] 1947:3–13) and then narrated the experiences of Pope and his friends in hunting small and big game animals in the American West. Pope commented that he and his friend Art Young had had "the extremely satisfactory feeling that we killed five of the finest grizzly bear in Wyoming" (Pope [1923a] 1947, 229).

Pope's later book, *The Adventurous Bowmen,* recounted his eight-month voyage and safari to Tanganyika (now Tanzania) in 1925 with two other American archers. There, besides other animals, they killed twenty-one lions, five of them solely with bow and arrow. The other sixteen lions were "dispatched" with rifles because they had charged the hunters or had already been wounded by arrows (Pope 1926:231). Later readers are more likely to feel horror at the deaths than admiration for the bravery of the archers.

Pope returned to San Francisco and resumed his teaching of surgery, but died quite suddenly of pneumonia in 1926 at the age of fifty. At the museum Gifford, on learning of his death, wrote to Peru, where Kroeber was on his sec-ond archaeological expedition, accompanied by his new wife, the former Theo-dora Kracaw Brown. Answering Gifford's question about an obituary for the *American Anthropologist,* Kroeber replied, "Pope's going hit me hard. I want to write the obituary" (Kroeber 1926). Pope was only a year older than he.

Over a half-century later in her oral history, Theodora Kroeber recalled that Kroeber said to her on the day they received the news, "He shouldn't have died. He need not have died. . . . You have to have a will to live, with pneumonia." She herself had met Pope only once or twice but had definite impressions of him: "He was a very handsome man. He was one of the few men you would call beau-tiful. And very gracious" (T. Kroeber 1982:81).

From Peru Kroeber sent a short obituary of Pope, saying that in the fourteen years since Pope began to teach surgery, he had crowded "a professional career, research investigation, a busy professional practice, the direction of medical or-ganizations, war work, travel and big game hunting, an intensive practical and historical study of archery, many friendships, and a happy family life" (Kroeber 1927:341–342).

Pope had also crowded in at least one private obligation. His wife, Dr. Emma Pope, told Gifford that in 1925 he had made a solitary trip back to the Lassen country whence Ishi had come, taking with him only his dog (E. Pope 1926).

A decade after writing Pope's obituary, Kroeber, with his gift for the elegiac, also wrote an obituary for Waterman when he too died at the age of fifty, having left Berkeley for the second time in 1921, going to the Heye Museum of the American Indian in New York and from there to a variety of other museum and teaching positions. Kroeber (1937:527) described him as "first of all a brilliant, incisive, colorful teacher, rarely systematic and sometimes erratic, but extraordinarily stimulating."

As eulogy for Ishi, Kroeber could bring himself to write only two paragraphs in his *Handbook of the Indians of California* (1925:344), ending with these words: "He was industrious, kindly, obliging, invariably even tempered, ready of smile, and thoroughly endeared himself to all with whom he came in contact. With his death the Yahi passed away."

As for the dependable, hardworking Gifford, late in his long career, in 1945, he was finally named a full professor in the Berkeley department, and in 1947 he was made director of the Museum of Anthropology, which had been moved back to Berkeley in 1931. George Foster, who had earned his doctorate at Berkeley in 1941, wrote a factual and affectionate obituary of Gifford, saying that he was "a modest, unassuming man who won the devoted friendship of all who knew him, and who made major scientific and human contributions to a community of scholars over nearly half a century" (Foster 1960:329).

NOTES

1. Gifford had told Kroeber that he and Waterman had agreed on the Pacific Islands room for Ishi (Gifford-Kroeber Letters, September 30, 1915).

2. The portrait photograph of Pope in Theodora Kroeber's *Ishi in Two Worlds* (1961, in group of photographs following p. 100), shows something of the shamanistic quality in Pope that may have intrigued Ishi, Theodora Kroeber, and others (see her comment about him later in this paper). Alfred Kroeber may also have seen an element of this quality in Pope, for in 1919, when Kroeber was conducting a graduate evening seminar at Berkeley in shamanism, he invited Pope to speak to the group and demonstrate some of his sleight-of-hand skills. Kroeber noted that the students had read reports by observers of shamans at work but not reports by the shamans themselves (Kroeber 1919). Whether Pope accepted the invitation is not known.

3. Pope's third monograph, *A Study of Bows and Arrows* (1923b), was a technical analysis of the designs and strengths of the weapons of archery from different cultures and time periods.

4. I gleaned this information from several sources: museum clerk Frances McMahon's report to Gifford (who was doing fieldwork in the central Sierra) that during a temporary absence of Loud's "Mr. Warburton and the boy [probably Richard Kretschmer] are combining on relieving the inside night man" (McMahon 1915); the Dolores Letters, 1912–26; and the Loud Letters, 1913–46, especially his letter to Kroeber, May 26, 1919: "I can stand to be kept in alternate nights but I am not prepared to stay in two nights in succession." I found no job descriptions or work schedules for the guards in the Department and Museum of Anthropology Archives.

5. In 1918–19 Juan Dolores was a research fellow with the Berkeley department, and collected Papago texts, such as myths, songs, and autobiographies, from Papago informants in Arizona. These form part of a large collection of Papago language and folklore materials made by Dolores and Kroeber (1909–51), most of it by Dolores, and held in the Ethnological Documents Collection of the Department and Museum of Anthropology Archives in the Bancroft Library. In his later years Dolores worked regularly at the museum as a preparator, as did Loud (see Kroeber 1947; Kroeber 1949).

6. Foster's letter (Foster 1999) and Hinton's article (Hinton 1999) both discuss the Kroeber-Hrdlička connection.

7. Kroeber was chary about divulging the year of his psychoanalysis or the name of his analyst. Desley Deacon, in her all-encompassing study of Elsie Parsons and her intellectual and social milieu, put the date at 1918 (Deacon 1997:202), as I did in my biographical article on Kroeber (Buzaljko 1999:928).

Since then I have come to see the year 1920 as the crucial one for new beginnings for him. He was experiencing another loss, as his close personal relationship with Elsie Parsons was coming to an end. Nevertheless, after a reunion with her in December 1919, he traveled back to California with a remarkable sense of anticipation, telling her, "For the first time in years I turn westward without the prison gate sense. That's a good deal to get out of a five weeks' trip. And there too you helped – so subtly that you may be unaware and I should find it hard to formulate. You see you really are a Liberator, even where you least expect" (Kroeber, January 7, 1920, quoted in Zumwalt 1992:180).

Having applied for a six-month leave of absence from Berkeley, Kroeber was about to start working as a lay analyst with selected patients at the Stanford neuropsychiatric clinic, under the supervision of physicians Saxton Pope and Henry Harris. But first he had to undergo a level of treatment himself by these "psychiatrically-minded doctors," who told him that he was not neurotic, as he reported to Sapir on February 2, 1920 (Golla 1984:332).

By early April, Kroeber was again in New York, where he remained until late May, managing to see Parsons at least twice during those weeks (Deacon 1997:212–213). It must have been in that period that he began full psychoanalysis with, first, Smith Ely Jelliffe (1866–1945), a well-known American physician, medical writer, and editor, who had begun to practice an eclectic style of analysis in about 1910. In 1915, in one of his many publications, Jelliffe stated that, in general, "patients who really need a psychoanalysis – who are not indulging in a luxury so to speak – need at least two to three months treatment" (Jelliffe 1915:79, quoted in Burnham 1983:75). Jelliffe's biographer, John C. Burnham, commented that this estimate conformed to the standards of the day. Julian H. Steward, in his fine memoir of Kroeber (Steward 1961:1050), says that he was psychoanalyzed for three months in 1920, though he does not give a source.

Jelliffe, in turn, referred Kroeber to a younger physician, Gregory Stragnell (1888–1963), a neuropsychiatrist and medical editor, who that same year married Jelliffe's eldest daughter, Sylvia. However, Stragnell was "strongly independent" of his father-in-law, according to Burnham (1983:156). Born in Colorado, he had graduated from Columbia University's College of Physicians and Surgeons in 1913. The next year he had volunteered as a military surgeon with the French army, serving until 1917. Returning to New York, he opened a private medical practice and also became an editor of the *Medical Record* (known by various titles) of New York City and associate editor of the *Journal of Nervous and Mental Disease* (see entries for him in *Who's Who in America* 1932 and *Who Was Who* 1973).

Among Stragnell's early psychoanalytical writings was a paper titled "The Golden Phallus" (Stragnell 1924), a study of the dream symbolism of five individuals, three of them his patients and the other two unknown persons who had sent him descriptions of their dreams. Symbols of gold, the sun, and the father – or mother – linked the dreams of all five. Stragnell ended with many conjectures. Too much had been attempted.

In June or early July 1920, Kroeber, back in California, sent Edward Sapir a printed announcement that he had opened "an office for the practice of psychoanalysis" in downtown San Francisco (Golla 1984:342). On July 14, at the end of his next letter, Kroeber wrote, "I may add that I've been analyzed and have had some clinical experience, but that I believe it is open to doubt whether this community is ripe for psychoanalysis" (Golla 1984:344).

It was Theodora Kroeber in her biography of her husband (T. Kroeber 1970:102) who provided the last names of the two analysts, enabling me to identify them. However, she was in error when she described them as Viennese and part of the group around Freud there. Jelliffe and Stragnell were American-born and -educated, though Jelliffe had met and corresponded with both Freud and Jung (Burnham 1983). What Theodora Kroeber did provide for her readers was this valuable personal insight of Alfred Kroeber's into his own psychoanalysis: He had once told her, she said, that "the analytic period had been for him a serene and absorbingly interesting one. . . . When I asked him what he 'got' from analysis, not over-all or intellectually or theoretically, but in immediate, concrete return, he answered, half in fun but only half, 'I got over my *Sturm und Drang* which had overtaken me twenty years late. I learned not to be so solemn' " (T. Kroeber 1970:104).

Alfred Kroeber, in a note of appreciation to Jelliffe (Kroeber 1935), confirmed that he and Stragnell were the analysts whose patient he had been; he gave the time as 1921, but his letter to Sapir had put it a year earlier.

REFERENCES

DA: Department and Museum of Anthropology Archives, Bancroft Library, University of California, Berkeley

UC PAAE: University of California Publications in American Archaeology and Ethnology.

Berry, Rose V. S. 1929. Dr. Saxton Temple Pope: his work and his play. UC *Chronicle* 31:126–156.

Brandes, Stanley. 1999. Assuming responsibility for Ishi, *Anthropology Newsletter* 40(5): 2 (May), correspondence column.

Burnham, John C. 1983. *Jelliffe: American psychoanalyst and physician and his correspondence with Sigmund Freud and C. G. Jung.* Ed. William McGuire. Chicago: University of Chicago.

Buzaljko, Grace W. 1999. Alfred Louis Kroeber. In *American national biography,* Vol. XIV. Ed. John A. Garrety and Mark C. Carnes. New York: Oxford University, pp. 926–930.

Deacon, Desley. 1997. *Elsie Clews Parsons: inventing modern life.* Chicago: University of Chicago.

Dolores, Juan. Letters. DA.

———. 1913. Papago verb stems. *UC PAAE* 10:241–263.

———. 1923. Papago nominal stems. Ed. J. Alden Mason. *UC PAAE* 20:19–31.

Dolores, Juan, and A. L. Kroeber. 1909–51. Papago language and folklore. Texts and field notes, 3519 pp. in longhand. Ethnological Documents Collection, DA. BANC FILM 2216, reels 134:1–5 and 135.

Eloesser, Leo, M. D. 1973. Saxton Temple Pope, M. D. *Surgery, Gynecology, and Obstetrics* 137:845–850.

Foster, George M. 1960. Edward Winslow Gifford, 1887–1959. *American Anthropologist* 62:327–329.

———. 1999. Dialogue: responsibility for Ishi. *Anthropology News* 40(7):5–6, October.

Gifford, E. W. 1915. Two letters to A. L. Kroeber, August 22. A. L. Kroeber Papers, Bancroft Library.

———. Gifford-Kroeber letters. Department of Anthropology Archives, DA.

Golla, Victor, ed. 1984. *The Sapir-Kroeber correspondence: letters between Edward Sapir and A. L. Kroeber, 1905–1925.* Survey of California and Other Indian Languages, report 6. Berkeley: University of California.

Heizer, Robert F., ed. 1970. *An anthropological expedition of 1913, or Get it through your head, or yours for the revolution: correspondence between A. L. Kroeber and L. L. Loud, July 12, 1913–October 31, 1913.* Archaeological Research Facility, Department of Anthropology, University of California, Berkeley.

Herman, Mary W. 1953. University of California anthropology personnel [Berkeley, 1901–1953]. Manuscript, 32 unnumbered pages. Copies on file with John H. Rowe and Grace W. Buzaljko.

Hinton, Leanne. 1999. Ishi's brain. *News from Native California* 13(1):4–9.

Hrdlička, Aleš. File. DA.

Jelliffe, Smith Ely. 1915. The technique of psychoanalysis. *Psychoanalytic Review* 2:73–80, 191–199, 286–296, 409–421.

Kroeber, A. L. File. DA.

———. Papers. Bancroft Library, University of California, Berkeley.

———. 1913. Proposed anthropology budget, with appended notes, 1913–1914. *In* Department of Anthropology Financial Accounts files. Box 4, folder 5.

———. 1915a. Letters to Wilson D. Wallis, March 30, 1915, and April 18, 1915. Wallis file, DA.

———. 1915b. Letter to Thomas T. Waterman, August 28. In Kroeber-Waterman letters, July 1913–October 1917, DA.

———. 1916. Letter to Aleš Hrdlička, October 27. In Hrdlička file, DA.

———. 1916–20. Letters to Elsie Clews Parsons. In Parsons Papers, American Philosophical Society, Philadelphia.

———. 1919. Letter to Saxton Pope, April 2. In Pope file, 1913–1922, DA.

———. 1921. Information regarding Juan Dolores and Papago work. Typescript, 2 pp., April 14. In Dolores file, DA.

———. 1925. *Handbook of the Indians of California.* Bureau of American Ethnology, Bulletin 78. Washington DC: Smithsonian Institution.

———. 1926. Letter to E. W. Gifford, September 18. In Kroeber file, DA.

———. 1927. Saxton Temple Pope. *American Anthropologist* 29:341–342.

———. 1935. Letter to Smith Ely Jelliffe, December 30. In Jelliffe file, DA.

———. 1937. Thomas Talbot Waterman. *American Anthropologist* 39:527–529.

———. 1942. Letter to James M. Rosenberg, February 21. In A. L. Kroeber personal file, 1936–42, DA.

———. 1947. L. L. Loud. *American Antiquity* 12(3):180.

———. 1949. Juan Dolores, 1880–1948. *American Anthropologist* 51:96–97.

———. 1952. *The nature of culture.* Chicago: University of Chicago.

Kroeber, Karl. 1999. Response to Berkeley. *Anthropology News* 40(7): 3 (October), correspondence column.

Kroeber, Theodora. 1961. *Ishi in two worlds: a biography of the last wild Indian in North America.* Berkeley: University of California.

———. 1970. *Alfred Kroeber: a personal configuration.* Berkeley: University of California.

———. 1982. Theodora Kroeber-Quinn: Timeless woman, writer, and interpreter of the California Indian world. Transcript of oral history conducted 1976–1978 by Anne Brower. Regional Oral History Office, Bancroft Library, University of California, Berkeley.

Loud, Llewellyn L. Letters. In Loud file, DA.

———. 1918. Ethnogeography and archaeology of the Wiyot territory. UC PAAE 14:221–436.

McMahon, Frances. 1915. Letter to E. W. Gifford, October 13. In Gifford and clerk file, DA.

Pope, Emma W. 1926. Letter to E. W. Gifford, November 2. In Emma W. Pope file, DA.

Pope, Saxton T. 1918. Yahi Archery. UC PAAE 13:103–152.

———. 1920. The Medical History of Ishi. UC PAAE 13:175–213.

———. [1923a] 1947. *Hunting with the bow and arrow.* New York: Putnam.

———. 1923b. A study of bows and arrows. UC PAAE 13:329–446.

———. 1926. *The adventurous bowmen: field notes on African archery.* New York: Putnam.

Rademacher, Kurt. 1993. Notes on visit with Virginia Pope Evans . . . , March 20. Copy in files of author.

————. 1994. Saxton Pope's reminiscences of Ishi. Paper presented at symposium, Ishi: the Man and His Times, Revisited. Oakland Museum, Oakland, CA. March 26.

Rockafellar, Nancy, and Orin Starn. 1999. Commentary: Ishi's brain. *Current Anthropology* 40(4): 413–415.

Sapir, Edward. 1910. Yana texts, together with Yana myths collected by Roland B. Dixon. UC PAAE 9:1–235.

Simonds, A. Allison. 1920. Letter, unsigned carbon copy, April 16. In Saxton Pope file, 1913–22, DA.

Steward, Julian H. 1961. Alfred Louis Kroeber, 1876–1960. *American Anthropologist* 63(5):1038–1060.

Stragnell, Gregory. 1924. The golden phallus. *Psychoanalytic Review* 11:292–323.

University of California. Department of Anthropology and Museum Accounts Files. Boxes 4 and 5, 1912–1915. DA.

————. 1915. *Announcement of courses of instruction. 1915–16.* Berkeley: University of California.

Warburton, Arthur. Letters. DA.

————. Notes to E. W. Gifford. DA.

Waterman, Thomas T. 1915a. Departmental readers and helpers roll, December 16. Department of Anthropology and Museum Accounts files. Box 5, folder 2, DA.

————. 1915b. Letter to Arthur Warburton, October 19. In Warburton file, DA.

Who's who in America, 1932–33. 1932. Entry for Gregory Stragnell. Vol. 17, p. 2210. Chicago: A. N. Marquis.

Who was who in America, 1969–1973. 1973. Entry for Gregory Stragnell. Vol. 5, p. 701. Chicago: Marquis Who's Who.

Zumwalt, Rosemary Lévy. 1992. *Wealth and rebellion: Elsie Clews Parsons, anthropologist and folklorist.* Urbana IL: University of Illinois.

PART TWO
The Repatriation Controversy

Previous page. Ishi in Oroville, September 1911.

Ishi in San Francisco, July 1912.

Introduction to Part Two

In the general introduction to this volume we have outlined the controversy over the repatriation of Ishi's remains, triggered by the discovery in the late 1990s that his brain had not been cremated with the rest of his body but had been preserved and sent to the Smithsonian Institution in 1917. The sequence of events and the conflicts of opinion aroused (particularly within the University of California, Berkeley, Anthropology Department) are lucidly narrated in George Foster's "Assuming Responsibility for Ishi: An Alternative Interpretation" (Chapter 7). Stuart Speaker's "Report and Recommendations for Repatriation" for the Smithsonian Institution (Chapter 5), with which this part begins, is the most judicious and scholarly assessment we have of the survival to the present day of people of Yana ancestry (the basis of the assessment, as Speaker notes, being Alfred Kroeber's 1955 collation of such information). Speaker's report is an impressive, because not oversimplified, articulation of processes of cultural loss and survival by which many Indian peoples have sustained themselves within hostile white American culture. One should notice, for example, how closely analogous are the social implications of Speaker's analysis of the linguistic and anthropological evidence of Ishi's heritage to those to which Shackley's assessment of projectile point making leads him (Chapter 11).

Speaker's report is valuable also in revealing how important were the persistent efforts of Art Angle, chairman of the Butte County Native American Cultural Committee, in moving the process of repatriation forward by making the slow wheels of bureaucracy begin to turn. Mr. Angle's perseverance, marked always by self-effacing dignity and good manners, came at the cost of considerable personal sacrifice, and all interested in Ishi and his history owe him a debt of gratitude, a slight payment toward which we make in our dedication of this volume to him.

What lies beyond what Speaker and Foster tell is the final successful repatriation of all Ishi's remains, his brain together with the ashes that had been kept in an urn at the Olivet Funeral Home (see Vizenor, Chapter 19, this volume). All were buried together in Ishi's native land in August 2000 by the American Indians to whom the brain had been returned by the Smithsonian. The site is unmarked, so that this final resting place may remain undisturbed. It is revealing of the process of healing activated by this simple action that the Indians charged with burial invited to join them in the ceremony the official from the Smithsonian who had flown from Washington to deliver the brain. In courteously declining this gracious gesture he reciprocated the feelings of respect and goodwill embodied in the offer. With Ishi's physical remains finally at peace in the earth he knew so intimately, it is the records of his voice and his words and the exemplarity of his spirit that become his enduring legacy to all Californians.

But the theoretical and methodological debates among anthropologists for which Ishi's repatriation served as a convenient focal point continue. They will continue, as they should, because vital intellectual disciplines renew themselves by processes of self-criticism, and the strength of an academic profession grows from its readiness to critique its own historical evolution. Professor Scheper-Hughes's essay (Chapter 8) is directed as much to speculations about Alfred Kroeber as about Ishi, because she is passionately concerned with an important development in anthropological theory and practice that has roiled the profession now for three decades. Occasionally some of Scheper-Hughes's assertions call for further consideration[1]: there is, for example, no evidence we know of for the claim that Ishi sought and was denied prostitutes. But a few such statements should not be permitted to obscure the indisputable fact that many within the discipline, like Scheper-Hughes, want aggressive engagement by ethnographers in the lives of their informants, and encourage their fellow professionals to participate as partisans in current political controversies, arguing that anthropology should liberate itself from old-fashioned ideas of scholarly detachment and primary concentration on past history. Such disciplinary self-reevaluation appropriately finds the case of Ishi a useful focus, especially because he intruded into, and may have indirectly influenced, the first great period of anthropological self-examination, which took place during the second decade of the past century. Because Alfred Kroeber played so energetic a part both in the political controversies of that time (for example, defending Franz Boas from attacks deriving from a combination of patriotic chauvinism, anti-Semitism, and professional antipathy)[2] as well as in the discipline's first intense intellectual self-criticisms, it seems almost necessary to consider how his experience with Ishi may have influenced his professional attitudes that contributed to the evolving character of anthropology during a crucial period of its early history. Scheper-Hughes delineates sharply an important fact: The profession was then so tiny that all personal relationships powerfully affected intellectual developments, and Alfred Kroeber at that time was becoming a major figure. That fact makes identifying Ishi's significance to the profession's history no easy task, however, because the intertwined personal and intellectual relations in which Kroeber engaged from 1914 to 1923 were, as historians of the profession such as George Stocking and Regna Darnell have shown, remarkably dense and complicated.

Although the period marks Kroeber's first intellectual foray into psychoanalysis, the 1914–1923 decade was perhaps quantitatively his most productive of anthropological work. During that period he published over eighty articles and reviews, as well as several books. It was then that he wrote *Anthropology* (1923), by far his most influential publication. Although he did not write it as a textbook, his publishers persuaded him to reshape it into one, and for the next quarter century, as Eric Wolf observed, Kroeber's *Anthropology* was in effect the *only* textbook in a burgeoning field. During that time Kroeber of course continued as curator of the Museum in San Francisco and was twice elected President of the American Anthropological Association; and even a cursory survey of his correspondence with Sapir, Parsons, Boas, Lowie, Goddard, and Dixon displays how his curiosity about every aspect of anthropology steadily increased.

In the latter part of the period he resumed ethnographic fieldwork in northern California, making studies of the Yanas' neighbors, the Maidu and Wintu, which resulted in substantial publications. Kroeber's growing interest in psychoanalysis then (as later in his career, first in association with Erik Erikson and subsequently with Frieda Fromm-Reichman) supplemented, rather than replaced his anthropological commitment. As early as 1920 his review of *Totem and Taboo* irritated Sigmund Freud into protesting at being treated as the teller of a *Just-So* story (a "felicitous" self-characterization, Kroeber observed in return).

Like many of his colleagues, Kroeber during those years engaged in arduous self-questioning, both personal and professional (exacerbated, as coincidentally were Boas's and Sapir's travails, by problems of physical health – in Kroeber's case Ménière's disease, which affects the inner ear and creates difficulties balancing and walking as well as a loss of hearing).[3] Not until 1920, when he underwent a three-month psychoanalysis, did he fully commit himself to a life and career in the American West. In 1914, after the death of his wife, who had been ill for five years (during which his father had died in 1911), Kroeber rejected the offer of a professorship at Harvard. But he continued to feel isolated in California, especially from the growing intellectual ferment among anthropologists in his native New York. He then began his focus on Zuni pueblo (where he spent the first weeks of his sabbatical in 1915),[4] a concentration that seems to have helped him formulate *his* disagreement with some fundamental Boasian assumptions. He was also shaping his challenge to the new psychologically oriented anthropology being developed by the Goddard-Parsons circle in New York, a challenge first articulated in his "Eighteen Professions" essay of 1915 and subsequently in "The Superorganic" of 1917. Kroeber's work (along with Lowie's) in 1914–15 seems largely responsible for bringing virtually every major ethnographer in the country to the Southwest during the next decade. Kroeber's principal insistence in these studies was that language competence is essential to ethnography in depth. Surely his experience with Ishi could only have encouraged that emphasis.

In New York Kroeber firmly established his lifelong friendship with Robert Lowie that led finally to Lowie's accepting a professorship at Berkeley in 1921 – the appointment that inaugurated the Berkeley department's extraordinary success. But Kroeber's most significant personal relationship begun during his sabbatical of 1915 was with Elsie Clews Parsons, the wealthy feminist and very popular writer who had become entranced by anthropology and who was a dynamic center of the circle of New York anthropologists. Parsons and Kroeber from the first struck up a teasingly provocative relation that aroused some jealousy among their colleagues. How intimate were Kroeber and Parsons (whom he could address with titles such as "Witch and Collaborator") is unclear. When they were at Zuni together, some Indians thought the two anthropologists went to the sacred mountain after sunset "to have a nice time." We hope they did, but if so, such intimacy did not endure. Yet until Elsie's death they remained genial friends, their letters displaying surprising openness about personal matters, although they never recovered the closeness of the World War I years.[5]

Any final judgment of Alfred Kroeber's role in American anthropology in the light of his relationship with Ishi must lie in the future, but Scheper-Hughes makes vividly enticing the rewards of investigation of the problem. The fundamental presupposition underlying her essay is significantly valid: it would be surprising if the last Yahi had not in perhaps subtle but important ways contributed, through his influence on Alfred Kroeber, to the historical evolution of a discipline many people have learned about only because of Ishi.

Yet it would be a shame if disciplinary self-assessments are allowed to obscure the larger significance of the history of Ishi and his people, Karl Kroeber argues in "The Humanity of Ishi" (Chapter 9). This is a transcript of his talk at the conference "Who Owns the Body" sponsored by the University of California in September 2000. This conference assembled experts from many disciplines and interested parties from all over the world to discuss a variety of issues relating to the treatment of human bodies, living and dead, and devoted an entire day to problems of the repatriation of Native American people and artifacts, with special attention to the case of Ishi, the day-long presentations being brought to a close by Kroeber's address. But as the conference made clear, the repatriation of Ishi is only one portion of an ongoing social struggle over the repatriation of Native American artifacts and bodily remains. Karen Biestman, in her sensitively nuanced evaluation of the conflicts which have been evoked by discussions of Ishi, "Ishi and the University" (Chapter 10), uses his case to persuade us how much still remains to be done to satisfy the legitimate demands of Native peoples that they be allowed to give fullest respect to their ancestors and what they created. She quietly convinces that the dynamic continuities of Indian cultures require that how and where their physical artifacts and the remains of those who made them are preserved must be determined primarily not by white academics or politicians but by the survivor-inheritors of those cultures.

NOTES

1. Ursula K. Le Guin has called into question the statements Dr. Scheper-Hughes attributes to her in Chapter 8: "These quotations appear to come not from conversation but from the talk I gave for the Anthropology Department Centenary at Berkeley in September 2001. Since they deal with a very delicate subject – what another person (my father) may have thought and felt – I chose my words and attention to nuance and accuracy; therefore I'd like to be accurately quoted. I did not say of Alfred Kroeber that 'by temperament he did not live in the past, and he did not like to think about the past.' I said, 'by temperament he did not live in the past and did not like to think about the past, but in the present, in the moment.' I did not say that my father tended to 'dislike whites who expressed identification with Indians, an attitude that struck him as "both sentimental and manipulative."' I said, 'I know my father distrusted whites – amateurs or professionals – who claimed emotional or spiritual identification with Indians. He saw such claims as sentimental and co-optive.' As for the words 'my father treated Ishi as a peer, and respected his distance and reserve,' I don't know from where Dr. Scheper-Hughes is quoting. I had a pleasant conversation with her at that meeting but have no memory of making such a statement."

2. Despite his German ancestry, Alfred Kroeber was not subjected to any of the ethnic prejudices common during World War I. His journalistic reports of his visits to both England and Germany in 1916 are shrewdly critical, but even-handed, and pessimistic: he saw the people of both countries entrenching themselves ever more deeply in an antagonism that would permit no accommodation. Exemplary is Kroeber's article "What an American Saw in Germany," published in the January 12, 1916, issue of *The Outlook*. Such popular writings also helped establish Kroeber's reputation among non-specialists on campus. (See John F. Garcia, "Milman Parry and A. L. Kroeber: American Anthropology and the Oral Homer," *Oral Tradition* 16:1 [2001], 58–84, 61.)

3. Alfred Kroeber told us that his principal fear when he was stricken with Ménière's disease and suffered hearing loss in his left ear was that he would later be afflicted in his

right ear and become totally deaf. He learned years after the disease had run its course that it almost never affects both ears.

4. Kroeber's landlady at Zuni recalled him introducing himself to her by saying, "I am willing to eat beans three time a day. Will you accept me to live here for the summer?" She agreed to rent him room because she thought he was "so cute." When in the field cooking for himself, Kroeber relied heavily on canned spaghetti; fortunately for him, his second wife became a splendid cook.

5. Although virtually all of Kroeber's correspondence is now easily accessible (some of it even in print), it should be noted that the personal portions of Parsons's letters to Kroeber are not with the rest of his papers in the Bancroft Library.

5

Repatriating the Remains of Ishi

Smithsonian Institution Report and Recommendation

STUART SPEAKER

I. INTRODUCTION

The brain of Ishi, a Yahi Indian from Tehama County, California, was preserved during an autopsy and sent to the Smithsonian Institution. It is currently in the collections of the Department of Anthropology in the National Museum of Natural History (NMNH). Ishi died of tuberculosis on March 23, 1916, and the autopsy was performed at the University of California medical school (Pope 1920). His body was cremated and placed in the Olivet Memorial Park cemetery in Colma, California, where his ashes reside today. The brain was sent to the Smithsonian Institution by the anthropologist Alfred L. Kroeber from the University of California at Berkeley. Kroeber had worked closely with Ishi from 1911 through 1914. Although it had long been reported that the brain was preserved, the published sources did not report the transfer to the Smithsonian Institution.

II. COLLECTION HISTORY

The brain of Ishi was donated to the United States National Museum (precursor of the NMNH) by the University of California at Berkeley, through Alfred L. Kroeber, a professor at the university. It arrived at the museum on February 26, 1917, as Accession 60884. Kroeber had written to Aleš Hrdlička, the museum's physical anthropology curator, in October 1916 to offer the remains to the museum. Hrdlička accepted and sent detailed instructions regarding the method of preserving the brain during shipment (Hrdlička 1916–17). The remains were catalogued into the Anthropology collections as No298736.

There is no known record that these remains were exhibited or included in research studies. From 1917 until about 1980 the remains were kept at the museum in an individual jar, wrapped in cloth and identified with two catalog number tags. Around 1980, the brain collection was moved to a series of large sealed tanks in which each set of remains was individually identified, and listed on the outside of the tank. Around 1992, the tanks were moved to the Museum Support Center, a research and collections complex where the majority of the anthropology collections are preserved.

III. HISTORY OF THE REPATRIATION PROCESS

In late February 1999, Mr. Art Angle, the chairman of the Butte County Native American Cultural Committee (BCNACC), contacted the Repatriation Office (RO) to begin discussion for the eventual repatriation of Ishi's remains. Mr. Angle had been given information on the remains by an independent researcher, Dr. Orin Starn, a professor of anthropology at Duke University, who had visited the RO in late January 1999. Dr. Starn had located records of the transfer of Ishi's brain from the University of California at Berkeley to the Smithsonian Institution in the University archives, and the RO gave him a complete copy of the Smithsonian accession and catalog records for these remains.

In telephone conversations and correspondence, the RO gave Mr. Angle detailed information on the remains, the National Museum of the American Indian (NMAI) Act, NMNH repatriation policy, an inventory of California human remains and archaeological artifacts, a Summary of the Maidu ethnological collection, and background information on NMNH history, research, and curation practices. Mr. Angle and a delegation of the BCNACC visited the NMNH on March 24–25 for consultations.

During the consultations at the NMNH, the RO emphasized that the museum was fully committed to the repatriation of Ishi's remains in a timely and appropriate manner. The RO explained the NMAI Act repatriation provisions, explained NMNH policies and the repatriation process, and distributed complete copies of the museum documents related to Ishi's remains and other materials (law, policy, inventories). At the conclusion of the consultations the RO and the BCNACC agreed on three basic points: (1) that Ishi's remains would be repatriated as soon as possible, (2) the need for broader consultation with tribes in northern California, and (3) to make progress toward repatriation of Ishi within two months.

The BCNACC did not formally request the return of Ishi's remains in the consultations. The BCNACC members expressed their concerns to see that Ishi's remains were repatriated and reunited with his ashes so that they could be buried in an appropriate location. They also asked a series of questions regarding the museum's curation and documentation procedures, what kind of research might have been conducted on Ishi's remains, the possibility of confirming the identity of the brain by DNA comparison to hair samples, and about the repatriation process. While at the NMNH, the BCNACC examined Ishi's brain and visited the Museum Support Center to look at the Maidu ethnology collections.

The RO initiated contacts with other California groups in February 1999 to notify them of the existence of Ishi's remains and to invite them to participate in the repatriation process. Through a series of telephone calls and correspondence with Redding Rancheria and the Pit River Tribe, the RO provided the same detailed information on the NMNH collections, the NMAI Act, and the NMNH repatriation policy. These exchanges were followed by a series of consultations in early April in northern California.

During the consultations with elders, spiritual leaders, and governmental officials of Redding Rancheria and the Pit River Tribe, the RO was given detailed information on the history and survival of the Yana people in Shasta County. The tribal representatives expressed a wide range of concerns regarding the repatriation of their ancestral human remains, protection of burials, and the importance of their cultural heritage. All present were completely in support of the repatriation of Ishi's remains and that the Yana people had to be included. The RO was able to let people know that the museum has a strong repatriation record and that there is a process in place, as well as to share information on the human remains of the Yana, Wintu, Achumawi, and Atsugewi peoples of northern California. These consultations concluded with agreements to continue to discuss the repatriation of Ishi's remains and other collections in the museum.

IV. LEGAL CONSIDERATIONS

The National Museum of the American Indian Act of 1989, as amended in 1996 (20 USC §80q [P.L. 101–185]), or NMAI Act, mandates the repatriation of culturally affiliated Native American human remains held by the Smithsonian Institution and outlines the process by which repatriation is to take place. Three principles that are detailed in the law are of particular importance in this matter. First, the law requires that only Native American descendants or tribal members that are culturally affiliated with the remains or objects (such as funerary objects, sacred objects, and objects of cultural patrimony) have sufficient "standing" to assert repatriation claims under the NMAI Act. Second, the law assigns priority in the assertion of repatriation claims to lineal descendants; in the absence of lineal descendants, remains and objects will be returned to members of a "culturally affiliated" tribe. Third, the law requires consultation, which is essential for the communication of Native concerns, priorities, and rights regarding the collections in the museum.

To have the required "standing" to assert a repatriation claim, a Native American must either be a lineal descendant or a member of a federally recognized Native American tribe that is culturally affiliated with the remains or objects, as more fully described in the NMNH "Guidelines for Repatriation," which has been provided to all Native groups consulted in this matter. For these purposes, this means that the person making a claim must be a member of a Native American group included on a list of recognized tribes administered by the Bureau of Indian Affairs (BIA) or be a member of an Alaskan Native community and regional corporation established under the Alaska Native Claims Settlement Act (ANCSA). Where a claimant is not a member of a federally recognized tribe, the Smithsonian will consider a claim provided that the requesting person or tribe can demonstrate that it is acting on behalf of a federally recognized tribe through an appropriate mechanism (such as a governmental resolution designating the tribe's repatriation representative or agent). Under the law, returns to culturally affiliated and federally recognized tribes are made on a government-to-government basis.

Establishing cultural affiliation ensures that human remains and objects are returned to the present-day Native people who share the closest cultural identity with particular human remains or objects. The law requires that the determination of cultural affiliation must be established " . . . by a preponderance of the evidence based upon geographical, kinship, biological, archaeological, anthropological, linguistic, folkloric, oral traditional, historical, or other relevant information or expert opinion . . . ." For known individuals, such as Ishi, the first priority of the RO is to find out whether there is any information related to lineal descendants. Lineal descendants take priority over any sovereign tribe if they can be identified.

The requirement for consultation means that the museum must seek out and listen to the concerns, evidence, and priorities of Native people as an integral part of completing a repatriation. Consultation is necessary to ensure that museums make informed decisions about repatriation with extensive input from the Native American people and communities with the most extensive and accurate information about these collections. This is a process of dialogue in which the museum shares the information it has available, discusses the legal and practical aspects of repatriation, and works with tribal representatives to identify and return their ancestral human remains and objects. Consultation begins with the sharing of information and ends with the arrangements for the appropriate return of their collections.

V. EVIDENCE BEARING ON THE
CULTURAL AFFILIATION OF ISHI

This section presents a variety of information that will be used as the basis for determining the cultural affiliation of Ishi, using the categories of evidence listed in the NMAI Act. The law mandates that human remains are to be repatriated to the most closely culturally affiliated Native American tribe. Furthermore, the law specifies various lines of evidence that can and ought to be used; the categories are intended to be broad and inclusive so that no significant source of information can be excluded from the evaluation process. Once the evidence is gathered, the legal standard of the preponderance of the evidence is then used to find whether an affiliation is more likely than not; the evidence does not need to overcome any reasonable doubt. Each of the categories included in this report is listed in the law, and they include all of the information, both published and oral, that is available. Other categories are listed in the law but have not been included because there is no relevant data (e.g., archaeology). The evidence presented in this section serves as the basis for the recommendations given subsequently in Section VI.

Kinship Evidence

Because the NMAI Act specifically gives priority to descendants for the repatriation of human remains, the NMNH policy is to attempt to locate family members where there is some likelihood of establishing a connection. Normally, in the case of a known individual, such as Ishi, this would be undertaken based on the available information, such as name, place of origin, dates of birth and death, family history, and any other known factors.

Although we know a great deal of Ishi's life, there is absolutely no reliable information that could lead to living relatives. The tragic nature of Ishi's life apparently made it difficult for him to discuss anything of his family or anyone else whom he had known prior to 1911. The University of California researchers, who conducted extensive anthropological interviews, did not press for such details in light of his apparent distress at speaking of such matters (T. Kroeber 1961; Waterman 1918:69). Because of this, there is no recorded information on Ishi's family, kin, or lineage. Kroeber inferred that the old woman found when surveyors accidentally found Ishi's camp in 1908 was Ishi's mother, and the linguistic information he provided suggested that the other woman seen in the camp was either Ishi's sister or a cousin (T. Kroeber 1961:109; Waterman 1918). Even this information cannot be verified.

Thomas T. Waterman (1918:57–58) and Theodora Kroeber (1961:86, 240–242) relate a claim by W. S. Seagraves, a rancher, that he could identify Ishi's family and that Ishi's mother and sister had been captured by Seagraves and Hiram Good in 1870. Seagraves, Good, and others were hunting Yahi and attacked a group that was gathering food. One man was killed, two women and a girl were captured, and a man and boy of about 16 fled. Later the man and boy briefly came to Seagraves's ranch. Seagraves made three claims: first, that he recognized Ishi when he saw him in San Francisco as the same boy he had seen in 1870; second, that the captured women were Ishi's sisters; and third, that the older man with the boy was Ishi's father. None of this can be confirmed in any way, and there is no evidence that Seagraves had any information to support his opinions. In the absence of any information to confirm this claim, including a complete lack of information from Ishi regarding his family and personal history, these claims cannot be substantiated.

Oral Tradition Evidence

In consultations with Native Californians, a variety of oral traditional evidence was presented that bears on the cultural affiliation of Ishi and the Yana people. The BCNACC has identified the interaction between the Yahi (Ishi's band of the Yana) and the Maidu as evidence of cultural affiliation. They note[1] that:

> Prior to the California Gold Rush, the Yahi were culturally affiliated with a number of California Indian tribes, including the Yana who lived to their north and the Maidu who lived to their south. Historically, these tribes, and others from as far away as Nevada, would gather each year at Foreman Creek where it intersected with the Middle Fork of the Feather River for purposes of trade, commerce, the performance of religious ceremonies and the exchange of information all of which were integral parts of the traditional lives of Native Americans of California.

This information confirms that the Yahi band of the Yana had positive and peaceful relations with the Maidu, in addition to more hostile interactions usually reported (Potts 1977:41–42; Johnson 1978:363). The BCNACC further notes that in 1911 Ishi "could have chosen to travel north, east, south or west to associate with neighboring tribes known to him, he chose to come south to the lands of the Maidu in his time of need," and that a Maidu boy and his father saw Ishi prior to his entry into Oroville in August 1911 (see also Dobkins 1997:45; Chapter 21, this volume). These facts demonstrate that the Yana had a variety of relationships, sometimes peaceful and sometimes hostile, with other tribes such as the Wintu, Nomlaki, Maidu, and Achumawi, but do not strongly support an interpretation that the Yana and these other tribes necessarily shared a common sense of identity.

During consultations with the Redding Rancheria and Pit River Tribe elders and representatives, individuals presented information regarding their own and others' *Noso* ancestry. The term *Noso* means the Yana people (the word is derived from Wintu), and has long been used by both the Yana and others. This information amplifies and confirms the historical records and accounts of Yana people surviving in the 20th century in Northern California (see the later sub-section "Historical Evidence"). Stories relating Ishi's knowledge of Achumawi words were also presented, although it has long been noted that Ishi also knew Atsugewi, Maidu, and Wintu words (A. Kroeber 1925:345).

Anthropological Evidence

Ethnographic, linguistic, and archaeological research on the Yana has documented an array of shared cultural elements common to all Yana groups. The Yana have probably been in northern California for much longer than the nearby tribes, especially the Wintu and Maidu. Yana is a language of the Hokan family, which appears to have been present in California for much longer than most other language groups. The nearest tribes, the Wintu and Maidu, speak languages of the Penutian family. The Wintu entered Northern California from the north, while the Maidu came from the east.

The Yana lived in small autonomous local social groups, each occupying a definite territory, having their own leaders and villages. This pattern characterized most, if not all, northern California tribes, and the term *tribe* therefore has a different meaning than when applied to more hierarchically organized peoples or where institutions such as clans served to unify related people across local boundaries. *Tribe* therefore should be considered analogous to *culture* in the sense of a group of people who share a common language and a set of distinctive values, institutions, kinship systems, ceremonial events, and myths.

Yana-speaking informants who worked with Kroeber, Waterman, Edward Sapir, and others distinguished between different Yana groups in only two ways: by village (which might be termed a "band" or "tribelet", following Kroeber 1925:830–832) and by dialect. Several publications and manuscripts list Yana villages, primarily in the Northern, Central, and Yahi areas (Sapir and Spier 1943; Harrington 1931a; A. Kroeber 1925:336–346). Each village represented a small, autonomous social and geographical group composed of related families, with a headman or chief.

On a "tribal" scale, the Yana themselves recognized two main subdivisions: the *Gari'si* and the *Gata'i* (Sapir and Spier 1943:243; A. Kroeber 1925:336–346). These are linguistic distinctions (discussed more fully below) representing the Yanas' own way of describing broad differences among Yana people. The *Gari'si* correspond to the Northern Yana, and the *Gata'i* correspond to the Central and Southern Yana. This classification suggests that the Yana themselves viewed all Yana speakers as a group while recognizing local (village) and general (dialect) differences.

Sapir's research emphasized linguistic aspects of Yana culture, but he also investigated the Yana kinship system (Sapir 1918). It is clear from his work with Ishi and his Northern Yana and Central Yana informants that the Yana of each dialect and local band shared the same kinship system, illustrated by the detailed descriptions of kinship terms and usages in Northern Yana and Yahi.

Linguistic Evidence

Linguistic evidence is the most significant body of documentation on the Yana available from the scholarly literature. Studies of the Yana language dialects began in the late 1800s, continued through the 1930s, and include major contributions by Sapir (1910, 1917, 1918), the most productive and influential linguist of his generation. Ishi himself was one of the most important sources for the documentation and understanding of the Yana language. In the absence of detailed information regarding the social relationships among Yana-speaking groups, the linguistic data are the most informative of the shared culture of the Yana people.

Yana is a Hokan language that is no longer spoken. Beginning with Sapir (1917), researchers have identified three or four geographical dialects of the Yana language: Northern, Central, Southern, and Yahi. Each dialect is considered to be part of a linguistic continuum rather than a sharply defined linguistic unit (Golla 1994; A. Kroeber 1925:338). Yana is clearly a single language in which all dialects share a basic common structure, lexicon, and phonology. Among the unique linguistic elements found in all Yana dialects is the rare use of gender specific forms, in which the speaker uses different dialects depending on whether he or she is speaking to a man or a woman (Miller 1996:230; A. Kroeber 1925:337). The fact that Ishi used these conventions is solid evidence of his essential Yana identity.

Differences between the geographical dialects are relatively minor lexical, phonological, and grammatical elements rather than structural, and all were mutually intelligible. The details of the Yana language as recorded from the Northern, Central, and Yahi dialects were so minor that there was never a clear definition of the differences or where one dialect changed to another. Sapir and Kroeber debated the existence and nature of the different dialects (Golla 1984). The shifts of usage from the north to the south were so subtle that sharp divisions cannot be established.

Sapir commented on the strong similarities between Northern and Central Yana, and at times treated them as a single dialect (Sapir in Golla 1984:187; Sapir 1918). He also frequently included Yahi and Southern Yana as a single dialect (e.g., Sapir 1917; Sapir 1923; also A. Kroeber 1925:345). Sam Batwi, a Yana-speaking informant, considered Southern Yana and Yahi to be the same (Sapir and Spier 1943), and Sapir once noted that he had no evidence to indicate any dialectical difference between Yahi and Southern Yana (Sapir in Golla 1984:206). At other times, Sapir and others noted the closeness of Southern and Central Yana (Sapir and Spier 1943:243–244).

The establishment of the Yahi dialect rests largely on the information given by Ishi during his years at the University of California, supplemented by other Yana informants. In fact, until Ishi's discovery the only substantial linguistic data available came from the Northern and Central groups. The destruction and displacement of the Southern Yana in the 1850s and 1860s left a gap in the anthropological record. The existence of differences between the Yahi and Southern Yana dialects is conjectural, and it is parsimonious and sensible to regard Ishi's Yahi information as the fullest account of Southern Yana available (Victor Golla, personal communication 1999).

It is well known that Ishi was unable to communicate with anyone when he arrived in Oroville in 1911, and that Waterman was able to use a Central Yana vocabulary to establish communication. There is no question that Ishi's Yahi was a Yana dialect and that the strong similarities between all Yana dialects was the basis for substantive conversation and understanding between Ishi and others. Sam Batwi, a Central Yana speaker, who had been a major linguistic informant for Sapir, was the first translator for Ishi upon his arrival in San Francisco. Batwi understood Southern Yana and translated extensively during Ishi's first weeks in the city; any difficulties in communication appear to have resulted more from personality differences rather than linguistic problems (Sapir in Golla 1984:187; Waterman 1918:65; see also Golla 1984:60–64).

Sapir, more than any other anthropologist, worked closely with Ishi and was able to communicate much better than any other non-Yana. His previous work with Northern and Central Yana speakers enabled him to speak and work directly with Ishi. Sapir was able to conduct detailed kinship, lexical, and grammatical research with Ishi because of the strong and systematic similarities between the Yana dialects (Sapir 1923).

The linguistic data amply demonstrate a strong cultural affiliation between all Yana people. Language is a very important element of cultural affiliation because it serves as the medium of communication, understanding, and shared experience between individuals and social groups. Language alone can contain and express the complexities and subtleties of cultural values, ideas, and relationships. The history, cultural influences, and cultural changes of a people are encoded in its language through differences and similarities. The strong similarities among the Yana dialects reflect the common history and culture shared by all Yana people.

Historical Evidence

The history of the destruction of the Yana people is well known. Vicious attacks on the Yana began in the 1850s, and by the late 1860s virtually all the Southern Yana and Yahi had been killed, deported, or taken captive (Johnson 1978; T. Kroeber 1961; Waterman 1918; Curtin 1898: Powers 1877). Individuals survived scattered among other Native American tribes or in the European American population. Only the much reduced Central and Northern Yana continued as intact social units, and even they were isolated by the immigrant population. By the 1880s the remnant Yana peoples were living in the Redding area, near Round Mountain, and at Montgomery Creek. From the earliest detailed accounts of these people, it is clear that the surviving Yana descendants were already intermarried among the more numerous Wintu and Pit River populations. The pattern of intermarriage between the Northern and Central Yanas probably represents a pattern which developed after the warfare and destruction of the mid-1800s (Chase-Dunn and Mann 1998:112–116).

When Jeremiah Curtin began his linguistic and ethnological fieldwork among the Yana in 1884, there were perhaps as few as thirty-five Yana speakers left in the area (Powell 1891:135). Curtin lived and worked at both Redding and Round Mountain on and off over a period of years, becoming quite familiar with the Yana, Wintu, and Pit River people, and collected a great amount of vocabulary and stories in Yana. In his notes, Curtin lists around two dozen Yana-speaking informants (Curtin 1884a, Curtin 1884b) and noted that "the Yanas and Wintus are so few in number that the members of each tribe are related to each other" (Curtin 1940:340).

By 1907 Sapir found only about a dozen Yana speakers, some near Redding and others at Montgomery Creek, where they were intermarried with the Pit River Indians (Sapir and Spier 1943:248). Linguistic work with Yana speakers continued into the 1930s, but by that time many of the informants were individuals who had both Yana and Pit River or Wintu heritage. Harrington encountered upwards of eleven Yana-speaking informants between 1922 and 1931 in the Redding, Montgomery Creek, and Hat Creek areas (Harrington 1922, Harrington 1931a; Harrington 1931b). Gifford and Klimek (1936:78) interviewed two Yana elders in the mid-1930s.

The most detailed information on people with Yana ancestry was compiled by Alfred Kroeber (1955) from the 1928 Bureau of Indian Affairs records. These data document the mixture of Yana, Pit River, and Wintu ancestry of people with Yana ancestry born in the late 1800s and early 1900s. None of these individuals had full Yana ancestry.

VI. RECOMMENDATIONS FOR REPATRIATION

The information presented in this report has been examined and discussed in order to establish facts that can be used to fulfill the repatriation provisions of the NMAI Act and its amendment. The Repatriation Office has engaged in a series of consultations with northern California tribes; this crucial step in the repatriation process ensures that all concerned parties with a demonstrated interest have a voice in the return of Ishi's remains. The law establishes a process for repatriation of human remains to either the family of an individual or to the culturally affiliated federally recognized Native American tribe. To this end, two points need to be summarized. It must be determined whether, first, there is any evidence that could establish a family connection to Ishi and, second, there exists evidence of cultural affiliation between Ishi and present-day federally recognized Native American tribes.

The impossibility of confirming a direct family relationship between Ishi and potential descendants has been discussed. Given the lack of any substantial knowledge from Ishi regarding any detail about his own family and relationships, or even the identity of any other Yana person, there is no possibility of confirming a relationship between Ishi and any other person. The little that is known strongly indicates that Ishi was the sole survivor of the few Yahi who remained in their traditional territory between 1870 and 1911 and that he had no children. The Yahi who were dislocated or captured prior to 1870 lived either among the immigrant European American population or with other Native American peoples. Since the Smithsonian is unable to trace Ishi's family history at all, establishing a relationship between Ishi and any other individual, past or present, is virtually impossible.

The evidence available on Ishi's cultural affiliation affirms his identity as a Yahi-Yana Indian. The bonds of shared language, identity, history, and culture united Ishi with other Yana people. Although the Yana language is not presently spoken, there are many Native Americans of Yana ancestry who share this cultural affiliation with Ishi. A great many Yana died in the open warfare of the 1850s and 1860s, and the survivors probably numbered less than 100 by the 1870s. These surviving Yana found refuge among the Wintu of the Redding area and in the Northern Yana territory of Montgomery Creek, adjacent to the Pit River tribe. Beginning in the 1870s, anthropologists and other observers began to record the history and culture of these Yana survivors and have left a record of the relationships between the Yana and the Wintu and Pit River peoples with whom they intermarried.

During our consultations with various northern California Native American tribes, the RO was given detailed information that the Yana descendants today are primarily represented by the federally recognized Redding Rancheria and

Pit River Tribe. Redding Rancheria includes Yana as one of its three official affiliations (Wintu and Pit River are the others), and perhaps half of its enrolled members have Yana ancestry. Given the large geographical extent of the Pit River Tribe and its larger population, a smaller percentage of Pit River people have Yana ancestry. The majority of Yana-descended Pit River members are from the Lower Pit River area, primarily the Big Bend territory of the Madessi band.

The tragic history of the Yana led to the virtual destruction of the tribe and the deaths of nearly all its members. Although the Yana tribe no longer exists as a social unit, and although people of Yana descent are scattered among several federally recognized tribes in northern California as well as among the unrecognized Native Americans, the Yana legacy continues to be a vital part of the Redding Rancheria and Pit River Tribe. Based on the facts of Ishi's Yana culture and the Yana heritage of the Redding Rancheria and Pit River Tribes, the RO recommends that the NMNH offer Ishi's remains to these two groups.

NOTES

This chapter is based on a report originally entitled *The Human Remains of Ishi, a Yahi-Yana Indian, in the National Museum of Natural History, Smithsonian Institution. Report and Recommendations for Repatriation, April 21, 1999*, available in full from the Repatriation Office, MRC-138, Department of Anthropology, National Museum of Natural History, Smithsonian Institution, Washington DC 20560.

1. "Claim for the Repatriation of Ishi's Remains, by the Butte County Native American Cultural Committee," Appendix 5 of the original report on which this chapter is based, not reproduced here.

REFERENCES

NAA: National Anthropological Archives, National Museum of Natural History, Smithsonian Institution, Washington DC.

UC PAAE: *University of California Publications in American Archaeology and Ethnology.*

Chase-Dunn, Christopher, and Kelly M. Mann. 1998. *The Wintu and their neighbors.* Tucson: University of Arizona.

Curtin, Jeremiah. 1884a. Vocabulary 1884, 1889. Manuscript 953, Numbered manuscripts 1850s–1980s (some earlier), NAA.

———. 1884b. Vocabulary October 11, 1884. Manuscript 2060, Numbered manuscripts 1850s–1980s (some earlier), NAA.

———. 1898. *Creation myths of primitive America in relation to the religious history and mental development of mankind.* Boston: Little, Brown and Company.

———. 1940. *Memoirs of Jeremiah Curtin.* Madison: State Historical Society of Wisconsin.

Dobkins, Rebecca. 1997. *Memory and imagination: the legacy of Maidu Indian artist Frank Day.* Oakland CA: Oakland Museum of California.

Gifford, E. W., and Stanislaw Klimek. 1936. Culture element distributions II: Yana. *UC PAAE* 37(2): 71–100.

Golla, Victor, ed. 1984. *The Sapir-Kroeber correspondence: letters between Edward Sapir and A. L. Kroeber 1905–1925.* Survey of California and Other Indian Languages, Report No. 6. Berkeley: University of California.

Golla, Victor. 1994. Ishi's language. Paper presented at conference, Ishi: The Man and His Times, Revisited, Oakland Museum, 26 March.

Harrington, John Peabody. 1922. Achomawai/Atsugewi/Wintu/Yana file. Microfilm reel 26/frames 56–63, John P. Harrington Papers, NAA.

———. 1931a. Yana/Achomawi/Wintu/Chimariko file. Microfilm reel 26/frames 64–81, John P. Harrington Papers, NAA.

———. 1931b. Biographical Notes/Yana Persons file. Microfilm reel 35/frames 353–375, John P. Harrington Papers, NAA.

Heizer, Robert F., and Theodora Kroeber, eds. 1979. *Ishi the last Yahi: a documentary history.* Berkeley: University of California.

Hrdlička, Aleš. 1916–17, Correspondence with Alfred L. Kroeber, 6 November 1916–5 January 1917. Box 38, Correspondence, papers of Aleš Hrdlička, NAA.

Johnson, Jerald Jay. 1978. Yana. In *California.* Ed. Robert F. Heizer. Handbook of North American Indians, Volume 8, Washington DC: Smithsonian Institution, pp. 361–369.

Kroeber, Alfred L. 1925. *Handbook of the Indians of California.* Bureau of American Ethnology, Bulletin 78. Washington DC: Smithsonian Institution.

———. 1955. Ethnological data of Yana Indians. Microfilm reel 157/frames 150–167 (BANC FILM 2049), Alfred L. Kroeber papers, 1869–1972 (BANC MSS C-B 925), Bancroft Library, University of California, Berkeley.

Kroeber, Theodora. 1961. *Ishi in two worlds.* Berkeley: University of California Press.

Miller, Wick R. 1996. The ethnography of speech. In *Languages.* Ed. Ives Goddard. Handbook of North American Indians, Volume 17, Washington DC: Smithsonian Institution, pp. 222–243.

Pope, Saxton. 1920. Medical history of Ishi. *UC PAAE* 13(5): 174–213.

Potts, Marie. 1977. *The northern Maidu.* Happy Camp CA: Naturegraph Publishers.

Powell, John Wesley. 1891. Indian linguistic families of America north of Mexico. In *Seventh annual report of the Bureau of American Ethnology, for the Years 1885–1886,* Washington DC: Smithsonian Institution, pp. 1–142.

Powers, Stephen. 1877. Tribes of California. In *Contributions to North American Ethnology,* Volume 3. U.S. Geographical and Geological Survey of the Rocky Mountain Region, Department of the Interior. Washington DC: Government Printing Office.

Sapir, Edward. 1910. Yana texts. *UC PAAE* 9:1–235.

———. 1917. The position of Yana in the Hokan stock. *UC PAAE* 13(1): 1–34.

———. 1918. Yana terms of relationships. *UC PAAE* 13(4): 153–173.

———. 1922. The fundamental elements of Northern Yana. *UC PAAE* 13(6): 214–234.

———. 1923. Text analyses of three Yana dialects. *UC PAAE* 20:263–294.

Sapir, Edward, and Leslie Spier. 1943. Notes on the culture of the Yana. *University of California Anthropological Records* 3(3): 239–286.

Waterman, Thomas Talbot. 1918. The Yana Indians. *UC PAAE* 13(2): 35–102.

6

Assuming Responsibility for Ishi

STANLEY H. BRANDES

The Department of Anthropology, U[niversity] of California Berkeley, in response to numerous inquiries from [m]embers of the profession, wishes to clarify for readers our considered opinion on the disposition of Ishi's brain. We
reached general agreement on these words at a regular faculty meeting March
29, 1999.

The recent recovery of a famous California Indian's brain from a Smithsonian warehouse has led the Department of Anthropology at the University of California Berkeley to revisit and reflect on a troubling chapter of our history. Ishi,
whose family and cultural group, the Yahi Indians, were murdered as part of the
genocide that characterized the influx of western settlers to California, lived out
his last years at the original museum of anthropology at the University of California, which was then located in San Francisco. He served as an informant to
one of our department's founding members, Alfred Kroeber, as well as to other
local and visiting anthropologists. The nature of the relation between Ishi and
the anthropologists and linguists who worked with him for some 5 years at the
museum was complex and contradictory. Despite Kroeber's lifelong devotion to
California Indians and his friendship with Ishi, he failed in his efforts to honor
Ishi's wishes not to be autopsied and he inexplicably arranged for Ishi's brain to
be shipped to and curated at the Smithsonian.

We acknowledge our department's role in what happened to Ishi, a man who
had already lost all that was dear to him. We strongly urge that the process of returning Ishi's brain to appropriate Native American representatives be speedily
accomplished.

We are considering various ways to pay honor and respect to Ishi's memory.
We regard public participation as a necessary component of these discussions
and in particular we invite the people of Native California to instruct us in how
we may better serve the needs of their communities through our research re-

lated activities. Perhaps, working together, we can ensure that the next millennium will represent a new era in the relationship between indigenous peoples, anthropologists, and the public.

NOTES

This letter is reproduced here by permission of the American Anthropology Association from *Anthropology News* 40(4), May 1999. Not for sale or further reproduction. The views expressed in this letter were those of the University of California, Berkeley, Department of Anthropology as a whole and do not necessarily reflect the personal opinion of then-Chair, Stanley Brandes.

7

Assuming Responsibility for Ishi

An Alternative Interpretation

GEORGE M. FOSTER

The brief statement, "Assuming Responsibility for Ishi," in the May 1999 *Anthropology Newsletter* (reprinted as Chapter 6 in this volume), reporting action taken at a University of California, Berkeley Anthropology Department faculty meeting held on March 29, 1999, implies that UC Berkeley anthropologists feel that there was something shameful about the way Alfred Kroeber, Thomas T. Waterman, Saxton Pope, M.D., and Edward Gifford treated Ishi and that a formal mea culpa is necessary. In this commentary I argue to the contrary: I believe that the behavior of the anthropologists (and of the University) was highly ethical and that apologies are out of order. I find, too, that a great many of my colleagues share this view, *including all who knew Kroeber and the Giffords,* who were the only people who had known Ishi well who were still living in the 1950s.

The story of Ishi is indeed dramatic. At dawn on August 29, 1911, butchers in a slaughterhouse near Oroville awakened to find a near-naked Indian cowering against the slaughterhouse corral fence. They called the sheriff, who, to protect the Indian, took him to the county jail, where speakers of several Indian languages tried in vain to communicate with him. The story of the "wild Indian" reached the San Francisco newspapers, where Kroeber and Waterman, professors at the University of California, read it. They surmised that the Indian was a speaker of Yana, two of whose four dialects had been studied and vocabularies recorded by anthropologists interviewing native speakers of the language.

On August 31, Waterman went to Oroville, where he tried to communicate with the Indian by reading words from the Yana vocabularies he had brought with him. The Indian listened impassively to a number of Waterman's attempts to pronounce the phonetically transcribed words. Only when he came to *siwini* ("yellow pine"), simultaneously tapping the pine frame of the cot on which they sat, did Ishi (as I will now call him) recognize the word. On the basis of additional words that Ishi recognized, Waterman concluded that he was Yahi, a

89

member of the southernmost Yana group, all of whose speakers had been pre-sumed dead. Batwi, one of two elderly Yana who had worked as informants for anthropologists, was still alive, living in Redding. Batwi came to Oroville, where, despite encountering substantial dialectical differences, he succeeded in communicating with Ishi. With the permission of the Indian Bureau in Wash-ington, and the concurrence of Ishi himself, Waterman brought Ishi to the Mu-seum of Anthropology in San Francisco, on Parnassus Heights, adjacent to the University of California, San Francisco, Medical School, where he lived until his death four years and seven months later on March 25, 1916.

Ishi's arrival caused great excitement in the San Francisco Bay area, but by the time I began graduate study under Kroeber and Robert Lowie in 1935, nine-teen years after Ishi's death, the story was already history. We students learned about Ishi in Kroeber's "Indians of California" course, but until the appearance of Theodora Kroeber's bestseller, *Ishi in Two Worlds,* in 1961, he was all but for-gotten by the community at large. Thanks to this book, a great many school-children have learned about Ishi, but his story did not again become front-page news until early 1999, when it was revealed that Ishi's brain had been removed during the autopsy performed at the UC Medical School prior to his cremation.

The present furor over Ishi began with a thoughtful article by *Los Angeles Times* staff writer Mary Curtin, entitled "Ishi: Group Seeks to Rebury Tribe's Last Survivor in Homeland," that appeared in the June 8, 1997, issue of the news-paper. The article reports, among other things, that a group of California Indi-ans known as the Butte County Native American Cultural Committee wished to repatriate Ishi's ashes to bury them near where he and his people had lived. Al-though the fate of Ishi's brain was unknown when Curtin wrote her story, her statement that it initially was held at the University of California, San Francisco, implicated the Medical School. Accordingly, Dorothy Bainton, M.D., vice chan-cellor of Academic Affairs, commissioned Nancy Rockafellar, Ph.D., a medical historian on the UC San Francisco faculty, to make a thorough investigation of the records at UC San Francisco and those in the Bancroft Library at UC Berke-ley. Her unpublished report, "A Compromise Between Science and Sentiment: A Report on Ishi's Treatment at the University of California, 1911–1916," issued February 17, 1999, is an invaluable source of information, revealing how a rumor concerning the whereabouts of Ishi's brain led to Duke University anthropolo-gist Orin Starn's verification in late January 1999 that Alfred Kroeber had in 1917 shipped Ishi's brain to Aleš Hrdlička, curator of physical anthropology at the Smithsonian, who added it to his collection of primate brains. It appears that, following Hrdlička's retirement in the 1930s, the brain was forgotten. During the nine years I was a Smithsonian employee (1943–1952), six of them in Washington, I can recall no occasion on which mention was made either of Ishi or his brain in connection with the Institution. (I might add that during my six graduate years, my twenty-six years as professor, and the first nineteen years of my retirement at Berkeley, the same held true in California: Ishi's brain was a nontopic.)

Starn's revelation that the Smithsonian, in spite of earlier denials, did indeed hold Ishi's brain led to a rash of articles and editorials in California newspapers demanding the return of Ishi's brain to Native Americans for proper reburial with his ashes. Many of the editorials were temperate statements stating the obvious: In simple justice the brain must be returned. Several were virulent in their attacks on the anthropologists who first established communication with Ishi and who cared for him until his death. *The Contra Costa Times* was the worst offender:

> This is the final indignity heaped upon Ishi by anthropologists. When he came out of the hills into Oroville in 1911, *they made him a curiosity.* They *studied him like a rat in a cage.* Then, when he died of tuberculosis, they *carved him up and sent his brain to the Smithsonian.* (issue of March 26, 1999, emphasis added)

After the Smithsonian agreed to return the brain, an editorial continued in the same vein:

> . . . the *butchered and scattered body* of California's most famous Indian is about to be joined together. (May 17, 1999, emphasis added)

Even some of the objective editorials imply that Ishi was exploited by the University of California and its anthropologists. For example, the *San Francisco Chronicle* wrote, "He [Ishi] was taken in by the University of California anthropological museum in San Francisco where he was a living exhibit of 'the last wild Indian in the United States'" (March 29, 1999) and that he "became a living exhibit in a San Francisco museum" (April 6, 1999).

On April 6, 1999, *Oakland Tribune* staff writer William Brand wrote:

> The rediscovery of Ishi's brain has put the UC Berkeley anthropology department in a tizzy. Professor [name omitted] read a strongly worded statement, approved by the department, expressing regret about the brain and urging its return to American Indians. 'Despite Kroeber's lifelong devotion to California Indians and his friendship with Ishi, he failed in his efforts to honor Ishi's wishes not to be autopsied and he inexplicably arranged for Ishi's brain to be shipped to the Smithsonian,' the statement said. 'We acknowledge our department's role in what happened to Ishi, a man who had already lost all that was dear to him.'

Brand here was speaking of the brief article in the Correspondence section of the May, 1999, *Anthropology News*, "Assuming Responsibility for Ishi" (Chapter 6, this volume)

Brand continues, "Nineteen professors approved an even more strongly worded statement outlining 'genocide and ethnic cleansing' of California Indians and apologizes [*sic*] for Kroeber's transgression." This document, "Statement by Members of the Department of Anthropology on the Proper Treatment of Ishi's Brain," dated March 17, 1999, was the final version of several earlier drafts which, for their content and intemperate language, seemed to a number of UC Berkeley active and emeritus professors to be unfair both to the University and to Kroeber and his associates at the time: Waterman, Pope, and Gifford. All of the drafts begin with the same phraseology as the published "Responsibility" paper:

> The recent recovery of a famous California Indian's brain from a Smithsonian warehouse has led the Department of Anthropology at the U of California Berkeley to revisit and reflect on a troubling chapter in our history. Ishi, whose family and cultural group, the Yahi Indians, were murdered as part of the genocide that characterized the influx of western settlers to California, lived out his last years at the original museum of anthropology at the U of California, which was then located in San Francisco. He served as informant to one of our department's founding members, Alfred Kroeber, as well as to other local and visiting anthropologists. The nature of the relationship between Ishi and the anthropologists and linguists who worked with him for some five years at the museum were[*sic*] complex and contradictory.

The "more strongly worded statement" spells out this relationship: "real friendship entwined with academic ambitions, *resulting in considerable insensitivity to Ishi's personal and medical needs*" (emphasis added). An earlier draft (March 3, 1999) includes the phrase "exploitation in the name of science."

The published version then continues:

> Despite Kroeber's lifelong devotion to California Indians and his friendship with Ishi, he failed in his efforts to honor Ishi's wish not to be autopsied and he inexplicably arranged for Ishi's brain to be shipped to and to be curated at the Smithsonian.

The draft of March 3, 1999 reads,

> Ishi had trusted Kroeber to ensure the sanctity of his remains after his death, and Kroeber, although unintentionally, ultimately betrayed this trust, failing to stop an autopsy. . . . The existence of this travesty is as shocking and surprising to our Department as it is to the rest of the public.

This draft continues with more of the same:

> We now realize that the anthropology that emerged in the early 20th century – so-called 'salvage anthropology' – was in reality, a human science that emerged and grew up in the face of American genocide. . . . We find abhorrent our department's role in our faculty's exploitation and betrayal of Ishi, a man who had already lost all that was dear to him at the hands of European colonizers. . . . We, the Anthropology Department of the University of California, Berkeley, wish to express its profound distress, anger, and sorrow for what happened to this tragic human being.

Clearly there is a sizable group, including anthropologists, at least some newspaper writers, and consequently some of their readers, who feel that the conduct of Kroeber, his colleagues, and the University of California in general, was highly unethical.

The most commonly voiced criticisms are the following:

1. Kroeber and Waterman took control of Ishi and placed him in a museum, where he was a major exhibit for as long as he lived. Other living arrangements (such as an Indian reservation) might have been more congenial to him.

2. By being brought to a city, with its air pollution and pathogens to which he had not been exposed, he was practically condemned to death. His death from tuberculosis is often cited in this context.

3. Anthropologists exploited Ishi, "pumping" him for information about his aboriginal life. The linguist Edward Sapir has been singled out for special condemnation, accused of hastening his death by "working" him long hours as informant when he fatigued quickly because of the ravages of tuberculosis.

4. By sending Ishi's brain to the Smithsonian, Kroeber violated a sacred trust with Ishi.

5. Theodora Kroeber's account of Ishi's life at the museum, and his relationship to the anthropologists and others with whom he associated, is overly sentimental and inevitably insensitive to Ishi's view of his role in the drama. Never having known Ishi herself, she relied largely on her husband for information, and he, by her own account, was reluctant to discuss Ishi.

I will address each of these charges in turn.

1. While acknowledging the tragedy of Ishi's story, I think he was fortunate to have as his closest friends anthropologists who, on the basis of data gathered from earlier Indian informants, were able to communicate with him, recognize his personal and psychological needs, and almost certainly make his last years more comfortable and satisfying than if he had been sent elsewhere. Viewed from the perspective of contemporary race relations and political correctness,

the decision to house Ishi at the museum has turned out to be symbolically unfortunate. Hotels, boarding houses, apartments, and homes are places where
human beings live. Museums are places where specimens are housed and cared
for, with facilities for study and exhibition. So it is probably inevitable that Ishi's
living at the museum conveyed the idea that he was stored there to facilitate his
roles as informant and exhibit. There is no doubt that Ishi attracted many people to the museum when, from time to time on Sunday afternoons, he and
Kroeber appeared together, Ishi demonstrating Yahi flint chipping and bow-
and arrow-making techniques and Kroeber answering questions and translating both for Ishi and museum visitors.

In reality, Ishi's situation did not conform at all to this popular perception.
In addition to rooms filled with artifacts of California tribes, the museum had a
bedroom where Indians stayed when they came to San Francisco, as well as
bathing and cooking facilities. Ishi differed from other Indians in becoming a
permanent rather than a transient resident. In addition to Indians, there were
two caretakers who always slept in the museum, as guards against fire. "So it
was," writes Theodora Kroeber (*Ishi in Two Worlds*, 1961, pp. 123–124), "that
when Ishi arrived, Indian guests were a normal part of museum living, and his
own sense of strangeness was made less acute through his new acquaintances'
feeling of ease and accustomedness."

Of those who criticize the decision to house Ishi at the museum, the question
must be asked: "What would *you* have done? Left him with the sheriff? Sent him
to an Indian reservation, where health conditions almost certainly would have
led to an early death?" One wonders, too, if perhaps in the final years of the 19th
and early years of the 20th centuries there were not other Ishis who fell into the
hands of less sympathetic white Californians than those of Oroville and who
quietly disappeared without public notice. I am convinced that Ishi was happier
and much better cared for at the museum than he would have been anywhere
else.[1]

2. Far from being a site of urban air pollution and pathogens, the museum's
location on Parnassus Heights was surely in 1911 as healthy an environment
as existed anywhere in the world. Even today the University of California, San
Francisco, campus, constantly bathed by ocean breezes off the Pacific Ocean a
mile or two to the west, must have the purest air of any urban institution in the
country if not the world. Moreover, the museum's location adjacent to the medical school was of great importance to Ishi's health. Pope, who joined the faculty
a year after Ishi arrived, was fascinated by the latter's skill as archer and bow-
maker. Ishi instructed Pope in the art and science of Yahi archery, and the two
men became fast friends. "Popey" also became Ishi's personal physician, and it
is unlikely that *any* San Franciscan had better, more constant, and more concerned medical care than Ishi.

3. As to whether Ishi was "exploited" by anthropologists depends on how one defines the term.[2] Ishi was indeed the source of a great deal of invaluable ethnographic and linguistic information for Kroeber, Gifford, Waterman, Sapir, Pope, and others. As to whether he felt exploited, we will never know. My impression – colored no doubt by my relationship with Eben Tillotson, a Yuki Indian friend during my first field work, in Round Valley, California, during the summer of 1937 – is that Ishi was pleased to help make the record of his language and culture as accurate and complete as possible. Tillotson, who was literate, always insisted on looking in my notebook to make sure that I correctly recorded names, places, and other data. "What my grandchildren will know of how we Yuki lived will depend on what you write, and you must be very careful in recording what I tell you." Had it not been for the cooperative efforts of California Indians telling anthropologists about their way of life, and the books, monographs, and articles that followed, all of us – Indians as well as non-Indians – would today know much less about aboriginal California than we do. A case in point illustrating this interdependence also comes from my 1937 research in Round Valley. Before I left Berkeley to begin my research, Kroeber suggested that I look up Ralph Moore, whom he had found to be an excellent informant. I did so, and found that Moore indeed knew a great deal about aboriginal Yuki culture. On the third or fourth day, however, I was rocked back when Moore, rather crossly, asked me, "Why do you ask me all these questions? Professor Kroeber has it all written down in the *Handbook of the Indians of California,* and I have to read about it each night to be ready for you in the morning!" "Mr. Moore," I said, "I'll give you ten dollars for that book!" Moore considered this offer to be reasonable, and for many years the volume, autographed by Kroeber to Ralph Moore, was in my library.

To me the most remarkable event of Ishi's last years was the month-long camping trip he made to his aboriginal home in May 1914 with Pope, eleven-year-old Saxton Jr., Kroeber, and Waterman. The attraction of the trip for Pope and his son was the excitement of serious bow-and-arrow hunting, as well as the romance of living like real Indians. For the two anthropologists the attraction lay in the unparalleled opportunity to see and photograph scenes of aboriginal life, until that time known only from informants' statements. Initially opposed to the trip, Ishi quickly was caught up in the excitement of the occasion and happily demonstrated to his friends many aspects of his former life. Was this "exploitation"? In the mid-1950s my wife, Mary, sat next to Saxton Pope, Jr., at a dinner party. When he learned she was an anthropologist, he told her many things about that trip, how he crossed a swift stream, holding on to Ishi's long hair as Ishi swam with strong strokes, how he and his father hunted with Ishi with bow and arrows, and the like. He felt that Ishi enjoyed the experience almost as much as he did. Certainly, photographs of this trip in *Ishi in Two Worlds* portray a happy person. After several weeks, however, he was ready to return "home" – to the museum.

4. With respect to "carving Ishi up and sending his brain to the Smithsonian," to use the *Contra Costa Times'* pungent expression, or that of the UC Berkeley draft of March 3, "Ishi had trusted Kroeber to ensure the sanctity of his remains. . . . Kroeber, although unintentionally, ultimately betrayed this trust," the following background is relevant. Kroeber, who, I assume, had final say about Ishi's care when he was in residence at the University, was on sabbatical leave in Europe and New York City during Ishi's last illness. Upon realizing that Ishi was near death, he wrote to Gifford:

> Please stand by our contingently made outline of action, and insist on it as my personal wish. . . . I do not see that an autopsy would lead to anything of consequence . . . As to disposal of his body, I must ask you as my personal representative to yield nothing at all – under any circumstances. If there is any talk about the interests of science, *say for me that science can go to hell. We propose to stand by our friends.* (*Ishi in Two Worlds*, p. 234, emphasis added; see also Chapter 4 in this volume.)

Although the letter arrived several days after Ishi's death, too late to strengthen Gifford's hand in preventing an autopsy, it makes clear that Kroeber had strongly opposed such action before he departed on sabbatical leave eight months earlier.

The autopsy was standard practice for all patients who died in the hospital, but the removal of the brain was not. Had Kroeber been present, he might have been able to prevent the autopsy, but it is unreasonable to expect that the young Gifford, whose formal education had ended several years earlier with a high school diploma, would be able to prevail over medical school regulations. The records do not reveal who ordered the removal of the brain. I find nothing in the record, however, to suggest that the removal of a brain following an autopsy was viewed as desecration of a body. The final paragraph of Pope's *The Medical History of Ishi* (1920), is a moving account of Ishi's burial and makes clear that his friends were greatly concerned that he have a proper and respectful burial:

> His body was carried to the undertakers where it was embalmed. No funeral services were held. Professor T. T. Waterman, Mr. E. W. Gifford, Mr. A. Warburton, Mr. L. L. Loud, of the Museum of Anthropology, and I visited the parlor, and reverently placed in his coffin his bow, a quiver full of arrows, ten pieces of dentalia or Indian money, some dried venison, some acorn meal, his fire sticks, and a small quantity of tobacco. We then accompanied the body to Laurel Hill cemetery near San Francisco, where it was cremated. The ashes were placed in a small Indian pottery jar on the outside of which is inscribed, 'Ishi, the last Yahi Indian, died March 25, 1916.'

Only in jest, in sick humor, could Ishi's death and burial be described as "carving up."

There remains the question of why Kroeber, in view of his forcefully expressed opposition to an autopsy, sent Ishi's brain to the Smithsonian Institution almost ten months after his death. Here we can only speculate, and what follows is my guess as to the factors involved. Kroeber, after having been absent from California for a year, returned to find the predictable pile of items demanding attention. What he had *not* expected to find was the brain of a close friend in a bottle of formaldehyde on a shelf in his office. This must have struck him as the last straw, the final indignity heaped upon him and a dear friend. The fact that he did nothing at all for five months after his return speaks to his fatigue and uncertainty. The thought of adding a bottled brain to the liter or two of ashes of its former bearer, or of cremating the brain separately, must have seemed bizarre to him. To Kroeber, as to many people, the physical remains even of a friend probably seemed distinctly secondary to the memory of that friend. But what to do about this problem? At that time it was believed that much could be learned from the study of human brains, in which, Kroeber knew, Aleš Hrdlička specialized. Why not let him study Ishi's? It must have appeared to Kroeber to be the ideal solution to this vexing problem: Ishi's last gift to science was his own brain! So, late in January 1917, Kroeber shipped the brain to Washington, where, following Hrdlička's retirement in the 1930s, it was forgotten for more than sixty years, until changing social conditions and concepts of justice made relevant the question of location and control of this bit of human protoplasm.

5. As for the charge that Theodora Kroeber's account is seriously flawed in some aspects of content and general portrayal, one can only respond with the obvious: Whatever the shortcomings of her descriptions and analyses, they constitute the basic source for *everyone* who writes on Ishi. Personally, I believe her account is fair and accurate, insofar as data were known and available. Edward and Delila Gifford were the two people closely associated with Ishi whom Mary and I knew best. As assistant museum curator "Gifford probably saw more of Ishi at least during museum hours than did the others [Kroeber, Waterman, Pope]; certain[ly] it was he [who] carried the brunt of responsibility for him during the last months of Ishi's life" (*Ishi in Two Worlds*, p. 153). From time to time Ishi was a weekend houseguest of the Giffords, and Delila often spoke to us of his impeccable manners and of his obvious pleasure of being in their company. Their accounts of Ishi's life at the museum and of his personality and behavior fully substantiate Theodora Kroeber's portrayal.

The reality of the genocide cannot – and should not – be denied. Theodora Kroeber's three chapters in *Ishi in Two Worlds*, pp. 40–100, are as graphic a description of the systematic extermination of a people as can be imagined. This is a stain on all of European American civilization, with its professed respect for human rights (as is the treatment of Africans brought to this country as slaves, their living descendants, and, in lesser degree, other ethnic minorities as well). Yet to suggest that the University of California, and Alfred Kroeber and other anthropologists in particular, bear a special blame strikes me as untrue and unfair. The UC Berkeley drafts pull out all the stops: through the use of loaded expressions such as "betrayed the trust," "the existence of this travesty," "we find abhorrent our department's role in our faculty's exploitation and betrayal of Ishi." They imply that the behavior of Kroeber and other anthropologists is a metaphor for the 19th-century genocide of the California Indians.

Everyone has a right to expect from history that its judgments be made against a background of total performance, not on the basis of a single episode, evaluated by the standards of a later point in time. In my view the documents discussed in this commentary deny Kroeber this right. Those who knew him well have not the slightest doubt as to his genuine affection for most of those with whom he worked, as well as for Indians as an ethnic minority.

How many anthropologists, like Kroeber, have had the courtesy to send their major publications to key informants, as illustrated by the case of Ralph Moore? How many have had their informants as houseguests, not just once but on many occasions? And how many onlookers during those Indian Claims cases of the mid-1950s held in Berkeley will ever forget Kroeber's vigorous support of the claims of California tribes to their ancestral lands?

The most troubling of all aspects of this story has to do not with Kroeber or Ishi but rather with the epistemology of anthropology. How is it possible for scholars with essentially the same training, and with access to the same data, to come to diametrically opposed conclusions? The most charitable answer to this question is that anthropology always has been, and continues to be, the search for the most plausible interpretations of data rather than the scientific testing of hypotheses to prove or disprove them. But how is plausibility determined? I know of no good answer to this question.

NOTES

1. In fact, Ishi did not live at the museum all the time; during the summer of 1915 he lived at the Watermans' home, as recounted in Chapter 4 of this volume.

2. Anywhere Ishi would live, he would have had to earn a living by using his skills for the benefit of others.

8

Ishi's Brain, Ishi's Ashes

Reflections on Anthropology and Genocide

NANCY SCHEPER-HUGHES

PREAMBLE

The following chapter is a critical reflection by a member of the Department of Anthropology at the University of California (UC), Berkeley, in response to demands by Native Californians for the repatriation of ancestral remains and sacred artifacts that are part of the permanent collections kept in the Hearst (formerly Lowie) Museum of Anthropology. After more than ten years under the 1990 Native American Graves and Repatriation Act (NAGPRA), the U.S. federal law that requires that all Native American human remains and sacred funeral objects be identified and repatriated to appropriately designated indigenous groups, at the date of this writing only two small material objects have been returned from the vast collections at Berkeley.

The tensions between Native Californians and university officials and anthropologists came to a head in the late 1990s when Art Angle, a Maidu Indian activist, asked that the brain of the famous California Indian known as Ishi, removed during autopsy at the University of California Medical Center in March 1916 (when Ishi was under the special protection of Alfred Kroeber and the Department of Anthropology) be located and returned to Ishi's cultural descendants in the area of Mt. Lassen along with his ashes, which were kept in a Pueblo jar in a cemetery in Colma, California. When it was discovered that A. L. Kroeber himself had sent the brain to be curated at the Smithsonian Institution, I was asked to chair a small departmental committee to review the data and to draft a formal response by our department. As I became more involved in the issue, I attended public hearings and began to visit leaders of Indian communities near Ishi's country in the area of Mt. Lassen. What follows, then, is not a research report but a foray into public anthropology – critically applied work by the anthropologist speaking and acting as an anthropologically informed citizen rather than as a specialist (which I am not with respect to either Native California or ethnohistory). The tone of the chapter reflects the emotionality of the subject for many, but especially older, California Indians.

INVISIBLE GENOCIDES

Modern anthropology was built up in the face of colonial and postcolonial genocides, ethnocides, mass killings, population die-outs, and other forms of mass destruction visited on the marginalized peoples whose lives, suffering, and deaths have provided anthropologists with a livelihood. Yet, despite this history – and the privileged position of the ethnographer as eyewitness to some of these events – anthropology has been, until very recently,[1] quite mute on the subjects of violence and genocide. Indeed, everything in the professional training of anthropologists predisposes them *not* to see the various forms of mass violence that have so often ravaged the lives of their subjects. Anthropologists are much better at analyzing the *psychological* (*see* Devereux 1961; Edgerton 1992; DeVos 1971; Scheper-Hughes 1993,[1979] 2000) and *symbolic* violence (see Bourdieu 1977; Bourdieu and Waquant 1992:111–205) that underlie so many normative institutions and ordinary social interactions.

Of course, genocides and mass violence predated Western colonization and are found in indigenous as well as in "civilized" Western societies. So the avoidance by anthropologists of the study of human violence, cruelty, and of evil, in general, was dictated by the wish to avoid further stigmatizing those marginal societies and cultures that were so often judged harshly and negatively in terms of Eurocentric values and aims. Those ethnographers who deviated from this general rule of avoiding the study of human violence, like Napoleon Chagnon (1968, 1988), often ended up harming their subjects. Chagnon's characterizations of the "fierce" and "savage" Yanomami Indians of the Venezuelan and Brazilian Amazon inadvertently created a useful rationale for the efforts of both national governments to further restrict Yanomami indigenous territories (Ramos 1987; 2001).

Consequently, a basic premise guiding twentieth-century ethnographic research was, quite simply, to see, hear, and record no evil (and very little violence) in reporting back from the field. Classical cultural anthropology and its particular moral sensibility orients anthropological ethnographers, like so many inverse bloodhounds, on the trail and on the scent of the good and the righteous in the societies that they studied. Some, like Paul Riesman (1987) even suggested that evil is not a proper subject for anthropology.[2] But the moral blinders that anthropologists wore in the one instance also shaded their eyes in other instances less appropriate for "hermeneutic generosity" – for example, marauding settlers and colonizers, fascist police states, unjust wars, and other instances of mass destruction. During the height of the Vietnam War some anthropologists united in arguing for a more politically astute and critically engaged anthropology (see Sanford and Comstock 1971, Hymes 1969). But overall, as Elliot Leyton (1998) pointed out, the contribution of anthropology to understanding *all* levels of violence – from criminal sexual abuse and homicide to political terrorism, "dirty" wars, and genocide – is extremely modest.

TRISTES ANTROPOLOGIQUES

In his professional memoir, *After the Fact,* Clifford Geertz (1995) notes somewhat wryly that he always had the uncomfortable feeling of arriving either too early or too late to observe the most significant and most violent political events in his respective field sites in Morocco and Java. Later in the same text he admits to consciously avoiding the pending conflicts by carefully moving back and forth between his respective field sites during relative periods of calm, always managing to "miss the revolution" (Starn 1992) – or the genocide – as it were.

Consequently, there is nothing in Geertz's ethnographic writings hinting at the "killing fields" that were beginning to engulf Indonesia soon after he had departed, a massacre of suspected Communists by Islamic fundamentalists in 1965 that rivaled more recent events in Rwanda. It was an extraordinary bloodbath – a political massacre of some 60,000 Balinese following an unsuccessful Marxist-inspired coup of 1965. Perhaps one could interpret Geertz's celebrated analysis of the Balinese cockfight as a coded expression of the fierce aggression lying just beneath the surface of a people whom the anthropologist otherwise described as among the most poised, controlled, and decorous in the world.

Today, the world, the objects of our study, and the uses of anthropology have changed considerably. Those privileged to observe human events close up and over time and who are thereby privy to local, community, and even state secrets that are generally hidden from view until much later – after the collective graves have been discovered and the body counts made – are beginning to recognize another ethical position: to name and to identify the sources, structures, and institutions of mass violence. This new mood of political and ethical engagement (see Scheper-Hughes 1995b) has resulted in considerable soul searching, even if long "after the fact."

Claude Lévi-Strauss (1995), for example, approaching the end of his long and distinguished career, opened his recently published photographic memoir, *Saudades do Brasil* (Homesickness for Brazil), with a sobering caveat. He warned the reader that the lyrically beautiful images of "pristine" rain forest Brazilian Indians about to be presented – photos taken by him between 1935 and 1939 in the interior of Brazil – should *not* be trusted. The images were illusory, he cautioned. The world they portray no longer exists. The starkly beautiful, seemingly timeless Nambiquara, Caduveo, and Bororo Indians captured in his photos bear no resemblance to the reduced populations one might find today camped out by the sides of busy truck routes or loitering in urban villages, looking like slums, carved out of a gutted wilderness. The Nambiquara and their Native neighbors have been decimated by wage labor, gold prospecting, prostitution, and the diseases of cultural contact: smallpox, tuberculosis, AIDS, and syphilis.

But the old master's confession goes further. These early photos capturing simple, naked Indians sleeping on the ground under romantic shelters of palm leaves, have nothing to do with a state of pristine humanity that has since been lost. The photos taken in the 1930s already show the effects of a savage European colonization on the once populous civilizations of Central Brazil and the Amazon. Following contact, these indigenous civilizations were destroyed, leaving behind only sad remnants of themselves – a people not so much "primitive," he cautions, as "stranded," stripped of their material and symbolic wealth. What Lévi-Strauss's camera had captured were images of a particularly virulent kind of human strip mining, an invisible genocide, the magnitude of which the anthropologist was at the time naïvely unaware.

Earlier, Lévi-Strauss (1966:126) had described the central quandary that *demands* that anthropology be a "vocation" (see also Sontag 1964:68–81) rather than just a scholarly pursuit. He wrote,

> Anthropology is not a dispassionate science like astronomy, which springs from the contemplation of things at a distance. It is the outcome of a historical process which has made the larger part of mankind subservient to the other, and during which millions of innocent human beings have had their resources plundered and their institutions and beliefs destroyed whilst they themselves were ruthlessly killed, thrown into bondage, and contaminated by diseases they were unable to resist. Anthropology is the daughter to this era of violence: its capacity to assess more objectively the facts pertaining to the human condition reflects on the epistemological level, a state of affairs in which one part of mankind treated the other as an object.

His statement is an indictment of those anthropologists who served as bystanders, silent and useless witnesses to the genocides and die-outs they encountered in the course of pursuing their science.

I implicate myself in this scenario. It took me over two decades to confront the question of overt political violence which, given my choice of early field sites – Ireland in the mid-1970s and Brazil during the military dictatorship years – must have required a massive dose of denial. While studying the madness of everyday life in the mid-1970s in a small, remote community in western Ireland, I was largely concerned with *interior* spaces, with the small, dark psychodramas of scapegoating and labeling within traditional farm households that was driving so many young bachelors to drink, depression, and schizophrenia. I paid scant attention to the political activities of Matty Dowd, from whom we rented our cottage in the mountain hamlet of Ballynalacken and who used our attic to store a small arsenal of guns and explosives that he and a few of his Sinn Féin buddies were running to Northern Ireland. Consequently, I left unexamined until very recently (Scheper-Hughes [1979] 2000) the links between the political violence in Northern Ireland and the tortured family dramas in West Kerry, which certainly had a violence of their own.

In Brazil I did not begin to study political violence until the late 1980s, when the half-grown sons of some of my friends and neighbors in the shantytown of Alto do Cruzeiro began to "disappear" – their mutilated bodies turning up later, the handiwork of police-infiltrated local death squads (Scheper-Hughes 1993: chapter 6). Up until that time I believed that the analysis of political violence occurring in the context of military dictatorships and police states, in times of political and economic transition, during and following civil wars and wars of liberation, were best handled by journalists. Anthropologists were (I thought) too slow, too methodical, too hesitant, too reflective, and our knowledge was too local and too culturally embedded to be of any use. Meanwhile, political upheavals and violent conflicts were too fast and unstable for the ethnographers' notebooks. By the time anthropologists had anything to say on such topics, it was usually too late or too complex an analysis to be of any practical use or good. But when Brazilian newspapers insisted on running stories about the "dangerousness" and "violence" of shantytown youths and street children, a representation that made the work of local death squads seem a necessary defense against the anarchy of the *favela,* I began to see the necessity of an anthropological intervention (see Scheper-Hughes 2001). I had the advantage of some mentors and older colleagues at Berkeley (for example, *see* Berreman 1969, 1982; Nader 1969, 1977) who had developed different, sometimes contestational, positions on pressing public issues.

KROEBER AND ISHI

Alfred Kroeber died before he could imagine, as Lévi-Strauss and other later anthropologists did, a radically different role for the anthropologist as an engaged witness rather than as a disinterested, "objective" spectator of scenes of human suffering, cultural destruction, and genocide. When Kroeber arrived in San Francisco in 1901 to take up the post of museum anthropologist at the University of California, it was at the tail end of a terrible, wanton, and officially sanctioned extermination of northern California Indians that began during the Gold Rush and culminated in the early decades of the twentieth century.

It was the fashion during the early twentieth century for historians and social scientists to take a coolly dispassionate approach toward their subject matter. For example, a biological historian and demographer of the period recorded the tragic events of the genocide in California as follows (see Cook 1978:91):

> Like all native people in the Western Hemisphere, the Indians of California under-went a very severe decline in numbers following the entrance of White civilization. From the beginning to the end of the process the native population experienced a fall from 310,000 to approximately 20,000, a decline of over 90% of the original number. This collapse was due to the operation of factors inherent in the physical and social conflict between the White and the Red races.

Disease epidemics were held responsible for "depressing the local population" (Cook 1978:92).

In fact, it was U.S. military campaigns and massacres, bounty hunts, debt pe-onage, land grabbing, and land enclosures by Anglo settlers and ranchers that were responsible for the greater toll of suffering and death on the native Califor-nia populations. In his letter to the Commissioner of Indian Affairs, a local agent, Adam Johnson (cited by Castillo 1978:107) reported the following about the so-called "Indian Wars" in California:

> The majority of the tribes are kept in constant fear on account of the indiscrimi-nate and inhuman massacre of their people for real or supposed injuries. They have become alarmed about the increased flood of [settlers] . . . it was just incom-prehensible to them . . . I have seldom heard of a single difficulty between the whites and the Indians in which the original cause could not be traced to some rash or reckless act of the former.

By 1860 American military attacks had taken the lives of 4267 Native Califor-nians, but even these were not the worst. During and after the California Gold Rush, Native Americans experienced a total assault on their communities from the "civilian" white population as well. For example, in May 1852 a mob of whites, led by the sheriff of Weatherville, California, attacked, without warning, a peaceful rancheria, indiscriminately killing men, women, and children. A lo-cal newspaper reported: "Of the 150 Indians that constituted the rancheria, only 2 or 3 escaped, and those were believed to be dangerously wounded. . . . none were spared except one woman and two children who were brought back as prisoners" (*Daily Alta California*, May 4, 1852, cited by Churchill 1997:220).

The devastating effects of the massacres were amplified by other assaults on the Native economy of the survivors. Settlers threw up fences that disturbed communal hunting for rabbit and deer and that restricted access to the oak groves where Native people gathered acorns, their staple food. In 1850 the California legislature passed a law that decreed that, on the word of a single white person, any Indian could be declared a vagrant, thrown in jail, and his labor sold at auction for up to four months without pay. In short, it was a form of legalized slavery.

These same new labor laws permitted the outright stealing of Indian children, a practice that was widespread in northern California through the end of the nineteenth century. An editorial published on December 6, 1861, in the local newspaper of Marysville, California, stated (cited in Castillo 1978:109):

> It is from these [local] mountain tribes that white settlers draw their supplies of kidnapped children, educated as servants, and women for the purpose of labor and lust. . . . It is notorious that there are parties in the northern countries of this state, whose sole occupation has been to steal young children and squaws . . . and to dispose them at handsome prices to the settlers, who being [largely] unmarried willingly pay 50 or 60 dollars for a likely young girl.

This particular form of settler predation, the abduction of Indian children, is bitterly remembered to this day by Maidu residents of Feather River, near Marysville. The late Rosalie Bertram shared the following painful memory with me in May 2000:

> When I was a little girl my grandmother and my great-aunt would interrupt whatever game I was playing to shout at me: "Rosalie – go hide!" If I didn't hide quick enough or if they didn't like my hiding place, they would pull me out and make me do it again and again until they were satisfied. Whenever I asked *why* I had to do this, my grandmother would say, "You'll understand when you are a grown woman".

As she remembered this, Rosalie began to cry silently.

The devastation suffered by Rosalie's Maiduan community (Maidu, Konkow, and Nisenan) is captured in the following numbers. In 1846 there were 8000 Maiduan people. In 1850 there were between 3500 and 4500. By 1910 only 900 Maidu people remained (Riddell 1978:386). The ethnocides continue to this day, though in different forms, the toll exacted from generations of structural violence: poverty, racism, social exclusion and geopolitical displacement, chronic unemployment, ill health, and family disorganization resulting from alcohol and drug addictions.

Kroeber, like most anthropologists of his day (including Margaret Mead, whose sense of urgency – "We must study them before they disappear!" – was dictated by the die-outs of "primitive" peoples, their languages, and their cultures) dedicated himself during his first two decades in California to what was then called "salvage ethnography." This was a concerted effort to document the cultures of rapidly disappearing indigenous peoples, largely by tapping the memories of the oldest members. It was North American anthropology's weak response to genocide, although it was never explicitly recognized as such. For Kroeber, salvage ethnography was a work of intense concentration based on the highest anthropological principles of his day. With the death of each cultural tradition, no matter how small, something uniquely precious and irreplaceable, a part of collective humanity, was irretrievably lost. And salvage ethnography was also a real labor of love. Kroeber's work culminated in his monumental, 925-page *Handbook of the Indians of California* (Kroeber 1925), which he delivered to the Smithsonian Institution in 1917, the year after Ishi's death, although it was not published until eight years later. The *Handbook* is considered by many to be Kroeber's most important and lasting contribution to his discipline.

In the *Handbook,* as in his more theoretical writings (see, for example, Kroeber 1917, 1952) Kroeber treated the decline of native populations and cultures as the result of an inevitable social evolutionary trajectory – the march of civilization, as it were. The technological complexity of Western civilization would simply overwhelm and replace the more technologically simple indigenous cultures. Today we might see this theory as an anthropological version of American Manifest Destiny, but that was not how Kroeber, the scientist, saw it. In his idealist view, history (understood teleologically) favored "massive", sturdy, and "tense" (as oppose to "flaccid") cultures,[3] characterized by an increasing complexity and "density" in patterned elements (1939:222). Cultural "intensity" leads, according to Kroeber, to greater material achievements and, therefore, to cultural dominance. Those few remaining scattered bands of small-scale hunting and gathering tribes in northern California would inevitably give way to white settler farming, ranching, and mining ventures. Some indigenous groups fell quickly; others resisted and fought bravely; small bands of survivors went into hiding.

That any indigenous people survived at all in California in the early twentieth century was, Kroeber ([1911a] 1972:9) wrote, "remarkable." He described the survival of the "elusive" Mill Creek Indians (discussed subsequently) in glowing terms. They were, Kroeber ([1911a] 1972:9) wrote, "the last free survivors of the American red man, who by an unexampled fortitude and stubbornness of character, succeeded in holding out against the overwhelming tide of civilization twenty-five years longer even than Geronimo's famous band of Apaches." But, he cautioned, the Mill Creek band of Yana Indians could not hold out forever, and their "final chapter" was fast approaching.

By the time Kroeber completed his *Handbook,* he came to view salvage ethnography – which he once famously described as "gathering the remembered remnants of dying aboriginal societies from survivors in blue-jeans living in ruined and 'bastardized' cultures" (Kroeber 1948a:427) – as less than satisfying work. He subsequently turned his attention to the American Southwest, where more vibrant and viable Native American cultures still flourished among Pueblo Indians. Kroeber also turned his back on "particularistic" ethnography in preference for more broadly theoretical writings – it is perhaps significant that he did so after the deaths of his first wife, Henriette Rothschild, in 1913 and of his key Yana Indian informant and friend, Ishi, in 1916, both from tuberculosis. Following the Boasian German idealist tradition (see Stocking 1996), Kroeber began to explore the collective "genius" of various cultural traditions, to which the individual was largely irrelevant.

In a forum assessing the contributions of Alfred Kroeber to anthropology as a whole, Stanley Diamond (1981:57) commented that in contrast to Robert Redfield, "Kroeber was never interested in the *carriers* of culture. [While] Redfield worried about *who* the people were who were communicating with one another … Kroeber had no interest in who was talking to whom." Indeed, what interested Kroeber as a mature anthropologist were cultural patterns, configurations, structures, and abstractions. At this same forum honoring Kroeber's legacy, Eric Wolf (1981:57–58) described Kroeber's impersonal approach to culture as "very abstract, very Olympian – frightening, ultimately." Indeed, there is a radical disjuncture between Kroeber the emotionally remote anthropologist (whose theoretical writings on culture are closer to Claude Lévi-Strauss's mid-twentieth-century structuralism, which they anticipate, than to any other American anthropologist) and Kroeber the warm and intimate family man, the personable colleague, supportive teacher, and good friend to his Indian informants, some of whom came to live with the Kroeber family in their summer compound (LeGuin 2001). Kroeber was a complex man who tried to balance a rich scholarly, academic, and field research–oriented life with an equally rich personal life that included a large family and many friends, some of them his native informants. Yet, he kept these two spheres, the personal and the "scientific," highly compartmentalized. The deep emotional reticence characteristic of his scientific research and writings bears no resemblance to his personal relationships, which were courtly, generous, and warmly affecting (see Steward 1961, especially pp. 104–105).

Perhaps confronting the suffering, devastation, and culture deaths of his native California informants was too difficult for Kroeber to bear, and he retreated into the safety zone of a theory that put their losses into a broader cultural historical perspective. Consequently, he could view the destruction of entire small populations of Native Californians from an Olympian perspective and distance as a small sidebar in the *longue durée* of social evolutionary time. Kroeber once famously described the genocide that reduced the indigenous population of California from 300,000 in the mid-1840s to less than 20,000 people at the close of the century as a thing of small import, "a little history . . . of pitiful events" (Buckley 1996). He admitted to an "unusual personal resistance" to "vehement" emotions, and he once confided to A. R. Pilling, another specialist in Yurok culture, that he did not delve into his Yurok informants' experiences of the contact era because he "could not stand all the tears" (Buckley 1966:277).

Moreover, Kroeber did not consider the native Californian genocide an appropriate anthropological topic. "After some hesitation," Kroeber wrote in 1925, "I have omitted all directly historical treatment . . . of the relations of the natives with the whites and of the events befalling them after such contact was established. It is not that this subject is unimportant or uninteresting, but that I am not in a position to treat it adequately. It is also a matter that has comparatively slight relation to aboriginal civilization" (cited by Buckley 1996:274). The vanquished peoples and cultures were already "ruined," anthropologically speaking, and could therefore cast little light on the "authentic" aboriginal civilizations that preceded them, which Kroeber viewed as the *true* subject of his discipline.

Alternatively, Kroeber's retreat into theory may have been an expression of his deep faith in science (see Kroeber 1948b:22–24). As with Freud, however, who made a similar move away from the social reality of his sexually abused women patients in favor of a more abstract and general theory of the unconscious (see Masson 1984), Kroeber's turning away from the suffering of his living informants in favor of a general theory of culture history[4] that "had no people in it" (Wolf 1981) could be seen as a betrayal.

It is difficult to know whether the tangled, intense, and ultimately tragic relationship between Kroeber and his Yahi informant and friend, Ishi, between 1911 and 1916 was a cause or a consequence of Kroeber's fatalistic views on the survival of indigenous peoples and cultures. This much is certain, however: The arrival of the Yahi Indian, Ishi, into Kroeber's life, and therefore into anthropological and historical consciousness, was uncannily overdetermined.

In the first of two pieces that Kroeber ([1911a,b] 1972) wrote about the Yahi Indians in the summer of 1911, he described the "discovery" in 1908 by California surveyors of a ragtag band of Mill Creek Indian Yahi survivors. The surveyors, working for a power company around Deer Creek, caught sight of a "naked Indian" standing still and poised before a stream with a double-pronged primitive fishing spear. It is believed that this person was Ishi. A few days later the surveyors came upon a cleverly concealed campsite in the tangled woods, which was the final refuge ("Bear's Hiding Place") of Ishi and his remaining family members including a middle-aged woman (believed to be Ishi's sister) and two elders, a man and a woman. The old woman, hiding under a pile of rabbit skins, was obviously ill and asked for water (in Spanish, indicating contact between the Yahi and earlier Mexican colonizers and settlers). After frightening the Indians away, the surveyors carried off the blankets, bows, arrows, cooking tins, and other supplies left behind in the Yahi hideaway. (These stolen "artifacts," later sold to the Anthropology Museum, were displayed as late as the fall of 2000 in the Hearst Museum of Anthropology at UC Berkeley.) Ishi's state of near starvation when he was captured in Oroville in 1911 (see below) was likely the result of the confiscation of his family's tools of subsistence.

Written for a popular audience, Kroeber's article is strewn with journalistic phrases of the sort he carefully avoided in his scientific writings. He referred, for example, to "a totally wild and independent tribe of Indians, without firearms, fleeing at the approach of the white man" (Kroeber [1911a] 1972:1). He described the Mill Creek Indians as "a handful of savages" while generously describing the truly savage white bounty hunters and Indian killers as "the enterprising pioneer and miner." Perhaps Kroeber was trying to seduce his Victorian readers by playing to popular stereotypes and then deftly overturning them. Anthropologists have often done so, realizing that anthropological views of the world are often too subversive for popular consumption.

Supporting the lesser of two evils – death and extinction being the other alternative – Kroeber argued for the capture of the Mill Creek Indians by a posse of U.S. soldiers sent by the Office of Indian Affairs: ". . . [but] a troop of cavalry might scour the region of Deer Creek and Mill Creek for months without laying hands on them. Possibly a gradually narrowing circle of men might enclose them and finally drive them to the center" (Kroeber [1911a] 1972:9). Then the captured Indians could be integrated with other remaining "survivors of landless tribes that have lived for many years as scattered outcasts on the fringes of civilization." Alternatively, the remaining Mill Creek band could be granted "a few square miles in the inaccessible and worthless cañon of Deer Creek where they now live." Otherwise, the future was grim: "If they continue their present mode of life, the settlers in the vacinity [sic] are likely to suffer further loss of property and livestock. If the Indians are ever caught in the act of marauding it may go hard with them, for the rancher in these districts rarely has his rifle far from his hand *and can scarcely be blamed for resorting to violence* when his belongings have been repeatedly seized" (Kroeber [1911a] 1972:8, emphasis added).

In October 1910 the young UC anthropologist and linguist Thomas T. Waterman led an expedition to the Mill Creek area in an attempt to find the "lost band" of Yahi; he reported "incontrovertible evidence of their existence in a wild state" (Waterman, in Heizer and Kroeber 1979:156).

Then, as if on cue, on August 29, 1911, the last member of that same Yahi Mill Creek band, the man whom Kroeber would later call "Ishi" (the Yahi word for man) appeared in Oroville. Possibly driven by hunger and desperation, the Indian emerged from hiding among the foothills of Mt. Lassen and was discovered cowering in the corner of an animal slaughterhouse. Barking guard dogs had given him away. He was taken and held at the Oroville jail until Kroeber and Waterman were contacted, and Waterman was able to identify him as a Yahi Indian. The "wild man" (as Ishi was described in the first newspaper accounts) whom Waterman encountered was cold, frightened, and suspicious. He refused at first to accept food and water. His clothing was a ragged canvas cloak, probably filched from an Anglo settler household or compound during the period of Ishi's life on the run.

In the first photo taken of Ishi just hours after his capture, shown in the introduction to Part II of this volume, Ishi appears startled and in a state of advanced emaciation. The photo is reminiscent of those taken of Holocaust survivors immediately after their liberation from concentration camps at the end of World War II. Ishi's hair is clipped or singed close to his head in a traditional sign of Yahi mourning. Had the old woman, possibly Ishi's mother, initially left behind at the abandoned hideaway at Mill Creek, died? His cheeks cling fast to the bones and accentuate his deep-set eyes. The photo shows a man of intelligence and of deep sorrow.

After Ishi's "rescue" by Waterman, he lived out his final years (1911–16) as a salaried assistant janitor (paid $25 week),[5] key informant, and a living specimen at the museum of anthropology at the University of California, San Francisco (UCSF), then located adjacent to the medical school. Ishi was given his own private quarters, but his room was located next to a hall housing a large collection of human skulls and bones that depressed him. Nonetheless, Ishi conveyed to his anthropological museum "guardians" that he wished to remain at the museum rather than face uncertainty elsewhere. He had few choices. He could not go home – his territory was occupied by the ghosts and wandering spirits of kin who had not died a peaceful death or been given a proper funeral.

During the period that Ishi lived among whites (doctors and anthropologists), he served as a willing informant to Kroeber (or the "big chief," as he wryly called the anthropologist) and other local and visiting anthropologists, including the brilliant linguist Edward Sapir of Yale University, whom Waterman (Theodora Kroeber 1964:234) and Kroeber (Darnell 1969:82) accused of overworking Ishi, already weak from illness. By all accounts, however (see Jacknis

2000; Hinton 2000), Ishi seemed to enjoy thoroughly his transcription sessions, which provided an opportunity for him to recall and recite the folktales, myths, gambling songs, and healing rituals of his youth.

Sustained contact with whites proved dangerous, however, and Ishi contracted tuberculosis, an urban disease, although his condition was not properly diagnosed until the final days of his life. Kroeber feared this outcome, because his first wife, Henriette, was felled by the same disease two years after Ishi arrived to live at the Museum. In a letter to Waterman (August 28, 1915), Kroeber expressed his anxiety and his frustration with Ishi's medical regime: "We have got to handle the case. The physicians go by the book and rule, and it's up to us to apply our knowledge of the individual and our judgement to their findings and advice. He [Ishi] undoubtedly has had TB since last winter, though for the last 6 months it has only been latent ... Pope alone barely admitted at last that he might have a non-important infection" (cited in Heizer and Kroeber 1979:237–238). Ishi succumbed in March 1916, while Kroeber was away in New York City on sabbatical leave.

Ishi has been described as Northern California's Anne Frank (Eargle 2000:115). Cruelly hunted, his group was reduced to five, then three, and finally to one when Ishi was discovered and captured. Hunger had flushed him out of his wooded hideout in search of meat at the Oroville slaughterhouse. Some local Indians speculate that Ishi may have been in search of refuge at the nearby Feather River (Maidu Indian) rancheria. The Maidu, like the Pit River rancheria people to the north of Mt. Lassen, were known to offer sanctuary to escaping Yahi. By this time, earlier enmities between Yahi, Maidu, and Wintu peoples were put aside in facing a more serious collective enemy (see also Shackley 2000:708–709).

"Ishi wasn't crazy," Art Angle, head of the Butte County Native American Cultural Committee (BCNACC) in Oroville, told me. "He knew where he was headed." But, betrayed by barking dogs, Ishi fell into the hands of whites instead. Another Maidu man suspected that Ishi's strange existence on the run had made him a "loner," fearful of all humans. A Pit River man said that Ishi, in his view, had perhaps "lost his bearings" and become disoriented. "Too many years alone" is what others have said. "He didn't trust anyone, white or Indian." "He suffered too much. It brought him to the breaking point," another Native Californian said. White people living near Ishi's family's Mill Creek hideaway also still talk about Ishi. A young white man, a deer hunter, whom I met in a general store overlooking Mill Creek, where he had stopped for supplies, commented angrily when he learned I was interested in the famous Yahi Indian: "They hunted Ishi just like a fox. I don't know how they could have done that to a man like him."

The unlettered Ishi did not write his own diary like Anne Frank, but he told parts of his life story to Kroeber and Sapir, both of whom recorded these fragments by hand and who captured Ishi's rendition of Yahi myths, origin stories, and folktales on primitive wax cylinders, then a great innovation, but many of which have since melted (Jacknis 2000). Ishi never broke the Yahi taboo against speaking of the dead, and he never spoke of his relatives, about the traumatic years he and his dwindling band spent in hiding, or about his own decision to travel south, alone, and beyond Yahi territory.

One of the original recordings that remains is Ishi's telling of the Yahi myth "Coyote Rapes His Sister," which has been transcribed by the Berkeley linguist Leanne Hinton. Hinton has remarked on Ishi's enthusiasm in telling this long tale, with its many subtexts filled with intimate details of everyday Yahi practices of acorn gathering, cooking, and housekeeping. Why Ishi, a man who was by all accounts excessively modest, chose to recount this particular tale – with its explicitly sexual content dealing with a profound Yahi taboo, brother-sister incest – remained a mystery to Hinton (see also Chapter 17, this volume). The theme of incest, however, must have been a powerful one for Ishi, who as an adult was forced to live, travel, and hide out with blood relations, all of them sexually taboo.

Among the many forms of violence suffered by Ishi during the years of hiding were the restrictions on his sexuality and on his right to reproduce – genocide in another form. Even after his "rescue" by whites, Ishi's sexuality was denied him by Kroeber, who refused, out of protectiveness, to allow Ishi access to local prostitutes. As mentioned in a subsequent paragraph, newspapers made Ishi's sexuality into a public joke.

In the second of the two short popular articles he wrote on the Yahi, Kroeber ([1911b] 1972) described Ishi's arrival in San Francisco on Labor Day, 1911:

> Ishi was a curious and pathetic figure in those [first] days. Timid, gentle, an almost ever-pervading fear held down and concealed to the best of his ability, he nevertheless startled and leaped at the slightest sudden sound. A new sight, or the crowding around of half a dozen people, made his limbs rigid. If his hand had been held and was released, his arm remained frozen in the air for several minutes. The first boom from a cannon fired in the artillery practice at the Presidio several miles away, raised him a foot from his chair. . . . His one great dread, which he overcame but slowly, was of crowds. It is not hard to understand this in light of his lonely life in a tribe of five.

In this poignant passage Kroeber describes what would today be considered the classical symptoms of post-traumatic stress disorder (PTSD). Ishi's startle reflex, his phobias, and his mobilization for flight are similar to the symptoms reported by many victims of sustained terror and warfare (see Herman 1992). Yet, despite Ishi's physical and psychological vulnerability and his strong fear of crowds, Kroeber allowed Ishi to perform as a living exhibit at the anthropology museum, which drew visitors in the thousands and for whom gaping at the "wild man of California" as he made arrows and fishing spears was a popular Sunday family outing in San Francisco. Kroeber also allowed Ishi to appear before much larger crowds at the Panama Pacific Trade Exhibition.

Despite the lurid title of Kroeber's Ishi piece ("Ishi the Last Aborigine: The Effects of Civilization on a Genuine Survivor of Stone Age Barbarism"), the article was meant to correct newspaper stories that portrayed Ishi as a comic figure. One feature story, written by an enterprising journalist, Grant Wallace (1911) of the *San Francisco Sunday Call,* portrayed the Indian as lovesick and wanting to "kneel at the feet of the first white goddess he had ever seen." Wallace had fabricated a comic love story based on Ishi's supposed infatuation with Lily Lena, a lowbrow music hall entertainer who appeared at the Orpheum Theater in San Francisco in the fall of 1911. Ishi's presence with Kroeber at one of Lily's performances gave endless amusement to journalists, among them Wallace. In his popular article Kroeber tried to set the record straight: Ishi, he wrote, was more impressed with the theater and with the crowds (he was seated next to Kroeber in the balcony) than he was with the performer, to whom he paid scant attention. (See also Chapter 2, this volume.)

THE DEATH OF ISHI

In 1915 Ishi began his decline, although his personal doctor from UCSF Medical School, Saxton Pope (1920:192), failed to notice until days before his death how thin and ravaged Ishi had become. Ishi seemed more an object of curiosity and romantic projection for Pope than his patient. In February 1916, a month before Ishi's death, Pope (1920:205) recorded the following: "All this time he had a moderate cough; but repeated examination failed to show any tubercle bacilli.... after taking food he apparently experienced great pain. Even water caused him misery and I have seen him writhe in agony, with tears running down his cheeks, yet utter no sound of complaint. At this period when he seemed to be failing so rapidly that the end must be near, *I coaxed him to get out of bed and to let me take his picture once more.* He was always happy to be photographed and he accommodated me. *It was only after the picture was developed that I recognized to what a pitiful condition he had been reduced*" (emphasis added).

Ishi's last hospital admission record reads, "Ishi – No. 11032. March 19, 1916. Well developed but extremely emaciated, dark skinned Indian lying in bed ... vomiting and retching occasionally, evidently in great distress ... broad and prominently arched nose; high malar bones and sunken cheeks; orbital depressions deep, apparently from wasting. Hair on scalp reaches to below shoulders, is thick, straight, and black with only a few grey hairs over the temples. . . . Extremities – very greatly emaciated" (Pope 1920:206–207).

When Kroeber was about to leave for a sabbatical year in New York City, he suspected that Ishi was gravely ill and, according to Theodora Kroeber, he had to be coaxed by Pope to go (T. Kroeber 1970:90–91). Kroeber was worried about the well-being of his mother-in-law and about Ishi's frail condition, and he feared that this might be his final leave-taking. Ishi told Kroeber not to worry: "I go, you stay." Kroeber communicated frequently from New York City by telegrams in which he demanded timely and frequent postings on Ishi's rapidly deteriorating condition. Ishi had entrusted Kroeber with the proper disposal of his remains – cremation. Realizing that Ishi's end was approaching, Kroeber posted an urgent telegram to his assistant, Edward Gifford, on March 24, 1916, demanding that Ishi's remains be treated honorably: "Please stand by our contingently made outline of action, and insist on it as my personal wish. There is no objection to a cast [death mask]. I do not however see that an autopsy would lead to anything of consequence . . . and I suspect that the autopsy would resolve itself into a general dissection. Please shut down on it. As to disposal of the body, I must ask you to be my personal representative on the spot and to yield nothing at all under any circumstances. If there is any talk about the interests of science, say for me that science can go to hell. We propose to stand by our friends" (letter cited in full in Heizer and Kroeber 1979:240). But Kroeber's telegram was "received too late to be of any use" (telegram to Kroeber from Gifford, March 30, 1916, Heizer and Kroeber 1979:240), and an autopsy was performed by Dr. J. V. Cooke a few hours after Ishi's death on March 25, 1916 (Pope 1920:209–212), during which Ishi's brain was removed – an event that Gifford described to Kroeber as "a compromise between science and sentiment" (Gifford to Kroeber, March 30, 1916, Heizer and Kroeber 1979:240).

By the time Kroeber returned to Berkeley, his ire had cooled considerably. Inexplicably, he even arranged for Ishi's brain to be packaged and shipped to the Smithsonian Institute for curation and to the care of Aleš Hrdlička,[6] a physical anthropologist of the old school, dedicated to collecting and measuring brain specimens from primates, human "exotics" (like Ishi), and Western "geniuses" (like John Wesley Powell, the first chief of the Bureau of American Ethnology).

Kroeber wrote to Hrdlička on October 27, 1916 (Bancroft Library, Records of the Department and Museum of Anthropology, cu-23): "I find that with Ishi's death last spring, his brain was removed and preserved. There is no one here who can put it to scientific use. If you wish it, I would be pleased to deposit it in the National Museum collection." Hrdlička replied on December 12, 1916 that he would be "very glad" to receive the brain and he would have it "properly worked up."[7] In another letter dated December 20, 1916, Hrdlička gave precise directions for the preparation of the brain for shipping: "The brain should be packed in plenty of absorbent cotton saturated with the liquid in which it is preserved, and the whole should be enclosed in a piece of oiled cloth . . . ." Then, in a letter dated February 20, 1917, the curator of the Museum of Anthropology at the University of California confirmed the transaction: "Ishi's brain was sent to the National Museum as a gift with the compliments of the University of California . . . If you will enter the donor as the Department of Anthropology of said University, I think your record will be as accurate as you can make it."

Kroeber knew that Ishi reviled the white man's "science" of skull and skeleton collecting. As to why he made such an abrupt about-face I can only speculate. Perhaps he thought it was too late for "sentimental" reservations. Ishi was dead, and the damage to his body was irreversible. Or perhaps – and to my mind this is the most probable explanation – Kroeber's behavior was an act of disordered mourning, of ravaged grief. Grief can be expressed in a myriad of inchoate and displaced ways,[8] ranging from denial and avoidance, as in the Yahi taboo on speaking the names of the dead, to the insistence that the death and loss experienced is a minor one (see Scheper-Hughes 1992 on "death without weeping" among Brazilian shantytown mothers), to the glee and rage of the Illonget headhunter intent on getting an enemy's head to "kill" the loss experienced on the death of a loved one, as described by Rosaldo (1989). Freud's (1957) classic essay on "mourning and melancholia" certainly comes to mind with respect to Kroeber's own "swallowed grief" following the deaths of his first wife and then soon afterwards of his friend and key informant, Ishi, both from the same disease. Added to this was the disturbing impact of World War I on an American of German ancestry who was sensitive to how the war might influence others' interpretation of his work.

Or perhaps Kroeber believed that the science to which he had unreservedly dedicated his professional life might be able to benefit from the tragedy of his friend and informant's death. If so, it was the triumph of science over sentiment. Kroeber had put his stock in anthropological science as the abiding faith in his life. Theodora Kroeber used to say (personal recollection) that whenever her husband was asked about his religion, he replied that he was an anthropologist. Still, Kroeber was not naïve about science. He had been through a similar situation when, as a 21-year-old student of Franz Boas at Columbia University, he was given full responsibility for the ethnographic and linguistic work-up on a small party of captive Greenland Natives brought to Boas by the Arctic explorer Robert Peary. When one of the adult men died of tuberculosis, members of the group were brought to mourn before a traditional earth mound that actually covered a counterfeit corpse made from a log. Without telling his mourners, the real body of the Eskimo had been whisked away to Bellevue Hospital College of Physicians and Surgeons for autopsy and scientific study (Thomas 2000:77). None other than Ales Hrdlička had assisted the autopsy performed by Dr. Harlow Brooks, and he wrote a brief report, "An Eskimo Brain" (Hrdlička 1901), published in *American Anthropologist.*

Support for the mourning thesis comes from Kroeber's second wife, Theodora Kroeber (1970:87), who gives an account of her husband's long period of depression and self-doubt between 1915 and 1922. According to Theodora, Alfred suffered greatly at the news of his friend's death, and he entered a pattern of flight that lasted a full seven years. A. L. Kroeber himself characterized this unsettling period in his midlife as a *"hegira"* – an intense period of journey, soul-searching, and melancholia, similar to what St. John of the Cross called a "dark night of the soul."

The period was marked by severe, possibly somatoform symptoms: physical disequilibrium, nausea, vertigo, strain, and physical and psychological exhaustion. His condition was similar to what used to be called (with a touch of Victorian delicacy) neurasthenia. Elaine Showalter (1985) might call it a classic expression of "male hysteria." Kroeber himself thought he might have a brain tumor or, worse, that he might be losing his mind (T. Kroeber 1970:87). When his vertigo was particularly severe, Kroeber moved sideways, like a crab, and bystanders sometimes moved aside, thinking he was an ordinary drunk.

Yet, in the midst of this dark interlude, brought on – if Theodora is correct – by the death of Ishi, which awaked a long delayed grief response to the death of his first wife, Kroeber completed his masterpiece: the *Handbook of the Indians of California.* Henriette died in the spring of 1913, two years after Ishi came to live in the anthropologists' antechamber. Immediately following Henriette's death Kroeber threw himself into his work as an antidote to his pain, spurred on, Theodora Kroeber suggests, by Ishi's example. Ishi dealt with his own grief and mourning by sitting in the museum, quietly singing fragments of Yahi funeral songs while he chipped and flaked arrowheads or made a fire with his fire drill. According to Theodora's account (1970:84–85):

> Sometimes [Ishi] went to Kroeber's home for dinner; he knew Henriette; he knew of her illness, of her death; he would never speak of these matters, his tact reinforced by inexorable Yana custom; neither would he forget them. Sitting beside him that day [the day of Henriette's death] while Ishi worked, Kroeber thought of Ishi's first coming to the museum, of their growing friendship. He recalled that after a few days Ishi was at work making Yana objects for the museum so that outside worlds would know something of his own Yana world. . . . Through the few words

that they exchanged, through the comfortable silences between the words, he felt Ishi trying to help him in his own loss, to comfort him, to transmit to him some of the strength and wisdom of his own Yana faith. There was much unfinished work for him and Ishi to do. There was other unfinished work in the full notebooks next door and, further away, with people about to disappear from the earth as had the Yana, their customs and language unrecorded. . . . Kroeber returned to his own room, to his desk. He took from the safe one of the Yurok notebooks. He worked for an hour, for two hours, the stubborn grammar imposing order on the writing hand, the directing brain. He put his work away at last. The sun had long since set . . . He had discovered, with Ishi's help, an anodyne – work – which from that day would rescue him when grief, worry, the agony of living threatened to engulf and overwhelm him.

After Ishi's death Kroeber took up a temporary position in the fall of 1917 at the Museum of Natural History in New York (made possible by a one-year exchange with Robert H. Lowie, then a curator of ethnology at the Museum of Natural History). While in New York he entered into a psychoanalysis with Dr. Smith Ely Jelliffe, a former student of Anna Freud. Kroeber recognized that his symptoms – the dizziness and nausea – were psychosomatic, a sign of his own disequilibrium (c.f. Chapter 4, this volume, and T. Kroeber 1970:86–87). With the death of Henriette his personal life was shattered, and with the death of Ishi his professional life seemed meaningless. At the age of forty, Kroeber questioned for the first time his choice of career and his long-term professional goals. According to Theodora Kroeber (1970:103), the source of her husband's discontent was that his "professional life no longer satisfied him. . . . [a] dissatisfaction [that] grew in part from the times, and from the changing face of anthropology itself, but there was [also] a pattern of exhaustion which was personal."

Though short by today's standards, Kroeber's analysis lasted a full nine months (c.f. Chapter 4 of this volume). He used that period to grapple with unresolved feelings about the direction of his personal and his professional life. On his return to Berkeley, Kroeber took another leave of absence from teaching and from chairing the department of anthropology, although he continued to direct the museum in San Francisco. During this partial leave he began to practice as a psychoanalytic therapist, first at the Stanford Clinic and then in a private practice in San Francisco, which he maintained for two years. His old friend Dr. Saxton Pope referred many patients to him.

Consequently, Kroeber never did write the definitive history of Ishi and his people. After the Indian's death, Kroeber avoided talking about his friend, and he put aside for a long while his materials and field notes on Ishi and Yahi culture. In her biography of her husband, Theodora Kroeber (1970) wrote that the subject of Ishi caused Alfred considerable psychological pain, so it was generally avoided in the Kroeber household.

Ursula Le Guin (2001), Kroeber's daughter by his second wife, Theodora, stated flatly that her father did not talk about Ishi. "He did not like to reminisce. By temperament he did not live in the past, and he did not like to think about the past." She added that her father tended to dislike whites who expressed identification with Indians, an attitude that struck him as both "sentimental and manipulative." "My father treated Ishi as a peer, and respected his distance and his reserve." Perhaps in his refusal to talk about Ishi, even to his own family members, Kroeber was observing the Yahi taboo on naming and speaking of the dead. I like to think so.

In the late 1950s, when Ursula was young, the idea of an Ishi biography was bandied about. Half in jest, Kroeber suggested that Theodora do it (Le Guin 2001). So, many years after the death of Ishi, Kroeber allowed his wife to use him as a key informant on Ishi's last years. Theodora told the story that her husband could not bring himself to write, for, as she wrote in her husband's biography, "he lived too much of it, and too much of it was the stuff of human agony from whose immediacy he could not sufficiently distance himself" (T. Kroeber 1970:93). Theodora Kroeber produced two moving literary accounts: *Ishi in Two Worlds* (1961) and *Ishi: Last of His Tribe* (1964), and what we know and remember about Ishi today is based largely on what she wrote down.

Ishi in Two Worlds directly confronted what Kroeber had avoided: the history of the genocide of California's Indians at the hands of white settlers and ranchers. Chapters 3 through 5 of her book stand as one of the most unflinching renditions of the brutality and savagery of California's white settler history. And because of Theodora Kroeber's compelling rendition of Ishi's life and times, Ishi lent a face, a name, and a personalized narrative to the hidden genocide of his people. Ishi came to represent more than the life of a single man and to symbolize, instead, the broader experience of Native Americans.

When Kroeber finally resumed his anthropological career full-time in 1922, he threw himself into new fields and approaches. He took up archaeology, and he experimented with statistical methods which afforded more distance from the subjective aspects of human life. Again, Kroeber's professional life evidenced his uncanny ability to compartmentalize: psychoanalytic and clinical work here; science and anthropology there. Despite his new engagement with psychological theory, Kroeber maintained a strong aversion to the application of behavioral or psychological approaches to anthropology.

Kroeber's embrace of the objective, the quantifiable, and the statistical could be seen as a flight into radical empiricism driven by a desire to map the ebb and tide of peoples and cultures, which Kroeber believed were as inevitable as night and day and birth and death. In the final years of his life, however, Kroeber returned to his collections of Mohave myths and Yurok folktales, which he had begun at the turn of the twentieth century. His monograph, *More Mohave Myths* (Kroeber 1972), was published posthumously through the efforts and skillful editing of Theodora Kroeber. In this final work Kroeber returned to his origins as a descriptive ethnographer and to what he called "scholarship in the old-fashioned sense . . . a work that one cannot do properly unless one likes the doing, and the doing can come close to becoming an obsessive addiction" (p. xii). In the end, Kroeber returned to the idea that ethnography was a job of saving and preserving what was in danger of being lost forever.

It is easy today with the advantage of hindsight to see the blind spots of our anthropological predecessors, including Kroeber's failure to recognize the ongoing genocide of Indians in northern California and to deal more humanely with Ishi's remains. With respect to the destruction of California Indians, in the 1950s, toward the end of Kroeber's career, he put aside his normal distaste for "applied anthropology," which he once described as "meddling," to argue the case of California Indians in a major land claims case (see *Indians of California v. the United States of America*, Docket 31–37). Although he found the case dispiriting, the Indians won the suit, and six years after Kroeber's death they were awarded a token sum for their collective losses (Shea 2000:50). Theodora described the land claims case as one conceived in white guilt and in bad faith. Eighteen years after the case was opened, President Johnson authorized a bill that awarded $800 to each "properly identified" and "qualified" Indian man, woman, and child alive in the United States as of December 1968. It was, wrote Theodora (1970:223), " just the sort of expensive but meaningless denouement that Kroeber had most feared."

Is it fair to ask what Kroeber might have done differently with respect to Ishi? What options did Kroeber have? Before Ishi became mortally ill, might Kroeber have considered broaching the topic of where Ishi had been headed when he was caught on the run? If it was indeed, as some Maidu Indians believe, to find sanctuary among related Native peoples, might that have been a possible solution? And, after Ishi's health began to fail, were the museum and hospital the best places for him?

To this day there is a strong investment in believing that Ishi was a happy man who enjoyed his new life among his white friends,[9] who was charmed by matches and window shades and was content in his roles of janitor and living museum exhibit. Perhaps he was. But the evidence (see especially Heizer and

Kroeber 1979:145–160) suggests another interpretation: that Ishi was simply at the end of his existential rope. Though not of his choosing, Ishi accepted his final destiny with patience, good humor, and grace. He was exceptionally learned in the art of waiting.

ISHI'S ASHES

Art Angle of Redding rancheria kept alive his family's "folklore" about Ishi's remains. He said that he had "always known" since a child about the desecration of Ishi's remains; stories had long circulated in his Maidu community about the Yahi man's brain sitting in a bottle somewhere. Though a practical, common-sense man with no claims to any specialized religious, ritual, or spiritual knowledge, Angle was driven by the story of Ishi. He clearly identifies with the lone Yahi survivor, to whom he bears an unmistakably strong facial resemblance, and he felt that it had somehow fallen to him to right the wrong that was done to Ishi: to locate the brain and to have it properly reburied (with his cremated remains) somewhere safely in Yahi country so that the Indian's wandering spirit could finally be at rest. In the mid-1990s Angle began to pursue the case in earnest, and he enlisted the help of other tribal leaders as well as the skills of Nancy Rockafellar, a UCSF medical historian, and Orin Starn, a cultural anthropologist from Duke University. It was Starn who unearthed the valuable correspondence in the Bancroft Collection at UC Berkeley that confirmed the transactions between Kroeber and Hrdlička about the transfer of Ishi's brain.[10]

The final chapter of this story opened in the spring of 1999 with the rediscovery of Ishi's brain, which had languished for three-quarters of a century in a vat of formaldehyde at a Smithsonian warehouse. Anthropologists at Berkeley differed in their opinions of what, if anything, should be said or done with respect to the discovery and the demands of the BCNACC for the immediate repatriation of the brain for burial. Some were embarrassed by the initial denials by the Hearst Museum of Anthropology and the University of California Administration. In a formal letter to Angle, October 27, 1997, from Ira Jacknis, the Hearst Museum's historian and archivist, and Rosemary Joyce, they state the University's official response to the repatriation demand: "There is no historical support for the idea that his brain was maintained as a scientific specimen."

Following the official news release indicating that Ishi's brain had indeed been traced to the Smithsonian, a departmental meeting was held, and a proposed statement was debated, many times revised, and finally accepted as the collective response of the Department of Anthropology at Berkeley. The unanimous statement, which falls short of the apology to Northern California Indians that a majority of the faculty had signed in an earlier draft, is reproduced as Chapter 6 of this volume.

However, I read the *full* statement, including the original apology, into the record of the California state legislature repatriation hearings held in Sacramento on April 5, 1999: "What happened to Ishi's body, in the name of science, was a perversion of our core anthropological values. . . . We are sorry for our department's role, however unintentional, in the final betrayal of Ishi, a man who had already lost all that was dear to him at the hands of Western colonizers. We recognize that the exploitation and betrayal of Native Americans is still commonplace in American society."

Some representatives of the Native Californian communities who were present accepted the apology. Art Angle, representing the BCNACC, acknowledged it as a "big step" for anthropology and for the University of California, adding, however, that "it did not go far enough." Others, like Gerald Vizenor, professor of Native American literature at Berkeley, dismissed the "pained rhetoric" and the apology as irrelevant, "too little and too late" (Shea 2000:53). Obviously, the mistrust between Native Americans and anthropologists founded in the history of genocide (and genocide ignored)[11] demands a great deal more than an apology or a scholarly conference held to honor Ishi and repatriation.[12]

Nonetheless, the return of Ishi's brain from the Smithsonian to representatives of the Pit River tribe on August 8, 2000, was an essential first step, paving the way for more constructive engagements between anthropologists and the survivors of California's genocides. Thomas W. Killion, an archaeologist and director of the Smithsonian Institution's repatriation program, was extremely helpful to representatives of Northern California tribes once the Smithsonian had located the brain among its holdings. Killion and his committee designated the Pit River tribe of Redding rancheria over the Maidu Indians of Enterprise rancheria as the recipients and new guardians of Ishi's brain, citing linguistic affinities between present-day Pit River people and the historical Yahi.[13]

The repatriation,[14] a first for northern California Indians, had profound and transformative effects on the many different Northern California peoples and tribes who came together on various occasions, crossing previously tense territorial and tribal boundaries, to pray and to prepare themselves and the land for the return of Ishi, and finally to celebrate the completed spiritual passage of their grandfather, Ishi.

Ceremonial fires burned brightly for several nights in May 2000 in the wooded foothills outside Oroville, anticipating Ishi's return. Maidu leaders took turns tending the fires with Pit River Indians, Mohawk Indian migrants to the area, and even a few anthropologists. Art Angle was both generous and philosophical about his tribe not having been selected by the Smithsonian anthropologists to receive the remains of their grandfather Ishi. The irony of white bureaucrats still making essential decisions about indigenous culture and cultural identity was not lost on those gathered around the purifying fires that Angle had organized according to his memory of "how things should be done." The ritual around the fire was simple and understated. Following it, those present were invited to look out over the rough terrain through which Ishi, hungry and barefoot, had traveled alone, and to find it in their hearts to thank "the grandfather" for teaching about human dignity during a period of profound suffering.

A few weeks after the secret burial of Ishi's brain with his cremated remains, a two-day celebration was held at Summit Lake on Mt. Lassen, a sacred Yahi site of human emergence. A communal feast was prepared. Whole salmon were roasted on stakes over slow coals while, nearby, a deer was prepared and roasted. A huge cauldron of savory and bitter acorn soup simmered over a fire. Old stories, interspersed with tall tales, were exchanged over tin cups of strong, black coffee ladled out of large pots. "Confessions" were made by holy men, who said they had not always lived "in a good way." "Ishi brought me back from the fire," one middle-aged man said, with reference to his former addictions to drugs, alcohol, and faction fights.

After the feast, dancers and spiritual leaders went into the bushes, where a sweathouse had been prepared. Meanwhile, talking circles were arranged at which Ishi and his Yahi culture were memorialized. At one of the circles Alfred Kroeber was "forgiven." Then an older woman, mindful perhaps of the presence of a few anthropologists, got up to chide those who might be tempted to criticize "their grandfather," whether Ishi *or* Kroeber. The old ones had their reasons, she said, for what they did. "And they needed to be respected." When darkness fell the group regathered in a circle under a bowl of stars. This time there was no talking. Then, the bear dancers announced their arrival with growls, snorts, and grunts. In deep trance the bear dancers brought strength and healing to those willing to be "brushed." Ishi *had* come home.

GETTING OVER: WRITING AGAINST GENOCIDE

The postcolonial critiques of anthropological ways of seeing and knowing have resulted in a relentless form of institutional and professional self-analysis. It is one thing to rethink one's basic epistemology, as many social sciences have done under the impact of deconstructionism. It is quite another to rethink one's way of being and acting in and on the world. Anthropologists have been asked to transform their central and defining practice of fieldwork, to decolonize themselves, and reimagine new relations to their anthropological subjects, some the victims and others the perpetrators of genocide and mass killings.[15]

The irony is that cultural anthropology is all about meaning, about making sense in a world that is so often absurd. Can one "make sense" of mass violence and genocide? In recent years an anthropology of suffering has emerged as a new kind of theodicy, a cultural inquiry into the ways that people attempt to explain, account for, and justify the presence of pain, death, affliction, and evil in the world (see Kleinman and Kleinman 1997, Farmer 1996). But the quest to "make sense" of suffering and chaotic violence is as old as Job, and as fraught with as moral ambiguity for the anthropologist as for the companions of Job, who demanded an explanation for suffering compatible with their need to believe in a just God (or a just world). As Geertz pointed out many years ago, the one thing humans seem unable to accept is the idea that the world may be ultimately deficient in meaning.

Yet, the gift of the ethnographer remains – as it was in Kroeber's day – some combination of thick description, eyewitnessing, and radical juxtaposition based on cross-cultural insight. The rules of our living-in and living-with peoples who are on the verge of extermination, however, remain as yet unwritten, perhaps even unspoken. What, during periods of genocide or ethnocide, is an appropriate distance to take from our subjects? What kinds of "participant-observation," what sorts of eyewitnessing, are adequate to the scenes of genocide and their aftermath? When the anthropologist is witness to such crimes against humanity, is scientific objectivity and empathy sufficient? At what point does the anthropologist as eyewitness become a bystander or even a coconspirator? Although these remain vexing and unresolved issues, the original mandate of anthropology and ethnography remains clear: to put ourselves and our discipline squarely on the side of humanity, world saving, and world repair, even when we are not always certain what that means or what is required or being asked of us at a particular moment in the lives of our friends and informants.

What, in the end, can we say about Alfred Kroeber and the man called Ishi? Not all Native Californians spoke well of Ishi, especially in earlier years. Some resented his acceptance of sanctuary with whites and with "the anthros." Young people, in particular, were quick to judge him: "Why didn't he escape?" Later, with age, they began to wonder how *they* might have behaved under the same circumstances. Today many Native people recognize in Ishi one way of surviving a holocaust: "We need to think in a good way, now, and to find ways to honor him." Anthropologists, too, need to respect our own ancestors, including "grandfather" Kroeber, recognizing in him one way of being an anthropologist (and a humanist) during a particularly fraught period in the history of California. Perhaps we all need to forgive each other, as we go about, once again, reinventing anthropology as a tool and practice of human freedom.

NOTES

1. Today there is a new generation of anthropologists who have not "missed the revolution" (Starn 1992) or turned their gaze away from genocides and who have positioned themselves squarely on the side of the victims and survivors of genocide and other forms

of communal violence and mass killings. See, for example: Binford 1996; Bourgois 1999; Das 1996; Feitlowitz 1998; Green 1999; Kuper 1982, 1985; Leyton 1998; Malkki 1995; Nelson 1999; Quesada 1998; Scheper-Hughes 1994, 1997, 1998, 1999; Smith 1990; Starn 1992; Stoll 1993; Suárez-Orozco 1987; Swendenburg 1995; and Taussig 1987, 1991.

2. A lively debate took place at the American Anthropological Association meetings in the late 1980s at which the late Paul Riesman concluded that when anthropologists try to intervene in critical situations (of life and death) in the field they betray their discipline, and they /we "leave anthropology behind . . . because we abandon what I [Riesman] believe to be a fundamental axiom of the creed we [anthropologists] all share, namely that all humans are equal in the sight of anthropology . . . . . . Once we identify an evil, I think we give up trying to understand the situation as a human reality. Instead we see it as in some sense inhuman, and all we try to understand is how best to combat it. At this point we leave anthropology behind and enter the political process" (Riesman 1987).

3. In his posthumously published *Yurok Myths* (Kroeber 1976:466), Kroeber comments on the "comparative lack of mental and physical tenseness in the life of the California Indian tribes, a slackness which is manifest in many phases of their civilization."

4. Ironically, we little remember Kroeber's theory of culture today, whereas his basic, descriptive ethnography remains an essential source for all specialists of Native North America.

5. At a preparatory meeting in Sacramento among several UC Berkeley administrators, public information officers, and university lawyers at which they discussed how the university should respond to the crisis around the repatriation of Ishi's brain, one administrator tried to inject some humor into the meeting by suggesting that the university should be praised for having hired Ishi at all. "As assistant janitor Ishi was" (she said) "UCSF's first affirmative action" hire. While gallows humor should not be counted as data, it reveals the anger felt at the demand to respond publicly to a sad event in which the university was implicated.

6. Kroeber included an essay written by Hrdlička on the skeletal remains of ancient man in *Source Book in Anthropology*, published in 1931, which he and Waterman edited.

7. There is no evidence that Ishi's brain was ever included in any anthropological or other scientific study (Jonathan Marks, personal communication). The brain was simply forgotten and left abandoned in a Smithsonian warehouse.

8. Although this section is speculative, my work for many years as a psychological anthropologist requires me to try to understand human motivation. The idea that Kroeber's quick disposal of Ishi's brain to Hrdlička might be a profound grief reaction emerged from my own experience. Upon arriving cross-country just two hours after my dear 95-year-old father died, I was completely distraught. I angrily demanded that his body be cremated in Baltimore that same day rather than transported, as previously agreed, to New York City for a conventional Catholic wake and family burial. "It's too late, too late for all that," I said to my older brother, who, with the help of a kindly Brook-

lyn funeral parlor director, helped walk me, step by step, out of an irrational position resulting from disorderly grief, anger, and despair. Grief had made me destructive, for in cremating my father and first mentor in life, I would have violated his own last wishes.

9. *See* Gerald Vizenor's (2000) satire, *Chancers: A Novel,* especially pp. 137–159.

10. Orin Starn is completing a book entitled *Ishi's Brain: Anthropologists, Native Americans and the Life and Death of the Last Yahi Indian.* It will be published by W. W. Norton.

11. See, for example, Deloria (1988) and Thomas (2000).

12. The University of California, Berkeley, sponsored three forums in response to the controversy over Ishi. The first, "Ishi's Brain," was held in the Department of Anthropology as a panel discussion, involving Nancy Rockafellar, James Clifford, Jonathan Marks, , myself, and (by phone) Orin Starn, on Monday, May 13, 1999; the second meeting, "Ishi: Past, Present, and Future," was held in Oroville, May 12, 2000 (cosponsored by the BCNACC); the third was a large international conference, "Who Owns the Body," sponsored by the Vice-Chancellor for Research, University of California, and held September 20–23, 2000.

13. The question of Ishi's actual tribal origins and identity is still debated among anthropologists and among California Indians. Ishi identified himself as a Yahi Indian, but some of his cultural traits, especially his production of projectile points, do not – at least according to one museum archeologist – "resemble ancestral Yahi forms but strongly resemble historic forms of Wintu/Nomlaki, a group that was in an amity relationship with the Yahi in the historic period" (Shackley 2000:708). Meanwhile, his physical appearance seemed closer to that of the Maidu, with whom the Yahi were not always on the best of terms.

Was Ishi, then, properly described by Theodora Kroeber as the last of the Yahi, the last of his tribe? Or was Ishi, as Shackley (2000) concludes, the survivor of a mixed culture that was the result of "dwindling gene pools" following Anglo genocides that forced bride stealing, intermarriage, intertribal child kidnapping, and cultural sharing as an indigenous survival strategy? According to my Native Californian informants, ethnic identity was maintained, despite intermarriage and adoptions. "No," I was told definitely by one key informant, "Ishi was not the last of the Yahi." Yahi survivors, fleeing genocide, were taken in by neighboring groups and given new identities to protect them (for the Yahi were particularly hated and hunted down by Anglo bounty hunters). "But even so everyone knew who among us were true Yahi and that information was passed down to their children and grandchildren, so that the Yahi would not disappear from this earth forever." Of course, that particular information will never be shared with outsiders.

14. Some Native Americans, such as the Iroquois of New York, have little interest or passion invested in repatriation, and they have even sometimes refused to accept human remains that have been offered to them from museum collections.

15. In "The Primacy of the Ethical" (Scheper-Hughes 1995) I tried to imagine a politi-

cally engaged and "militant" anthropology in which anthropology as a disciplinary field and as a field of action converged. The notion or conceit of the anthropologist as *companheira* emerged out of the practice of liberation theology in Brazil, where one could, for a brief while, be both priest and partisan.

REFERENCES

Berreman, Gerald. 1969. Bringing it all back home. In *Reinventing anthropology.* Ed. Dell Hymes. New York: Random House.

——. 1982. *The Politics of truth: essays in critical anthropology.* Amherst NY: Prometheus.

Binford, Leigh. 1996. *The El Mozote massacre.* Tucson: University of Arizona.

Borneman, John. 1997. *Settling accounts: violence, justice, and accountability in postsocialist Europe.* Princeton NJ: Princeton University, pp. 111–135.

Bourdieu, Pierre. 1977. *Outline of a theory of practice.* Cambridge UK: Cambridge University.

Bourdieu, Pierre, and Loic Waquant. 1992. *Invitation to reflexive sociology.* Chicago: University of Chicago.

Bourgois, Philippe. 1999. Reconfronting violence in El Salvador and the U.S. inner city with a Cold War hangover. Paper presented to the Society for Cultural Anthropology. San Francisco, May 1999.

Buckley, Thomas. 1989a. Kroeber's theory of culture areas and the ethnology of northwestern California. *Anthropological Quarterly* 62(1): 15–26.

——. 1989b. Suffering in the cultural construction of others: Robert Spott and A. L. Kroeber. *American Indian Quarterly* 13(4): 437–445.

——. 1996. "The little history of pitiful events": the epistemological and moral contexts of Kroeber's Californian ethnology. In *Volksgeist as method and ethic: Essays on Boasian ethnography and the German anthropological tradition.* Ed. George Stocking. History of Anthropology series, vol. 8. Madison: University of Wisconsin.

Castillo, Esward. 1978. "The impact of Euro-American exploration and settlement." In *California.* Vol. 8. Ed. R. Heizer. Washington DC: Smithsonian Institution, pp. 99–127.

Chagnon, Napoleon. 1968. *Yanomamo: the fierce people.* New York: Holt, Rinehart & Winston.

——. 1988. Life histories, blood revenge, and warfare in a tribal population. *Science* 239:985–992.

Churchill, Ward. 1997. *A little matter of genocide: holocaust and denial in the Americas, 1492 to the present.* San Francisco: City Lights Books.

Cook, Sherburne F. 1978. Historical demography. In *California.* Vol. 8. Ed. R. Heizer. Washington DC: Smithsonian Institution, pp. 91–98.

Das, Veena. 1996. Language and body: transactions in the construction of pain. *Daedalus* 125(1): 67–92.

Darnell, R. 1969. The development of American anthropology 1979–1920. Doctoral Dissertation, University of Pennsylvania.

Deloria, Vine. 1988. *Custer died for your sins.* Norman: University of Oklahoma.

Devereux, George. 1961. *Mohave ethnopsychiatry and suicide.* Smithsonian Institution, Bureau of American Ethnology Bulletin No. 175. Washington DC: Government Printing Office.

DeVos, George. 1971. Conflict, dominance and exploitation. In *Sanctions for evil.* Ed. Nevitt Sanford and Craig Comstock. Boston: Beacon, pp. 155–173.

Diamond, Stanley. 1981. Discussion following essay by Fritz Wolf on Alfred Kroeber. In *Totems and teachers: perspectives on the history of anthropology.* Ed. Sydel Silverman. New York: Columbia University, pp. 55–64.

Eargle, Dolan. 2000. *Native California guide: weaving the past and present.* San Francisco: Trees Company.

Edgerton, Robert B. 1992. *Sick societies: challenging the myth of primitive harmony.* New York: Free Press.

Farmer, Paul. 1996. On suffering and structural violence: a view from below. *Daedalus* 125(1): 245–260.

Feitlowitz, Marguerite. 1998. *A lexicon of terror: Argentina and the legacies of torture.* New York: Oxford University, pp. 48–62.

Feldman, Alan. 1991. *Formations of violence: the narrative of the body and political terror in Northern Ireland.* Chicago: University of Chicago.

Fein, Helen. 1990. Genocide – a sociological perspctive. *Current Sociology* 38:23–35.

Finnagan, William. 1992. *A complicated war: the harrowing of Mozambique.* Berkeley: University of California.

Freud, Sigmund. 1957. Mourning and melancholia. In *The standard edition of the complete works of Sigmund Freud,* vol. 14. London: Hogarth, pp. 243–258.

Geertz, Clifford. 1995. *After the fact: two countries, four decades, one anthropologist.* Cambridge MA: Harvard University.

Gourvitch, Philip. 1998. *We wish to inform you that tomorrow we will be killed with our families.* New York: Farrar, Strauss and Giroux.

Green, Linda. 1999. *Fear as a way of life.* New York: Columbia University.

Heizer, Robert F., and Theodora Kroeber, eds. 1979. *Ishi the last Yahi: a documentary history.* Berkeley: University of California.

Herman, Judith. 1992. *Trauma and recovery.* New York: Basic Books.

Hinton, Leanne. 1999. Ishi's brain. *News from Native California* 13(1): 4–9.

———. 2000. Paper and comments delivered at the conference, "Ishi: Past, Present and Future," hosted by the Butte County Native American Cultural Committee, Oroville, California, May 12, 2000.

Hrdlička, Aleš. 1901. An Eskimo brain. *American Anthropologist,* n.s. 3:454–456.

———. 1931. The most ancient skeletal remains of man. In *Source book in anthropology.*

Ed. A. L. Kroeber and T. T. Waterman. New York: Harcourt, Brace and Company, pp. 43–66.

Hymes, Dell, ed. 1969. *Reinventing anthropology.* New York: Random House.

Jacknis, Ira. 2000. From performance to record: Ishi's music and speech. Paper presented at the international conference, "Who Owns the Body," University of California, Berkeley, September 20–23.

Kleinman, Arthur, and Joan Kleinman. 1997. The appeal of experience; the dismay of images: cultural appropriations of suffering in our times. In *Social suffering.* Eds. A. Kleinman, V. Das, and Margaret Lock. Berkeley: University of California.

Kroeber, Alfred L. [1911a] 1972. The elusive Mill Creeks: a band of wild Indians roaming in northern California today. *Travel* 17(4): 510–513,548,550. Reprinted in *The Mill Creek Indians and Ishi: early reports by A. L. Kroeber.* Berkeley: University of California.

Kroeber, A. L. [1911b] 1972. Ishi, the last aborigine. *World's Work Magazine* 24(3): 304–308. Reprinted in *The Mill Creek Indians and Ishi: early reports by A. L. Kroeber.* Berkeley: University of California.

———. 1917. The superorganic. *American Anthropologist* 19:163–213.

———. 1925. *Handbook of the Indians of California.* Smithsonian Institution, Bureau of American Ethnology. Bulletin 78. Washington DC: Government Printing Office.

———. 1939. *Cultural and natural areas of native North America.* Berkeley: University of California.

———. 1948a. *Anthropology: race, language, culture, psychology and prehistory.* New York: Harcourt, Brace and World.

———. 1948b. My faith. In *The faith of great scientists: a collection from the American Weekly.* New York: Hearst, pp. 22–24.

———. 1952. *The nature of culture.* Chicago: University of Chicago.

———. 1972. *More Mohave myths.* Anthropological Records, Vol. 27. Berkeley: University of California.

———. 1976. *Yurok myths.* Berkeley: University of California.

Kroeber, Alfred L., and Thomas T. Waterman. 1931. *Source book in anthropology.* Revised edition. New York: Harcourt, Brace and Company.

Kroeber, Theodora. 1961. *Ishi in two worlds.* Berkeley: University of California.

———. 1964. *Ishi, last of his tribe.* Berkeley: Parnassus.

———. 1970. *Alfred Kroeber: a personal configuration.* Berkeley: University of California.

Kuper, Leo. 1982. *Genocide: its political use in the twentieth century.* New Haven CT: Yale University.

———. 1985. *The prevention of genocide.* New Haven CT: Yale University.

Le Guin, Ursula. 2001. A conversation with Ursula LeGuin – author and daughter of A. L. Kroeber. Distinguished Lecture in honor of the centenary of the Department of Anthropology, University of California, Berkeley.

Lévi-Strauss, Claude. 1966. *Tristes tropiques.* New York: Athenaeum.

Lévi-Strauss, Claude. 1995. *Saudades do Brazil: a photographic memoir*. Seattle and London: University of Washington.

Leyton, Elliot. 1998. Discussant comments following plenary panel on the Anthropology of Violence, Canadian Anthropological Society Meetings, St. John's, Newfoundland.

———. 1998. *Touched by fire: Doctors Without Borders in a Third World crisis*. Toronto: McClelland and Stewart.

Malkki, Lisa H. 1995. *Purity and exile: violence, memory, and national cosmology among Huti refugees in Tanzania*. Chicago and London: University of Chicago.

Masson, Jeffrey. 1984. *Assault on truth: Freud's suppression of* The Seduction Theory. New York: Farrar, Straus and Giroux.

Nader, Laura. 1969. Up the anthropologist: perspectives gained from studying up. In *Reinventing anthropology*. Ed. Dell Hymes. New York: Random House, pp. 285–311.

Nelson, Diane. 1999. *A finger in the wound: body politics in quincentennial Guatemala*. Berkeley: University of California.

Pope, Saxton. 1920. The medical history of Ishi. *University of California Publications in American Archaeology and Ethnology* 13(5): 175–213.

Quesada, James. 1998. "Suffering child: an embodiment of war and its aftermath in post-Sandinista Nicaragua. *Medical Anthropology Quarterly* 12(1): 51–73.

Ramos, Alcida. 1987. Reflecting on the Yanomami: ethnographic images and the pursuit of the exotic. *Cultural Anthropology* 2(3): 284–304.

———. 2001. Old ethics die hard: the Yanomami and scientific writing. Lecture delivered at the Townsend Center for the Humanities, University of California, Berkeley, October 22, 2001.

Riddell, Francis A. Maidu and Konkow. In *California*. Vol. 8. Ed. R. Heizer. Washington DC: Smithsonian Institution, pp. 370–386.

Rieff, David. 1996. An Age of genocide. *The New Republic* 29(January): 27–36.

Riesman, Paul. 1987. Power, action, and critique: comments on "The Madness of Hunger" (Scheper-Hughes). American Anthropological Association Meeting, Chicago.

Rosaldo, Renato. 1989. Grief and the headhunter's rage. In *Culture and truth: the remaking of social analysis*. Ed. R. Rosaldo. Boston: Beacon, pp. 1–21.

Sanford, Nevitt, and Craig Comstock, eds. 1971. *Sanctions for evil*. Boston: Beacon.

Scheper-Hughes, Nancy. 1993. *Death without weeping: the violence of everyday life in Brazil*. Berkeley: University of California.

———. 1994. The last white Christmas: the Heidelberg pub massacre. *American Anthropologist* 96(4): 805–832.

———. 1995a. Who's the killer? Popular justice and human rights in a South African squatter camp. *Social Justice* 22(3): 143–164.

———. 1995b. The primacy of the ethical: propositions for a militant anthropology. *Current Anthropology* 36(3): 409–440.

———. 1997. Peace-time crimes. *Social Identities* 3(3): 471–497.

———. 1998. Undoing: social suffering and the politics of remorse in the new South Africa. *Social Justice* 25(4):114–142.

———. 1999. The body and violence. *Theater Symposium* 7(1): 7–30.

———. [1979] 2000. *Saints, scholars and schizophrenics: mental illness in rural Ireland.* Berkeley: University of California.

———. 2001. Human rights and death squads in northeast Brazil. *Newsletter of the Center for Latin American Studies, University of California, Berkeley,* Fall 2001, pp. 6–7, 18–19.

Schulz, Paul E. 1988. *Indians of Lassen.* Mineral CA: Loomis Museum.

Shackley, Steven M. 2000. The stone technology of Ishi and the Yana of Northern California. *American Anthropologist* 102(4): 613–712, reprinted with modifications as Chapter 11 of this volume.

Shea, Christopher. 2000. The return of Ishi's brain. *Lingua Franca* (February): 46–55.

Showalter, Elaine. 1985. *The female malady: women, madness and English culture.* New York: Pantheon.

Smith, Carol, ed. 1990. Conclusion: history and revolution in Guatemala. In *Guatemalan Indians and the state: 1540 to 1988.* Austin: University of Texas.

Sontag, Susan. 1964. The anthropologist as hero. In *Against interpretation.* New York: Dell, pp. 68–81.

Starn, Orin. 1992. Missing the revolution: anthropologists and the war in Peru. In *Re-reading cultural anthropology.* Ed. George Marcus. Durham NC and London: Duke University, pp. 152–179.

———. 2001. The ghosts of Kroeber Hall: anthropology and Native America. Department of Anthropology Centenary Speaker series, December 4, 2001.

Steward, Julian. 1961. Alfred Louis Kroeber: obituary. *American Anthropologist* 63:1038–1087.

Stoll, David. 1993. *Between two armies in the Ixil towns of Guatemala.* New York: Columbia University, pp. xi-xviii, 61–91.

Suárez-Orozco, Marcelo. 1987. The treatment of children in the Dirty War: ideology, state terrorism, and the abuse of children in Argentina. In *Child survival.* Ed. Nancy Scheper-Hughes. Dordrecht and Boston: D. Reidel, pp. 227–246.

Swendenburg, Ted. 1995. Prisoners of love: with Genet in the Palestinian field. In *Fieldwork under fire: Contemporary studies of violence and survival.* Eds. Carolyn Nordstrom and Antonius C. Robben. Berkeley: University of California, pp. 25–40.

Taussig, Michael. 1987. *Shamanism, colonialism and the wildman.* Chicago: University of Chicago, pp. 3–73.

———. 1991. Terror as usual: Walter Benjamin's theory of history as state of siege. In *The nervous system.* New York: Routledge, pp. 11–35.

Thomas, David Hurst. 2000. *Skull wars: Kennewick Man, archaeology, and the battle for Native American identity.* New York: Basic Books.

Vizenor, Gerald. 2000. *Chancers: a Novel.* Norman: University of Oklahoma.

Wallace, Grant. 1911. Ishi, the last aboriginal savage in America, finds enchantment in a vaudeville show. *San Francisco Call,* October 8, 1911.

Waterman, Thomas T. [1918] 1979. The Yana Indians. Republished in *Ishi the last Yahi: a documentary history.* Ed. Robert F. Heizer and Theodora Kroeber. Berkeley: University of California, pp. 131–160.

Wolf, Eric. 1981. Alfred L. Kroeber. In *Totems and teachers: perspectives on the history of anthropology.* Ed. Sydel Silverman. New York: Columbia University.

———. 1982. *Europe and the people without history.* Berkeley: University of California.

9

The Humanity of Ishi

KARL KROEBER

Although, like most teachers, I talk too much, I speak to you on this occasion with reluctance. I claim no expertise as an anthropologist, no specialized knowledge of California Indians, nor any competence in the study of repatriation. Were I not the son of Alfred and Theodora Kroeber, I would not have been invited here. Moreover, I have doubts about the value of this conference, beginning with its title, because I fear it may obscure the qualities of humanness Ishi so uniquely exemplified. To explain my anxieties, I begin, as I shall end, by quoting my mother, who spent several years trying to understand a Yahi man (whom she never knew) both as an individual and in his relations to people she had come to respect and love. One result was a poem in which she tried to articulate what might have been the feelings of a California Indian such as Ishi confronting his death.

> When I am dead
> Cry for me a little.
> Think of me sometimes,
> But not too much.
> It is not good for you
> Or your wife or your husband
> Or your children
> To allow your thoughts to dwell
> Too long on the dead.
> Think of me now and again
> As I was in life
> At some moment which it is pleasant to recall.
> But not for long.
> Leave me in peace

As I shall leave you, too, in peace.
While you live
Let your thoughts be with the living.

I am the only speaker today whose relationship to Ishi is thus familial and affectional, and this has exposed me to unpleasant experiences. I hope, anyway, that few of you have had to endure seeing *your* father grotesquely maligned in profiteering fictions and dramas misrepresenting Ishi's life. It's naive, I suppose, to complain about imaginative disfigurings by the reduction of characterization to cartooning, since that is the hallmark of postmodernism. And I recognize that these creative falsifiers, like their academic counterparts, may be inspired by good intentions. Unfortunately, I lived in Wisconsin half a century ago, when the state's best known politician was similarly inspired. Senator Joseph McCarthy was often cynical, but I do not doubt that he also believed some of his personal attacks on individuals were justified by the nobility of his ideological commitments, and certainly for his time nobody could have been more politically correct.

Nevertheless, I appear here, because I cannot deny my family is implicated in what has been done in Ishi's name. My father, along with Waterman, and Pope, and Gifford, and Warburton, and the rest at the Museum, bear responsibility for most of what is said and written of Ishi today. They gave him housing, gainful employment, and the friendship of co-workers, along with medical attention in the hospital next door. Had they followed the preference of some Washington bureaucrats then, and some anthropologists today, and sent him to an internment center for Indians, Ishi would not be a topic for discussion here. My mother also bears responsibility, because her book *Ishi in Two Worlds* has been the primary source – if often misused and inadequately acknowledged – for most of the plays, TV movies, video docudramas, and fictional fantasies that discomfit me and my siblings while obscuring the difficult but precious truth about Ishi. There would be no conference today on Ishi had not Theodora Kroeber, rather like E. B. White's wonderful spider-woman, not been so staunch a friend and so skillful a writer.

I should ignore personal discomfort, because I realize that offensive pseudo-dramatizings are of no lasting importance. In the realm of art, dishonest imagining usually self-destructs with gratifying speed. More dangerous are public pronouncements by professional scholars schematizing Ishi's history in the service of current ideological agendas. Such academics, however noble their intentions, may perpetuate falsification of history, not least by encouraging supposedly nonfictionalizing feature writers and filmmakers. Their disconnected factoids and pseudofactoids multiply the difficulties of recovering the subtle co-

herence of historical truth. How TV-type history diminishes the chances of recovering something of Ishi's real uniqueness is illustrated by a California newspaper report after an interview with a video documentarian telling us Alfred
Kroeber came from the East in order to study Ishi (that is, ten years before Ishi
came out of hiding!) and maliciously "locked up" unspecified materials until
1985, a neat trick for somebody who died in 1960.

My dislike of academic and popularizing distortions, however, is not brought
forward in defense of my father. A person of genuine integrity, I believe, is not
truly injurable by public detractors, however shrill. I have for years taught my
students that Socrates, who was executed by the Athenians on the grounds of
patently false accusations, was correct in insisting even as this happened that his
fellow citizens were damaging *their* integrity, not his. He argued that any group
which creates a scapegoat to evade self-evaluation weakens its moral power as a
collective, whether it be a city-state, a political or ethnic party, or a profession.

But if my motives are not filial, they sure as hell are personal. I have been an
academic scholar-teacher for half a century, and I deplore any degrading of the
humanistic scholarly enterprise – which I believe has been (and I hope will continue to be) profoundly valuable to our multiethnic democracy. To me, professional profiling is nearly as repugnant as racial profiling. Humanistic scholarship is primarily committed to understanding and nurturing the diversified
complexity of all that it has ever meant – and all that it ever *might* mean – to be
an individual human being. Humanistic scholarship is essentially historical,
which means it accepts Frederic Maitland's principle that events now long past
were once in the future. It devises means by which we may do more than exercise
current prejudices upon circumstances, actions, and motives of people different
in time, place, or culture from ourselves. By enhancing self-awareness of precisely how *we* are biased, historical humanism enables us to understand and
evaluate even remote circumstances, actions, and motives in a mode productive
of more than self-gratification.

Such scholarship must begin in the humility that misunderstanding is easier
than understanding. We will seek to judge especially those who lived before us
only in terms of the richest context we can reconstitute, in terms of all we can
discover as to what forces brought about the changing conditions of *their* lives,
and how exactly those conditions were evolving – eventually into the circumstances of our life that determine our perspective on theirs. Good history, as
much as good ethnography, is dialogic, but it is a dialog with those who are un-
answering. Only by recreating a full context of the past life of the dead can we
hope to hear authentic echoes of their voices. This object of the historian's passion may never be entirely attained, but unless we are driven by that aspiration,

our claims to historical understanding are hypocrisy, our learning just a new form of falsification serving current, and critically unexamined, prejudices.

Recently I talked with a woman I believe to be the last person who encountered Ishi as a living man. That testimony is to me precious, but in part because *this* last survivor confirms that, in the twenty-first century, Ishi and his people, the Yahi, are about to become entirely historical, no longer to hold a place in *any* living memory. That is why I wish to encourage ongoing careful historical studies of Ishi and of his people. These will and should bring modifications of our present understanding, revisions and reevaluations of the circumstances and the actors, in a drama far more significant than either openly fictional or pseudoacademic sensationalizings suggest. Every member of my family favors such continuously revisionary historical research.

The original plan for a conference on Ishi's repatriation arose out of a statement publicly issued by members of the Anthropology Department at Berkeley. In response, my brother, Clifton Kroeber, a professional historian, addressed a letter to the signatories through its chairman offering a list of sources of information and basic historical procedures he hoped would help them in their worthy endeavor of "pursuing and understanding those matters now so remote in time while so evocative of issues with which we must still contend today."

I want to add to my brother's listing of useful sources and procedures the proposal that the final years of Ishi's life be examined in the context of the full history of anthropology in this country. One might begin with institutional history, because the Berkeley anthropologists imply so nasty an interpretation of their own heritage. My research has led me to perceive originating practices and purposes of American anthropology radically different from that of any other I know. American anthropology has been decisively shaped by its concentration, beginning in the nineteenth century, upon the Native American peoples of this country. American Indians (as I'll from now on refer to them) determined in a variety of ways the special character of American anthropology, linguistics, and folklore. More than a century ago, there were American Indian professional anthropologists whose work is still admired, for example that of the Tuscarora Hewitt and the Omaha La Flesche. The Fox Indian William Jones is the first of our anthropologists, so far as I know, to be killed by the people who were the object of his inquiry. In my study of American Indian mythologies, moreover, I have been so impressed with the speed and sophistication with which so-called informants understood and exercised the ethnological principles of their interlocutors, that I make this reflexivity one focus of my teaching these materials.

This nativist orientation of the American form of the discipline has been superseded by recent American anthropologists, some of whom use the term "salvage anthropology" with an implied sneer. By deliberate policy effectuated through hirings, anthropology departments have steadily diminished the proportion of their faculty whose principal concern is specific American Indian cultures, and have offered fewer and fewer courses, especially for undergraduates, concentrating on American Indians. These hiring practices and curriculum changes have in effect announced to students and the public that American Indians are relatively unimportant. I don't want to oversimplify this development, which, for example, is caught up in the vast expansion of anthropology after the Second World War. A century ago there were fewer than a hundred full-time American anthropologists. But effects of hiring policy appear when you discover that, in the past fifty years, undergraduate courses in specific American Indian cultures have dwindled from above twenty percent of the anthropology departmental offering to less than five percent. And the Berkeley department only manifests a national "anti-Indian" trend. At my home institution, in the past decade I have frequently offered the only course in Columbia College dealing exclusively with American Indian cultures.

This continuing de-emphasis on Indian cultures by American anthropologists illuminates their critique of their predecessors, while it contrasts with the intellectually powerful revaluation of traditional American Indian oral artistry during the past thirty-five years, spearheaded by revisionary Boasian anthropologists and linguists. Their dramatic reassessment of ethnographic texts accompanied what has been called the Native American literary renaissance of poetry, fiction, and drama in English by contemporary Indians – among whom Gerry Vizenor is one of a cluster of distinguished writers. As someone who tried to help in this effort, at the beginning of this new century I find it is pleasantly surprising to remember that even twenty years ago it was difficult to find publishers for *any* Indian writing, however excellent, and how one had to battle to get the major academic anthologies to include only a few pages of American Indian materials within collections of *American* literature.

My personal research, however, has been in the records of oral materials. Exploring the diversity of American Indian myths, I have encountered something among the Boasians for which I find no parallels in equivalent collections from British, French, German, Scandinavian, or Russian folklorists and ethnographers. That is, American ethnologists, linguists, and folklorists frequently established long-term and intimate relationships with individual American Indians whose languages or social practices they were learning. Their accounts echoed my personal experience. My latest book is dedicated to the memory of Juan Dolores, a Papago Indian whom I knew when I was a child. He was a frequent visitor to our home here in Berkeley and annually spent his vacation at our summer place, Kishamish, in the Napa Valley. I and my siblings still refer to the front bedroom as "Juan's room." The Yurok Robert Spott, who collaborated with my father for three decades, built the outdoor fireplace at Kishamish, and, as I've recounted elsewhere, took delight in my childish insistence that he tell me his people's myths exactly as I had heard them from my father. First I attributed these relationships to what I came to recognize as my parents' remarkable gift for creating enduring friendships. When I started to read in the myth collections of "salvage anthropologists," however, I discovered everywhere emotional tributes and expression of deep affection revealing analogous personal experiences. Among these I cite here only Barre Toelken's account of his life with the Navajo Yellowman and his family, affecting in itself and distinguished by Toelken's subtle analysis of the intricate nature of that long relationship – an account that anyone attempting to assess Ishi's relations with his friends in San Francisco ought to consult.

If we are to develop any understanding of Ishi as an individual, we must begin by recognizing that his general situation is not unparalleled. Most terribly, he is not – and shame that it should be so – the only final survivor of his people destroyed by the Old World's invasion of the New. One of the most notorious of American novels, after all, is *The Last of the Mohicans.* But Ishi has become significant to many Native peoples, even those whose ancestors were sometimes hostile to his, because, although indubitably the last of the Yahi, Ishi lived out his life in a manner that contradicts the victimizing *myth* of the vanishing American Indian, what I call the Fenimore Cooper fallacy. That fallacy, too often internalized by Native Americans, has been a terrible burden on them. Someone like Gerry Vizenor here has been forced to be almost belligerent about his persistent corporeality – for Gerry, even to the point of returning to the Berkeley campus after disappearing into a Tricksterish tour of lesser intellectual institutions.

The fallacy of the vanishing Indian as noble victim – noble *because* a victim – however, has been a greater burden to whites. That is why it is important that we establish to the best of our imperfect abilities the individual historicity of Ishi. For if we do not attend to the idiosyncrasies of Ishi's experience, we will create another red ghost, the kind D. H. Lawrence said haunts the American imagination. Lawrence was correct, if our literature is a valid indicator. From Philip Freneau's "The Indian Burying Ground," published the year our Constitution was adopted, to Stephen King's vastly popular and quite repulsive *Pet Sematary* two hundred years later, we do indeed see the American imagination as self-spooked by dead/undead Indians, because their reality has in absolutely classical Freudian fashion been repressed. Berkeley anthropologists denouncing their predecessors present us with an intriguing version of guilt's false face, a version of Fenimore's fallacious noble savagery, a mental restructuring that may incarcerate Indians more cruelly than any physical restraints, while morally corroding its proponents, who must deny refabricating the condition they claim to deplore. If prisons are built of stones of law, and brothels with the brick of religion, reservation-internment camps were enclosed by the fences of science.

My mother's book on Ishi, which depicts with agonizing detail the extermination of California Indians, was written before there was widespread awareness of those horrors in this beautiful land. She did not employ the term "genocide," now used so casually everywhere. Because I am myself a humanist, and therefore committed to regarding with equal skepticism faddish demonizations and faddish sanctifications embodied in clichés, I urge that we discriminate more carefully, especially when dealing with genuine, not factitious, horrors suffered by other people. The Yahi were less fortunate than the Jews under the Nazis, or the Armenians under the Turks. All of the Yahi were destroyed. Ishi truly was the last Yahi, and he knew it. Although he was not the only Indian who became possessed of such terrible knowledge, his individual actions and their particular consequences make his experience not only poignant but also exemplary.

His behavior urges upon us, Indian and white alike, the responsibility not to debase the *uniqueness* of what he was and what he did. I'm drawn toward the economic term *debase* because I want to protest against the commercialized politicizing of Ishi in something of the same spirit that notable Jewish scholars such as Michael Bernstein have protested against commodifications of the Holocaust. Appropriate here are the words of the Israeli novelist A. B. Yehoshua, who had the courage to tell his countrymen, "Our having been victims does not accord us any special moral standing. The victim does not become virtuous for having been a victim. . . . The murderers were amoral; the victims were not made moral. To be moral you must behave ethically. The test of that is daily and constant." The powerful truth of Yehoshua's words derives, first, from the novelist's unblinking recognition that his people were victims. Analogously, anyone who denies that Native Americans were victimized by invading European American culture is either a liar or a fool. But beyond this first horror lies a subtle, insidious satisfaction in celebrating victimization – especially if the sufferer is not oneself.

For a long time this phenomenon has puzzled me. Why were Berkeley anthropologists, for example, so anxious publicly to demonize their predecessors by representing Ishi as sheer victim? I have come to suspect that in a society as pervasively narcissistic as ours, especially among the affluent, for whom all the pronouns have atrophied except the first-person singular, claiming victimization for self or others offers the profound pleasure of self-righteousness. This may be why religious fundamentalism flourishes today. Nothing, after all, warms the ego like the feeling of moral superiority, especially in a world where ethical standards seem continuously to dissolve. As a long term, continuous source of satisfaction, self-righteousness even beats sex. But I believe it is exactly such self-righteousness that Ishi's behavior challenges, challenges appealingly and inspiringly. If there was ever anyone entitled to feel himself an innocent victim, it was Ishi. Instead, he quietly but definitively rejected the role that seemed forced upon him, just as he preferred to wear Western clothes and resisted being photographed in "primitive" garb and "savage" postures. He refused to be merely a victim, not through dramatic posturing or flamboyant rhetoric, but through simple. modest, ordinary behavior in the course of daily living. This is why the story of his life in the museum, the part of his story we know best, has captivated the imagination of so many peoples around the world. I suspect that many people understand better than the ideologically sophisticated that an admirable ethical character is exhibited less significantly by spectacular actions and melodramatic pronouncements than by consistent conduct in the course of everyday life. Ishi, as my mother observed, seizes our imagination by the mysteriousness which abides in the simplicity of his behavior. He exemplified the invisibility of what William Wordsworth called the best part of a good man's life – "little, unremembered acts of kindness and of love." And this is why the humanity of Ishi is falsified by those who turn him into a symbol, abstract him into some sort of universal icon. His behavior was shaped by his specific Yana/Yahi heritage, which, like many Indian cultures, most honored respectful sensitivity to the dynamics of daily interrelations with familiar people. Esteem for the truly individual qualities of any human being entails esteem for that person's particular cultural heritage, the bedrock of the historicity of human individuality.

Such a view sounds, and I hope is, generous, but it is also humbling, even troubling. It reminds us that much that ostensibly celebrates Ishi is in fact self-disguised exploitation. Or so it seems to me, perhaps because of my personal experience. I have tried as a teacher to make broadly accessible the unusual accomplishments in verbal storytelling of various Indian cultures. I have emphasized the special qualities of their understanding of the natural world and the beauty and emotional complexity of their diverse imaginative creations. Yet again and again I return to asking myself, by what right am I doing this? I – of course with the best intentions – seem to make use of their accomplishments for my benefit, and to the benefit of those who profited from their destruction, for the benefit of people who, in spite of what they profess, do not really desire to engage with the strange difficulties of so different a way of life. I cannot soothe my conscience with the flattering unction that I work with Indian imaginative materials exactly as I do with works by Keats, Jane Austen, Shakespeare, or Emily Dickinson, because the historical facts of how my people have devastated Indian peoples is part of my consciousness. My efforts to restore and increase appreciation of their mythologies seem never entirely to escape the suspicion of personal advantage from the destruction of their cultures, with which perhaps even my praise implicates me.

What gives *me* the right, as historical necessity forces me to do, even as I speak *of* these people to seem to speak *for* them? Perhaps because I have never been able to put away these self-doubts, I ungraciously urge them on others. Specifically, to focus on the subject of this conference, I suggest that all those, including Indians, who like me sought the return of all Ishi's remains to his native countryside, should not exempt themselves from examination of their motives for "redeeming" and repatriating what belongs to none of us. In this respect, I praise the manner in which Ishi's descendants carried out the repatriation, without media hype or public fanfare, and in a fashion that precludes another white invasion, this time of tourists, curiosity seekers, and wannabe mystics. Ishi is honored by this return to his long concealment.

Let me offer a few thoughts as a literary humanist on the idea of repatriation of the dead. My thinking begins with discomfort at the title of this conference: "Who Owns The Body?" More than of Agatha Christie it reminds me of that fascinating five-thousand-year-old man whose crushed body was clumsily torn from a glacier in the Alps near the Italian-Austrian border a decade ago. This so-called "Iceman" became the object of nauseous territorial disputes, even though he manifestly antedated both Austria and Italy. Such fighting over the possession of a dead body revolts me, because it tries to deny the reality of death. Death destroys the possibility of ownership. A dead body is un-ownable. Death is terrible because it renders the very idea of possession impossible – whether possession of a body or of a *patria*, a territory, an arbitrarily delimited space of the natural world claimed as "mine" or "ours." In the face of death, even "Italy" and "Austria" shrivel to triviality. Forgive these dark thoughts of an old man, but they may help to explain why so many people have not insisted on repatriating their dead. There must be in this lively audience at least a few other people who go back to the Second World War, who had, if not relatives, perhaps friends who died in the invasion of Normandy and whose bodies lie in French cemeteries alongside the remains of other Allied troops, and even of Germans whom they fought against. For many of us of their generation at least, this is appropriate burial ground. Our contemporary fetishizing of the body, I fear, reveals a loss of confidence in the reality of spirit.

Such reflections carry me as a literary scholar back to a foundation of Western literature, Homer's *Iliad*, which is full of fighting over dead bodies. The physical heroism of these battles is Homer's ironic dramatizing of how we deface a world overflowing with natural and cultural beauty. And the poem's climax, as if Homer knew this conference had been planned, recounts Trojan Priam's begging the killer of his son Hector, Achilles, to allow the old man to carry the corpse back to Troy for crematory funeral rites. Achilles in his furious anger not only killed Hector; he attempted to mutilate the body, dragging the corpse through the dust around Troy behind his chariot. But in this endeavor Achilles failed. He was unable to disfigure the body of his dead enemy, thanks to the interference of some gods. Divine intervention in the Homeric poem always is to highlight a fundamental truth about human behavior. In this case, the point is that once you have killed your enemy, you have put him out of your power. You can hack the body to bits, but the man is gone.

The desire to repatriate the dead entails taking on a burden of moral responsibility, because the claim of right for final disposition of what *was* a human being defines the ethical quality of the claimant. Priam makes a dangerous expedition alone through the hostile Achaian army to the tent of Achilles. There he makes no appeal to conventional pieties, historical precedents, or religious sanctities. He appeals to Achilles simply as an old father so grief-stricken that he kisses the hands of the man who killed his son. Priam's courageous simplicity succeeds as nothing else could have, because it restores Achilles to sanity, brings him back to his true self. Priam touches Achilles' profound emotional sensitivity and understanding of the horror of the human condition, the horror epitomized by the perverse idealism of warfare, of which Achilles is the supreme practitioner. It is, in fact, the unique acuity of his sensitivity to human life as intrinsically an existence of suffering and grief which drove Achilles into the insanity of his unmitigated anger. Priam's appeal recalls him to the terrible bond that binds his fury to Priam's sorrow. But, contrary to what we would be told by any modern writer – with faith in nothing but the spurious refuge of physical contact – Homer does not have the two men embrace. Achilles pushes away the old man kneeling before him, and the two mourn silently, apart.

Achilles sends Priam back to Troy with Hector's body and halts the war until the mourning ceremonies are completed, but repatriation occurs within circumstances that compel us to assess the uncertainties and ambiguities which inhere in this most fundamental of cultural institutions. The episode forces us honestly to reexamine what makes worthwhile such assertions of spirit against the irresistible processes of physical nature. How, in honoring the dead body, do we honor the individual human spirit?

This excursus on the *Iliad* has not taken me far from Ishi. Indeed, it is impossible to talk about Homer and get very far from the central problems of humanity. If the *Iliad,* in current jargon, is life-affirming, it is so only because it so unflinchingly dramatizes the inescapable agonies, terrors, and griefs that are the lot of every person. Ishi equally exemplifies how conditions of pain and suffering make precious each human life – but in a different way. No one has had more bleakly to confront, in total isolation, the destruction of everything that makes life worth living. To these circumstances he responded, I will say not heroically, but hopefully, even though his must have been a hope originating in desperation. After a life of concealment, to put himself at the mercy of those who had so viciously destroyed his people and family and driven him into a life of perpetual hiding required of him not only a rare courage but also an unusual resiliency of spirit that obliterated all traces of self-pity.

During his life at the museum more of his virtues flowered out of these qualities – above all, his ability not merely to adapt swiftly to radically new conditions but also to discover in them new interests, new pleasures, and new means for giving scope to his affections, his curiosity, his humor. He made giving himself up to the Western world much, much more than an act of physical survival. This is the feature of Ishi's story which has made my mother's telling of it fascinating to so many different people. Ishi is exemplary because he confronted the consequence of his most fateful act, not with mere stoicism, but with creative hope for good possibilities even in the worst of circumstances, rejecting the role of victim, even though hideously victimized.

To me, the most impressive feature in Ishi's behavior is the speed with which he chose the museum as his new home, even before those around him were sure that it should be. From the very beginning he refused to be passive, just as *his* people, almost alone and against overwhelming odds, had fought the white invaders. Consistently, with the calmness drawn from the reserve of personal integrity that is the complement of his volatility, he refused to be anything but himself. Quietly and patiently he continued shaping his own life from the inside, whatever the outside pressures might be. Evidence of his success in self-fashioning was his delight later at returning to his native country, a delight accompanied by his assertion at the end of his visit that his former way of life was irretrievable, that he had made his home in another time, another place. He was the first of the camping party to board the train to carry them back to San Francisco, and from the train he made his only public speech – a beauty. He leaned out the window of the train, extended his arms to the large crowd of Northern Californians who had assembled to see the Wild Indian depart, and called out: "Ladies and gentlemen, goodbye!"

Ishi made his terrible experience yield positive rewards – not for himself alone but also for those with whom he associated. All the evidence we have proves how much he enriched the lives of those he lived with and worked with at the Museum, each of whom came to respect him and to enjoy his company. These effects of Ishi's modest, unassertive, but unwaveringly active integrity demand an equivalently tough-minded and antisentimental response from us. We respond inadequately unless we respect Ishi the individual, and through him his

Native Yahi culture, which provided him with the forms by which to manifest in so unique a fashion the primary virtues of patience, courage, a lack of self-pity, and a sensitivity to others, leading to a capacity for deep personal friendship based on esteem for people entirely different in education and life experience.

Only if we honor Ishi's individuality will we avoid sentimentalizing him. I do not see how we can speak of his life as anything but tragic, yet I have come to feel that he himself did not so regard it. We debase by overuse the term *tragedy* and, by so doing, diminish understanding of those who suffer the genuine experience. But even authentic tragedy is not ultimate. For a very, very rare few there is the experience beyond tragedy. For Sophocles, beyond *Oedipus the King* there was *Oedipus at Colonus*; for Shakespeare, beyond *Lear* and *Hamlet* there were *The Winter's Tale* and *The Tempest*. That, I have come to feel, was the realm of Ishi's experience to himself, an experience beyond fear and pity, beyond tragedy. Another Indian once wrote, "What a man learned, and it was all he learned in a lifetime, was a degree of fitness for the things he had to do." Ishi could not have anticipated what he would have to do during the final years of his life, but he learned quickly to perform with grace and competence – and enjoyment that delighted others – the fundamental acts required by a new civilization. These acts were unspectacular, commonplace tasks of daily life. Ishi compels the imagination because with such unassuming ease he affirms the supreme importance of ordinary human life. Ishi's modestly cheerful demeanor rebukes our current fondness for finding profound meaning only in acts of sensational violence and in apocalyptic scenarios. Saxton Pope, his doctor, describes how Ishi "quietly helped the nurses" in the surgical department to "clean instruments," and how "he came into the women's wards quite regularly, and with his hands folded before him, he would go from bed to bed like a visiting physician, looking at each patient with quiet concern or with a fleeting smile that was very kindly received and understood."

It is easy for those who have motives for melodramatizing Ishi's life to forget that its last summer was spent not in the museum but as a houseguest with the Watermans. Distraught at Ishi's death, Waterman ignored the tuberculosis bacilli in blaming himself for letting Sapir overwork the one whom Waterman called "the best friend I ever had." Sapir's report of their collaboration brings to bear another perspective, one that had been earlier suggested by my father's warning of the potency of Ishi's enthusiasm for this work. He wrote Sapir that Ishi would rather "tell customs or myths than eat." And, sure enough, Sapir reported that in going over his texts for interlinear translations, "it proved a difficult task to hold Ishi in leash in the matter of speed of dictation – I endeavored to use every tittle of evidence that I could muster, [to keep up with] Ishi's 'explanation' of single words, his accompanying gestures. . . ."

Sapir's words strike me forcibly, because they point toward distinctive qualities in the translations of stories told by Ishi that I have read. These are driven by a energetic self-reflexivity that gives vivid form to combinations of apparently incongruent psychological states and physical activities. A linguist who has worked closely and patiently for years with Ishi's texts finds him in his native language a subtle and sophisticated storyteller, confidently articulate. Analogously, the distinguished musicologist Bruno Nettl analyzed recordings of Ishi's songs, judging that they revealed the Yahi singing style to be "a curious mixture of severe limitation and amazing variety." But, like everyone else who somehow comes in contact with Ishi, Nettl concludes on the note of the personal. "These recordings are an amazing personal document. Ishi was presumably not an outstanding singer in his tribe – indeed he did not live in a truly tribal environment. Yet he was able to sing over fifty songs, and to sing them . . . in an assured and self-confident manner. How many members of Western civilization, left alone as the only survivors of their culture, would be able to do the same?"

Last year I wrote the chair of the Berkeley anthropology department that I would be delighted if Ishi, through the effect of repatriation efforts, should help to reverse the policy of diminishing American Indians' role in American anthropology of the past two generations. But whether or not that happens, the task of all who truly wish to honor Ishi in and for himself is to insist that we be allowed to hear his words and his voice. Ishi's words and voice were recorded by those terrible, terrible anthropologists of long ago, and for some years dedicated scholars such as Ira Jacknis in the Hearst Museum have preserved these materials. In the twenty-first century it is time to make Ishi's stories and songs widely available. To me, repatriation of Ishi's physical remains in his native land is incomplete without the recovery of his voice, his songs, his words, his stories. To dedicate our energies to *that* restoration, furthermore, accords with the positive, forward-looking character Ishi exhibited in his genially reserved, gregariously patient conduct of the ordinary businesses of life.

Walter Benjamin was right: a significant existence requires neither historical success nor even survival of one's name. We will never know Ishi's real name, but we can and should allow him to speak for himself in the twenty-first century. From his words we will surely find reasons and opportunities to reevaluate overly simple assumptions about what his final years may teach us. The more we hear from Ishi himself, I am certain, the more will we appreciate the generous reciprocity of giving and receiving that characterized the last years of his life in the museum – a reciprocity that makes especially cogent John Steinbeck's comment that receiving is superior to giving, because "receiving . . . if it be well done, requires a fine balance of self-knowledge and kindness. It requires humility and tact and great understanding of relationships. In receiving you cannot appear, even to yourself, better or stronger or wiser than the giver, although you must be wiser to do it well."

As my mother wrote, "Howsoever one touches on Ishi, the touch rewards. It illuminates the way."

NOTE

This address was presented at the Conference "Who Owns the Body?" at the University of California, Berkeley, September 28, 1999.

10
Ishi and the University

KAREN BIESTMAN

Whereas the discovery of Ishi sparked the interest of anthropologists at the University of California, who brought him from the Oroville jail to San Francisco, where he was examined, studied, and ultimately employed as a janitor at the Anthropology Museum . . . (California State Assembly 1999)

Just as Ishi's encounter and early institutional relationships were complex, so too are the recent chapters in the Ishi legacy as scholars, politicians, activists, and advocates position themselves within and around the Ishi camp. The above preamble to California Assembly Concurrent Resolution (ACR) 25: the Remains of Ishi (California State Assembly 1999), was introduced in 1999 in response to the revelation that Ishi's brain, autopsied and removed against his wishes in 1916 by medical personnel at the University of California (UC) San Francisco Medical School, was gifted to the curator of Physical Anthropology at the Smithsonian Institution in 1917 by Professor Alfred Kroeber of the University of California's Anthropology Department. There it dwelled inconspicuously for over eighty years until inquiries from Butte County Native Americans and scholars Orin Starn and Nancy Rockafellar unlocked the mystery of Ishi's preserved brain. This time, in the spirit of institutional accountability and oversight, Ishi's image provided the platform for the State of California to question the university's treatment of Native American human remains in teaching and research. Was the State of California simply flexing its governmental muscles over the powerful and often independent University of California Regents, or does ACR 25 reflect genuine institutional change?

This was not the first time, nor undoubtedly the last that Ishi's name would be invoked for opportunistic purposes. Throughout the twentieth century, Ishi's memory has been enlisted to serve various political, media, sentimental, and institutional ends. Surely UC anthropologists Alfred Kroeber and Thomas

T. Waterman and surgeon Saxton Pope were interested in Ishi as an informant who could unlock Yahi cultural mysteries. Without question, Ishi brought with him a personal history of severe hardship and isolation, having survived the wave of dispossession and violence that characterized California Indian Country at the turn of the century and brought its population to the brink of extinction. Although Friends of the Indians organizations were actively indicting the federal government's treatment of Native Americans, most Westerners continued to view tribal people as obstacles to progress and enemies of righteousness. In this climate, what is unique about Ishi's relationship with university personnel is its profound lack of victimry, force, or guilt. In fact, Ishi's five-year life at the museum distinguishes an otherwise tarnished historical record as a largely humanitarian chapter. He came to the museum as a living relic but soon became a companion and colleague to his "keepers," who remember him fondly. He developed a public celebrity status based both on curiosity and affection. Such attentions were also patronizing and commodifying, but nonetheless tolerable, as Ishi selectively participated in San Francisco activities only if they fit within his understanding of a proper Yahi construct. He measured his words, his memory, and his privacy with steadfast dignity and patience.

In death, however, the bonds of friendship failed to protect him from the indignity of autopsy. In the final analysis, the interest of science in the Yahi specimen prevailed. The great irony of this tragedy is not just that Ishi's remains were disrespected in death, but that thousands, potentially millions, of anonymous Native Americans suffered this desecration regularly, silently, and without recourse. Legions were collected and studied almost universally without consent. Many were harvested from graves or decapitated on battlefields and sent under orders by the Surgeon General to the Army Medical Museum for study. Ishi put a human face on the history of disparate treatment of Native American dead, a face that would surprise many by emerging eighty-three years after his death to champion the repatriation cause.

In the years following his death, the Ishi collection became a featured teaching and research tool at the University of California, safely fixed in time and material cultural artifacts. Save from his friends, the story of Ishi the man was all but forgotten in the twentieth century. It was not until Theodora Kroeber penned *Ishi in Two Worlds* in 1961 (Kroeber 1961) that Ishi's memory was resurrected. Again he became a celebrity as Mrs. Kroeber's biography interpreted his unusual life. But was it all that is "surely and truly known" about him, as indicated in the text?

A critical analysis of Mrs. Kroeber's text suggests dilemmas posed by translation and perspective. Mrs. Kroeber never met Ishi, having arrived in Berkeley long after his death. She acknowledged a deep interest in Indian history and culture dating back to her Colorado childhood, but conducted none of the primary research about Ishi herself. Instead, she relied on her husband's research and recollections, indicating that he was at her side during the writing and read the final draft manuscript before his death in 1960. She engages in what historians call controlled speculation, in which collateral records of scholars, museum curators, newspapers, and even Waterman's widow were used to weave the narrative. Berkeley anthropologist Ira Jacknis describes the text as part fictional, part historical. Markedly absent is a native voice. Although several tribes survived in the Mt. Lassen region, no members were interviewed. This is due undoubtedly to the presumption that Ishi was the sole survivor of an extinct people, a designation that enhanced his celebrity status as a primitive, Stone Age Indian.

Had Mrs. Kroeber consulted Natives in the region, such as the Pit River, Maidu, and Wintu peoples and the ancestors of the present Redding Rancheria, she might have heard narratives of intermarriage, shared experiences, and mutual histories. Ishi's life and Yana existence are alive in the oral tradition of these people, several of whom testified about these cultural intersections at the 1999 California Assembly hearings on the remains of Ishi. Claims by the Pit River and Redding Rancheria peoples convinced the Smithsonian to repatriate Ishi's brain directly to them. Even contemporary archaeological studies by such scholars as Berkeley's Steven Shackley (Chapter 11, this volume) of Ishi's arrowpoints suggest that they resemble more the styles of neighboring tribes and less the classic Yana style, giving credibility to the idea that Ishi was not an isolated tool maker.

Despite these omissions, which subject Mrs. Kroeber to critical evaluation today, her work was revolutionary in the 1950s and reflected the prevailing ethics and research standards of the time. The political and cultural climate of this era was one of intolerance. Responding to fears that there was something "un-American" about Indian culture, sovereignty, and holding land in common, Congress enacted "termination" legislation that severed the Federal Trust Relationship with 109 bands and tribes, leaving many disenfranchised squatters on their own land. This and other 1950s legislation was unilateral. Tribal voices did not count and were, in fact, invisible to the general public. The exception was cinematic, where Indians emerged as single-dimensional obstacles to progress, Christianity, and chastity, trapped indefinitely on nineteenth-century Western soundstages. Both constructs undermined tribalism.

Theodora Kroeber's *Ishi in Two Worlds* was an exception to the stereotypes. Her telling was a life story about the translated remembrances of the relationship between Ishi and her husband Alfred, whom Ishi called "Big Chiep." Albeit romantic at times, she wrote in the spirit of respect and admiration for Ishi the human being. She wrote candidly about the violence and dispossession that characterized California Indian history. In so doing, she challenged the prevailing research, political tenor, and popular culture sentiment of the day. Her interests were familial rather than institutional, but the Kroeber legacy at Berkeley cannot be separated from the evolution of the anthropology discipline and the Museum collection. Surely this connection, and the fact that the book was well written, influenced the University of California Press to publish it. That UC Press published the book in the midst of controversial times for Indian affairs suggests that their interests were in other than supporting status quo political and racial sentiments.

Unanswered questions remain, however. Why Mrs. Kroeber makes no mention of the brain being deposited with the Smithsonian remains a mystery. Possibly, it represented an episode so painful for her husband that she chose to omit it. Possibly she chose to emphasize his life rather than treatment in death as the focus of the narrative. Although curious, the omission does not undermine the value of the book. The consequence of this omission or misplacement in the University of California's archives, however, is professionally damning and facilitated yet another chapter of Ishi's legacy in the repatriation debates.

Whereas a federal statute known as the Native American Grave Protection and Repatriation Act of 1990 provides protection for Native American remains and cultural items and provides for the repatriation of those remains and items, and. . . . Whereas it is the explicit policy of the State of California that all Native American remains be repatriated . . . (California State Assembly 1999)

When the public debate on repatriation reached the Berkeley campus in the late 1980s, neither side raised Ishi's name. Anthropologists such as Dr. Frank Norick acknowledged that reburial might happen in the future, but not, as Norick noted, "without a fight." He spoke for many skeptical scientists when he suggested that Indians' interest in skeletal remains were based on politics, "plain and simple" (Heimoff 1989):

> Let's just say that I don't think their arguments are religious at all, since most of them are nominally Christian, if nothing else. Any ties to aboriginal religion are purely fabricated. And so these demands are going to be settled in the political sphere. The courts are going to decide this. It's also a great way for Native American lawyers to get their names in the books. I think it makes them feel better, to jump up and down on this.

Norick's prediction was in part correct. There was opposition. In contrast to Stanford University, whose administration voluntarily repatriated its collection of 550 Ohlone skeletal remains in April 1989, it took an act of Congress to shift the University of California's practices, if not its institutional values. Campus and state initiatives alone proved unsuccessful in facilitating institutional change, and there seemed to be no common ground. In October 1989 the campus established an American Indian Skeletal Remains Advisory Committee, chaired by law professor Rachel Moran, to recommend a policy for the disposition of Native remains. University of California anthropologists Susan Anton, F. Clark Howell, G. D. Richards, and Vincent Sarich wrote their colleagues in November 1989, asking for letters supporting the "jeopardized" collection due to lobbying of the administration by faculty of the Native American Studies Department and Native American groups. They received 150 letters of support. At risk was not only research and teaching material, but potentially $300,000 in National Science Foundation grants provided to the Lowie Museum (later renamed the Hearst Museum) for curatorial work. For this reason, uc faculty lobbied heavily and successfully against the passage of California Assembly Bill 2577, also known as the Katz Bill, which favored repatriation. An amended state law favoring repatriation was eventually passed in 1991 (Thornton 1998). The creation of a systemwide Joint Academic Senate-University Committee on Human Remains in April 1990 preempted the campus's policy efforts. In its final report to the Office of the President, the systemwide committee recommended that, first and foremost, the university needed a deaccession policy with specific criteria that balanced the respect for Native dead and their descendants with the university's mission in teaching, research, and community service. Native scholars also noted the value of scientific inquiry in such a balanced policy but suggested, in Russell Thornton's words (Miller 1990), that "science can't be the tail that wags the dog. Ethics has to be the ultimate authority." The policy also called for ongoing and respectful consultation with Native Americans, the creation of new programs in Archaeology and Museum Studies, and educational support for Indian youth (Associated Students 1992).

In 1989 Congress passed the National Museum of the American Indian (nmai) Act (Public Law 101–185), which established both the Museum and a comprehensive repatriation policy for the country's largest Native American collection, housed at the Smithsonian. It was expanded into a comprehensive national policy in 1990 with the passage of *the Native American Grave Protection and Repatriation Act* (nagpra; Public Law 101–601), which superseded state and university policy efforts. Yet, even when the spirit and mandate of federal law favored repatriation, University of California opponents continued to resist. Delays in compliance with the required inventory and challenges to the definitions and standards of proof of "culturally affiliated" groups prolonged the now antagonistic relationship between Native Americans and the university. But some anthropologists, and the discipline itself, were changing. In June 1990,

University of California Department of Anthropology chair William Simmons told the Academic Senate that there was no unanimous position within the discipline, that social anthropologists tended to be more concerned with Native American claims, whereas "physical and biological anthropologists would be more concerned with the preservation of the collection" (Academic Senate 1990). The early NAGPRA debates were silent as to the role and presence of Ishi.

The University of California, Berkeley, missed the first inventory deadline in 1995, was granted an extension by the National Parks Service to complete it, and was declared in a state of "forbearance" with the act (National Park Service 1999). Since that time, demands for accountability and shifting professional sentiments are changing the museum landscape. In the last five years, honorable museum leadership by directors Rosemary Joyce, Kent Lightfoot, and Patrick Kirch, along with institutional support from the Office of the Vice Chancellor for Research, have moved the University of California closer to compliance with NAGPRA. In June 2000, the university completed its human remains inventory. Save for a minority of anthropology faculty who continue to insist that Native dead are university property, the institutional posture is changing as well.

Whereas the fate of Ishi is an example of the cruelty and injustice dealt to every tribe in California by those who came here and displaced them, and . . . Whereas an expression of a desire for the unification and return of Ishi to his homeland would constitute an expression of remorse on the part of the State of California for its actions that contributed to this injustice . . . (California State Assembly 1999)

Nothing propelled the issue of repatriation faster and more poignantly than the discovery of Ishi's brain. It was a compelling reminder of the disparate treatment of Native dead. This time the relationship was undeniably personal, not scientific, and intricately interwoven with the evolution of anthropology at Berkeley. It also forced the State to rethink its own role in the dispossession and destruction of the California Indian population in the early years of statehood. Ishi again became an icon and catalyst for social and political change.

At the 1999 California Assembly hearings on the remains of Ishi, the Anthropology Department offered a public apology for its role in his "final tragedy" and indicated a desire for renewed cooperation with the California Indian community. Was this a gesture of goodwill and a commitment to accountability? Critics of the apology, controversial even among the departmental faculty, argue that it too is part of an extended exploitation, evidence of the university capitalizing on Ishi's legacy to assuage institutional guilt and enhance its own reputation. Nor are activists free of responsibility for co-opting Ishi's image in pursuit of larger institutional and political goals. Capitalizing on Ishi's mistreatment in death, repatriation activists point to Ishi as evidence of continued systemic discrimination.

Whether driven by the dictates of NAGPRA, by the gradual shift in the anthropology discipline toward inevitable accommodation, or by the emergence of scholars and administrators committed to both implementing the law and acting ethically, the University of California is changing its actions. In September, 2000, the university sponsored a three-day conference aptly named "Who Owns the Body?" Born from the idea of an intellectual forum to analyze the Ishi experience and general treatment of Native dead, it grew to embrace faculty in various fields of science and the humanities. The dilemma Ishi posed for the academy was one of balancing science and sanctity and of institutional versus human rights. It crossed disciplinary, cultural, and international lines. Such paradoxes are raised in worldwide forums concerning bioethics, biopiracy, mass graves, and communities of loss. In May 2001, the University of California Office of the President released its revised Policy and Procedures on Curation and Repatriation of Human Remains and Cultural Items. Finally, in October 2001, the California Legislature passed A.B. 978, the California Native American Graves Protection and Repatriation Act. Sponsored by Assemblyman Darrell Steinberg, A.B. 978 was designed to enhance NAGPRA and create a State Repatriation Oversight Commission with Native American representation. It is safe to assume that the memory of Ishi informed the dialogue and influenced the final product in each of these developments.

Now therefore be it resolved by the Assembly of the State of California, the Senate thereof concurring, that the Legislature urges the Regents of the University of California to immediately take any and all actions necessary to ensure that the remains of Ishi be returned to the appropriate tribal representatives . . . so that a proper Indian burial ceremony may take place and closure may be brought to this indignity. (California State Assembly 1999)

In August 2000 Ishi's brain was reunited with his cremated remains and buried privately in an undisclosed location in the shadow of Mt. Lassen. His legacy, like his relationship in life with scholars and museum professionals, is complex. If Theodora Kroeber's translation and remembrance of Ishi's philosophy is accurate, he cautioned the living not to think too often of the dead, that to do so was healthy only occasionally. If true, many affiliated with the university have ignored his warning – some to promote a romantic, celebrity caricature of him; others to iconify him for the purposes of activism. Still others have invented Ishi as a New Age deity whom they revere and worship. Finally, some continue to exploit him by defying the institution in his name in order to remedy or promote their own professional standing.

Ishi's real legacy, ultimately, can best be remembered as that of a human being whose selective disclosure of knowledge and experience constituted active resistance; a man who was intellectually curious and generous of spirit in reciprocal relationships. He was an imaginative survivor of one of the most lethal chapters in American history, but never a victim. Instead, with only a 600-word vocabulary, Ishi adapted early twentieth-century San Francisco society into a relative Yahi construct with dignity, poise, and humor.

In recent years Ishi has also personalized the debate between research and human interests and challenged scientists to think and act beyond institutional boundaries. More than any advocate, activist, lawyer, scholar, or politician who has invoked his image in this debate, Ishi became a catalyst for accountability and integrity.

The memory, however, of this Yahi man whose name remains a mystery may best be served in the academy by a connection to place. Thanks to the decade-long efforts of Anishinaabe scholar Gerald Vizenor, Ishi has an architectural presence at the university. Nestled in the interior structures of Dwinelle Hall on the UC campus is Ishi Courtyard, a place for remembering Ishi, the first Native American to give his life in service to the University of California. In the spirit of Vizenor's performative piece "Ishi and the Wood Ducks," Ishi's presence in this place constitutes an act of trickster survivance (Vizenor 1995).

REFERENCES

Academic Senate. 1990. Proposed state law brings skeletal remains issue front and Center. *Notice* 14(8).

Associated Students of the University of California Academic Affairs Office. 1992. *Informational guide to the repatriation of human skeletal remains at the University of California.*

California State Assembly. 1999. Concurrent Resolution 32: The remains of Ishi. Introduced by Assemblyman Darrell Steinberg.

California State Assembly. 2001. A.B. 978: California Native American Graves Protection and Repatriation Act of 2001. Introduced by Assemblyman Darrell Steinberg.

Heimoff, Steve. 1989. Angle of repose. *East Bay Express,* Berkeley, July 12, 1989.

Kroeber, Theodora. 1961. *Ishi in two worlds.* Berkeley: University of California Press.

Miller, Christian T. 1990. Bill may mandate return of bones. *Daily Californian,* September, 1990.

National Park Service. 1999. National NAGPRA Review Committee minutes. Eighteenth Meeting, November 18–20, Salt Lake City UT.

Thornton, Russell. 1998. Who owns our past? The repatriation of Native American human remains and cultural objects. In *Studying Native America: Problems and prospects*. Ed. Russell Thornton. Madison: University of Wisconsin Press.

Vizenor, Gerald. Ishi and the wood ducks. In *Native American literature: a brief introduction and anthology*. New York: Harper Collins.

PART THREE

Ishi's World Revisited

Previous page. Ishi preparing fire drill, 1914.

Ishi with fire drill, 1914.

Introduction to Part Three

About Ishi's life from his birth (around 1860) until 1911 we have no certain first-hand or documentary evidence. Anyone, Indian or white, genuinely interested in Ishi soon realizes that the only possibility of learning significant truths about his first half-century of life depends upon reconstructions built up from the kind of unspectacular, painstaking scholarly analysis that Steven Shackley applies to Ishi's making of arrowpoints (Chapter 11). Shackley demonstrates that precise scientific study of apparently unimportant artifacts can lead to revealing inferences about the man and complexities in his cultural heritage. Artifacts he crafted show Ishi to have been a masterful flint knapper, and the character of his skill leads to intriguing inferences as to how and from whom he may have learned it. Meticulously systematic analyses of how projectile points were shaped by Ishi and other, unknown Northern California Indians enable Shackley to infer a fluidly troubled socio-historical background as Ishi's native heritage. That his knapping practices seem closer to those of some Wintu than to traditional Yahi techniques opens the way to speculations on the effects, in the decades immediately preceding Ishi's birth, of social disruptions among Northern California hunter-gatherer societies, disruptions created by intensifying historical and environmental stresses. The very rigor of analysis necessary for identification of stone technology practices leads a thoughtful scholar toward evaluations of the intricate historical changes that may help to account for the individuality of a gifted man's work, because, as Shackley observes, every anthropologist always confronts diverse evidences of the extraordinary adaptability of human beings. Thus Ishi – like most Indians who made arrowpoints – preferred to use manufactured glass when it became available through the intrusion of white culture, even though he went on making arrowpoints using techniques he had learned from native forebears. The transmission of these techniques, however, had itself undergone changes reflecting the effects of historical turmoil produced by shifting processes of social conflict and cooperation among tribal groups. The difficulties and rewards of scientifically studying such adaptive complexities Shackley dramatizes by observing that contemporary understanding of Ishi's knapping techniques has been obscured by his very fame as a projectile point maker. Because his work offers the *single* product of an identifiable aboriginal knapper, white archaeologists, teaching themselves arrowpoint making, have often imitated Ishi's idiosyncratic practices as described by observers and photographs taken of him at work.

Nowhere does human adaptability appear more vividly than in the records of linguistic discourse, the focus of essays by Victor Golla and Orin Starn. Starn's discussion (Chapter 12) of the presence of a few Spanish words in Ishi's language, noticed by the ethnographers and linguistics with whom he worked, has the special virtue of reminding us of the enormous importance of the Spanish-Mexican presence in California for many years before its conquest by the United States. John Rollin Ridge's 1854 novel *Joaquin Murietta* turns on the fact that the Spanish were mining gold long before the forty-niners arrived, and virtually all California Indian languages have adopted Spanish loanwords – another evidence of the adaptability Shackley dramatizes.

Victor Golla (Chapter 13), as a professional linguist, has long been interested both in Ishi's native language and the ways in which he both adopted and resisted English when he came to San Francisco. Golla's studies have made him aware that the recovery of an extinct language is a ferociously difficult process, requiring often exasperatingly meticulous analyses of evidence even more fragmentary than old arrowpoints. Like Shackley, Golla understands that what a conscientious scholar can accomplish today depends largely on what he has learned from his forebears in his discipline. To describe accurately how Ishi used his language one has to know exactly how it was recorded and described by earlier linguistic investigators. Study of Sapir's study of Ishi's language, in fact, led to Golla's receiving a National Science Foundation grant in 1986 to supervise the editing of stories Ishi had told to Sapir. As is illustrated in the next section of this volume, that project is now beginning to come to fruition. This work, however, requires even more time-consuming, painstaking scholarship than projectile point analysis. Yet Golla's unpretentious demonstration (among other matters) of how Ishi's "pidgin" English in fact reflects forms of his native Yahi/Yana tongue demonstrates how careful and informed scholarship opens up possibilities for understanding Ishi's mind and cultural heritage that seemed unattainable a few decades ago.

11

The Stone Tool Technology of Ishi and the Yana

M. STEVEN SHACKLEY

The recent "excitement" over the discovery of Ishi's preserved brain at the Smithsonian Institution, and the resultant response from some members of the Native American community, a few academics, and the media, has brought Ishi's story, yet again, into the mainstream (Bower 2000; Rockafellar and Starn 1999; Hinton 1999; Shea 2000). As this volume attests, no other Indian in the history of North America generates more commentary, much of it based solely on assumptions and statements of the obvious, than Ishi. But there is yet much in the empirical world that may actually provide some illumination for Ishi as an individual as well as our understanding of cultural process, identity, and change in the late prehistoric and early historic Yahi world.

This chapter is the result of a long-term project based on Ishi's stone technology curated in the Phoebe A. Hearst Museum of Anthropology at the University of California, Berkeley. The project suggests a number of new possibilities for Ishi's origin; the long-term relationship of the Yahi to surrounding, often hostile, prehistoric Native Californians, as well as the following Anglo population; and our understanding of the relationship between stylistic attributes in projectile points and cultural identity.

The use of stylistic attributes in prehistoric lithic assemblages for identifying ethnic affiliation and even individual style has been hotly debated in archaeology, particularly as it relates to projectile point form (Clark 1989; Close 1989; Flenniken 1985; Flenniken and Raymond 1986; Flenniken and Wilke 1989; Hoffman 1997; Shackley 1990, 1996b; Shott 1996, 1997; Thomas 1981, 1986; Whittaker 1987; Wiessner 1983, 1990). Typical of many, Clark (1989:32) is skeptical as to the possibility of ever identifying ethnic affiliation or particularly symbolic behavior from prehistoric lithic assemblages:

> In default of live informants or an exceptionally detailed historical record, I can-
> not understand how an archaeologist, removed by millennia from the subjects of
> interest, could generate hypothetical interpretations of symbolic behaviour that
> could be subjected to any conceivable kind of empirical test.

The data and inferences presented here, derived from the analysis of Ishi's projectile point technology, are as close as we can come to an "exceptionally detailed historical record" and a "live informant" as recommended by Clark (1989:32). Additionally, a parallel analysis of projectile points from two Late Prehistoric/Protohistoric sites in Yahi and Southern Yana territory (see map, Figure 11.1) in north central California (Kingsley Cave – 4TEH1; Payne's Cave – 4TEH193), as well as a historic ancestral Wintu (Nomlaki) site (4TEH58), are equally enlightening as to the differences in form and style employed by Ishi in various settings (Shackley 1996a).

In addition, the recent controversy over Ishi's brain and his cultural affiliation, and the presentation of historic morphological evidence of Ishi's possible non-Yana ancestry, raises important questions as to the actual genetic and cultural origin of Ishi as a Yahi, and the social dynamics present in the northern Sacramento Valley for over 1000 years (Johnson 1973, 1978, 1984, 1994; Rockafellar and Starn 1999; Shea 2000).

The consummate ability of Ishi as a stone toolmaker has become nearly legend in the literature (Kroeber 1961; Nelson 1916; Pope 1918; cf. Titmus 1985; Whittaker 1994). Although there is definite empirical support for these claims, there has been virtually no systematic examination of the artifacts produced by Ishi other than the early work directly with him by Nelson (1916) and Pope (1918), and these attempts are certainly not representative of our recent understanding of stone technology and cultural identity. With respect to projectile point style, the arrowpoints Ishi produced have never been analyzed with a consideration of the cultural milieu from which they were derived. This omission is unfortunate, because the style and attributes portrayed in the projectile points produced by Ishi are (theoretically) directly traceable to his group of origin. Furthermore, we have one hafted arrowpoint that was in all likelihood produced by Ishi before he became directly influenced by European American culture at the University of California, as well as the many projectile points produced by him after his arrival at the university in 1911.[1] Virtually nowhere else in the North American ethnological and archaeological record does this particular and peculiar circumstance exist.

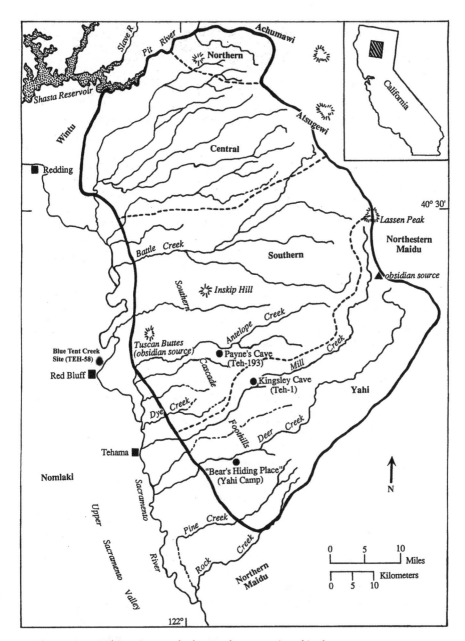

Fig. 11.1. Yana/Yahi territory and relevant places mentioned in the text.

A WORD ABOUT THE CONTEMPORARY CONTEXT

For the nation, Ishi's death meant that the last "free" Indian had died. Despite everything mainstream America had done to hasten that demise, there was a certain sadness when the inevitable finally happened. [Thomas 2000:90]

After the first version of this essay was completed, Shea's (2000) review of the controversy over the repatriation of Ishi's brain, which had been recently found at the Smithsonian Institution, and Rockafellar and Starn's (1999) commentary were published. Although Shea's examination (which I consider mainly balanced) of the issue and the academic polemic surrounding it is not directly germane here, it is worthy of some attention, particularly given the inference of Ishi's ambiguous cultural identity. I would refer the reader to these two papers and to Leanne Hinton's (1999) review. To summarize, Ishi's brain, thought by a number of Indian groups to have been removed during the autopsy before his cremation, but never found in either the museum or the San Francisco campus of the University of California, was found to be in the collection of the Smithsonian Institution. It had been transferred there by an agreement between Alfred Kroeber and Aleš Hrdlička after Ishi's death (Hinton 1999). The paper trail of this sad incident is detailed best in Hinton's commentary (1999; see also Bower 2000).

Disturbingly, the most vocal and critical anthropologists (and historians) in this entire debate have been those who do not work with Native Americans as colleagues or consultants, nor teach courses on Native American subjects. Leading statements in commentaries, such as "Ishi remains one of the most haunting chapters in American history" (Rockafellar and Starn 1999:413) – besides the obvious fact that Ishi was not the haunting subject here – seem to be generated mainly to draw attention to the authors rather than the story proper; they are symbolic of many of the more critical statements. Any attempts to offer new empirical data that may actually provide edification for both anthropological and Native interests are relegated to the uninteresting heap of minutiae (Shackley 1996a; Foster in Shea 2000:53). Virtually none of these critics has acknowledged that these early twentieth-century anthropologists, so vainly despised now, "were understandably protective" of Ishi in a Western society with many members who still wanted to exterminate all Indians (Hinton 1999:5). My research in the archives at Berkeley and elsewhere on Ishi's relationship with Kroeber, and particularly with the Waterman family, suggests that Ishi considered them his new family, despite problems of language (see Chapter 14 in this volume). The statement in Berkeley's Anthropology Department open letter, that Ishi had already "lost all that was dear to him," ignores his positive relationships to members of the department and museum and to other members of the community in which he lived (Hinton 1999:9; see also Shea 2000:52–53). As described in the introduction to Part I of this volume, when Charles Kelsey, a Bureau of Indian Affairs agent, offered Ishi his choice of where he wanted to live, Ishi emphatically stated his preference to live out his days among the anthropologists and die in his new home (Thomas 2000:87).

In the end, the Smithsonian's recommendation that Ishi's preserved brain should go to the Pit River and Redding Rancheria, where Yana descendants now reside, effectively ended the turmoil. Although I would disagree with Art Angle's statement that the brain belongs to "all the California Indians" (Hinton 1999:9), my research indicates that Ishi could be descended from any number of groups that were living in the upper Sacramento River Valley. So, in a way, Angle is correct, and his group could make a legitimate claim for the remains, although the Smithsonian's decision was the most rational, given the current political climate.

Some of the more critical in the group at Berkeley convinced Darrell Steinberg in the California Legislature to draft an Assembly Concurrent Resolution (ACR 35) to urge the Regents of the University of California to "immediately take any and all actions necessary to ensure that the remains of Ishi . . . be returned to the last surviving member of the Yahi Indians," further stating that "Ishi died of tuberculosis, a European disease against which he was almost defenseless." Not concerned with reality or recent epidemiological studies of the history of tuberculosis in the Americas, the resolution ignores the facts that Ishi's remains were placed in a private cemetery not controlled by the University of California and that several recent studies have discovered tuberculosis in *prehistoric* remains throughout the Americas (Buikstra 1981; Salo et al. 1994; Stead et al. 1995). This disregard for factual evidence is all too typical of recent posturing by anthropologists on the issue of Ishi's brain. Many of us find the recent reaction as embarrassing and vexing as Kroeber's behavior over eighty years ago. Unfortunately, the more adversarial and absurd press releases and articles have overshadowed the more balanced treatments like Hinton's (1999) or Shea's (2000), as well as Thomas's (2000) short summary in the context of repatriation in the United States. While Ishi lived at the museum, "he was protected from people trying to use him for commercial interests" (Hinton 1999:5). It is too bad that intellectuals today cannot afford Ishi the same courtesy given to him by those whom they so resoundingly criticize.

The decisions made by Kroeber and others concerning the disposition of Ishi's brain is certainly a disturbing chapter in the history of anthropology, and something that (we hope) could never happen today. It is time to move beyond the grandstanding and realize that where we are today is, in large part, a result of what we learned from our forebears in anthropology.

ISHI AND TECHNOLOGY

Certainly, Ishi has received the most detailed observation of any single Native American. This situation was partly an effect of circumstance, and partly an effect of the social climate of the early twentieth century (Heizer and Kroeber 1979; Kroeber 1961; Waterman 1918). The objects he produced are indeed nearly deified in some circles as manufactures of the last aboriginal Native American (John Whittaker, personal communication, June 2004). This categorization is perhaps unfortunate, because an examination of his technology in light of current advances in lithic technology has simply not occurred, possibly as a result of the rather romantic effect of this historical figure.

Ethnographic Observation of Ishi's Arrowpoint Production

From the text description [Holmes 1919:329] and the photograph, one gains an idea of Ishi's probable notching procedure. Ishi used the "side of tool" method of flake removal and tied a leather pad over his left thumb to protect it from the removed notching flake and from penetration by the notching tool at the time of detachment. He rested his hands on his legs to gain more control and stability and used his legs to apply additional pressure. [Titmus 1985:252]

Ishi's arrowpoint production trajectory was observed directly by both Nels Nelson (1916) and Saxton Pope (1913, 1918) and was indirectly discussed by Holmes (1919). Both direct studies were based on observations made over multiple episodes of production. Each observed similar methods used by Ishi, suggesting that these observations are probably quite accurate, at least by early twentieth-century anthropological standards, and that Ishi's methods were standardized. There is much more that we in the early twenty-first century wish they would have recorded. Evidently knapping was quite enjoyable to Ishi, as noted by Nelson (1916:398):

Among other things suggested to him, partly to satisfy the interest of the visiting public, was that of chipping arrowpoints, and probably nothing else that he undertook proved of equal interest and satisfaction to visitors as well as himself.

Generally, Ishi employed a biface production trajectory quite similar to that described for much of Native America (Crabtree 1973; Hoffman 1997; Holmes 1919; Kelly 1988; Schumacher 1877; Whittaker 1987, 1994). It must be noted here, however, that much of our original concept of North American stone tool making is derived from observations and oral history connected to the Ishi image. In my experience, many archaeologists, both in the field, flintknapping, and in print, refer to Ishi's stone tool making as "the first" or "original" or use him in an appeal to authority, as Titmus's quote above suggests. Many archaeologists

employ the same types of tools and body positions today as Ishi did, partly because of the physics and fracture mechanics required by the work but also because of a tradition of anthropological flintknapping that can be traced to Ishi.
This could certainly make an interesting and likely fruitful project on the social
psychology of archaeologists who are stone tool makers, but it is beyond the
scope of this chapter.

Most of the observations by Pope and Nelson were made while Ishi was
working with obsidian, although he also used bottle or window glass for the
large side-notched points, probably because the obsidian nodules available were
too small to derive appropriately sized flakes (Pope 1913,1918). As discussed below, there is an indication that the pressure technique used on the long glass
points was somewhat different than on the smaller obsidian points.

Both Nelson (1916) and Pope (1918) observed that Ishi reduced obsidian
cores by throwing the nodule against another stone and reducing the pieces
through indirect percussion using an antler punch. Ishi also employed direct
hard-hammer percussion on obsidian cobbles, as shown in Figure 11.2 (Pope
1913).[2] Nelson states that direct freehand percussion was used "especially if only
small flakes are wanted," whereas indirect percussion with an antler punch was
used when "a large spearpoint or knife-blade is ultimately desired" (1916:399).
This may simply be Nelson's opinion, because either method can ultimately be
used for the same end, and direct freehand is often more efficient for manufacturing large flakes for larger biface production (see Ahler 1989; Andrefsky 1998;
Whittaker 1994). It is possible, although conjectural, that Ishi used an antler billet for direct freehand work, but there is no evidence of this process in the literature, nor any billets present in the Hearst Museum collection. Indeed, the large
bag of obsidian debitage (waste fragments) curated at the Hearst Museum,
saved by someone from an unknown number of reduction episodes, appears to
represent mainly direct freehand percussion with a hard hammer (crushed and
destroyed platforms, large platforms when present, and relatively thick larger
flakes; see Ahler 1989). Nor are there any statements in the literature as to how
Ishi held the core mass during indirect percussion, but it was presumably *sous le
pied* (see Crabtree 1972:88).

According to Nelson and Pope, Ishi preferred to use untempered or de-tem-
pered iron pressure flakers and notching tools with rounded chisel-shaped
points, lenticular in cross-section. These tools are still in the collection at the
museum (Figure 11.3). There is some evidence that this type of flaking tool was
regularly employed by the Yahi during the Protohistoric period. In 1889 D. B.
Lyon of Red Bluff came upon a Yahi individual (possibly Ishi) in the bush along
Big Antelope Creek (Waterman 1918:60). He never actually saw the person in the
heavy chaparral, but the Yahi dropped a bundle and ran away after Lyon threw

Fig. 11.2. Ishi employing direct hard hammer percussion at Deer Creek in 1914. Photo by A. L. Kroeber. Courtesy of the Phoebe A. Hearst Museum of Anthropology and the Regents of the University of California.

a rock into the bushes where he had heard a sound. Suddenly, while Lyon was examining the bundle, arrows flew overhead, and he realized it would be only a short time before the archer had the distance and an arrow found its mark. Lyon escaped with the bundle. Within the bundle was a smaller cloth bag that contained a pressure knapping kit (see Waterman 1918:92). The kit contained pieces of glass and chinaware presumably for point production, a leather palm pad, and three iron pressure flakers in three sizes with chisel-shaped points that ap-

Fig. 11.3. Pressure knapping tools produced and used by Ishi at the museum. Top two are edging flakers; third from top is a notching tool; bottom is an antler punch. Photo by G. Prince.

pear nearly identical to those produced by Ishi and now in the Hearst Museum collection (see Figure 11.3). The location of the bundle appropriated by Lyon is unknown. Ishi's tools were made by inserting the iron rods in wood and wrapping the wooden handles with cordage for strength.[3] Importantly, Ishi, and presumably the Yana, did use both the long "Ishi stick" pressure flakers, as is commonly assumed in knapping circles, as well as smaller pressure flakers (Pope 1913; see also Holmes 1919).

There was at least one more instance of Ishi interacting with local Anglo settlers from the region. In November 1908 a party of engineers surveying a pipeline along Deer Creek came upon a small band of Yahi (four individuals) living at a site called *Wowunupo'mutetná* (Bear's Hiding Place; Waterman 1918). Ishi fired arrows at the engineers, frightening them away. They returned later and found the camp deserted except for one old woman, probably Ishi's mother. The engineers stole most of the transportable articles, including a quiver with arrows. This loss of important items of technology was likely fatal for the remnant band of Yahi, given that winter was approaching and there was no time to

Fig 11.4. Obsidian production failures (*top row*) and probable preforms (*bottom row*). Photo by G. Prince.

retool. Fortunately for an understanding of Yahi material culture, some of the articles, including the arrows, are now in the Hearst Museum collection. The arrows were most probably made by Ishi, because it appears he was the only Yahi knapper left by that time. One of the arrows exhibits a glass corner-notched point. This projectile point is one of the few (perhaps only) projectile points attributable to a specific known aboriginal knapper.

As noted earlier, Nelson's study suggests that Ishi did not use an antler billet in early stages of biface production. He apparently used the larger pressure tools to edge and thin the bifaces. Some of the preforms in the museum, however, could have been reduced by billet flaking early in the production trajectory (see Figure 11.4). The photographs taken at Deer Creek indicate the "palm holding with soft pad" method of biface pressure reduction as described in Plew and Woods (1985:216–217; Figures 11.5 and 11.6). Note in Figure 11.6 that the chisel end of the tool was rotated nearly perpendicular to the platform margin on the preform, concentrating pressure on a very small surface area. There is no evidence on the preforms at the Hearst Museum or in the literature that Ishi

Fig. 11.5. Ishi pressure-reducing an obsidian biface preform at Deer Creek. Photo by A. L. Kroeber. Courtesy of the Phoebe A. Hearst Museum of Anthropology and the Regents of the University of California.

abraded the margins during reduction, even when using obsidian and glass, but to produce the oblique parallel effect he was so proficient at doing, he must have prepared the marginal platforms (see also Whittaker 1994:140).

Ishi's notching tool was a smaller version of the edging and retouching pressure flaking tools (see Figure 11.3). The notching technique appears to be the "end of tool" method described by Titmus (1985:252–253). Ishi would wrap the left thumb in soft leather and punch the notch in perpendicular to the margin of the biface or from the corner while holding the object between the left thumb and index finger (Figure 11.7; Nelson 1916:402). Ishi's staged position shown in Figure 11.7 would make it difficult to remove a notching flake, but the general position is correct (cf. Titmus 1985:252).

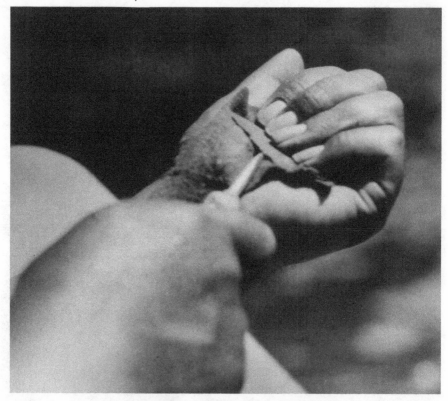

Fig. 11.6. Close-up of biface-thinning technique. Note right-handedness and that the chisel-shaped tool end is perpendicular to the biface margin. Photo by A. L. Kroeber. Courtesy of the Phoebe A. Hearst Museum of Anthropology and the Regents of the University of California.

ANALYSIS OF ISHI, YAHI/YANA, AND WINTU/NOMLAKI PROJECTILE POINTS

Unlike most current studies in lithic technology, the historic or ethnographic portion of this analysis is not focused on specific regional or technological problems per se. In this study, only a single knapper is involved; a knapper who was technically influenced by the remnants of Yahi and possibly surrounding Native society and the beginnings of early twentieth-century technology.

We have spent much energy on the study of modern knappers as a portal to the understanding of prehistoric lithic technology. Some are concerned, however, that modern stone tool replications do not necessarily mirror the myriad decisions and exigencies of prehistoric knappers (Thomas 1986; Young and Bonnichsen 1984). Others base much of their interpretation of prehistoric flaked lithic assemblages on experimental design (Flenniken 1985; Flenniken

Fig. 11.7. Notching an obsidian preform using the "side of tool" method. Photo by N. C. Nelson. Photo courtesy of the American Museum of Natural History.

and Raymond 1986; Flenniken and Wilke 1989; Plew and Woods 1985; Titmus and Woods 1986; Whittaker 1994). Unfortunately, this study cannot resolve that issue to either side's satisfaction, although some of what Ishi produced at the museum appears to be a reflection of cultural influences outside the Yahi group (see Clark 1989; Sackett 1982,1990; Wiessner 1983).

Analytic Methods and Source Provenance of Artifact Raw Material

The collection of Ishi's material at the Hearst Museum includes portions of all stages in the production trajectory, from one refit core to all classes of debitage, point preforms, and finished projectile points. Unfortunately, the obsidian debitage was thrown into one large bag with no reference to the number of production episodes it contained. However, all stages of production seem to be present, and a number of obsidian sources are present in the material (see Origer 1989).

Tom Jackson analyzed by x-ray fluorescence a grab sample of obsidian debitage produced by Ishi during his stay at the museum, some of which are late-stage biface thinning flakes (in Origer 1989). The obsidian was procured from five sources and seven geochemical groups including Napa (2 groups), Mt. Konocti (2 groups), Medicine Lake Highlands (Grasshopper Flat/Lost Iron Wells/Red Switchback group), Borax Lake, and Tuscan (Origer 1989:75; see also Hamusek-McGann 1993; Hughes 1983; Jackson 1986). All these sources are in northern California, and the pieces were apparently procured by Ishi during trips around the region or given to him as gifts (see Kroeber 1961). The Tuscan source was within Southern Yana territory (see Figure 11.1) and was probably used by the Late Prehistoric Yahi knappers, perhaps even Ishi (Hamusek-McGann 1993). An x-ray fluorescence analysis of seventeen of Ishi's projectile points indicated that three of these sources are reflected in the assemblage: Mt. Konocti (12 percent), Napa Glass Mountain (41 percent), and Medicine Lake Highlands (47 percent). See Shackley (1995) and Davis et al. (1998) for a discussion of energy-dispersive x-ray fluorescence spectrometric applications in archaeology and in this analysis.

The projectile points produced by Ishi at the museum, the points from the upper levels of Kingsley and Payne's caves (4TEH1 and 4TEH193), a sample of points from the historic-period Wintu/Nomlaki Blue Tent Creek site near Red Bluff (4TEH58), and the hafted point on the one arrow likely made by Ishi in 1908 in Yahi country were all analyzed using the same attributes. These attributes loosely follow Thomas's (1981) scheme, adapted to the dominance of shouldered and corner-notched points of the region, and incorporating technological attributes. Technological attributes include descriptive projectile point types (see Table 11.1), bifacial flake pattern, presence of obvious rejuvenation,

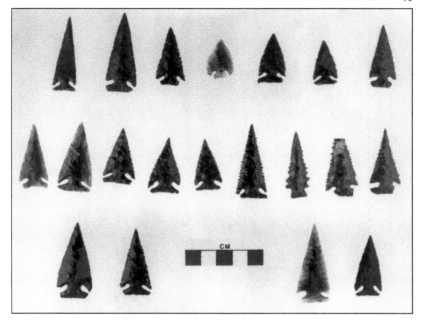

Fig. 11.8. Obsidian corner-notched, expanding-stemmed point styles produced by Ishi at the museum. Photo by G. Prince.

and raw material. Metric attributes included maximum length, width, thickness, and weight, basal indentation ratio, notch opening index, basal width/maximum width ratio, proximal shoulder angle (PSA), and distal shoulder angle (DSA). Each specimen was examined under a 10× magnifier lamp and weighed on a digital scale. The data were entered into Excel for Windows and translated into SPSS 8.0 for statistical manipulation.

Ishi's Projectile Points
Some of Ishi's projectile points produced at the museum have been illustrated in a number of places (see Kroeber 1961; Pope 1918). Many of the points produced were given away at various demonstrations for the public (Kroeber 1961). The specimens remaining in the museum are certainly illuminating.

Two general projectile point forms were produced by Ishi while at the museum: triangular corner-notched, with an expanding stem and straight base, and triangular side-notched, concave based. Figure 11.8 exhibits the range of variation of the corner-notched forms. Most of these obsidian points exhibit straight margins, although some are convex and some were serrated. The specimen third from the right in the second row is a rather different form, possibly a copy of something observed in the museum. Note the regularity of the notch

Table 11.1. Cross-Tabulation of Projectile Point Type and Origin/Site

POINT TYPE		ORIGIN/SITE					TOTAL
		Ishi>1911	TEH-193	TEH-1	Ishi-1908	TEH-58	
Desert Side-notched	Count	42	2	3		2	49
	% within PTYPE	85.7%	4.1%	6.1%		4.1%	100.0%
	% within ORIGIN	56.8%	11.1%	18.8%		50.0%	43.4%
	% of Total	37.2%	1.8%	2.7%		1.8%	43.4%
Desert Side-notched, serrated	Count	2	1	3		2	8
	% within PTYPE	25.0%	12.5%	37.5%		25.0%	100.0%
	% within ORIGIN	2.7%	5.6%	18.8%		50.0%	7.1%
	% of Total	1.8%	0.9%	2.7%		1.8%	7.1%
Corner-notched, expanding-stem	Count	16			1		17
	% within PTYPE	94.1%			5.9%		100.0%
	% within ORIGIN	21.6%			100.0%		15.0%
	% of Total	14.2%			0.9%		15.0%
Corner-notched, expanding-stem, serrated	Count	4	1				5
	% within PTYPE	80.0%	20.0%				100.0%
	% within ORIGIN	5.4%	5.6%				4.4%
	% of Total	3.5%	0.9%				4.4%

POINT TYPE		ORIGIN/SITE					TOTAL
		Ishi>1911	TEH-193	TEH-1	Ishi-1908	TEH-58	
Cottonwood, concave base	Count	10					10
	% within PTYPE	100.0%					100.0%
	% within ORIGIN	13.5%					8.8%
	% of Total	8.8%					8.8%
Basal-notched, contracting-stem	Count		10	8			18
	% within PTYPE		55.6%	44.4%			100.0%
	% within ORIGIN		55.6%	50.0%			15.9%
	% of Total		8.8%	7.1%			15.9%
Basal-notched, contracting-stemmed, serrated	Count		4	2			6
	% within PTYPE		66.7%	33.3%			100.0%
	% within ORIGIN		22.2%	12.5%			5.3%
	% of Total		3.5%	1.8%			5.3%
TOTAL	Count	74	18	16	1	4	113
	% within PTYPE	65.5%	15.9%	14.2%	0.9%	3.5%	100.0%
	% within ORIGIN	100.0%	100.0%	100.0%	100.0%	100.0%	100.0%
	% of Total	65.5%	15.9%	14.2%	0.9%	3.5%	100.0%

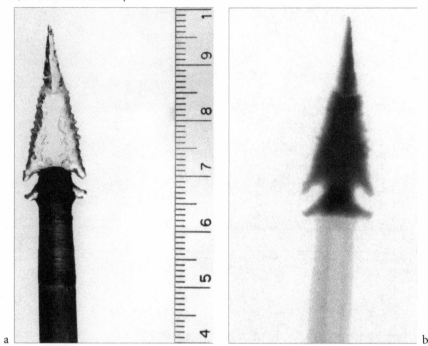

Fig. 11.9a. Hafted glass projectile point produced by Ishi in 1908 or earlier. Photo by G. Prince. Note probable recent tip repair and Ishi's sinew wrapping. Fig. 11.9b. X-ray of point. Note half-element configuration: corner-notched, expanding-stem.

angles (i.e., distal and proximal shoulder angles) in the corner-notched specimens. There is some indication that this was the style most familiar to Ishi when he came to the museum.

As discussed earlier, some of Ishi's arrows stolen in 1908 from the Yahi encampment on Deer Creek found their way to the museum. One of these arrows exhibits a clear glass projectile point (Figure 11.9a). The tip of this point is broken and was apparently mended in the museum. It is not clear whether this was mended with a new piece of glass later or was the original tip, because the marginal angle is different and there is a lack of serrations on the mended portion. This issue is not relevant here, however; the haft element is of interest. The point itself is only marginally retouched; no flake scars even reach the midline. The general shape, however, is quite similar to those in Figure 11.8, produced by Ishi three to seven years later (the precise chronology of the specimens produced in the museum is impossible to determine). An x-ray of the tip of the arrow indicates a notch angle very similar to those in Figure 11.8 (Figure 11.9b). Interestingly, the notches in the glass 1908 specimen appear to have been produced with a larger tipped notching tool rather than the smaller notching tool used at the museum and present in the kit recovered by Lyon in 1889. Unfortunately, only this one "aboriginal" example of Ishi's projectile points is available. It is possible that he produced other styles before 1911, but this we will never know. The corner-notched, expanding-stem points with straight bases appear to have been a favored style of Ishi when using obsidian as a raw material.

The other general projectile point form produced by Ishi was the side-notched, concave-based point that appears to be a variant of the Desert Side-notched form, called the "Redding subtype" (see Baumhoff 1957; Baumhoff and Byrne 1959; Lanning 1963; Thomas 1981). Within this group there appear to be two more specific styles. The first group, produced from obsidian, exhibits the general range of variability of the Desert Side-notched series in the Great Basin and much of California (mean weight = 2.99g $\pm$ 0.98, basal width/max width ratio = 1.00 $\pm$ 0; Figure 11.10a). Note that some of the notches are "keyhole" notches, an effect of the notching technique discussed above, and that both straight-angled notches and more acute-angled notches occur.

Ishi also produced side-notched points from bottle and window glass (Figures 11.10b and 11.11a). These points are surely the most exquisite and eccentric and obviously reflect a style definitely "Ishi." These points were made from clear, amber, and cobalt blue bottle glass and from large pieces of window glass. Although the points exhibit the general nominal attributes of Desert Side-notched points, they are most remarkable for their symmetry and length, some reaching over 11 cm in length. Also remarkable is the number of long points exhibiting oblique parallel flaking. The oblique direction appears to be up and to the left (on the top of the biface), an indication of a right-handed knapper.

The smaller obsidian specimens all exhibit random flake patterns, but many of the large glass specimens exhibit nearly perfectly symmetrical oblique parallel flake scars on both surfaces. These longer points in the collection are likely some of Ishi's attempts to produce more fanciful styles for the public. Other than length, however, the attributes are essentially the same as the shorter obsidian points, and both "classes" would be classified as Desert Side-notched forms.

Ishi's ability to create extremely symmetrical points is quite notable. All points in the museum exhibit a mean thickness of 4.69 mm with a standard deviation of 0.93 mm. The glass points are somewhat more variable, with a mean thickness of 4.86 mm and a standard deviation of 1.69 mm. These points, however, are considerably longer than the obsidian specimens.

A few very late-stage glass preforms remain in the Hearst collection. Figure 11.11b exhibits clear and cobalt blue glass late-stage preforms that apparently lack only notches. The inference that these are late-stage preforms rather than finished specimens seems valid given the presence of early-stage notches that are

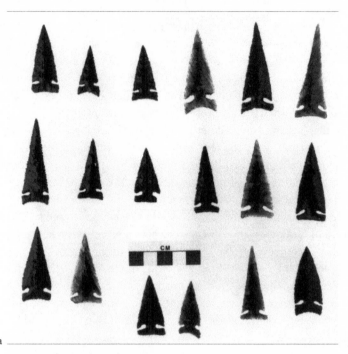

Fig. 11.10. Obsidian and glass side-notched points produced by Ishi at the museum. Photos by G. Prince. (a) Obsidian points. (b) Glass points.

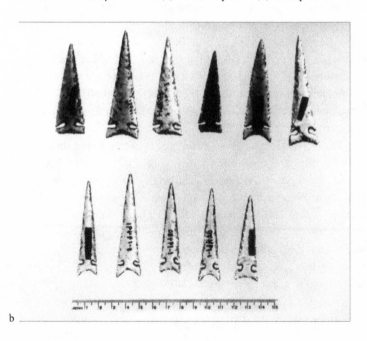

removed from the damaged specimen shown in Figure 11.11a, third from right, bottom row, and the lack of Cottonwood Triangular type unnotched forms in this part of prehistoric California, although they certainly could be the result of experimentation by Ishi. Apparently, this specimen was rejected due to the damage. No "finished" cobalt blue specimens remain in the Hearst collection. It is, of course, possible that these were considered finished by Ishi. Many exhibit the same fine oblique parallel flaking present on the notched specimens. Indeed, these points are more regular in thickness (mean = 4.33 mm ± 1.21), although there may have been other idiosyncratic variables that related to finished quality.

While Ishi can surely be considered a master knapper, most of the rather exotic (long) point forms appear to have been a product of influence while living at the museum. Most likely he was stimulated to produce these forms by the public that visited the museum and watched him produce points (see Kroeber 1961; Nelson 1916). It may not be coincidental that he produced more "traditional" styles from obsidian rather than glass. But how truly "traditionally Yahi" was the style of these obsidian points produced by Ishi at the museum, and even more importantly, how are these and the glass point made in 1908 representative of traditional Yahi and Yana styles?

Late Prehistoric and Protohistoric Yana Projectile Point Styles

Until recently, the investigation of prehistoric sites in the Southern Yana and Yahi region has been sporadic and not necessarily problem oriented (Baumhoff 1955, 1957; Greenway 1982; Hull et al. 1991; Johnson 1973, 1978). Baumhoff excavated two important sites in Southern Yana and Yahi territory while working for the University of California Archaeological Survey at Berkeley, and the excavated material is currently curated at the Hearst Museum (Baumhoff 1955, 1957). The results of these excavations, at Kingsley Cave (4TEH1) and Payne's Cave (4TEH193), were both published in *Archaeological Survey Reports* of the University of California, and although a detailed synopsis of these reports will not be given here, a few aspects of the excavations are relevant to the problem at hand.

The upper portions of these two sites should represent very late prehistoric if not protohistoric occupations. Both sites reveal flaked glass, even glass arrowpoints, in the upper levels. The protohistoric projectile point styles from these two sites in Southern Yana and Yahi territory should represent the styles familiar to Ishi if not actually produced by him. They do not, however.

Kingsley Cave is a rock shelter located approximately 30 km east of Red Bluff, California, on the southwestern slopes of the Cascade Mountains, along a tributary of Mill Creek (see Figure 11.1). The site was known to Ishi as *t'ena* (Baumhoff 1955:53) and is within ethnohistoric Yahi territory (Johnson 1978; Water-

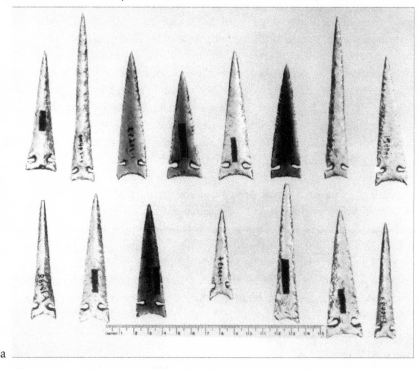

a

Fig. 11.11. Large glass points produced by Ishi at the museum. Photos by G. Prince. (a) Side-notched points. Note refined "keyhole" notches. (b) Clear and cobalt blue glass points, possibly preforms.

man 1918). Approximately one-half of the site was excavated during two field seasons. The rock shelter is considered by some to be the resting place of a number of Yahi who were massacred in this area in 1871, but the material recovered in the excavations cannot definitely be tied to this incident based on archaeological evidence alone (see Baumhoff 1955:42; J. Johnson, personal communication, 1990). According to Baumhoff, the deposit varies from about 10 cm near the rear of the shelter to nearly two meters deep near the mouth. The deposit proper is disturbed, partially due to bioturbation and partially due to the prehistoric excavation of pits for various purposes (Baumhoff 1955:60). Bottle glass and possible flaked glass material exists in the deposit; my inspection indicates glass material present down nearly one meter, although the vast majority is present in only the first 20 to 30 cm. For this study, only obsidian and glass projectile points were examined from the upper 50 cm of the deposit from both sites.

Figure 11.12a shows eighteen of the points selected from Kingsley Cave. There appear to be three general forms here. The basal-notched, contracting- and straight-stemmed points seem very common in the upper levels of the cave.

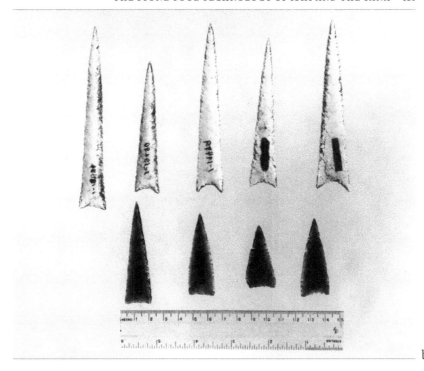

b

These are considered locally to be variants of the Gunther series (Greenway 1982; Hull et al. 1991; Nilsson 1991). The side-notched and corner-notched deeply serrated points also appear to be common, colloquially called "Mill Creek points," whereas the rather "typical" Desert Side-notched point is rare. The Desert Side-notched shown in Figure 11.12a, bottom row center, actually is made from a brown jasper, a very rare raw material in this site, and would be considered a "general subtype" by Baumhoff and Byrne (1959); it may be a point from another region somehow making its way into this context. Note the absence of the corner-notched, expanding-stemmed points made by Ishi.

Payne's Cave is located in an outcropping of rock above Antelope Creek in ethnohistoric Southern Yana territory not far from the northern border of Yahi territory (Figure 11.1). This shelter is considerably smaller than Kingsley Cave, and the deposit was almost entirely excavated (Baumhoff 1957). The deposit reached depths of nearly 3.5 m, but most areas it was less than one meter. The upper 10 cm were dry, and the lower deposit was quite damp. As at Kingsley Cave, obsidian dominated the projectile point assemblage. At Payne's Cave,

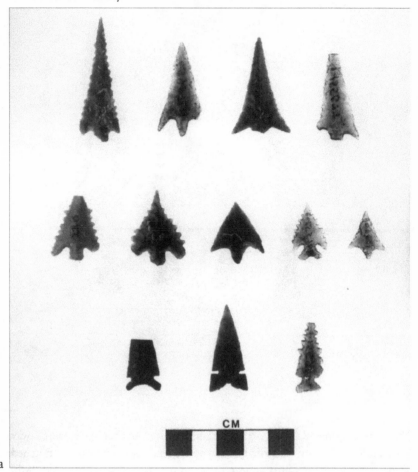

a

Fig. 11.12. Samples of Late Prehistoric/Protohistoric projectile points recovered from (a) Kingsley Cave (4TEH1) and (b) Payne's Cave (4TEH193). Photos by G. Prince.

however, two bottle glass projectile points were recovered (Figure 11.12b, bottom row, second and third from left).

Generally, the point forms recovered from the Late Prehistoric and Protohistoric contexts at Payne's Cave are not significantly different from the Kingsley Cave material. The assemblages are dominated by contracting-stem points, although side-notched points are somewhat more common in the upper levels at Payne's Cave (see Table 11.1). These side-notched points are not what most researchers consider to be "Desert Side-notched" points. As evident in Figures 11.12a and 11.12b, these points are generally deeply serrated, with a dominance of straight bases, and quite small; they are locally called "Mill Creek points." Some consider this small side-notched point to be rather typical of the Yahi and

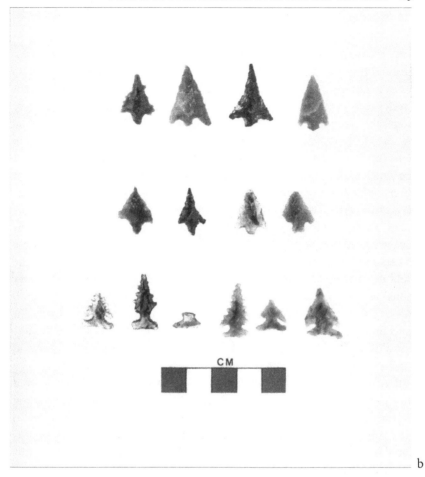

b

southern Yana, and the production of these points from bottle glass lends some credence to this notion (J. Johnson, personal communication, 1990; see also Johnson 1978). The more "classic" Desert Side-notched was, at least, known to these groups, as indicated by its presence in the upper levels at Kingsley Cave (Figure 11.12a, bottom row, two left specimens). The "typical" Yahi-Yana side-notched points could certainly be variants of the Desert Side-notched points, although recent excavations in Late Prehistoric/Protohistoric sites in Central and Northern Yana territory recovered "typical" Desert Side-notched points and not "Mill Creek" points (Hull et al. 1991; Nilsson 1991). This recent work seems to further indicate that the Gunther series and the Mill Creek styles are rather typical of the Yahi, particularly the Mill Creek forms.

Wintu/Nomlaki Projectile Point Styles:
The Blue Tent Creek Site (4TEH58)

After the initial discovery that point forms differ between the ancestral Yana sites and those produced by Ishi at the museum, another site nearby, protohistorically occupied by the Wintu or Nomlaki, was investigated. The Blue Tent Creek site located just across and somewhat north along the Sacramento River from Yahi territory near Red Bluff, was excavated by A. E. Treganza as part of the National Park Service–funded salvage of sites to be inundated by the Redbank Reservoir (Treganza 1954; see Figure 11.1). The excavated material is curated at the Hearst Museum. The site stretched at least 400 meters along the Sacramento River at Blue Tent Creek and included habitation areas as well as a defined cemetery; some of the site has been destroyed by the construction of Interstate Highway 5. Rapid fluvial deposition from the river created a deep context reaching over 2.4 meters, even though the presence of glass beads and other historic material indicated an occupation between C.E. 1800 and 1850, just before the Gold Rush and the removal of upper Sacramento River Indian groups to regional reservations. Spanish influence in the upper Sacramento River region was very slight; most of the impact came during the Gold Rush and subsequent ranching activities (Johnson 1978). Most importantly here, this places this ancestral Wintu/Nomlaki site contemporaneous with the two rock shelter sites in Yana territory to the east, and within the range of the birth date of Ishi.

Treganza's (1954) report illustrates a sample of projectile points recovered from the historic period contexts. His Plate 2 illustrates two general point types: Gunther Barbed and both large and small Desert Side-notched. Indeed, two of the figured Desert Side-notched points are seemingly identical to those produced by Ishi at the museum (Treganza 1954:Plate 2; Figure 11.13, top row). Additionally, Baumhoff and Byrne used this assemblage as a "type site" in their constructed typology of the Desert Side-notched, in this case their "Desert-Side notched, Redding sub-type" characterized by the keyhole notches (their "comma shaped") and "bell shaped" bases (Baumhoff and Byrne 1959:38). Treganza's observation of the projectile points is telling (Treganza 1954:6):

> In refined pressure techniques involving light ribbon-flaking [oblique parallel], narrow basal notching, and near perfect symmetry, it would be difficult to surpass the better made specimens from this site. There is represented here real technological achievement in pressure control, a feature frequently exhibited in the Late Horizon sites of central California

As shown in Figure 11.13, these specimens exhibit the same highly refined execution and attributes of those points produced by Ishi at the museum, including the notch angles, keyhole notches, and oblique parallel flaking. An image of

CA-TEH-58

CM

ISHI >1911

Fig. 11.13. Five of the obsidian Wintu/Nomlaki points from 4TEH58 (*upper row*) and five of Ishi's points (*lower row*). All of Ishi's points are obsidian except second from right, which is an amber bottle glass.

both the Blue Tent Creek site side-notched points and a sample of Ishi's side-notched points certainly indicates their similarity (Figure 11.13). Parenthetically, Figure 4 in LaPena's (1978) chapter on the Wintu in the California volume of the *Handbook of North American Indians* illustrates two arrows "collected in 1885" (LaPena 1978:330). One of the arrows has a hafted stone point. The one notch exposed enough to discern is certainly a keyhole notch form, and the style would be classified as a Redding subtype of the Desert Side-notched in the

Baumhoff and Byrne (1959) classification. The "Redding subtype" certainly seems to be associated with the Wintu/Nomlaki in the historic period. Additionally, the arrow figured exhibits the same parallel ring markings below the fletching as the arrows produced by Ishi in the museum.

Multivariate Statistical Analysis of Ishi and Yana Projectile Points
Based on observable attributes alone, it appears that the projectile points produced by Ishi differed from those produced by his likely direct ancestors (Yahi) but were nearly identical to those produced at at least one site by historic period Wintu/Nomlaki.

Exploratory multivariate analysis is one method that can be used to verify observable attributes (Baxter 1994, 1999; Johnson and Wichern 1982). Often used to investigate structure in the data, it can also be useful in detecting "outliers": those cases that do not fit within the multivariate groups (Baxter 1999; Shott 1997). For this data set, 113 specimens from the four groups plus the one point made in 1908 were subjected to a discriminant analysis using Mahalanobis distance as the grouping method with SPSS 8.0 (five cases were rejected from the analysis for missing cases). All the nominal and metric variables discussed above were used in the analysis except length and weight, because many of Ishi's glass points are of considerably greater size than the archaeological examples, creating more potential multivariate distance based on these two variables. These variables included point type, flake pattern, thickness, basal indentation ratio, basal width/maximum width ratio, proximal shoulder angle, and distal shoulder angle. Although the data are not perfectly multivariate normal, mainly due to variable group sample sizes, the analysis does exhibit exploratory potential (see Rose and Altschul 1988). Cross-validated (jackknifed) analyses yielded essentially the same results, indicating some multivariate normality (Table 11.2).

In an assessment of group structure, a plot of the first two canonical discriminant variables (97.2 percent of population variability) does indicate considerable group separation, particularly with the Ishi group produced after he arrived at the museum (Figure 11.14). Note especially, that the Payne's Cave (TEH-193) group is nearly completely contained by the Kingsley Cave (TEH-1) group. The Ishi group centroid is a considerable multivariate distance from the former two groups. There is an overlap between the Ishi point group and Kingsley Cave due to the small side-notch attributes shared by both groups. As is visually evident, the corner-notched points produced by Ishi at the museum, and apparently before coming to the museum, are most dissimilar to the Kingsley Cave and Payne's Cave material. Because of its lack of invasive flake removals, thinness, and possibly other variables, the "Ishi point" produced before he arrived at the

Table 11.2. Discriminant Classification Matrix for Projectile Point Data [a]

Classification results [b,c]

		PREDICTED GROUP MEMBERSHIP					TOTAL
	Origin	Ishi>1911	TEH-193	TEH-1	Ishi-1908	TEH-58	
Original	Ishi>1911	62	2	1	5	4	74
count	TEH-193	0	13	1	1	1	16
	TEH-1	0	10	0	2	3	15
	Ishi-1908	0	0	0	1	0	1
	TEH-58	0	0	0	1	3	4
Percent	Ishi>1911	83.8	2.7	1.4	6.8	5.4	100.0
	TEH-193	0.0	81.3	6.3	6.3	6.3	100.0
	TEH-1	0.0	66.7	0.0	13.3	20.0	100.0
	Ishi-1908	0.0	0.0	0.0	100.0	0.0	100.0
	TEH-58	0.0	0.0	0.0	25.0	75.0	100.0
Cross-	Ishi>1911	59	2	1	6	6	74
validated	TEH-193	1	9	4	1	1	16
Count	TEH-1	0	10	0	2	3	15
	Ishi-1908	0	0	0	0	1	1
	TEH-58	0	0	0	1	3	4
Percent	Ishi>1911	79.7	2.7	1.4	8.1	8.1	100.0
	TEH-193	6.3	56.3	25.0	6.3	6.3	100.0
	TEH-1	0.0	66.7	0.0	13.3	20.0	100.0
	Ishi-1908	0.0	0.0	0.0	0.0	100.0	100.0
	TEH-58	0.0	0.0	0.0	25.0	75.0	100.0

a. Cross validation is done only for those cases in the analysis. In cross validation, each case is classified by the functions derived from all cases other than that case.

b. 71.8% of original grouped cases correctly classified.

c. 64.5% of cross-validated grouped cases correctly classified. 97.2% of variability contained in the first 2 canonical variables. Box's M = 112.805, p= .00 for the seven variable solution (see Baxter 1994:199).

museum forms a separate group, although it is closest to the large Ishi group. What is most illuminating is the classificatory similarity between the historic Wintu/Nomlaki specimens from TEH-58 and the side-notched points Ishi made at the museum (Figure 11.14 and Table 11.2).

The classification matrix further illuminates the group separation and the similarity between the Wintu/Nomlaki specimens and Ishi's points (Table 11.2). Because the Wintu/Nomlaki group and Ishi's points are so similar and thus grouped together, there is only a 64.5 percent correct multivariate classification in the cross-validated solution. Six (8.1 percent) of Ishi's points were classified as Wintu/Nomlaki points in this analysis. Consequently, the first two canonical

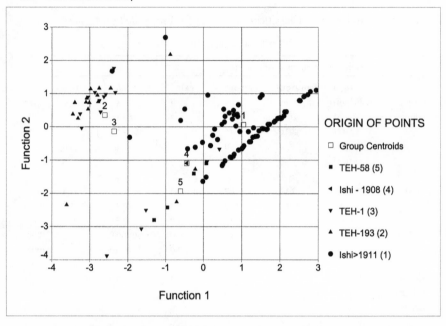

Fig. 11.14. Plot of the first two canonical discriminant variables for the projectile point data. Numbers after group name are group numbers on biplots.

functions indicate that the Ishi and the Wintu/Nomlaki group centroids strongly overlap (Figure 11.14).[4]

Both readily observable projectile point morphology and discriminant analysis indicates considerable difference in style between projectile points produced by Ishi both before and after arriving in the "Western world" and by his assumed direct Yahi and Yana ancestors, and considerable similarity between historic Wintu/Nomlaki points and what he produced after 1911. It may not be fair to compare what might be called "active" point assemblages in the archaeological case with the "inactive" points Ishi made at the museum. However, the Blue Tent Creek site points (certainly an active assemblage) and Ishi's side-notched points are so similar that this caveat may not be that valid.

Ishi and Hunter-Gatherer Cultural Identity

Thus *Ishi* [Kroeber 1961] contains both the reductive and romantic flaws inherent in its own literary and anthropological past and the painful historical awareness that characterizes more recent works about Native California. [Buckley 1996]

The data presented above indeed suggest that Ishi produced projectile points using styles surely not representative of the Late Prehistoric or Protohistoric

Yahi and Southern Yana. The samples from Kingsley Cave and Payne's Cave do, however, suggest that these particular groups did produce points that appear rather standardized. The small corner-to-side notched deeply serrated points (Mill Creek points), often produced from obsidian, seem rather endemic to the Yahi territory in very Late Prehistoric to historic contexts (Greenway 1982; Johnson 1978). This pattern is further supported by the lack of this style in Central and Northern Yana Late Prehistoric sites, where Gunther Barbed points are more common (Hull et al. 1991; Nilsson 1991). Ishi's production of what Baumhoff and Byrne (1959) would consider Desert Side-notched, Redding subtype, is most similar to those styles recovered from historic Wintu/Nomlaki contexts at the Blue Tent Creek site.

So, if this is all true, what possible explanation can be generated to account for what could be called Ishi's "deviant" technological behavior? Much of this remains inferential, because Ishi was bound to never speak of the dead; whoever taught him how to make stone tools could not be revealed. Ishi did state, however, that men would congregate "in a circle in a warm sunny place" to make projectile points, often away from the rest of the group (Pope 1918:117). Among the !Kung, hunting and exchange partners would often produce arrows together, and the styles would become somewhat standardized and readily recognizable to the partners (Wiessner 1983:262; see also Olive and Pigeot 1992; Roux et al. 1995). Similar behavior may have occurred among the Yahi and Wintu/Nomlaki. Producing arrows in a group may have served to standardize point and arrow styles such that a Yahi point style was readily distinguishable from a Wintu/Nomlaki style. Recall that only 25 percent of the contemporaneous point forms were similar at Kingsley Cave and Payne's Cave according to the multivariate analysis (Table 11.2). These stylistic attributes may have been recognizable to Yahi and non-Yahi alike. The most readily observable point differences among the !Kung San were between linguistic groups, and not between bands of the same language. A similar case may have occurred among the Yahi and their linguistically distinct neighbors such as the Maidu and Wintu/Nomlaki, or even, it appears, the Central and Northern Yana (i.e., Mill Creek points versus Gunther Barbed points).

Based on this assemblage and analysis, Ishi did not produce projectile point styles similar to the "Yahi style"; rather, many of his points are statistically and observationally identical to Wintu/Nomlaki points from the Blue Tent Creek site, as well as some collected from the Wintu in 1885. While it is tempting at this juncture to state emphatically that the most rational explanation is that Ishi was not really a Yahi, Sapir's linguistic analysis of Ishi's spoken language, as well as published references by other trained anthropologists, suggest that he considered himself a Yahi. As noted by Jacknis (Chapter 14, this volume), Ishi could speak a number of words and sing songs derived from surrounding groups. Kroeber stated, however, that Ishi "never met a soul of any of the three [surrounding] stocks." although he did note that the Wintun [Nomlaki] and Yahi were on "friendly terms" and that they "came up Deer Creek as far as Ya'muluk'u" (A. Kroeber 1925:345). Regional oral history, and Ishi's functional morphology, as well as the stone tool data presented here, however, suggest a number of alternative inferences for Ishi's origin.

Recently, Jerald Johnson (1994) reported a compilation of metric data of Ishi's stature and cranial/facial morphology taken by Pope, as his physician, suggesting that Ishi's physical self was much more similar to Maidu or Wintu speakers than Yana, speakers of a Hokan language. An often published photograph of Ishi, Alfred Kroeber, and Sam Batwi, a northern Yana (Figure 11.15; cropped to eliminate Batwi in Kroeber 1961:125) indicates the greater stature of Ishi. Even barefoot he was nearly the same height as Kroeber, and Batwi was noticeably much smaller and stouter. According to Johnson (1994), Ishi's craniofacial morphology is much more similar to Maidu or Wintu than Yana and presumably Yahi, based on Pope's data and this photograph. Although this kind of phenotypic assessment is hazardous, it does suggest a genetic background for Ishi that may be different from most Yana/Yahi.

Because of having to live in such a marginal environment, the Yahi were never on good terms with any surrounding groups for any length of time. Regional archaeological evidence suggests that speakers of Hokan languages, probably what could be called proto-Yana, lived in a much larger territory that included the upper Sacramento River Valley as well as the southern Cascade foothills until the "Penutian intrusion" at some point over 1000 years ago (Johnson 1973,1984,1994). These groups speaking Penutian languages were the ancestors of the Maidu and Wintu/Nomlaki who lived in the river valley at the time of Spanish and Anglo contact. Considerable violence is suggested at this time in the archaeological record, and the proto-Yana evidently did not move into a smaller, more marginal habitat willingly. Violence at the hands of outsiders was not new with the coming of Anglos after 1850; the Yahi had maintained long-term enmity relationships with the groups speaking Penutian languages who had forcibly removed them from bottom land and surrounded them for some time (Lambert 1994). Johnson (1978:363) noted that during the historic period the Yahi were "apparently on good terms" with the Wintu who hunted and camped on lower Deer Creek (see also Dixon 1905:206; DuBois 1935; Kroeber 1925:345), but were not on good terms with the Maidu. This circumstance could certainly have included the Wintu/Nomlaki group who lived at the nearby Blue Tent Creek site, and this amity relationship could explain the presence of the Wintu-type Desert Side-notched point at Kingsley Cave, noted

Fig. 11.15. Sam Batwi, a northern Yana, left; A. L. Kroeber, center; and Ishi, right. Photo taken in 1911. Courtesy of the Phoebe A. Hearst Museum of Anthropology and the Regents of the University of California.

earlier. Ishi noted that the Yahi had a name for the Red Bluff area where the Blue Tent Creek site is located: *Mimlosi,* evidently containing the Nomlaki term *mem* for water (Kroeber 1925:345). Johnson also noted that Maidu oral history indicates that the Yahi would raid their camps near the frontier and steal women and children (Johnson 1994; personal communication, 1994). This state of affairs could be one vector for the incorporation of Ishi as a young Maidu or Wintu into Yahi society. Alternatively, Ishi could have been a Wintu-Yahi half-blood who learned to produce projectile points from a Wintu father or father figure. Few male Yahi were left for Ishi to communicate with quite early in his life. While Ishi noted that "the men" would congregate in a warm place to flintknap, he never elucidated the ethnic affiliation of those knappers. Kroeber's statement that Ishi "never met a soul of any of the three stocks" in the area remains vexing, particularly since his notes in the Bancroft Library do not elaborate on the point (Kroeber 1925:345).

Edward Sapir, the linguist who closely worked with Ishi for so long, never mentioned that he spoke any language other than Yahi or English (1910, 1917, 1918, 1922, 1923; see also Waterman 1911). If Ishi was originally a Wintu/Nomlaki, then one would expect a trained linguist to detect this easily, although Sapir's time spent with Ishi was quite limited in 1915.

So, we are left with several possible inferences. While at the museum, and apparently before he came to live there, Ishi produced projectile points in forms that do not resemble ancestral Yahi forms but strongly resemble historic Wintu/Nomlaki forms, a group that was in an amity relationship with the Yahi in the historic period. Ishi apparently more closely resembles the phenotype of the groups speaking Penutian languages, such as the Nomlaki, who surrounded the Yahi, rather than other Yana.

My general inference here is that Ishi represents in his physical self, and in what he produced as a hunter-gatherer, the adaptation of a hunter-group under severe environmental and social stress. By the 1850s, the concept of a "Yahi" versus a "Maidu" or "Wintu" had changed radically from that of a thousand or even two hundred years earlier. Archaeological data suggest that, although territoriality and social boundary defense was typical five hundred or more years ago in the upper Sacramento Valley, by the early nineteenth century constant conflict and contact between the earlier Hokan-speaking groups and the Penutian "interlopers" had begun to dissolve the old enmity relationships, and intermarriage probably became more common. After the Anglo intrusion into the region and the systematic genocide perpetrated on the Yana as well as other groups in the region, the gene pool dwindled to the point where, although the old aboriginal enmities became unsupportable and intermarriage became necessary, the kidnapping of women and children apparently increased. Finally, these groups were herded onto reservations in 1853, approximately the time Ishi would have been born. While the Wintu (Nomlaki) and Maidu living in the Sacramento Valley were moved onto reservations, a remnant band of Yahi hid in the foothills. This severed any positive contact and support that the Yahi may have enjoyed with the Nomlaki.

What emerges from these historical details and archaeological inference is a picture of an amalgam culture by the early to mid-nineteenth century, where a Wintu/Nomlaki-Yahi boy learned to produce projectile points as a Wintu/Nomlaki but lived the life of a Yahi in the Lassen foothills until no more Yahi remained.

Ishi's lithic technology and entire persona, then, are a reflection of the adaptability of humans, and particularly the Yahi, to tremendous long-term cultural stress. In this light he offers us a picture of human adaptability well beyond what the early anthropologists could ever have imagined.

NOTES

Acknowledgments: This chapter is an expanded version of a paper presented at the 56th Annual Meeting of the Society for American Archaeology in New Orleans, Louisiana, April 1991 (Shackley 1991), and published in *American Anthropologist* (Shackley 2001). Copyright (2000) American Anthropological Association. Reproduced by permission of the American Anthropological Association from *American Anthropologist* 102(4). Not for sale or further reproduction. I thank the American Anthropological Association for permission to use its text and images. Thanks to Karl and Clifton Kroeber for inviting me to publish it in this volume. Figures 11.2, 11.5, 11.6, and 11.15 are courtesy of the Phoebe A. Hearst Museum of Anthropology, University of California, Berkeley, and the Regents of the University of California. I thank the American Museum of Natural History, and Barbara Conklin specifically, for the photo used in Figure 11.7. Betty Clark, Radiology Supervisor at Cowell Hospital, now the Tang Center, University of California, Berkeley, graciously and patiently x-rayed the hafted glass point. Gene Prince, Principal Museum Photographer at the Hearst Museum, photographed the glass and obsidian specimens and offered some helpful advice. Thanks to Jenna Weinkam for drafting Figure 11.1. Meg Conkey, Gene Prince, Bill Simmons, Mike Shott, Phil Wilke, Peter Mills, Kathleen Butler, Steven Lucas-Pfingst (Kwaymii/Kumeyaay), and Burton Benedict read various portions of drafts of this paper and offered valuable critique. Phil Wilke and John Whittaker, *American Anthropologist* reviewers, were especially helpful in clarifying some of my lithic technology prose and logic. Phil has been a particularly good sounding board on this issue. Ira Jacknis, my research colleague in the museum, pointed me toward some recent social anthropological references and shared his ideas on Ishi's "Yahiness." Thanks to

Tim White for references on the introduction of *Mycobacterium tuberculosis* to the Americas. I especially thank Jerald Johnson for extended discussions about Ishi, Yana archaeology, and perceptions of the media and public about these subjects. All of the above were helpful, and even though we did not all agree, I am grateful. The inferences and conclusions presented here are entirely my own.

1. As discussed later, Ishi produced projectile points for the public on Sundays at the museum; a very popular museum program. These projectile points are now in private and institutional hands throughout the world – the museum is frequently contacted by an heir whose parents or grandparents had an "Ishi point." Locally, the California State Museum in Sacramento, and the Department of Anthropology, California State University, Sacramento, have examples produced by Ishi. These are generally the side-notched variety discussed here, with a few exceptions. Because their provenance is not as secure as those in the Hearst Museum collection, they were examined but not included in the analysis. I doubt that their attributes, if measured and included in the analysis, would change my inferences.

2. In the photographs in the Hearst Museum archives taken by Kroeber and Nelson, Ishi is shown reducing a core with direct freehand percussion with the hammerstone in his left hand, but pressure flaking various bifaces with his right hand. If Ishi was ambidextrous in knapping, it is not noted anywhere. It is highly unusual for a knapper to employ ambidexterity in this manner, in my experience. It could be that Ishi was legitimately ambidextrous, or the photographer had Ishi stage it this way. The photo negatives are not reversed.

3. Phil Wilke noted in the review of the earlier paper that this is different from most known aboriginal flakers from California, Nevada, and Baja California, where iron rods were affixed to the outside of the stick and both wrapped. Phil feels that it would have been more difficult to drill longitudinally through wood without the benefit of the technology available to Ishi at the museum. Given the evidence for prehistoric drilling through stone as well as wood in the prehistoric northern California collections in the Hearst Museum, I doubt that it would be difficult to do. Without flakers from prehistoric or protohistoric Yana contexts or historic text on the subject, the problem remains unresolved.

4. Some may take issue with the inference that Ishi's projectile point forms were most similar to the TEH-58 (Wintu/Nomlaki) points rather than the other "Yana" sites, based on the classification matrix. While a 71.8 percent correct classification with over 97 percent of the variability contained in the first two canonical variables is certainly not perfect, how often do we approach a 72 percent correct classification in anthropology (see Shott 1997)? More importantly, the multivariate overlap between the points Ishi produced and the TEH-58, points is indisputable. I stand by the multivariate statistical confirmation of my observation of the morphological attributes.

REFERENCES

Abler, S. A. 1989. Mass analysis of flaking debris: studying the forest rather than the tree. In *Alternative approaches to lithic analysis*. Ed. D. O. Henry and G. H. Odell. Archaeological Papers of the American Anthropological Association. vol. 1, pp. 85–118.

Andrefsky, William, Jr. 1998. *Lithics: macroscopic approaches to analysis*. Cambridge: Cambridge University.

Baumhoff, M. A. 1955. Excavation of Site Teh-1 (Kingsley Cave). *Reports of the University of California Archaeological Survey* 30:40–73.

———. 1957. An introduction to Yana archaeology. *University of California Archaeological Survey Reports* 40.

Baumhoff, M. A., and J. S. Byrne. 1959. Desert side-notched points as a time marker in California. *University of California Archaeological Survey Reports* 48:32–65.

Baxter, M. J. 1994. *Exploratory multivariate analysis in archaeology*. Edinburgh: University of Edinburgh.

———. 1999. Detecting multivariate outliers in artefact compositional data. *Archaeometry* 41:321–338.

Bower, Bruce. 2000. Ishi's long road home: a California Indian's preserved brain accentuates his tragic, mysterious life. *Science News* 157:24–25.

Buckley, Thomas. 1996. "The little history of pitiful events": the epistemological and moral contexts of Kroeber's Californian ethnology. In *Volksgeist as method and ethic: essays on ethnography and the German anthropological tradition*. Ed. G. W. Stocking, Jr. History of Anthropology, vol. 8. Madison: The University of Wisconsin, pp.257–297.

Buikstra, J. E., ed. 1981. *Prehistoric tuberculosis in the Americas*. Evanston IL: Northwestern University Archaeological Program.

Burrill, Richard. 1990. Ishi: America's Last Stone Age Indian. Sacramento: The Anthro Company.

Clark, G. A. 1989. Romancing the stones: biases, style and lithics at La Riera. In *Alternative approaches to lithic analysis*. Ed. D. O. Henry and G. H. Odell. Archaeological Papers of the American Anthropological Association, vol. 1, pp. 27–50.

Close, A. E. 1989. Identifying style in stone artefacts: a case study from the Nile Valley. In *Alternative approaches to lithic analysis*. Ed. D. O. Henry and G. H. Odell. Archaeological Papers of the American Anthropological Association, vol. 1, pp. 3–26.

Conkey, M., and C. Hastorf, eds. 1990. *The uses of style in archaeology*. Cambridge: Cambridge University.

Crabtree, Don E. 1972. An introduction to flintworking. *Occasional Papers of the Idaho State University Museum* 28.

———. 1973. Experiments in replicating Hohokam points. *Tebiwa* 16(1): 10–45.

Davis, M. K., T. J. Jackson, M. S. Shackley, T. Teague, and J. H. Hampel. 1998. Factors affecting the energy-dispersive x-ray fluorescence (EDXRF) analysis of archaeological obsidian. In *Archaeological obsidian studies: method and theory.* Ed. M. S. Shackley. Advances in Archaeological and Museum Science. vol. 3. New York: Kluwer/Plenum, pp. 159–180.

Dixon, R. B. 1905. The Northern Maidu. *Bulletin of the American Museum of Natural History* 17:119–346.

Du Bois, C. 1935. Wintu ethnography. *University of California Publications in American Archaeology and Ethnology* 36(1).

Flenniken, J. Jeffrey. 1985. Stone tool reduction techniques as cultural markers. In *Stone tool analysis: essays in honor of Don E. Crabtree.* Ed. M. G. Plew, J. C. Woods, and M. G. Pavesic. Albuquerque: University of New Mexico, pp. 265–276.

Flenniken, J. J., and A. Raymond. 1986. Morphological projectile point typology: replication experiments and technological analysis. *American Antiquity* 51(3): 603–614.

Flenniken, J. J., and P. J. Wilke. 1989. Typology, technology, and chronology of Great Basin dart points. *American Anthropologist* 91(1): 149–158.

Greenway, Gregory B. 1982. Projectile point variability at Dead Man's Cave (CA-Teh-290) in the Southern Cascade Mountains of northeastern California. Master's thesis, Department of Anthropology, California State University, Sacramento.

Hamusek-McGann, Blossom. 1993. What X equals: the archaeological and geological distribution of "Source X" Tuscan obsidian in northern California. Unpublished Master's thesis, Department of Anthropology, California State University, Chico.

Heizer, Robert F., and Theodora Kroeber, eds. 1979. *Ishi the last Yahi: A documentary history.* Berkeley: University of California.

Hinton, Leanne. Ishi's brain. *News from Native California* 13(1): 4–9.

Hoffman, Charles M. 1997. Alliance formation and social interaction during the sedentary period: a stylistic analysis of Hohokam arrowpoints. Ph.D. dissertation, Arizona State University. Ann Arbor MI: University Microfilms.

Holmes, William H. 1919. Introductory: the lithic industries. In *Handbook of Aboriginal American Antiquities, Part 1.* Bureau of American Ethnology, Bulletin 60. Washington DC: Smithsonian Institution.

Hughes, Richard E. 1983. Exploring diachronic variability in obsidian procurement patterns in northeast California and south central Oregon: geochemical characterization of obsidian sources and projectile points by energy dispersive x-ray fluorescence. Ph.D. dissertation, Department of Anthropology, University of California, Davis.

Hull, K. L., E. Nilsson, and M. S. Kelly. 1991. Understanding Yana prehistory: application of multiple analyses. Paper presented at the 25th Annual Meeting of the Society for California Archaeology, Sacramento.

Jackson, T. L. 1986. Late Prehistoric obsidian exchange in central California. Ph.D. dissertation, Department of Anthropology, Stanford University.

Johnson, Jerald J. 1973. Archaeological investigations in northeastern California (1939–

1972). Ph.D. dissertation, Department of Anthropology, University of California, Davis.

———. 1978. Yana. In *California*. Ed. R. F. Heizer. Handbook of North American Indians, vol. 8. Washington DC: Smithsonian Institution, pp. 361–369.

———. 1984. The Dutch Gulch Lake, Cottonwood Creek Project and the prehistory of north central California. In *Intensive cultural resources survey, Dutch Gulch Lake*. Submitted by the Foundation of California State University, Sacramento, and Theodoratus Cultural Research, Fair Oaks CA, to the U.S. Army Corps of Engineers, Sacramento District, pp. 187–220.

———. 1994. Ishi's ancestors. Paper presented at the symposium Ishi: The Man and His Times Revisited. Oakland CA: Oakland Museum.

Johnson, R. A., and D. W. Wichern. 1982. *Applied multivariate statistical analysis*. Englewood Cliffs NJ: Prentice Hall.

Kelly, Robert L. 1988. The three sides of a biface. *American Antiquity* 53(4): 717–743.

Kroeber, A. L. 1925. *Handbook of the Indians of California*. Washington DC: Bureau of American Ethnology Bulletin 78.

Kroeber, Theodora. 1961. *Ishi in two worlds*. Berkeley: University of California.

Lambert, Patricia M. 1994. War and peace on the western front: a study of violent conflict and its correlates. Ph.D. dissertation, Department of Anthropology, University of California, Santa Barbara.

Lanning, Edward P. 1963. Archaeology of the Rose Spring site, Iny-372. *University of California Publications in American Archaeology and Ethnology* 49(3): 237–336.

LaPena, Frank. 1978. Wintu. In *California*. Ed. R. F. Heizer. Handbook of North American Indians, vol. 8. Washington DC: Smithsonian Institution, pp. 324–340.

Nelson, Nels C. 1916. Flint working by Ishi. In *Holmes anniversary volume: anthropological essays presented to William Henry Holmes*. Ed. F. W. Hodge. Washington DC: Washington DC: J. W. Bryan, pp. 397–402.

Nilsson, Elena. 1991. Flaked stone artifacts. In K. L. Hull, E. Nilsson, and M. S. Kelley. *Archaeological Investigations at CA-Sha-1720, CA-Sha-1723, CA-Sha-1724, and CA-Sha-1752, California-Oregon Transmission Project, Shasta County, California*. Chico CA: Dames & Moore, Appendix A.

O'Connell, J. F., and C. M. Inoway. 1994. Surprise Valley projectile points and their chronological implications. *Journal of California and Great Basin Anthropology* 16:162–198.

Olive, Monique, and Nicole Pigeot. 1991. Les tailleurs de silex magdaleniens d'Etiolles: vers l'identification d'une organisation sociale complexe. In *La pierre préhistorique: actes du séminaire du laboratoire de recherche des Musées de France 13 et 14 decembre 1990*. Ed. M. Menu and P. Walter. Paris: Laboratoire de Recherche des Musées de France, pp. 173–185.

Origer, Thomas M. 1989. Hydration analysis of obsidian flakes produced by Ishi during the historic period. In *Current directions in California obsidian studies*. Ed. R. E.

Hughes. Contributions of the University of California Archaeological Research Facility, vol. 48, pp. 69–78.

Plew, M. G., and J. C. Woods. 1985. Observation of edge damage and technological effects on pressure-flaked stone tools. In *Stone tools analysis: essays in honor of Don E. Crabtree.* Ed. M. G. Plew, J. C. Woods, and M. G. Pavesic. Albuquerque: University of New Mexico, pp. 211–228.

Pope, Saxton T. 1913. Making Indian arrow heads. *Forest and Stream,* December 20, 1913.

———. 1918. Yahi archery. *University of California Publications in American Archaeology and Ethnology* 13:103–152.

Rockafellar, Nancy, and Orin Starn. 1999. Ishi's brain. *Current Anthropology* 40:413–415.

Rose, Martin R., and Jeffrey H. Altschul. 1988. An overview of atatistical method and theory for quantitative model building. In *Quantifying the present and predicting the past: theory, method, and application of archaeological predictive modeling.* Ed. W. J. Judge and L. Sebastian. Washington DC: U.S. Government Printing Office, pp. 173–256.

Roux, V., B. Bril, and G. Dietrich. 1995. Skills and learning difficulties involved in stone-knapping: the case of stone bead knapping in Khambhat, India. *World Archaeology* 27:63–87.

Sackett, J. R. 1982. Approaches to style in lithic archaeology. *Journal of Anthropological Archaeology* 1:59–112.

———. 1990. Style and ethnicity in archaeology: the case for isochretism. In *The uses of style in archaeology.* Ed. M. Conkey and C. Hastorf. Cambridge University, pp. 32–43.

Salo, W. L., A. C. Aufderheide, J. E. Buikstra, and T. A. Holcomb. 1994. Identification of *Mycobacterium tuberculosis* DNA in a pre-Columbian Peruvian mummy. *Proceedings of the National Academy of Sciences* 91:2091–2094.

Sapir, Edward. 1910. Yana texts, together with Yana myths. *University of California Publications in American Archaeology and Ethnology* 9(1): 1–235.

———. 1917. The position of Yana in the Hokan stock. *University of California Publications in American Archaeology and Ethnology* 13(1): 1–34.

———. 1918. Yana terms of relationship. *University of California Publications in American Archaeology and Ethnology* 13(4): 215–234.

———. 1922. The fundamental elements of Northern Yana. *University of California Publications in American Archaeology and Ethnology* 13(6): 1–235.

Schumacher, Paul. 1877. Methods of making stone weapons. *U.S. Geographical and Geological Survey Vol. III, Bulletin* 3.

Shackley, M. Steven. 1990. Early hunter-gatherer procurement ranges in the Southwest: evidence from obsidian geochemistry and lithic technology. Ph.D. dissertation, Arizona State University. Ann Arbor: University Microfilms.

———. 1991. Projectile point technology of Ishi and the Yahi-Yana: inferences for hunter-gatherer style and ethnicity. Paper presented in the Session, Researching Symbolism,

Style, and Ritual at the 56th Annual Meeting of the Society of American Archaeology, New Orleans.

———. 1994. Projectile point technology of Ishi and the Yana of north central California. Paper presented at the symposium, Ishi: The Man and His Times Revisited. Oakland Museum, Oakland, California.

———. 1995. Sources of archaeological obsidian in the greater American Southwest: an update and quantitative analysis. *American Antiquity* 60:531–551.

———. 1996a. Ishi was not necessarily the last full-blooded Yahi: Some inferences for hunter-gatherer style and ethnicity. *Berkeley Archaeology* 3:1–3.

———. 1996b. Elko or San Pedro?: a quantitative analysis of Late Archaic projectile points from White Tanks, Yuma County, Arizona. *Kiva* 61:413–431.

———. 2001. The stone tool technology of Ishi and the Yana of north central California: inferences for hunter-gatherer cultural identity in Historic California. *American Anthropologist* 102:693–712.

Shea, Christopher. 2000. The return of Ishi's brain. *Lingua Franca* 10(1): 46–56.

Shott, Michael J. 1996. Innovation and selection in prehistory: a case study from the American bottom. In *Stone tools: theoretical insights into human prehistory.* Ed. G. H. Odell. New York: Kluwer/Plenum, pp. 279–309.

———. 1997. Stones and shafts redux: the metric discrimination of chipped-stone dart and arrow points. *American Antiquity* 62:86–102.

Stead, W. W., K. D. Eisenach, M. D. Cave, and M. L. Beggs. 1995. When did *Mycobacterium tuberculosis* infection first occur in the New World? An important question with public health implications. *American Journal of Respiratory and Critical Care Medicine* 151 N4:1267–1268.

Thomas, David H. 1981. How to classify the projectile points from Monitor Valley, Nevada. *Journal of California and Great Basin Anthropology* 3(1): 7–43.

———. 1986. Points on points: a reply to Flenniken and Raymond. *American Antiquity* 51(3): 619–627.

———. 2000. *Skull wars: Kennewick man, archaeology, and the battle for Native American identity.* New York: Basic Books.

Titmus, Gene L. 1985. Some aspects of stone tool notching. In *Stone tool analysis: essays in honor of Don E. Crabtree.* Ed. M. G. Plew, J. C. Woods, and M. G. Pavesic. University of New Mexico, pp. 243–264.

Titmus, Gene L., and James C. Woods. 1986. An experimental study of projectile point fracture patterns. *Journal of California and Great Basin Anthropology* 8:37–49.

Treganza, Adan E. 1954. Salvage archaeology in Nimbus and Redbank Reservoir areas, central California. *University of California Archaeological Survey Report* 26.

Waterman, T. T. 1911. Field notebooks of text and vocabulary dictated by Ishi. Berkeley: Bancroft Library, University of California.

———. 1918. The Yana Indians. *University of California Publications in American Archaeology and Ethnology* 13:35–102.

Whittaker, John C. 1987. Individual variation as an approach to economic organization: projectile points at Grasshopper Pueblo, Arizona. *Journal of Field Archaeology* 14:465–480.

———. 1994. *Flintknapping: making and understanding stone tools.* Austin: University of Texas.

Wiessner, P. 1983. Style and social information in Kalahari San projectile points. *American Antiquity* 48:253–276.

———. 1990. Is there a unity to style? In *The uses of style in archaeology.* Ed. M. Conkey and C. Hastorf. Cambridge: Cambridge University, pp. 105–112.

Young, D. E., and R. Bonnichsen. 1984. *Understanding stone tools: a cognitive approach.* Peopling of the Americas Process Series. vol. 1. Orono: University of Maine.

12

Ishi's Spanish Words

ORIN STARN

A reporter from the *San Francisco Examiner* in 1911 described Ishi as "absolutely innocent of modern life" and "unspotted by the world."[1] This view of the man discovered at Oroville's slaughterhouse just two weeks before as a member of an untouched aboriginal people has persisted across the decades. A belief in Ishi as "the last Stone Age Indian in North America" has indeed been part of the fascination, sadness, and romance of his story for many Americans. In 1979 Theodora Kroeber and Robert Heizer still insisted that Ishi was a "true forest person . . . who existed quite outside white civilization."[2]

But were Ishi and the Yahi really so completely cut off from the rest of the world? Ishi certainly possessed a storehouse of Yahi myths, music, and knowledge that must have come down through the generations, even if recent research shows he knew Maidu and Atsugewi as well as Yahi songs.[3] Yet much evidence now suggests that the story of Ishi and his people is far from a saga of primordial isolation, of unbroken tradition and cultural conservatism. Especially revealing has been the rediscovery of Bear's Hiding Place in the early 1990s by researchers Brian Bibby, James Johnston, and Jerald Johnson in the course of making *Ishi the Last Yahi,* filmmaker Jed Riffe's important documentary. Bear's Hiding Place was the camp in Deer Creek's ravine inhabited by Ishi and the other last survivors of his band in the late nineteenth and early twentieth centuries. Bibby, Johnston, and Johnson found a house pit, metate, and other signs of Native occupation there. Yet Bear's Hiding Place was also littered with cans, Log Cabin syrup tins, bottles, coffee pots, and other white goods, all likely pilfered from settler cabins. These finds strongly suggest that Ishi and the others by no means subsisted by the traditional methods of hunting and gathering alone.[4] To be sure, they gathered acorns, hunted deer with bow and arrow, and harpooned salmon; yet they also pilfered liberally from white homesteaders, cooking acorn mush in discarded coffee tins, using an old saw blade to make brush shelters, glass to chip arrowheads, and square nails to tip harpoons. Ishi and his people, in other words, resourcefully amalgamated the Yahi and the Western, the old and the new, the handmade and the manufactured, in order to survive their long, hard concealment. It is simply wrong to label Ishi a Stone Age man: machine-age goods like glass and saws were an integral part of his lifeway.

In what follows, I will focus on another line of evidence for mixture and change in the experience of Ishi and the Yahi, namely the existence of Spanish loanwords in their speech.[5] Strong evidence exists that a number of Spanish words entered the Yahi language in the nineteenth century, with some Yahi perhaps even learning to speak a bit of this European tongue. Consider, for example, the diary of J. Goldsborough Bruff. In 1850, this gold seeker stranded for the winter near Deer Creek, met a "a party of squaws with large conical baskets on their backs, 2 men with them." "I found they understood some Spanish," Bruff explained, and in this language they asked for food and directed the lost man to the nearest ranch.[6] Thirty years later, according to Thomas T. Waterman's account, a ranchhand named Frank Norvell surprised four half-clothed Indians breaking into a cabin not far from Mill Creek. One woman gestured toward the bush saying "*dos chiquitos papooses*" by way of explaining that the group had children back at their camp. Then there was the old woman, the one who may have been Ishi's mother, discovered by a party of surveyors in 1908 at Bear's Hiding Place. One report had it that she had asked for water in a "few words of broken Spanish," and that she repeated *malo* and even *muy malo* to describe her legs' painful condition.[7]

There were certainly many Spanish loanwords in Ishi's vocabulary. Saxton Pope, the doctor, estimated that his friend and archery companion learned about three hundred English words: "hullo," "nice day," "too cole," "too hot," and other basics.[8] Ishi was a favorite with San Francisco's children; from them, he also picked up children's colloquialisms, among them the all-purpose "Sure, Mike." Yet Pope also noted that Ishi knew three words derived from Spanish nouns: *camisa*, shirt, *paka*, cow, and *papello*, paper.[9] Although apparently not recognizing the possible Spanish connection, Juan Dolores, the Papago man who befriended Ishi in San Francisco, also reported in a letter to Alfred Kroeber that Ishi complained "*tci'kita, tci'kita*" when a nail he was using to flake a spear point "was too small or short."[10] The linguist Leanne Hinton believes this suggests that Ishi's word for "small" was the same Spanish borrowing, of the word *chiquita*, as that of the Yahi woman encountered by Norvell in 1885.[11] Ishi's term for white people, *saldu,* may also have come from Spanish. As the linguists Edward Sapir and Leslie Spier suggested in a 1943 article, it probably derived from *soldado,* Spanish for "soldier," an understandable connection insofar as the first whites the Yana spied may have been Spanish or Mexican troops early in the nineteenth century.[12]

Spanish might have entered Yahi by two possible routes. One was indirectly, by way of interaction with other Indians who had picked up loanwords. California's Indians often took loanwords from their contact with Spanish speakers, then passed them on to other Native groups that did not have any actual contact with the outsiders. Language resembled disease in this sense; it could fan out in advance of the actual physical arrival of Europeans, just as the smallpox of 1837 raced up from Mariano Vallejo's ranch in Sonoma to kill hundreds, perhaps thousands, of Indians in the Sacramento Valley who had never yet encountered a white man in the flesh.

Thus the Yahi could have acquired words like *malo* and *chiquito* without ever meeting a Spaniard or Mexican. One possibility is that they picked up the terms from their southern neighbors, the Maidu. It is unclear whether the Maidu themselves absorbed Spanish loanwords indirectly from the Patwin and other groups closer to the missions on the Pacific Coast or directly from Spanish soldiers, Mexican cowboys, or others. At any rate, however, at least twenty-five Spanish loanwords appear in Oroville's Maidu dialect. It may even be that some nineteenth-century Maidu spoke the language as a survival strategy amidst the terror of the Gold Rush, or so some observers have speculated. "One old-timer," the part-Maidu medicine man and cultural activist Joe Marine reports, "told me that way they could pretend to be Mexican instead of Indian when the whites were out Indian hunting."[13]

Yet the Yahi may also have had direct interaction with Spanish speakers. One tantalizing bit of support for this theory comes from Waterman's field notes. In 1915 an Antelope Creek sawmill owner, Darwin B. Lyon, told the anthropologist this story:

> I know from what I have heard my father, grandfather, and mother say that these Indians used to work for the Mexicans, and that is where they learned a few words of Spanish. My mother saw them working in the fields near Red Bluff, the same tribe of Indians that Ishi belongs to. There are old grant line marks up there; piles of stones that are said to have been piled by the Indians for the Mexicans. They were not wild and were not afraid of the first white man who came into the country. I have heard my grandfather say that he has seen large camps of them along the Sacramento River in the fall, fishing for salmon. They were friendly at that time and were not afraid of whites. I think they used to steal from the whites, and that first started the trouble. They made petty raids, and the whites retaliated by following them into the hills and killing as many as they could, irrespective of size,

sex, or age. There were probably fifteen years, from 1890 on, that I don't remember any of them ever being seen or heard of, until the camp was found where Ishi came from.[14]

Lyon's story calls to mind the case of the Bushmen, the people of South Africa's Kalahari Desert more properly known as the !Kung. The !Kung were once believed to have stuck to the same desert lifeway for thousands of years. A picture of a pristine Stone Age tribe appeared in the hit movie *The Gods Must Be Crazy* – and many anthropology studies. Yet more recent research suggests that !Kung also worked on ranches and farms in the late nineteenth century.[15] It was only new restrictions on native labor and other changes that forced the people back exclusively into the Kalahari in the early twentieth century. In this sense, the !Kung underwent a "reprimitivization," namely reverting to seclusion and the hunting and gathering that they were abandoning a century before. The view of the !Kung as marooned forever on their own was a mirage that concealed history's more messy realities. It was an invention of whites invested in romantic mythologies about lost tribes and the state of nature.

Could the Yahi have undergone the same kind of "reprimitivization" as the !Kung? The testimony of Lyon suggests one possible sequence of events along these lines. By such a scenario, the Yahi of Ishi's parents' or grandparents' generation would have worked in the Sacramento Valley during Mexican rule in the 1840s. This was a period across California when it was more common to exploit the labor of Indians than to try to exterminate them. After the Gold Rush and California's seizure by the United States, the Yahi and other Indians were expendable, all the more so with the new flood of Chinese laborers into the state. The campaigns of Robert Anderson, Hi Good, and others began in the 1850s in retaliation for real and imagined attacks on white settlers. The violence led the last survivors to seclude themselves on Deer Creek, an emergency measure in a changing, more hostile world. A scenario of engagement followed by withdrawal would explain why Ishi and the others knew a few Spanish words, but none in English, since they would have already gone into hiding by the time the forty-niners' tongue became California's dominant language in the late nineteenth century. Ishi himself probably never had contact with any Mexican. The vestiges of Spanish in Ishi's speech would have come down from his mother and others of earlier generations, a ghostly trace of a forgotten chapter of Yahi history before the bloody arrival of the U.S. Americans.

It would be a mistake, of course, to put too much stock in the single account of D. B. Lyons. A further objection is that standard accounts have always reported that the Sacramento Valley adjacent to Yana country was settled by Anglo-Americans, not Spaniards or Mexicans. The valleys of the Sacramento

River and its tributaries, or so historian Robert Cowan contended, were "too far north for the Spanish Californians, who declared any lands north of Sonoma were not fit for human habitation."[16] Indeed, the best-known ranchers of the 1840s were all Anglo-Americans or of northern European extraction: John Bidwell, Peter Lassen, Pierson Reading, Albert Toomes, among others. These men established big ranches in the 1840s with land titles granted by Mexico's government to try to secure what was then the country's northern frontier against the Russians, English, French, and U.S. Americans.

Yet a closer look at the records suggests that Spanish was often spoken nonetheless in the northern Sacramento Valley as a lingua franca. After all, the area was Mexican territory in these years just before the U.S. seizure of California. Official business was transacted in Spanish; Bidwell, the most influential rancher, was proud of his fluency in the language. He went by Juan Bidwell with Spanish-speaking friends. It is even incorrect, as it turns out, to say that there were no Mexican rancheros in the northern valley. Aguas Frías south of Butte Creek was granted to Salvador Osio in 1844; Dionisio and Maceimo Fernández in 1846 received a grant in the far south of Butte County, just below the area today occupied by the town of Oroville.[17]

A reminiscence of a future Oroville judge and city father, Charles Lott, also details the employment of Mexican cowboys on the northern valley ranches. In 1849, Lott visited Peter Lassen's property, which stretched up Deer Creek well into ancestral Yahi land. According to Lott, Lassen had "from fifteen to twenty Mexicans and Indians to take care of his cattle and horses."[18]

Were Yahi among the Indians working on Peter Lassen's ranch or on other ranches in the area? Is that where Spanish words entered into the Yahi tongue? Like so much about Ishi, it is impossible to say for sure. The literary critic Gerald Vizenor titles an essay "Ishi Obscura," a way of calling attention to the many parts of Yahi history that will and perhaps should forever go unresolved.[19] Instead of simply seeking to establish the facts of Ishi's story, Vizenor suggests, it would be wise also to reflect about the reasons for the sometimes prying, obsessive curiosity that leads white scholars, history buffs, and others to feel the compulsive need to uncover every secret, every truth about Native peoples.

It may well be that the Spanish words in Yahi came only secondhand by way of contact with other Indian groups. Even this explanation, however, cuts against the grain of the usual ways of understanding Ishi. The Yahi were supposed to be a prickly people isolated in their own territory and hostile to their Wintu and Maidu neighbors, a tribe unto themselves. Yet there would have had to have been significant contact with Indians of other groups for the Yahi to pick up Spanish loans. For that matter, as some scholars have recently suggested, the last survivors in Deer Creek may not all have been Yahi. Amidst the violence, terror, and dislocation of the 1850s and 1860s, Mill and Deer Creeks became a region of refuge for many Indians who were not Yahi. It is certainly possible that Ishi or others in the band of survivors that concealed themselves until the early twentieth century at the very least descended from mixed unions, albeit with Yahi as their principal language and cultural referent.

The Spanish words underscore the inadequacy of a view of the Yahi as messengers of primordial aboriginal culture, cut off from other Indians and the rest of the world. Ishi was proud of his knowledge of songs, hunting, and others traditional arts. Although having burned off his hair in mourning just before being found in Oroville, Ishi grew it long again in San Francisco in the customary Yahi style. Yet he was also quick to embrace matches, mattresses, and other amenities of white society – in this sense shattering the stereotype of Indians as forever wedded to the tradition and the past. The full story of the Yahi will never be known. There can be no doubt that intermixture, improvisation, and reinvention were part of the experience of Ishi and his people in the long decades when they managed against the odds to survive in the face of invasion and conquest.

NOTES

1. Philip Kinsley, "Untainted Life Revealed by Aborigine," in Robert Heizer and Theodora Kroeber, *Ishi the Last Yahi: A Documentary History* (Berkeley: University of California, 1979), p. 101.

2. *Ishi the Last Yahi*, p.7.

3. See Chapter 14, this volume.

4. Jed Riffe's 1997 short film *Bear's Hiding Place: Ishi's Last Refuge* documents and discusses these finds.

5. For a fine discussion of Ishi's language more generally, see Chapter 13, this volume. I am very grateful to Victor Golla, Jean Perry, Herb Luthin, and Leanne Hinton for their guidance in thinking about language in Native California.

6. These excerpts from Bruff's diary appear in *Ishi the Last Yahi*, p. 8.

7. A. L. Kroeber, "The Elusive Mill Creeks," in *Ishi the Last Yahi*, p. 83.

8. Linguist Victor Golla (Chapter 13, this volume) explains that Ishi also invented a "personal pidgin," mixing English nouns and phrases with Yahi grammatical markers. An example was his word for hat, *hatna*, the result of his taking the English noun and adding the Yahi suffix *na*, roughly equivalent to English *the*.

9. Saxton Pope, "Characteristics of Ishi," in *Ishi the Last Yahi*, p. 231.

10. Juan Dolores to Alfred Kroeber, October 23, 1912, Series 5, Box 12, Department of Anthropology Papers, Bancroft Library, University of California, Berkeley.

11. Leanne Hinton, personal communication, 1999.

12. Edward Sapir and Leslie Spier, "Notes on the Culture of the Yana," *Anthropological Records* 3(3):243, 1943.

13. Joe Marine, personal communication, 1999.

14. Ethnological Documents Collection, Reel 199, p. 527, Bancroft Library.

15. See, for example, Robert Gordon, *The Bushman Myth: The Making of a Namibian Underclass* (Boulder CO: Westview, 1992).

16. Robert Cowan, *Ranchos of California* (Fresno CA: Academic Literary Guild, 1956), p.16.

17. Krista Deal, "The Mexican Land Grants of Butte County," unpublished paper on file in the regional archive in the library at Chico State University.

18. Charles Lott, "As It Was in the Days of '49," *Diggins*, Summer 1999, 30 [published by the Butte County Historical Society]. I am very grateful to Michele Shover for passing along this reference. Shover herself has published a series of path-breaking articles in the *Dogtown Territorial Quarterly* about the history of the Chico area.

19. The essay appears in Vizenor's *Manifest Manners: Postindian Warriors of Survivance* (Hanover: Wesleyan University, 1994).

13
Ishi's Language

VICTOR GOLLA

ISHI AND YANA

Yana is an extinct language. The last known speakers, Kate Walson and Malcolm
Cayton, were eighty and seventy-three years old, respectively, when they were
interviewed by Edward W. Gifford and Stanislaw Klimek in 1934 (Gifford and
Klimek 1936:78), and they are now long gone. The documentation of Yana, the
work primarily of Edward Sapir in 1907 and 1915, with important secondary
materials collected by Jeremiah Curtin (in 1884 and 1888), Roland B. Dixon (in
1900), C. Hart Merriam (in 1907), Thomas T. Waterman (from 1911 to 1916), and
J. P. Harrington (in 1922 and 1931), can never be increased.[1] However, because of
the excellence of Sapir's materials in particular, Yana is actually one of the better
known languages of Native California.

Although all Yana dialects were probably mutually intelligible (Sapir and
Spier 1943:244), numerous phonological and lexical differences, and at least a
few distinctions in grammar, separated a northern group of dialects from a
southern group, with the boundary between the two lying somewhere in the vi-
cinity of Battle Creek. The northern dialect area was further subdivided into
what Sapir called Northern Yana (spoken in a relatively small area near Round
Mountain and Montgomery Creek on present-day U.S. Highway 299, a few
miles from the Pit River) and Central Yana (spoken on Clover Creek and the
various forks of Cow Creek, apparently as far south as the modern Shasta-
Tehama county line). Although they differed in a number of phonological par-
ticulars (most of which appear to be Northern Yana innovations), Northern and
Central Yana shared almost all of their vocabulary. Speakers of one could understand speakers of the other "without difficulty" according to Sapir (1923:263),
and it is clear from what is preserved of their traditional culture and literature
(Sapir 1910; Sapir and Spier 1943) that they shared a common ethnic heritage.
Powers (1877:275) referred to them jointly as the "Nozi," a term possibly of

Wintu origin (Sapir and Spier 1943:242) but more likely a Maidu epithet, *nusí* "the short (people)."[2]

The speakers of the southern dialects were outside the "Nozi" group. Powers called them the "Kombo," another Maidu term,[3] and wrote of them as if they were a distinct tribe (1877:277–81). The territory they occupied, in the dry lava bed country from Battle Creek southward to the canyons of Antelope, Mill, and Deer Creeks, was less hospitable than the country to the north, and their numbers were small even in precontact times. The extent of linguistic diversity in this southern area will always be uncertain, since we have little attestation of the Yana spoken here except for Ishi's speech. In 1907 Sapir obtained a number of words and phrases from Betty Brown, his Northern Yana consultant, which she said represented the dialect spoken around Antelope Creek, and on the basis of this fragmentary attestation Sapir identified a "Southern Yana" dialect coordinate with Northern and Central Yana.[4]

After working with Ishi in 1915, Sapir wrote to Kroeber that Betty Brown's Antelope Creek material was "evidently much more closely related to Ishi's forms than to those of either Northern or Central Yana" and that if any dialect difference existed in the area south of Battle Creek it was almost certainly "slighter than that which . . . exist[ed] between Northern and Central Yana." In this letter he suggested a three-dialect classification of the language into Northern Yana, Central Yana, and Yahi (or Southern Yana), and tentatively divided the last into Northern Yahi (Antelope Creek) and Southern Yahi (Ishi's speech), although his preference was "to ignore the possible difference altogether, as far as linguistics is concerned" (Sapir to Kroeber, January 10, 1916, in Golla 1984:206–207). In *Text Analyses of Three Yana Dialects* (1923), apparently surrendering to what had become general usage, Sapir publicly adopted a four-dialect scheme for Yana (Northern, Central, Southern, and Ishi's "Yahi") while suggesting that the virtually undocumented Southern Yana dialect was "a link between the Central and Yahi dialects, with a leaning, I surmise, to Yahi rather than to Central Yana" (1923:263).

Whatever the exact dialectological map, it is clear that there were significant linguistic differences between the Yahi dialect that Ishi spoke and Northern and Central Yana. Although, as noted below, the Central Yana speaker Sam Batwi served as Ishi's interpreter for a few weeks, communication between the two was not easy. Yahi was, in Sapir's estimation, the most "archaic" of the attested dialects and "appreciably harsher to the ear" (1923:263). Perhaps the most salient characteristic of Yahi (and the source of its name) is the existence of a restricted class of nouns that take a special form of the absolutive suffix, -*hi* (e.g., *galaa-hi* "fish," *yaa-hi* "person"), alongside the much larger class of nouns that take the standard -*na* suffix (e.g., *ba-na* "deer," *chu-na* "eye, face"). In Northern and Central Yana the -*hi* class is not distinguished; -*na* is used with these nouns as well (*galaa-na, yaa-na*).[5]

COMMUNICATING WITH ISHI

The middle-aged Southern Yana man who wandered into Oroville on August 29, 1911, was, almost from the first, assumed to be a "Kombo" from the Deer Creek area. For his first interview with Ishi in the Butte County jail in Oroville, Thomas T. Waterman apparently took with him the most accurate and comprehensive vocabulary of Yana then available, a list of approximately 200 Northern and Central Yana words that had been prepared the previous year by Edward Sapir (Sapir to Kroeber, April 7, 1910, in Golla 1984:50–52).[6]

The scene was vividly described by Waterman (1918:64):

> The first impression received of the wild Indian was the sight of him, draped in a canvas apron they had hurriedly put on him at the slaughter-house, sitting on the edge of a cot in his cell, still uncertain of his fate, and answering in a few words of Yana all questions, hundreds of which were being fired at him in English, Spanish, and half a dozen Indian languages, by visitors of all complexions. The present writer's amateur attempts at Yana were equally unintelligible to him for a long time. An agreement was finally reached, however, on the word for the material of which his cot was made, *siwin'i*, or yellow pine. His face lightened up at this word, though he evidently could hardly trust his senses. These were perhaps the first intelligible sounds he had heard from a human being in three years.

In fact, a considerable number of the words in Sapir's list, like *siiwin'i* "yellow pine," were identical with, or very close to, Ishi's Yahi forms, including *ba-na* "deer," *buuni* "feather," *sawa* "arrow," *chu-na* "face," and many others. In some cases there were small phonetic differences: for Northern (N.) and Central (C.) Yana *diitil-la* "quiver" Ishi had *diitel-la*; for *wu-na* "pine-nuts" he had *hu-na*. There were, however, several instances in which the N. and C. Yana forms given by Sapir corresponded to Yahi words of a totally different shape: for N. and C. Yana *doobun-na* "panther," for example, Ishi had *hooch'ul-hi*; for *kewach'i* "storage basket" Ishi had *baanu* (a word which in N. Yana meant "twine").

Sapir's short vocabulary, accurate and useful as it was, could not serve more than rudimentary functions of communication. A Yana-speaking interpreter was needed, and the obvious choice was Sam Batwi.

In his sixties by that time, Batwi had served as a consultant or interpreter to nearly every ethnographer or linguist to pass through the area, beginning with Jeremiah Curtin in 1889. In 1900 he worked briefly with Roland Dixon (Dixon and Kroeber 1903:22), and he and Betty Brown were Sapir's two principal consultants in 1907 (Sapir 1910:6). Although a very knowledgeable source of information on Yana language and culture (Sapir found him "the only one . . . at all acquainted with the mythology"), his dialect background was somewhat obscure. He had presumably lived most of his life in the Cow Creek area and spoke only Central Yana, but he also told Sapir that he had known Southern Yana in his childhood and had once lived around Battle Creek.

Batwi was brought to Oroville in time to accompany Ishi and Waterman on their trip to San Francisco. While it was immediately clear that the two spoke different dialects, Ishi was able to understand Batwi's Central Yana, and Batwi was quick to become Ishi's mouthpiece. How well Batwi was able to facilitate communication during Ishi's first days in civilization can be judged from the following excerpts from an article in the *San Francisco Call* of September 6, 1911 (reprinted in Heizer and Kroeber 1979:79–100):

> Crossing the bay was a wonderful experience, and yesterday morning as he stood in front of the Affiliated colleges [Ishi] asked Batwee as to the direction of where he crossed the big water. Batwee said: "First, yesterday, he frightened very much, now today he think all very funny. He like it, tickle him. He like this place here. Much to see, big water off there" and he waved his hand toward the ocean, "plenty houses, many things to see."
>
> The first time that the unknown refused to obey orders was yesterday. He was to be photographed in a garment of skins, and when the dressing for the aboriginal part began he refused to remove his overalls.
>
> "He say he not see any other people go without them," said Batwee, "and he say he never take them off no more."
>
> The battery of half a dozen cameras focused upon him was a new experience and evidently a somewhat terrifying one. He stood with his head back and a half smile on his face, but his compressed lips and dilated nostrils showed that he was far from happy.
>
> "Tell him, Batwee, white man just play," said Waterman, and the explanation seemed to reassure him.
>
> He talked to Batwee freely, but would tell little that was personal. His name, if he knows it, he keeps to himself. . . . He is so desirous of "doing as the Romans do" since he arrived in civilization that it was thought he might be induced to tell his name when he knew that all white men had them. Batwee told him it was customary in the best circles, or words to that effect, and in response he declared his entire willingness to have a name. He had none, he reiterated. . . . Batwee calls him John, but Doctor Kroeber declared that lacking in individuality.
>
> When he is asked anything about his wife, he begins to tell Indian myths or legends.

Despite Batwi's passable ability to interpret for Ishi, his services were dispensed with after only a few weeks. Kroeber found Batwi "too old to make himself ac-

quainted very readily with a new form of speech" and "nearly hopeless" at providing reliable translations for Ishi's mythological narratives (Kroeber to Sapir,
October 7, 1911 and November 18, 1911, in Golla 1984:62–64). Another complica-
tion seems to have been mutual dislike between the two Indians.[7]

But without Batwi's aid, Kroeber, Waterman, Gifford, and the others working with Ishi were left with a serious communication problem. Kroeber described the difficulty early along (Kroeber [1911] 1979) in these terms:

> I have tried to teach him English, but he will not learn it. He repeats the words after
> me readily enough, but when he is told to use them, he refuses. It is embar-
> rassment, self-consciousness or timidity, but it is not inaptitude. I try to teach
> him to count and he understands the meaning of the words, but he refuses to use
> them. I thought at first that if he were thrown upon his own resources he would
> learn to take care of himself, but he has been alone so long that it does not seem
> to matter to him whether any one understands him or not. When he talks to me,
> although Sam Batwee may not be present, he uses his own tongue and appears to
> be just as happy although he knows I can not understand, as though I understood
> it all.

Nearly a year later Kroeber was continuing to remark on Ishi's "dislike of the
English language" (Kroeber [1912] 1979):

> One remarkable fact so far has stood out against his progress toward real civiliza-
> tion: a reluctance to learn English. In several months of association only with peo-
> ple of English speech . . . one would expect a tolerable proficiency in the new lan-
> guage, an ability of expression at least lively and fluent if not correct. But a few
> dozen names of objects and persons are all that have crossed his lips. It is not
> inability that is at fault, for his pronunciation, when called upon to repeat what
> is spoken to him, is excellent, and some words, such as "water," "money," and
> "chicken," blossomed from him in a very few days.

ISHI'S PIDGIN ENGLISH

During the next three years, as he became more and more habituated to living
and working in the museum (also venturing into the city), Ishi's repertoire of
English words expanded somewhat. More precisely, he seems to have worked
out a personal pidgin, mixing English nouns and phrases with Yana grammatical markers. Theodora Kroeber gives a good account of Ishi's "broken English"
in *Ishi in Two Worlds* (1961:225–228). The fullest published documentation,
however, comes from Saxton T. Pope, Ishi's physician, friend, and fellow archer,
who compiled the following list of the terms Ishi commonly used (Pope
1920:188):

Hullo; nice day; too cole; too hot; too much water-tee; too much lazy-auna-tee; hims good; hims no good; bad man; sleep; eat; work; sing; dance; I go; you go; you likey him?; lice (rice); pishy (fish); bean-us; honey; labit (rabbit); big one; little one; led (red); white; black; hat-na (hat); shoes; camisa (Spanish for shirt); mahale (mujer, Spanish for woman); lopa (rope); lopa pikta (rope picture or moving pictures); candy-tee; soda wata; whiskey-tee; smoke; doctor; big cheap (big chief); dog; kitty-tee; coyote; chicken-a-tee; egg; apple; owanga-tee; lemon; barnarna-tee; cracker; soap; powder; medicine; chair; sit down; talk; how much money-tee?; money; shoot; cut em; die man (death); sick man; ole man; lady; mama; papa; sister; papoose (baby); too much I smoke (fog); I all a time smoke; put em away; you go get em; what's a matter-tee?; you go pretty soon; long time; automobile; horse; telephone; fire; pistol (gun); pike (fight); evleybody happy; him cry; too much pina (pain); sheep-na; paka (vaca, cow); tea; koppy (coffee); milik (milk); nipe (knife); axa (axe); hatch (hatchet); papello (paper); light; all a same.

The ending -na in hat-na and sheep-na is the general form of the Yana absolutive suffix, noted earlier. Although Pope notes it only in these two words, Ishi probably used it with greater frequency. Another carryover from Yana is the suffix that Pope writes -tee (too much water-tee; too much lazy-auna-tee; candy-tee; whiskey-tee; kitty-tee; chicken-a-tee; owanga-tee; barnarna-tee; what's a matter-tee?). This is the Yahi quotative enclitic, -ti, used in stories to mark direct discourse and in conversation to flag words and phrases spoken "in quotes" (Sapir 1923:289, note 182). Thus, when Ishi said candy-tee, he was essentially saying what you call "candy"; similarly, what's a matter-tee is probably to be understood as "what's the matter", as you say.

The element -auna- in too much lazy-auna-tee is the Yahi noun for "fire" (the stem 'au- and the absolutive suffix). This apparently was one of the few substantive words from Yana that Ishi regularly employed in his pidgin, using it to mean variously "hot," "burning," "sunshine" and allied concepts.[8]

Four of the words on Pope's list are of special note: camisa, paka, papello, and mahale. The first three are from Spanish camisa, vaca, and papel. The last is possibly a form of Spanish mujer, as Pope suggests, but could also be derived from Yokuts, another Central California Indian language.[9] All four words were probably known to Ishi before coming to San Francisco, and are likely to have their origin in a trade jargon that was known in the Yahi community before and during the Gold Rush. Kroeber mentions that Ishi "knew . . . a few words of Spanish learned from his own people and considered by him part of his native tongue" (1925:343). Also according to Kroeber, Ishi seemed to know "a fair number" of words and place names in neighboring Atsugewi, Maidu, and Wintu. "Since he had never met a soul of any of the three stocks, this is a fact of interest, evidencing that the California Indians in their native condition took some interest in each other and spent more or less time in the home circle telling one another about strangers and their ways" (Kroeber 1925:345–346).[10]

STUDYING ISHI'S LANGUAGE

However inadequate his translations, Sam Batwi did give Kroeber and his colleagues some minimal access to Ishi's dialect of Yana. During the few weeks that Batwi remained in San Francisco, Waterman in particular worked intensively with him and Ishi. He compiled a lengthy vocabulary and transcribed and translated at least one complete myth text, the "Wood Duck" story (Valory 1971:7, items 35–36). Ishi's original dictation of the narrative was recorded on wax cylinders; Waterman then played these back to Ishi, who "repronounced" the words one by one, enabling Waterman to transcribe them with fair accuracy and Batwi to give them an (unfortunately dubious) English rendering (Kroeber to Sapir, May 29, 1915, in Golla 1984:193). A number of Ishi's songs were also recorded on wax cylinders, some with spoken texts, but most of these were made after Batwi's departure, and little analysis was done at the time (see Nettl 1965; Keeling 1991:269–280, 292–294).

The only other significant collection of linguistic data from Ishi before 1915 consisted of the place names (and map) that Kroeber and Waterman obtained from Ishi before and during their trip with him back to Yahi territory in 1914. Some of these place names, and a copy of the map drawn by Ishi, were published by Kroeber in the section on Yahi geography in his *Handbook of the Indians of California* (1925:344–346). The full list was later published by Baumhoff (1957; reprinted in Heizer and Kroeber 1979:217–220).

Beyond this, very little was learned of Ishi's language until the appearance on the scene of Edward Sapir.

From virtually the day of Ishi's discovery, Kroeber had been eager to enlist Sapir's aid. Although he was still in his twenties, in 1911 Sapir was probably the most accomplished field linguist in North America (Darnell 1990a). He was certainly the only scholar who had a good grasp on the workings of Yana phonology and grammar, which he derived from his fieldwork on Northern and Central Yana carried out under Kroeber's supervision in 1907–08. This work had also given him considerable acquaintance with traditional Yana culture and society. Although he had worked extensively with only two speakers – Betty Brown, a Northern Yana from Montgomery Creek, and Sam Batwi – he had been able to make an impressive collection of mythological and ethnographic texts (Sapir 1910).

On the day of Ishi's arrival in San Francisco, Kroeber sent Sapir an urgent telegram (Kroeber to Sapir, September 6, 1911, in Golla 1984:59):

HAVE TOTALLY WILD SOUTHERN YANA AT MUSEUM ALSO SAM BATWI FAIRLY
SUCCESSFUL INTERPRETER DO YOU WANT TO COME AND WORK HIM UP IF SO
BOTH AT YOUR DISPOSAL IF NOT WOULD APPRECIATE IMMEDIATE SENDING
OF LIST OF YANA GRAMMATICAL ELEMENTS FOR BETTER UNDERSTANDING
OF LANGUAGE AND ANALYSING OF TEXTS.

Sapir (who was at that time chief of the Ethnological Survey of Canada and deeply involved in field studies of the Nootka and other Canadian groups) was unable to break off his work and come to California on short notice. He did, however, send Kroeber an extensive list of Yana inflectional and derivational elements – in essence, a capsule description of Yana verbal and nominal morphology. Kroeber and Waterman seem not to have made any significant use of this list, which was eventually published as "The Fundamental Elements of Northern Yana" (Sapir 1922).

Kroeber and Sapir kept in fairly close contact during the following three years (see their correspondence in Golla 1984:63–194), but it was not until 1915 that plans were finally made for Sapir to come to California to work with Ishi (Darnell 1990a:80–81). Sapir arrived in mid-June, about two weeks after Kroeber had left on a year's sabbatical that was to take him to New York and Europe. Since Sapir was also teaching a summer session course, it was more convenient for him to work with Ishi on the Berkeley campus than at the museum in San Francisco, and arrangements were made for Ishi to spend the summer with Waterman's family in south Berkeley. Sapir and Ishi worked daily in the Anthropology Building near College Avenue and Bancroft Way, continuing without significant interruption for two months until, in mid-August, the tuberculosis that was soon to kill Ishi made its appearance. As Saxton Pope summarized the events (Pope 1920:198):

> In the summer vacation of [1915] Ishi [lived] at Professor T. T. Waterman's home under the most hygienic conditions with plenty of outdoor recreation, sleeping, proper food, and diversion. Nevertheless, his health suddenly began to fail, and on August 22 he was returned to the University Hospital in San Francisco.

Waterman appears to have harbored the suspicion that the rapid pace Sapir set in his work with Ishi contributed to the latter's collapse (Kroeber 1961:234). Although Sapir was notoriously thorough and persistent in field elicitation, there is no evidence to suggest that he and Ishi had anything other than a comfortable working arrangement. Even so, Sapir found the problems of communicating with Ishi to be daunting. As he later wrote to Kroeber (Sapir to Kroeber, September 23, 1915, in Golla 1984:194):

> At first the task seemed perfectly hopeless. . . . I despaired for a while of being able
> to get text from him at all, but found before very long that he could be made to dic-
> tate reasonably good texts. The difficulty was not so much in writing down Ishi's
> words, as in getting him to interpret them. As a matter of fact, what success I have
> had is due almost entirely to brute memory of stems and grammatical elements fa-
> miliar to me from Northern and Central Yana.

In a published description he characterized "the language of discussion" between himself and Ishi as "a crude jargon composed of English, quasi-English,
and Yahi" (Sapir 1916:329, note 4). He expanded on this later (Sapir 1923:264):

> It should be remembered by anyone who makes a study of [the Yahi text] in this
> paper and who may be inclined to feel annoyance at the gaps in my analysis that
> Ishi's English was of the crudest. "Him's no good" did duty for "He (or it) is bad"
> or "That is not correct," while "sista" might mean equally "sister" or "brother."
> Ishi was perfectly willing to dictate and to interpret; the difficulties followed
> unavoidably from the circumstances. In going over his texts for interlinear
> translations – and it proved a difficult task to hold Ishi in leash in the matter of
> speed of dictation – I endeavored to use every tittle of evidence that I could muster,
> Ishi's "explanation" of the single words, his accompanying gestures, the context of
> the myth itself, and, most important of all, the analogies of the northern dialects.
> Had Yahi proved to be less closely related to these dialects than it is, it is difficult to
> believe that it would have been feasible to secure from Ishi more than merely lexi-
> cal information.

What Sapir attempted to accomplish in this work – and partially succeeded
in doing – was to document Ishi's Southern Yana in the text-and-translation
format that had been pioneered in American linguistics by his teacher, Franz
Boas (Darnell 1990b). Sapir himself was a master of this technique, which called
for both superb phonetic skills and enormous patience.

Essentially what a linguist following this procedure did was ask a fluent
speaker – preferably one who also had a wide acquaintance with the oral literature of his or her group – to dictate extensive "texts." These were usually myths
or stories, although sometimes also descriptions of traditional practices. The
narrator would be asked to speak normally, but at a pace slow enough to allow
the linguist to make an accurate phonetic transcription. Some linguists of that
era attempted to make phonograph recordings, but the process (wax cylinders
until the 1930s) was slow and cumbersome, and the usefulness of the recordings
was minimal except for very short texts or songs. In the training of linguists
great emphasis was placed on rapid and accurate phonetic stenography, and an

experienced and skillful fieldworker could transcribe speech at something approaching normal narrative speed.

After a text had been dictated, the usual procedure was for the linguist to check the phonetic transcription word by word with a fully bilingual interpreter, frequently someone other than the speaker from whom the text was obtained. The goal was to obtain exact translations of all of the elements of the text. These translations were usually written between the lines of the phonetically transcribed original text (see Figure 13.1). In the process of obtaining these interlinear translations, the linguist would collect supplementary information on general linguistic structure and on ethnographic matters.

Sapir's field notebooks from his summer with Ishi are now in the Bancroft Library at the University of California, Berkeley. There are six notebooks of fifty pages each, although the last of these is only half-filled. The first forty-four pages of the first notebook contain individual words and phrases and a few grammatical paradigms. The first text begins on page 45, and the remainder of the notebooks are filled – sixteen lines to the page – with detailed phonetic transcriptions of Ishi's narratives.

There are 3296 lines of text, containing approximately 13,000 words (many of them morphologically complex verbs requiring several English words to translate). This is, by any standards, an impressive documentation of a language. Its usefulness is diminished, however, by the incomplete translation of many of the texts, in part the result of Sapir's difficulty in communicating with Ishi but largely due to the suddenness with which their work ceased when Ishi became ill. Only about a third of the lines of transcribed text have interlinear translations, and many of these lines are only incompletely translated.

WORKING WITH SAPIR'S MATERIALS

Sapir himself had little opportunity after 1915 to work with the notes he collected from Ishi. He published only three papers that drew on the material in any significant way. The first two of these (Sapir 1916, 1918) focused on the remarkably good data on kinship terminology that Ishi had provided (Sapir 1916:329, note 4):

> I consider the full data on kinship terms that I obtained from [Ishi], aside from a few doubtful points, as thoroughly reliable. This is due to the fact that the terms were collected very slowly and with the utmost care and circumspection, with repeated checking whenever opportunity was offered; further to the fact that data already obtained from the Northern Yana helped me to follow the informant. . . .
> The work was rendered possible by the use of counters, differing in appearance for males and females, arranged in the form of a genealogical tree; this device put the whole investigation on a directly visible footing.

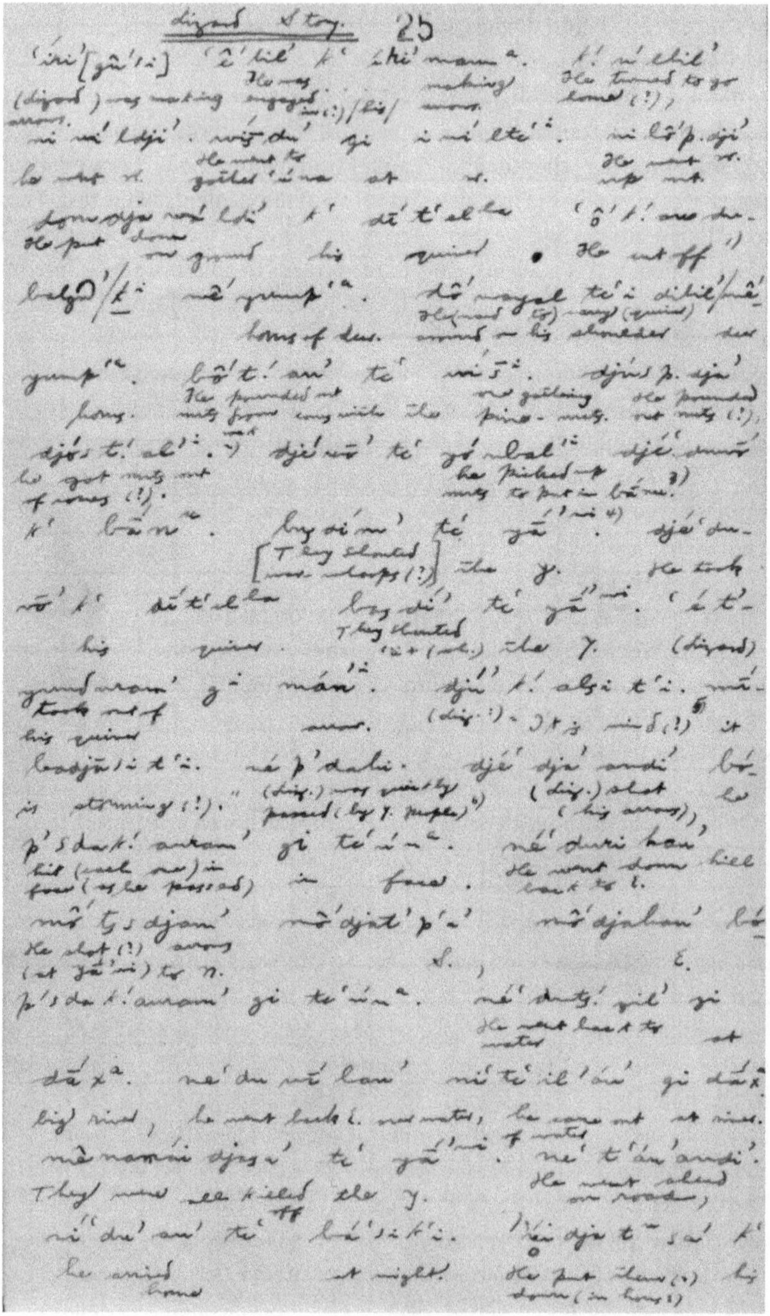

Fig. 13.1. Sample page from Edward Sapir's linguistic field notes on Yahi. Courtesy of the Bancroft Library, University of California, Berkeley.

Sapir also presented a short, but extremely valuable, general discussion of Ishi's dialect in "Text Analyses of Three Yana Dialects" (Sapir 1923), one of his most remarkable papers. This tour de force of compact linguistic analysis provides a synopsis of Yana grammar and phonology in the form of a cross-referenced set of notes (229 in all) to three short excerpts from texts obtained from Betty Brown, Sam Batwi, and Ishi. The text sample from Ishi is the first two dozen lines from "A Story of Lizard" (p. 25 ff. of notebook 5).

Sapir used none of Ishi's material in his well known paper, "Male and Female Forms of Speech in Yana" (Sapir [1929] 1990), although he remarks that "the main facts apply to all four [dialects]."

After Sapir's death in 1939, his original Yana notes (both those from his 1907–08 work and those he obtained in 1915 from Ishi) were returned to the University of California, where they remained in the Anthropology Department archives until the late 1960s. In 1969 they were transferred for safekeeping, along with the rest of the departmental archives, to the Bancroft Library (Valory 1971).

When plans were made in 1984 to prepare a standard edition of Sapir's writings (*The Collected Works of Edward Sapir,* under the general editorship of Philip Sapir), it was decided that a number of Sapir's previously unpublished manuscripts should be included. The narrative texts obtained from Ishi were among those deemed worthy of publication, and in 1986 this writer (then at George Washington University) received a grant from the National Science Foundation to supervise the necessary editorial work on this and several other manuscripts. An editorial project for the Yahi manuscripts was set up in 1986–87 at the University of California, Berkeley, under the direction of Prof. Leanne Hinton. The goals of the project were, first, to prepare all of the translated portions of the texts for publication; second, if possible, to provide translations for at least some parts of the untranslated materials through the use of concordances and other computer-based strategies; and third, to carry out the linguistic analysis of the data necessary for the editing.[11]

As noted earlier in this chapter, the general structure of Yana is relatively well known, thanks largely to Sapir's publications on the Northern and Central dialects already mentioned, and to a dictionary based on Sapir's materials that was compiled by Morris Swadesh and edited by Mary R. Haas (Sapir and Swadesh 1960). Using these materials, as well as notes on Yana grammar taken by Stanley S. Newman when he was a student in a course taught by Sapir at Yale in which Yana was extensively discussed (Newman ms.), the Berkeley team was able to construct a nearly complete morphemic analysis of the translated portions of Sapir's Ishi texts. Much of this preliminary work was done by Kenneth Whistler, who then entered the analyzed texts in a multilinear text concordance. Working with this concordance, another member of the editorial team, Jean Perry, was able to provide schematic glosses for the substantial portion of the texts for which Sapir had provided no translation. A third participant, Herbert Luthin, focused on identifying the rhetorical structure of Ishi's narratives, relying on Sapir's punctuation and markings of stress and other prosodic phenomena, as well as on an analysis of syntactic consistency and alternations in register.[12]

Funding for the Berkeley project came to an end in 1989 before a complete edition of the materials had been prepared. The editorial effort has continued, however, although to date only secondary publications of the materials have appeared. Hinton has published a children's book based on a portion of one of the texts (Hinton and Roth 1992). Luthin's doctoral dissertation (1991) is a general study of the oral-literary structure of Yana narrative that incorporates significant amounts of the Yahi material.

DOES ISHI'S LANGUAGE HAVE A FUTURE?

Ishi has been dead, and his dialect silent, for more than eighty-five years. The last known fluent speakers of any Yana dialect probably died in the 1940s. There are a few elderly people still alive who once heard Yana spoken, and who may remember a few words, but otherwise the language has vanished from living memory.

However, all over Indian California – all over Indian America – there is an intense interest in retaining a speaking knowledge of traditional languages, and some tribes even think about reviving languages that have become extinct. Although there is no Yana Tribe to sponsor such efforts, a few individuals have given some thought to reviving Yana – in large part because Ishi spoke it. That this is not an impossible task is demonstrated by a film made in the early 1990s for the cable channel HBO, *Ishi: Last of His Tribe*. Although this film was not a documentary but a dramatization, and many liberties were taken with the historical truth of Ishi's story, in one regard the producers were scrupulously accurate. They decided that the American Indian actor who portrayed Ishi, Graham Greene, should be given lines to speak in real Yana. To accomplish this they turned to a linguist, William Shipley, an expert on Northern California languages who taught for many years at the University of California, Santa Cruz. Shipley, using Sapir's publications on Yana and a few of the Berkeley project's materials, was able to construct a fairly close Yana translation of the lines Greene was to speak. This translation was as accurate as Shipley could make it, both in grammar and in vocabulary, and he gave Greene and the other actors extensive coaching in Yana phonetics. The result of this diligence was a few minutes of movie dialogue that, probably, Ishi himself could have understood with little difficulty. For a few brief moments, on the lips of a versatile actor, Ishi's language flickered back to life, not by magic but as the result of some hard, focused work.

Surely it is not beyond the realm of possibility that others in the future will invest similar effort to rekindle Ishi's language in a more meaningful, sustained way. Let us hope so.

NOTES

1. With the exception of some of Sapir's and Dixon's materials (the latter incorporated into Sapir 1910), all of the documentation of the Yana language remains in manuscript form. Waterman's notes on his work with Ishi are housed in the Bancroft Library, University of California, Berkeley. Merriam's vocabularies (a general vocabulary and a natural history word list) and other notes, mostly on ethnogeography, are also housed in the Bancroft Library (Heizer 1969). Curtin's notes (from several Northern and Central Yana speakers) are in the National Anthropological Archives, Smithsonian Institution (BAE MSS 269-a, 953, 1296, and 2060). Curtin obtained a number of texts in addition to direct elicitations of vocabulary and grammatical materials, and English versions of some of these were published in Curtin (1898). The originals of Harrington's notes (from eight speakers of Northern and Central Yana) are also housed in the National Anthropological Archives but are more generally accessible in a microfilm edition (catalogued in Mills 1985:56–81). Harrington, a skilled phonetician, devoted a considerable part of his work on the language to re-eliciting the Yana vocabulary in Sapir's published work.

2. The Northeastern Maidu verb stem *nus* (or *nys*) means "short, low, stooped over" (Shipley 1963:156); the Yana were traditionally characterized by their neighbors as unusually small of stature. The Northern and Central Yana apparently did not use "Nozi" or an equivalent term among themselves (Sapir and Spier 1943:242), but instead made a distinction between Northern Yana (*gari'i*) and the Central and Southern Yana (*gataa'i*) (Sapir and Spier 1943:243–244). Ishi, however, grouped Northern, Central, and possibly some Southern Yana – that is, most if not all non-Yahi Yana – together in a single category, *garis'i* (Kroeber 1925:345).

3. Maidu *k'ómbo* "tribal name for the Yana Indians" (Shipley 1963:140).

4. Some of these forms are in the table of "Parallel Forms in Three Dialects" in Sapir and Spier (1943:244), without specific attribution to Betty Brown. Sapir mentions her Antelope Creek material in a letter to Kroeber (Sapir to Kroeber, January 10, 1916, in Golla 1984: 206).

5. The morphology of the Yana absolutive suffix (which is roughly equivalent in function to the English definite article) is somewhat more complicated than this summary indicates. There is an assimilation of *-na* to *-la* when the stem ends in *l* (*dal-la* "hand," *diitil-la* "quiver"), and polysyllabic nouns ending in a short vowel take no absolutive suffix at all (*daati* "child," *sawa* "arrow"). It should also be noted that the absolutive suffix was normally used only by men when speaking to other men. It was never employed by women or by men in speaking to women. Thus a woman would say *yaa* "person," *ba* "deer," and so forth (for a full discussion see Sapir [1929] 1990). The situation in Ishi's di-

alect was further complicated by his habit of whispering or omitting final vowels, so that his pronunciation of a noun with the *-hi* absolutive suffix, such as *yaah* for *yaa-hi* "person," was hard or impossible to distinguish from the unsuffixed "female" form of the word. In this chapter Yana forms are cited in the orthography of Sapir and Swadesh (1960), but with *ch* in place of their *c*.

6. Sapir had provided Kroeber with this list for a very different project. Between 1910 and 1912, in collaboration with Roland B. Dixon, Kroeber had amassed vocabularies of sixty-seven California Indian languages in order to identify patterns of borrowing or "in the event of any relationship existing between languages then considered unrelated, to determine this fact" (Dixon and Kroeber 1919:49). The comparative study of these vocabularies, entered in columns on large sheets of butcher paper, led to the discovery of the Hokan, Penutian, and Ritwan families (Dixon and Kroeber 1913).

7. Waterman comments that "they never learned to care for each other." Batwi "had very little tact or adjustability, and Ishi regarded him as a tiresome old fool, though he was too polite to say so." In general, Ishi seemed "readier to make friends with whites than with other Indians," probably because "the Yahi had learned to view all other peoples with suspicion and hostility" (Waterman 1918:65).

8. Pope also quotes Ishi as saying of alcohol, "Whiskey-tee crazy-aunatee, die man" (Pope 1920:186).

9. According to William Bright, "*mahala* (pronounced [məhálə]) was used in California during the Gold Rush to mean 'Indian woman,' and the term still exists as a California place name (Mahala Creek, Humboldt County). One hypothesis is that it derives from Spanish *mujer*. Another is that it is from one of the dialects of Yokuts that were spoken in the gold mining area, such as Chowchila *mokheela* 'woman' or Yawelmani *moxelo* 'old woman' (Geoff Gamble, p. c.). *Mahala mat* is the name of a native shrub in the Pacific Coast states" (posted on-line in the ssila *Bulletin* 94.1, September 11, 1999).

10. If this information can be recovered from Kroeber's (and Waterman's) notes, a list of the non-Yana words and place names that Ishi knew would shed considerable light on the precontact relationships of the Yahi.

11. Preparation of manuscript material for publication in *The Collected Works of Edward Sapir* has been supported, in part, by awards from the National Science Foundation (grant # bns-86–09411) and the Wenner Gren Foundation for Anthropological Research.

12. Hinton has published a description of the Berkeley project (Hinton 1988a) and a short statement of its results (Hinton 1988b). Another summary is Golla 1988.

REFERENCES

Baumhoff, Martin. 1957. *An introduction to Yana archaeology.* University of California, Archaeological Survey, Report 40:49–54.

Curtin, Jeremiah. 1898. *Creation myths of primitive America in relation to the religious history and mental development of mankind.* Boston: Little, Brown and Company.

Darnell, Regna. 1990a. *Edward Sapir: linguist, anthropologist, humanist.* Berkeley: University of California.

———. 1990b. Franz Boas, Edward Sapir, and the Americanist text tradition. *Historiographia Linguistica* 17: 129–144.

Dixon, Roland B., and A. L. Kroeber. 1903. The native languages of California. *American Anthropologist* 5:1–26.

———. 1913. New linguistic families in California. *American Anthropologist* 15:647–655.

———. 1919. Linguistic families of California. *University of California Publications in American Archaeology and Ethnology* 16:47–118.

Gifford, Edward W., and Stanislaw Klimek. 1936. Culture element distributions: II, Yana. *University of California Publications in American Archaeology and Ethnology* 37:77–100.

Golla, Victor, ed. 1984. *The Sapir-Kroeber correspondence: letters between Edward Sapir and A. L. Kroeber 1905–1925.* Survey of California and Other Indian Languages, University of California, Berkeley, Report 6.

———. 1988. Sapir's Yahi work: an historical perspective. In *Papers from the 1987 Hokan-Penutian Workshop and Friends of Uto-Aztecan Workshop.* Ed. James E. Redden. Occasional Papers on Linguistics 14. Carbondale: Department of Linguistics, Southern Illinois University, pp. 2–6.

Heizer, Robert F. 1969. *Catalogue of the C. Hart Merriam collection of data concerning California tribes and other American Indians.* With the assistance of Dennis Bailey, Marke Estis, and Karen Nissen. Berkeley: University of California, Department of Anthropology, Archaeological Research Facility.

Heizer, Robert F., and Theodora Kroeber, eds. 1979. *Ishi the last Yahi: a documentary history.* Berkeley: University of California.

Hinton, Leanne. 1988a. A report on the Yanan Project, University of California, Berkeley: introduction. In *Papers from the 1987 Hokan-Penutian Workshop and Friends of Uto-Aztecan Workshop.* Ed. James E. Redden. Occasional Papers on Linguistics 14. Carbondale: Department of Linguistics, Southern Illinois University, p. 1.

———. 1988b. Yana morphology: a thumbnail sketch. In *Papers from the 1987 Hokan-Penutian Workshop and Friends of Uto-Aztecan Workshop.* Ed. James E. Redden. Occasional Papers on Linguistics 14. Carbondale: Department of Linguistics, Southern Illinois University, pp. 7–16.

Hinton, Leanne (translator) and Susan L. Roth (illustrator). 1992. *Ishi's tale of Lizard.* New York: Farrar, Straus, Giroux.

Keeling, Richard. 1991. *A guide to early field recordings (1900–1949) at the Lowie Museum of Anthropology.* University of California Publications: Catalogs and Bibliographies 6.

Kroeber, A. L. [1911] 1979. It's all too much for Ishi, says the Scientist. *San Francisco Call*. October 8, 1911. Reprinted in Heizer and Kroeber 1979: 111–112.

———. [1912] 1979. Ishi, the last aborigine. *The World's Work*. July 1912, pp. 304–308. Reprinted in Heizer and Kroeber 1979: 119–123.

———. 1925. *Handbook of the Indians of California*. Bureau of American Ethnology, Bulletin 78.

Kroeber, Theodora. 1961. *Ishi in two worlds*. Berkeley: University of California.

Luthin, Herbert W. 1991. Restoring the voice in Yanan traditional narrative: prosody, performance and presentational form. Doctoral dissertation, University of California, Berkeley.

Mills, Elaine L. 1985. *A guide to the field notes: the papers of John Peabody Harrington in the Smithsonian Institution, 1907–1957*. Vol. 2, *Native American history, language and culture of northern and central California*. White Plains NY: Kraus International Publications.

Nettl, Bruno. 1965. The songs of Ishi. *Musical Quarterly* 51(3): 460–477.

Newman, Stanley S. ms. Yana notes from Sapir's course. [Notes taken by Newman from Sapir's lectures on Yana grammar in Linguistics 132, Yale University, March-April 1932. 57 pp. (4″ x 6″ slips).] Originals in Golla's possession.

Pope, Saxton T. 1920. The medical history of Ishi. *University of California Publications in American Archaeology and Ethnology* 13:175–213.

Powers, Stephen. 1877. *Tribes of California*. Contributions to North American Ethnology, vol. 3. Washington DC: Government Printing Office.

Sapir, Edward. 1910. Yana texts, together with Yana myths collected by Roland B. Dixon. *University of California Publications in American Archaeology and Ethnology* 9:1–235.

———. 1916. Terms of relationship and the levirate. *American Anthropologist* 18:327–337.

———. 1918. Yana terms of relationship. *University of California Publications in American Archaeology and Ethnology* 13:153–173.

———. 1922. The fundamental elements of Northern Yana. *University of California Publications in American Archaeology and Ethnology* 13: 215–234.

———. 1923. Text analyses of three Yana dialects. *University of California Publications in American Archaeology and Ethnology* 20:263–294.

———. [1929] 1990. Male and female forms of speech in Yana. In *Donum natalicium Schrijnen*. Ed. St. W. J. Teeuwen. Utrecht: Nijmegen, pp. 79–85. Reprinted in *Selected writings of Edward Sapir in language, culture and personality*. Ed. David G. Mandelbaum. Berkeley: University of California, 1949, pp. 206–212. Also reprinted in *The collected works of Edward Sapir*. Vol. 5, *American Indian Languages 1*. Ed. by William Bright. Berlin and New York: Mouton de Gruyter, 1990, pp. 335–341.

Sapir, Edward, and Leslie Spier. 1943. Notes on the culture of the Yana. *University of California, Anthropological Records* 3(3): 239–298.

Sapir, Edward, and Morris Swadesh. 1960. *Yana dictionary.* Ed. Mary R. Haas. University of California Publications in Linguistics 22. Berkeley: University of California.

Shipley, William F. 1963. *Maidu texts and dictionary.* University of California Publications in Linguistics, vol. 33. Berkeley: University of California.

Valory, Dale. 1971. *Guide to ethnological documents (1–203) of the Department and Museum of Anthropology, University of California, Berkeley, now in the University Archives.* Berkeley: Archaeological Research Facility, Department of Anthropology.

Waterman. Thomas T. 1918. The Yana Indians. *University of California Publications in American Archaeology and Ethnology* 13: 35–102.

PART FOUR

Ishi's Stories

Previous page. Ishi at Mill Creek, 1914.

Ishi in San Francisco, 1914.

Introduction to Part Four

KARL KROEBER

Ishi seldom spoke directly to others about his personal history; we possesses scarcely any more autobiographical data from him than we have from William Shakespeare. Artistic expression, however, may reveal to a skilled and open-minded interpreter much about an individual's inner being. Herbert Luthin and Leanne Hinton demonstrate this to be so with Ishi. The songs he sang and the stories he told were his unique renderings of conventionalized forms, the supra-personal structures through which the primary forces of Yahi culture flowed. Traditional songs and stories provided the framework by which the individuality of each tribal member could develop itself. We today know only print culture, and a hypervisual one to boot; so we fail to understand how an oral culture (such as Ishi's Yahi one) is principally constituted and kept alive by singing and storytelling. Through songs and stories the interdependencies of the individuals of the culture manifest themselves by speech acts that are also personally expressive. Thanks to the skill and diligence of anthropologists a century ago, it is possible for us (and our descendants) not merely to hear Ishi's voice and read the words he spoke, but even (if we are willing to make the effort) to learn much about the inner nature of a remarkable man and of the cultural heritage that he cherished and desired passionately to preserve – not least because of the nourishing strength it had given him in all the sufferings and strangeness of his life.

Ira Jacknis's "Yahi Culture in the Wax Museum: Ishi's Sound Recordings" (Chapter 14) tells two stories. One is of how, in San Francisco nearly a hundred years ago, recordings were made of Ishi singing songs and telling stories, how these recordings have been organized and preserved for nearly a century, and what their specific value is for those interested in Ishi and Yahi/Yana language and culture. The other story is of the changing technology that made possible the making and preserving of these records of Ishi's voice – it appears that anthropologists at the Hearst Museum were, almost by accident, recording pioneers. Despite the fragility of the recording cylinders of a century ago, 90 percent have been preserved or transcribed on to more durable forms. Although Jacknis's modesty may conceal the point, it should be noted with admiration that because of the dedication and skill of the curators at the Hearst Museum, no significant material Ishi recorded has been lost. Both stories are fascinating, and inseparably intertwined, yet probably most of us will share Jacknis's feeling that primarily "we owe it to Ishi to listen to his words," for in these recordings he "was sending off a personal message to the future, even when he was narrating the journey of the Dead."

Jacknis's essay is followed by translations of stories that Ishi told to Kroeber and Waterman or dictated to Sapir (see Chapter 13). Jean Perry, who has worked with Ishi texts for more than a decade, presents two translations (Chapter 15) as literal as she could make them. This literalness may for some readers interfere with easy understanding, but I urge those unfamiliar with Native American storytelling to take the time to reread these stories. They offer an astonishingly vivid dramatization of Yahi cosmology. "The Journey of the Dead" fits the death of individuals into the ongoing cycle of creation that constitutes the dynamic of the Yahi universe, which is articulated in the "Long, Long Ago" myth. Like all such myths of beginnings, it is simultaneously a story for *now*, the moment of telling. The dead enter into a hole in the earth leading to the south (where fire appears) and then are whirled up through a hole in the sky opening into the place of continual origin of all created life as we know it, both in its natural and in its cultural forms.

Perry rightly observes that these are traditional, not personal, narratives, but why Ishi chose to tell them seems apparent. They succinctly but evocatively display Yahi conceptions of the elemental forces always operating throughout the world in which we live and die, and thus provide the basis for his understanding of the purposiveness of all Yahi patterns of behavior. In both stories, moreover, idiosyncratic qualities of Ishi's storytelling are, I believe, perceptible: signs of his manipulation of Yana/Yahi narrative style. That style seems to me unusually elliptical; it not infrequently demands imagining of details the teller omits. Strong contrasts of tonality are common, often accompanied by abrupt temporal flashbacks that disrupt narrative linearity. Ishi's stories deploy these characteristics with unusual concentration and intensity, even at comedic moments, as when Coyote sees his burnt paws as Pit River grasshoppers.

Herbert Luthin, who also has worked with Ishi's narratives for more than ten years, adds to his and Leanne Hinton's lucid translation of Ishi's remarkable "Lizard" story (Chapter 16) an analytical interpretation whose full value becomes apparent when one turns to the final selection in this section. This analy-

sis by Professors Hinton and Luthin of parts of "Coyote Rapes His Sister" is perhaps the most significant critique yet made of any traditional Native American
text (Chapter 17). They demonstrate that serious attempts to understand the
art of oral storytelling of Native Americans must take account of the traditions
of rhetorical form through which each particular telling takes shape. Simultaneously, however, informed attention must be paid to the personal character of
the teller, along with the context within which each unique telling was delivered,
and, above all, the exact fashion in which the story's language is structured to
achieve specifically definable effects upon its audience. For traditional Native
American stories much, sometimes all, of this basic information today can be
reconstructed solely through linguistic analysis. Because of the ruining of Native American cultures, most of their traditional stories are lost forever. But a
tiny fraction (which nevertheless comprises thousands of stories) were salvaged
by Boasian anthropologists in the first half of the twentieth century. In the second half of the century some "belated" Boasian linguists, ethnologists, and folklorists, with the help of Native Americans and a few literary critics, began to
develop methods of linguistic analysis for recovering the social potency and
imaginative richness of Indian storytelling. The Hinton-Luthin essay illustrates
dramatically both the difficulties and the rewards of this revisionary enterprise.

The artistry of many traditional Native American narratives until very recently was generally unrecognized, for causes both formal and ethnocentric. Indian oral stories were constructed in a fashion so different from that of our written texts that few modern readers could unaided perceive the artistic structuring
that endows Indian tales with imaginative potency.[1] There is, moreover, an in-
grained ethnocentric resistance in Western culture (as in many others) to ad-
mitting artistic impressiveness in unfamiliar literary forms. Western readers are
likely to think, for example, that an Indian teller (Ishi or someone like him) was,
after all, just an "ordinary" Indian telling stories well known in his tribe, so why
should we expect any artistic merit in his recitations? I am tempted to counter
by asking why we should expect any particular artistic merit in the writings of
the spinster daughter of an unimportant English clergyman named Austen? The
basic problem, however, is the profound difference between storytelling in an
oral culture and storytelling in a print culture. Any Native American (such as
Ishi) recounts stories that his people had told and retold for decades, even hundreds, perhaps thousands, of years – in that process sometimes developing and
refining the structuring of themes into an exquisitely shaped and deeply meaningful narrative. Such stories may be called examples of aesthetically superior
communal art, if one understands "communal" to refer to a relationship between creative individuals and their social traditions that is totally unlike any
such relationship in Western print culture today.

As with the amazing cave paintings of 30,000 years ago, we are just beginning to gain an understanding of the principles by which individual artistry
functioned in Native American oral cultures. To the enhancement of such understanding Chapter 17 is a benchmark contribution. It demonstrates that the
problems to be overcome are both linguistic and rhetorical. When there are no
longer speakers of a language such as Yahi, and the recorded corpus in the language is small, comprehension of the meaning of words and phrases can be attained only through excruciatingly laborious analyses. These require what John
Keats praised as the rare power of "negative capability," the power to keep one's
mind open, to test and retest every possibility, to accept that one will continually
make mistakes requiring painstaking correction, and to recognize that each
small advance in understanding may also modify hard-won previous conclusions – in short, scholarship at its most intense. Without such linguistically accurate comprehension of minute details of a teller's rhetoric, however, no significant judgment as to aesthetic purpose or effect of a story can be offered – any
more than one of today's literary critics would claim the power to evaluate a
poem in a language of which she is not completely a master.

The rhetorical problems posed by Indian stories are daunting. We do not yet
know the history of the storytelling of *any* Native American culture well enough
to define the place in its rhetorical traditions of any single story, let alone a single
recitation. Lacking this knowledge, we can pass only sketchily tentative judgments on the peculiar accomplishments of any individual teller. Seldom have
commentators on Native American stories known enough about the personal
history of tellers or about their rhetorical conventions to define precisely how
individual style is manifested through traditional forms, as Luthin and Hinton
are able to do so persuasively with Ishi's recounting of "Coyote Rapes His Sister."

They succeed because they make so detailed a formal contrast between the
tellings of Batwi and Ishi. They rightly focus upon a central feature of oral storytelling that has almost disappeared from our written narratives: *repetition.* Just
as Indian stories are retold over and over (every time at least slightly differently),
so phonological, lexical, syntactic, and discursive repetitions determine the artistic shape of every Indian narrative. Attention to various levels and forms of
repetition highlights how Ishi, in contrast to Batwi, downplays the broadly
ribald aspects of the tale. Ishi concentrates on social consequences of natural
impulses that produce sexual behavior his culture defines as inappropriate,
"incestual." The "normal" life Coyote's act disrupts is constituted by carefully
defined cultural conventions. This seems to be why Ishi first heavily emphasizes
customary activities, most of them conventionally gendered, and at the climax
of the deception, in sharp contrast to Batwi, has Coyote instruct his sister on
how to adorn herself and how to recognize an "appropriate" sexual partner at

the dance (himself disguised). At the dance, again unlike Batwi, Ishi gives us what Luthin and Hinton call a deftly managed scene of double-duplicity as disguised Coyote and adorned sister discuss her "absent" brother. The complexity of interplay between protagonist and sister is essential to Ishi's telling because, rather than exploiting as Batwi does the bawdy features, Ishi's version, although it does not eliminate comedic elements, foregrounds the fragility of conventional control of a force so naturally powerful as sexuality. Coyote can succeed because his sister (like most people) is looking for sexual satisfaction. The *need* for social control, however, Ishi affirms with equal dramatic (if humorous) vividness by his conclusion. Batwi's "conclusion" has Coyote with ludicrous ineptitude failing to save the children his sister produced, finally simply telling them to grow up, and then heading off into another unrelated adventure. Ishi, according to the material Luthin and Hinton present, with beautiful irony rounds off his story of violated convention by having the sister-mother curse the children, whom Coyote saves and then cares for and nurtures in what traditionally would have been woman's work.

Ishi, who never willingly described his life of concealment, does indeed, as Luthin and Hinton insist, tell us much about himself and Yahi culture in this story – which was not elicited but which he chose to tell. Why choose this story, which, incidentally is called "Coyote Rapes His Sister" not by him but by the white linguists (Sapir called Batwi's version simply "Coyote and His Sister," although Batwi, as Hinton and Luthin show, emphasizes sexuality more than Ishi)? It seems reasonable to suppose that a tale about the bad results of violating a major cultural convention might have seemed to Ishi an excellent way of dramatizing the preciousness of Yahi behavioral traditions, which are means for shaping natural impulses into socially productive channels.

Such an understanding of Ishi's storytelling, however, is made possible only by the analytic depth and exactness of Luthin and Hinton's conscientious study. It is their carefulness which validates the suggestion of factoring into any interpretation of Ishi's storytelling what we know about his life experience. This in turn requires adherence to their wise caution: after all, "what do I know about Yana psychology?" And what do we know about Yana storytelling practices? My own linguistically unsophisticated study of other Yana narratives, especially those of Betty Brown and some of Jeremiah Curtin's unpublished tales, leads me to suspect that Ishi was both a subtle and not entirely unconventional, though always original, Yana/Yahi storyteller. I therefore believe to be entirely valid Luthin and Hinton's conclusion that in his manner of telling stories Ishi "was in fact telling us a good deal about himself and about the way his people . . . lived. They survived for so long because these life-giving rhythms kept playing, day after day after day." The prime implication of this view, as they rightly assert, is that careful study of Ishi's own words makes his unique individuality stand forth clearly – and thereby frees him from the equally falsifying stereotypes of archetypal victim or archetypal ideal natural man.

NOTE

1. In my *Artistry in Native American Myths* (University of Nebraska Press, 1998), I present the case for this view in detail and with diverse exemplifications.

14
Yahi Culture in the Wax Museum
Ishi's Sound Recordings

IRA JACKNIS

When the Yahi man now known as Ishi wandered into the corral of that Oroville slaughterhouse on August 29, 1911, he was discovering more than a new social world. During his life he had come to know the white man's iron tools, glass, and woven cloth. What he certainly had no experience of, however, was its rapidly developing recording technology. Within days, he encountered his first camera (developed in 1839) and sound recorder (invented in 1877). "It was on Ishi's second day in San Francisco," noted Theodora Kroeber, "that the American Phonograph Company proposed making records by and about him, the bonus to be a gold-mold master record from the Edison Company. No commercial recordings were made, then or later" (Kroeber [1961] 1976:132).[1] Instead, the University of California (uc) Anthropology Museum decided to make its own, and later in the week Ishi began to record the first of 148 wax cylinders.

This chapter explores those recordings, documenting both Ishi's music and his speech. As such, it is a case study in the objectification of musical and verbal performance (cf. Jacknis 1996b).[2] Although I will suggest some aspects of a more formal analysis of Ishi's speech and music (cf. Nettl [1965] 1979; Luthin 1991), this essay focuses instead on contextual issues of ethnographic inscription. How did these ephemeral performances (as well as ephemeral Yahi culture in general) become objects, how were they transcribed and made available for analysis, and what have been the implications for the preservation of these objects over the past century? And what relation do these collections bear to the rest of Yahi culture, poorly documented and now extinct? These issues are made even more critical when we realize that these records of the Yahi sound world are the only ones extant and are the only ones there will ever be.[3]

NATIVE AMERICAN SOUND RECORDINGS BEFORE 1911

The phonograph used to record Ishi in 1911 was only one of several technologies then available. A machine that could record sounds was devised by Thomas A. Edison in 1877, but the inventor's interests soon went elsewhere, and it was not until 1887 that a practical version of the device was widely available (Gelatt 1977:34). During the next decade or so, the technology underwent two simultaneous changes: discs replaced wax cylinders as the primary format, and commercially prerecorded music supplanted individually recorded music and speech (Gelatt 1977:46).[4]

The history of sound recording has always been more than just the story of commercial music recordings (cf. Morton 2000), and the Ishi recordings are part of this largely unstudied topic. Although they do include music, an important part is devoted to formal texts and discursive narrations. Edison, as well as others, commonly referred to his invention as a "talking machine" (literally "sound writer," phono + graph). As this machine could record sounds as well as play them back, Edison encouraged its use for office dictation and hoped that it would be used as a recorder for telephone messages. However, passive listening gradually overwhelmed active transcription as companies rushed to earn a profit from the technology.

By the turn of the twentieth century, when the University of California was beginning to record, the university was a fairly small part of the recording universe, using rather outmoded devices. Yet the wax cylinder machine was the most suited of the available technologies for field recording. These machines were inexpensive, fairly light, and portable, and, most important, they could be used for recording as well as playing. One drawback, however, that had important implications for preservation was that such a recording existed only as a unique positive; making duplicates was difficult and compromised.

The first recordings of Native American speech and music were made among the Passamaquoddy of Maine in 1890 by Jesse W. Fewkes, under the auspices of Boston philanthropist Mary Hemenway.[5] In fact, Fewkes's "field recordings were the first made anywhere in the world" (Hickerson 1982:68). He followed this test with recording among the Zuni in 1890 and the Hopi in 1891.[6] The most important institution for the recording of American Indian music during its first decade was the Smithsonian's Bureau of American Ethnology (BAE), and the most prolific of its recordists was Alice C. Fletcher. Fletcher, who had been studying Native American music since the early 1880s, focused on the Omaha and other Plains groups. She was succeeded in 1907 by Frances Densmore, who recorded and studied Indian music for the next fifty years. Though starting slightly later than the Smithsonian, the American Museum of Natural History under Franz Boas soon became a leader, especially in quantity and regional scope. Unlike the Smithsonian's more individual practice, the American Museum was the first American anthropology museum to collect sound recordings systematically. In addition to New York and Washington, there were other miscellaneous recordists such as the Southwest Museum's Charles F. Lummis.[7]

Of these recordings, the overwhelming majority were devoted to music, although a few ethnographers, particularly those associated with Franz Boas, attempted to record Native speech (Golla 1995). In 1902 Boas instructed his student H. H. St. Clair to use the phonograph to record Comanche speech (Stocking 1974:460). Summarizing the experiment to the Bureau of Ethnology's William H. Holmes, Boas suggested that "the phonograph makes it easy to collect good texts by having old men dictate into the phonograph" (Boas to Holmes, June 2, 1903, BP). By 1914, however, he had to admit that "so far, no extended series has been collected in this manner" (Boas [1914] 1940:452; cf. Jacknis 1996b:196). Beginning in 1912, the BAE's John Peabody Harrington became perhaps the most active recorder of Native American language on the phonograph.[8]

A commercial market for American Indian music did not develop until the 1950s. Although ethnic recordings had been produced for a general audience before 1900, they were soon marketed primarily to immigrant audiences so that they could make money for the record companies. American Indian records could not have much of an appeal because of the relatively small size of its diverse community, its poverty, and its lack of electricity. Later acts of crossover appropriation – for African American "race records" and jazz and for central European dance music – started in college communities. However, a few scattered commercial discs of Indian music were made in these early years. mostly of groups from the Southwest, Plains, and East, in the 1910s and 1920s (Spottswood 1990:2927–2934). California was conspicuous by its absence.[9]

BEFORE ISHI: UNIVERSITY OF CALIFORNIA, BERKELEY, SOUND RECORDINGS, 1901–11

By 1911 the University of California, which had been using the phonograph in the field for a decade, was one of the leaders in the documentation of American Indian music. Undoubtedly, the practice of Franz Boas at the American Museum was a model for the work of his first Columbia doctoral student, Alfred L. Kroeber (1876–1960). After earning his Ph.D. in June 1901, Kroeber came to Berkeley in the fall with the founding of the anthropology department and museum.

With the ultimate goal of reconstructing the unwritten histories of Native Americans, Franz Boas and his students aimed to create a consultable archive for traditions that they believed were threatened with inevitable extinction. This

they accomplished by acquiring or creating various kinds of discrete objects –
artifacts, texts, photographs, sound recordings.[10] Despite music's ephemeral
nature, anthropologists tended to treat it like other kinds of cultural documentation. Psychologist Benjamin Ives Gilman, who analyzed Fewkes's Pueblo cylinders, likened them to specimens in a museum. Like artifacts, they could be
collected systematically; that is, gathered according to some coherent principle,
and, once objectified, they could be preserved for future generations. Always
available, they could be repeatedly analyzed, even by someone who had not recorded them (Brady 1999:81).[11]

Linguist Pliny E. Goddard, just appointed instructor, made the department's
first sound recordings in October 1901 among the Hupa and Wailaki (and perhaps others) (Long 1998:39). Goddard, who was hard of hearing, was always attracted to the use of technological aids in his studies. He may have been the one
to encourage Kroeber to use the phonograph, which his colleague did for the
first time in February 1902 (of the Yuki Ralph Moore, probably in San Francisco). Kroeber's first field recording was of Costanoan singers in Monterey,
made that April; his first recording of the Yurok came in July.

During the first decade, at least, Kroeber was the most active of the California
recordists, followed by Goddard, field associate Constance Goddard DuBois,
and students Samuel Barrett and Thomas T. Waterman.[12] Waterman – who
would make most of the Ishi recordings – first used the phonograph among the
Diegueño in September 1907.[13] Most of the recording in this decade was done
primarily in the years 1901–03 and 1905–11.[14] Naturally, the university focused
its work on Native California, but geographical coverage was quite broad, as
Kroeber strove for a comprehensive inventory. Outside of the state, the museum
recorded in nearby Oregon, Nevada, and Arizona, and even made cylinders
from visiting Siberian and Pacific Island peoples.[15] Although most were field recordings, some were made at the museum in San Francisco.[16] The University of
California department was unusual in the amount of recording that it did of
Native myth and narrative accounts. Moreover, Kroeber especially was interested in experimenting with the phonograph in order to determine its limitations and to maximize its efficiency.[17] By the arrival of Ishi in September 1911, the
museum had almost 1600 catalogued cylinders.

ISHI'S RECORDING SESSIONS: A SUMMARY
Ishi's sound recordings were not made steadily throughout his life at the museum; instead they were bunched, particularly to his first months there. Although our sources are not precise, he seems to have had four principal recording sessions: early September 1911, recorded by Waterman (the first and longest);
January 1912, by local musician William F. Kretschmer; February 1912, by

Kroeber; and the last in April 1914, also by Kroeber. Ishi's entire body of recorded music and speech was contained on 148 wax cylinders, with a total of about 5 hours and 41 minutes (not counting several cylinders that are now unplayable).[18]

According to the catalog, Waterman made the first recordings of Ishi some time in September 1911 (series 55, 57). Our best indications of their specific dates are the several newspaper accounts that describe them (*San Francisco Examiner* [1911] 1979; Miller [1911a] 1979, 1911b; Kinsley 1911). Ishi left Oroville on Labor Day (Monday, September 4), arriving in San Francisco before midnight. On Wednesday afternoon, he started telling the Story of Wood Duck (U-tut-ne), which he continued the following morning. Then in the afternoon of Thursday, September 7, he repeated the story for the phonograph, for a total of fifty-one cylinders, lasting two and a quarter hours (134 minutes, 55 seconds).[19] Although Waterman and others at the museum had been recording California Indian music for a decade, the speed and, even more, the extent of this recording is amazing.

Surviving documentation on the recording sessions is vague; it does not allow us to determine precisely how long each session lasted, but from newspaper accounts we know that they sometimes took place over several days. Exact recording dates are often missing from the catalog, but an important clue are the numbers given for each series: "Wood Duck Myth (D1–51, 134'55")," "Account of the fate of souls after death (F1–28, 71'53")," "Account of a ceremony for adolescent girls (A1–7, 18'44")," plus nine more cylinders, some with multiple songs and speech, for a total of ninety-five cylinders during September 1911. Three songs for the adolescent girls' ceremony were evidently recorded on September 22 (Kroeber and Valory 1967:20).[20] Although these were undoubtedly recorded over several days, it is very likely that the entire series was recorded more or less continuously.

In January 1912, William Kretschmer made four cylinders of songs for a woman's dance in the girls' adolescence ceremony, and for gambling and dance; the latter two repeated songs that Ishi had sung earlier for Waterman (series 59). Beyond this minor recording, Kretschmer is important for making transcriptions of many of Ishi's songs. Born in 1861, in Vienna, Austria, where he trained at the Conservatory of Music, William F. Kretschmer was a composer and arranger for musical publishers in Philadelphia and New York before moving to Oakland to teach theory and harmony. He died in San Francisco in September 1914, not long after recording Ishi.[21]

A month after the Kretschmer cylinders, Alfred Kroeber made another cluster of Ishi recordings: twenty cylinders in February 1912.[22] Later in the year, on August 27, Kroeber made another five (series 60), and on April 14, 1914, he made the final recordings of Ishi: nineteen cylinders (series 66). Some of these cylinders contained more than one song on a cylinder, and some, especially in Kroeber's last session, contained repetitions of songs that Ishi had already recorded.[23]

We do know that, some time in the spring of 1914, Ishi was filmed singing into the phonograph, and it is highly likely that these last recordings were made then. This film, made by the California Motion Picture Corporation, was released in November of 1914 (acc. 475, cf. Kroeber [1961] 1976:133). It was to include 25 feet of film on "Singing in phonograph," as part of "Ishi as a scientific specimen," as well as 75 feet on "speech record-lip movements." In the final list of scenes are: "Singing his ancient melodies into the graphophone," and "Listening to his song 'coming back' to him." Unfortunately, accession information reports that the nitrate negative had to be destroyed in 1928 because the emulsion was gone.

Also in 1911, probably that September, Waterman produced some kymograph tracings of Ishi speaking.[24] This specialized machine produced a paper tracing recording the position of the tongue as it formed sounds. Pliny Goddard, before he left for the American Museum in 1909, was one of the most active users of this machine (Goddard 1905).

These 148 cylinders may seem like relatively little for the four-plus years Ishi lived in San Francisco, but the sound recordings were only one medium out of a total array of Ishi documentation, and that time included extended periods of Ishi's illness, as well as lengthy absences on the part of both Waterman and Kroeber.

RECORDING AS SOCIAL PERFORMANCE

Like all sound recordings until recently, the Ishi cylinders document unique performances, not more general cultural forms.[25] In explaining the limitations of phonograph recordings as a representational medium, anthropologist Jaime de Angulo pointed to the many practical and performative problems that could occur during any given recording: the machine runs slowly, there is distracting ambient noise, the singers forget the words or sing too softly, and so on (de Angulo and d'Harcourt [1931] 1988:25).[26] This has been a special problem for Native Californian song and story, where "Each telling ... is a performance, and no two performances are the same" (Silver and Miller 1997:123). Although many Boasian ethnographers stressed the paradigmatic over the performative (Brady 1999:63, cf. 81), these issues of representation and sample – acute for Ishi – were of keen concern to Kroeber and Goddard.

All acts of ethnographic transcription are social acts, and even more so when they involve the recording of myths and songs. Ishi's cylinders were the result of a collaborative effort of several individuals, each playing a distinct role. For these recordings, the actors included the performer, Ishi; the various recordists; and, for at least the first sessions, a Native audience of Sam Batwi. Of mixed Central Yana and Southern Yana–Maidu parentage, Batwi had traveled down from his home in Redding to Oroville, so that he could help as an interpreter. He then accompanied Ishi and Waterman to San Francisco, where he seems to have remained "for three weeks or so" (Kroeber 1976:151).[27] In addition to issues of personnel and audience, for traditional performances, key variables include posture and gesture, temporal practices of season and hour, motivation and compensation – all external to the sound waves impressed in the wax, but critically important in creating them.[28]

The phonograph was only one of the many novel mimetic technologies to which Ishi was exposed in a matter of days. Whether still or movie camera, telephone or phonograph, news accounts dwell repeatedly on his feelings of surprise and amusement. For instance, after looking at a photo of himself, taken upon his arrival in Oroville, "a look of astonishment spread over his face. He still gazed upon it, and with a half credulous look showed it to the callers and with wonder pointed at himself. When they nodded an expansive smile broke over his features, and with great awe he carefully laid the paper aside" (*Oroville Register* 1911a).[29] Similarly, in Oroville, "On Saturday Professor Waterman introduced the aborigine to the telephone. The professor went to the Marshall's office and rang up the Sheriff's office. They then took the Indian to the phone and put the receiver to his ear. Professor Waterman then said a few words in the Yana tongue. In astonishment and fright the Indian dropped the receiver" (*Oroville Register* 1911b).[30]

Of Ishi's first encounter with the phonograph, one reporter noted that the recording "caused Ishi much amusement, and he thought at first that the records were something to eat. It was feared that there would be difficulty in inducing him to speak into the phonograph, but as soon as he comprehended he began his narrative in his best chest tones and told it consecutively" (Miller 1911b). Reports of astonishment are a standard trope in the literature on sound recording, as are attempts to assimilate the new medium to Native cultural categories (cf. Brady 1999:27–51). Comments by Kroeber and Waterman reveal a more nuanced reaction, or at least one that evolves. According to Kroeber, during his first month in the city Ishi did not understand most things, but after a while his surprise vanished and he just accepted them. He would then do just about anything one asked of him (Heizer and Kroeber 1979:111; cf. 157–158).

For sound recording, the reaction is double; first to the act of inscription, but even more importantly, reflexively to the playback. We know that these cylinders were replayed soon after their recording so that Waterman could get transcriptions and then translations. Like many Americans at the turn of the century, Ishi was hearing his voice for the first time. Unlike so many others, however, who were quite unhappy with the sound of their voices (as, in fact, many are still today), Ishi seems to have been untroubled, judging from the reported enthusiasm he displayed. No doubt, for Ishi, all these experiences were so radical and transformative that the sound of his voice was the least of his problems.

Ishi's emotions may have been responsible for the slight delay in his recording. For whatever reason, Ishi first recounted the Wood Duck story for seven-plus hours over two days before he began to record it.[31] Perhaps this was due to Waterman's trepidation and a desire to make Ishi feel comfortable with his strange, new surroundings. According to one account: "To-day an attempt will be made to get Ishi to talk into a stenographer's phonograph. His voice is so low that the success of this experiment is doubtful. Waterman will further gain the Indian's confidence before bringing in the phonograph, as, if Ishi comes to the conclusion that there is witchery in it, there may be no records, and they, Waterman says, would be unparalleled in the history of anthropology" (*San Francisco Examiner* [1911] 1979:106).

The rapport the pair established must have been solid, for the dominant emotion that comes through our meager sources is Ishi's deep enthusiasm:

> Both the Indians [Ishi and Batwi] are deeply interested in Waterman's efforts to evolve a vocabulary for the unknown [Ishi] and will talk by the hour. Yesterday while they were at work and Waterman was writing down the words as rapidly as he could gain them he was called to the telephone. The unknown began a lengthy harangue, pointed to the book and pencil used for the list, and apparently complaining. Sam Batwi said, when questioned, that the Indian thought if they were going to work it should be steadily done. "He say better work all time, no leave, go away, stop," said Sam. [in Heizer and Kroeber 1979:104]

According to a similar report, Ishi told Batwi "that the head man Waterman would better stay and listen if he wanted to hear the rest of the story" (Heizer and Kroeber 1979:106). Here Ishi may have also been responding to a Yahi rule of storytelling. For example, among the Karuk (with a related Hokan language), once having started a story, "a narrator had to finish it. To fail to do so would cause his back to become crooked" (Silver and Miller 1997:124).

Four years later, when linguist Edward Sapir worked with Ishi to secure Yahi texts by manual transcription from oral dictation, Ishi's impatience again surfaced. Waterman reported to Kroeber (July 12, 1915, DA) that "Ishi has never been unwilling to work, but he was profoundly unwilling to dictate texts. The whole trouble was in putting on the breaks enough to record what he said." In a similar vein, Kroeber commented to Sapir (May 17, 1915; cf. Golla 1984:188),

"You will find Ishi bursting with mythological, ethnological, tribal, and geographical information, which he is delighted to impart, but he may need a little training before he will dictate connected texts slowly enough for writing. All that we have satisfactorily got of this sort has been through the wearisome process of having him repeat, word by word, speeches previously delivered into the phonograph."

Although we can only speculate as to Ishi's deepest thoughts and motivations, one has to view this recording activity as a response to his previous experience. For his entire life, white men had tried to destroy his people and his culture; more personally, he had just come from an extended period of "solitary confinement," in which he had lived alone for perhaps three years, without speaking Yahi to anyone. Besides the sheer pleasure in finally being able to speak his language to a receptive group (noted by Waterman, in Heizer and Kroeber 1979:130), Ishi's feelings of loss may have motivated him to want to leave a permanent record of his vanished life in objects (texts, vocabularies, artifacts, sound recordings, photographs, and film). Thus Ishi's experience as a holocaust survivor may help explain his excitement and commitment to the project.

As far as the anthropologists were concerned, one possible reason for their intensity in the work at this moment may have been doubts about the extent of Sam Batwi's participation. His aid, limited though it may have been, was the only way to obtain a translation from Ishi effectively, and they probably realized that he could not stay for an extended time. As it was, even Sapir, with his great linguistic abilities, had a very difficult time getting translations. Mere sound recordings were just the first step. Unlike previous forms of transcription, the phonograph allowed one to make sound recordings relatively easily without having the professional skills needed for either linguistic or musical transcription, let alone translation (Brady 1999:86). Waterman and Kroeber had these skills, but they must have realized how much harder it would be without Batwi.

Although they were innovative, one cannot fairly say that these recorded performances took place "out of context." Yet what relationship did they bear to Ishi's experiences growing up? Concerning the songs, we know that California Indian music was rarely produced in isolation, for its own sake, as it would have been for the phonograph. Rather, it invariably accompanied activities such as hunting and gathering, curing, or communal celebration (Wallace 1978:642). This shift undoubtedly affected the performances in ways we cannot precisely determine.

Of all the conventions for storytelling, the ones concerning seasonal and daily time are the best known. "Stories set in the prehuman, mythical era had to be told only in the proper season and at the proper time: in the winter and at night. According to many northern California groups (e.g., Modoc, Shasta, Atsugewi, Achumawi, Wintu, Northeastern Maidu), myth-telling in the summer attracted rattlesnakes." Another consequence for the wrong season was hastening the arrival of winter, and telling a myth during daylight would make the teller a hunchback (Silver and Miller 1997:125).

Although we do not know as much as we would like, we do have some indications of Ishi's performative expectations. According to one account, Ishi's telling of the story of Wood Duck occupied nearly all afternoon. "All of this took some hours, but it was explained that Indians tell stories merely to pass the time, and see no necessity to hurry. Night is the usual time for story telling, and Ishi said yesterday that it was no time to be telling stories, it was not dark enough" (Heizer and Kroeber 1979:104–105; cf. 106). Although we have no indication of Ishi's sense of appropriate season, his telling did occur near the beginning of autumn. However, the rules for a story such as Wood Duck were probably less rigid: "The restrictions that pertained to myth-telling did not apply to ordinary stories. Among the Shasta, for instance, adults used story fragments to illustrate points in conversation. . . . In addition, parents, or more often, grandparents, told children ordinary stories any time the children wanted to hear them" (Silver and Miller 1997:126).

Posture was also conventional for Native California narration. In some groups the teller remained seated, whereas among others he stood (Silver and Miller 1997:124). Ishi seems to have done both: "Sam Batwee evidently takes a pride in his friend's performances for he urged the unknown to sit up straight when he sang" (Heizer and Kroeber 1979:104). When Ishi sang Wood Duck's song he stood, but "while he told U-Tut-Ne's story he sat in a chair or squatted on the floor" (1979:105). Naturally, the phonograph was incapable of recording the elaborate gestures that invariably accompanied the dramatized telling of California Indian myths.

Finally, audiences were also expected to follow proper behavior. Smoking during myths might be forbidden; listeners might have to lie down. Frequently, active listener participation was demanded, with vocal expressions of approval or disapproval, but sometimes silence was enjoined (Silver and Miller 1997:124). The San Francisco sessions would have been strange to Ishi, to say the least. At least for the Story of Wood Duck he had a Yana speaker present, which must have encouraged him enormously. What he made of Waterman and the reporters is uncertain, but one gets the impression that Ishi was so overjoyed to have the opportunity to tell a story in Yahi that he just forged ahead.

In time, Ishi and his anthropologist friends ended up exchanging music. On at least one occasion, Ishi went to a musicale, although he was more impressed with the audience than the performance (Heizer and Kroeber 1979:107–12). Reportedly, "the voice of Caruso," which he probably heard on cylinders, "delighted Ishi" (Riffe and Roberts 1992). From the other direction, one cylinder contains Waterman singing an Indian song; and Kroeber noted "having sung the melody" of a girl's puberty song "with Ishi many times."[32]

These formal recording sessions were not the only occasions on which Ishi sang. On at least one Sunday he presented a song recital. Although it attracted a huge crowd, the "reviewer" for the *San Francisco Chronicle* (1911) found little to like, as indicated by the subtitle, "Selections Well Chosen, but Rendition Proves Indian No Rival of Caruso." Perhaps not understanding the conventions of Western performance, Ishi laughed when the crowd applauded. Ishi also sang to more appreciative listeners at the nearby University of California hospital: "He accompanied Pope on his rounds and often sang healing songs in Yahi to the patients" (Riffe and Roberts 1992; cf. Kroeber [1961] 1976:178; Pope in Heizer and Kroeber 1979:225).

BEYOND THE LIMITATIONS

The early acoustic mode of recording used until 1926 meant that the impressions in the recording surface were made by the mechanical action of sound waves. Early phonographs were thus generally limited in their capture of pitch and volume. String orchestras as well as high and low voices encountered difficulties, but a high male voice, like Ishi's, was suited perfectly. Ishi's recordings are almost all unaccompanied. The Yahi had several kinds of musical instruments – elderwood flute, split-stick rattle, cocoon rattle, and deer-hoof rattle (Johnson 1978:368). Although most California Indian singing is accompanied by rattles, only for two girls' adolescence songs (14–1699, 1700) did he use an instrument: beating time with a stick, probably as a substitute for the deer hoof rattle.

For ethnographic recordings, the primary limitation was duration. Although recording time for a wax cylinder in 1890 could be extended up to nine minutes, depending on the size of the cylinder and how it was recorded (Brady 1999:22), the usual duration was three to four minutes (a length that lasted through the era of 78-RPM discs, until the introduction of the long-playing record in 1948). Therefore, most recordings of the time were of short, self-contained songs or extracts from longer works. These temporal limitations thus acted to establish the "song" as the unit of analysis (Shelemay 1991:280). Ethnographers and others making individually recorded cylinders had somewhat more freedom. Boas, for example, had used two cylinders to record a Kwakwaka'-wakw (Kwakiutl) song at the Chicago World's Fair in 1893 (Jacknis, forthcoming).

Among the few ethnographers to employ multiple-cylinder recording regularly were Alfred Kroeber and his UC colleagues. They had used this approach often over the first decade of their work to record songs in series and lengthy myths and narratives. Before 1911, the longest was Kroeber's recording of the Yurok "Myth of the Origin of the Jumping Dance at Weitchpec" (38'49") on sixteen cylinders, and the one with the largest number of items was his recording of the Yurok "Medicine for the Dead," on nineteen cylinders (37'30"), both from 1907 (series 9). Even Waterman had recorded the Yurok "Death Purification Medicine from Wertpit" on ten cylinders in 1909 (22'54"; series 35).

Most California Indian songs, however, were "quite brief, some of only 20 to 30 seconds duration. If they were longer, it was from repetitions or stringing together a series of short melodies" (Wallace 1978:642). An examination of Ishi's songs reveals the common repetition of short segments, up to twenty times in a song (Nettl [1965] 1979:207). What is not clear, however, is whether such repetition was inherent in the song, correlated to the ongoing function that the song was meant to accompany (such as dancing), or conditioned by the length of the cylinder. According to one source (Heizer and Kroeber 1979:105), Ishi sang the three-note song of the Wood Duck "for hours with dignity and sweetness," which might account for the length of the session. Another report said that one rendition of the song went on for five minutes (1979:106).

While Ishi's Story of Wood Duck was narrative and not music, it was long. Among Native Californians, "persons who excelled as tellers of stories had so much literary material stored in their memories that they could perform for hours at a time and night after night without repeating themselves" (Silver and Miller 1997:123). In fact, it was by far the longest connected performance that uc anthropologists had yet attempted. Even so, the recorded version was quite a bit shorter than the first version he narrated, of which we have only the sketchiest summary. As with textual dictation, Ishi was undoubtedly constrained by the necessity to stop every three minutes or so for Waterman to switch the cylinders. The first version was probably more elaborate, with more repetition and greater detail. Given the difficulties of communication, it is likely that Ishi and Waterman just went ahead, each with his own task, with little adjustment between the logic of the story and the limitations of the cylinder.

Still, this performance is especially remarkable when one considers the recording history of Western classical music. The first complete recording of an extended work in this tradition was of Beethoven's Fifth Symphony, which lasts about 30 minutes, recorded in Germany in late 1911 and released on four double-sided discs (Brunner 1986:487).[33] The leaders in such efforts were Europeans; there were no American precedents for Berkeley's Ishi recordings except those by Kroeber himself. Ironically, Ishi's recordings may actually have been "liberated" by being noncommercial, because sets of multiple recordings were barely marketable at the time.

ISHI'S REPERTOIRE

Ishi's sound recordings may be grouped into three categories: mythological texts, discursive narration, and music. For the phonograph, Ishi recorded only one myth, the Story of Wood Duck.[34] In 1915, however, he was able to dictate another six mythological texts to Sapir: (1) an untitled fragment, not translated; (2) "A Story of Lizard," (3) "Coyote and Old Quail Woman," (4) "Coyote Rapes His Sister," (5) "Creation," (6) "Untitled [Panther and Coyote]." These texts remain in manuscript, although they are being prepared for eventual publication by a team of linguists led by University of California professor Leanne Hinton (1988; see also Chapters 13, 16, and 17, this volume).[35] According to Theodora Kroeber, "Pope recalled that Ishi had, one time or another when they were together, told him some forty distinct tales, recalled from the body of oral literature, story, and myth of the Yana people" (Kroeber [1961] 1976:206). In addition to this story, Waterman recorded four narrative accounts: the fate of souls after death, the ceremony for adolescent girls, the nature and causes of earthquakes, and a description of fishing.

The most numerous items, each no longer than two and a half minutes, are the sixty-five songs. This number includes eleven repeat performances of the same song, yielding a total of fifty-four unique songs.[36] As Nettl ([1965] 1979:204) comments, they appear to document virtually the entire musical repertoire of one Indian singer.[37] This was simultaneously a strength and a weakness of the Ishi recordings. On the one hand, such a thorough documentation of one singer had probably never been attempted before. On the other hand, because there are no other Yahi recordings with which to compare them, it is impossible to know what is characteristic of Ishi as an individual and what of Yahi music in general. They can be compared, at least, to the three cylinders that Sam Batwi made for Waterman some time during September 1911 (series 56, 58). For Yana myths, there is some comparative material, gathered by Jeremiah Curtin in 1884 and 1889, Roland Dixon in 1900, and Edward Sapir in 1907 (Sapir 1910).

In an attempt to control for these limited sources, Kroeber especially had Ishi rerecord songs that he had sung earlier, principally in his last session of 1914. This attempt, an outgrowth of Kroeber's earlier experiments to test the capacities of the phonograph, was fairly sophisticated for the time. It was obviously encouraged by the knowledge that these would be the only possible recordings of Yahi music. Nettl ([1965] 1979:205) notes the range of identity among these repetitions, some being clearly the same but others quite different. The classification of a song as being "the same" comes from Ishi, but it remains unclear in what sense Ishi meant these categorizations.

Judging by Ishi's identification of the songs, as taken down in the catalog, he had knowledge of many distinct functional genres of Yahi music.[38] Some of the most direct songs were those identified with hand-game gambling. A cluster of songs were ceremonial: girls' adolescent ceremony (with multiple components, including songs for dances), men's and women's sweathouse, the dead. Among the many songs related to curing were those for a doctor's bow, a doctor's arrow (for extracting arrows from the body), man's and woman's flint songs, and a doctor's song against rattlesnake bite. Somewhat related were several protective songs; there was a "bow" song for warding off enemy bullets or arrows, and a foot song preventing fatigue in travel. There are also a few songs that are hard to characterize: a song associated with dentalium money and one for thunder.

Many songs are identified with animals: owl, wood duck, deer (for dancing and not for dancing), and a fish song for shooting fish with arrows. While Nettl speculates that these songs were associated with hunting, at least some were probably the myth-related songs described by de Angulo: "Almost every animal has its own special song. There is the deer's song, the coyote's song, the song of the grasshopper, the earthworm, the vulture, the cocoon, etc. . . . These songs have nothing to do with the animals in question in terms of natural history. They hearken back to the mythical times when mankind-animals were not yet separated into human and animals. The great part of these songs are taken from some mythological episode" (de Angulo and d'Harcourt [1931] 1988:25). Certainly the latter would apply to the song of Wood Duck.

The Wood Duck song, as well as those for the girl's puberty ceremony and the dancing song of the dead in the other world, were closely related to mythological or ritual texts. In Native Californian performance, songs commonly alternate with oral recitation or dance. In the Wood Duck story, the protagonist sings a song to attract each of his prospective brides; the song consisting of three "words" sung on three tones: Wi-no-tay. Ishi seems to have sung Wood Duck's song for each telling of the story, including the recording session, although he may have repeated it at other times as well.[39]

Within Ishi's repertoire were songs for other genders and other tribes. He sang several female doctor songs and recounted at length customs and songs for the girl's puberty ceremony. Little is recorded about this rite (Sapir and Spier 1943:272–273), but it probably resembled the customs of the neighboring Achumawi. A girl dances for several nights (ten among the Achumawi, six among the Yahi), during which guests sing selections from a body of hundreds of songs (de Angulo and d'Harcourt [1931] 1988:23). Nettl ([1965] 1979:204) found no stylistic difference among the male and female songs, but speculated that women might have had distinctive songs, which Ishi did not know. While this was likely the case, song knowledge may also have resembled Yana speech styles. Although men and women had distinctive ways of speaking, men apparently controlled both.[40]

Six of Ishi's songs are associated in the catalog with neighboring tribes: three Maidu doctoring songs and three Atsugewi gambling songs (their foreign status is perhaps reflected in the fact that they seem to have been recorded consecutively). These tribal identifications may refer to the music, the words, or both. While both groups border Yana territory, the Atsugewi (to the northeast) speak a language in the same Hokan family as Yana, while the Maidu (to the southeast) speak a Penutian language and were traditional enemies of the Yahi. According to Kroeber, "Ishi knew a fair number of Atsugewi, Maidu, and Wintun words, about in the proportion of this order. Since he had never met a soul of any of the three stocks, this is a fact of interest, evidencing that the California Indians in their native conditions took some interest in each other and spent more or less time in the home circle telling one another about strangers and their ways" (Kroeber 1925:345–346; cf. Golla 1984:193). Borrowing of songs, especially for gambling, was frequent among California Indians (de Angulo and d'Harcourt [1931] 1988:23), and "words or lyrics borrowed from an alien language were often used" in songs (Wallace 1978:643).

We cannot know how Ishi acquired these songs and stories, but like most other Native Californian performers, he probably learned them informally by years of listening. "Storytelling in California was not a specialized occupation; nevertheless, gifted storytellers were greatly admired and their services were much in demand" (Silver and Miller 1997:123). The role of specialists of all kinds varied from region to region and tribe to tribe, and, again, it difficult to know where the Yahi and Ishi fit in. Generally, Yahi social organization was egalitarian (Sapir and Spier 1943:275), and in any case, Ishi certainly did not grow up in a normally functioning society. For the California region as a whole, "a large share of the songs represented common property, known and sung by any member of the tribe. Others, owned by individuals or social groups, had more limited circulation" (Wallace 1978:642). Again, a clue to Yahi practice was the customs of their Achumawi neighbors. Their shamans did sing some songs in public and had the assembled join in. "These shaman songs are thus not esoteric. Everybody knows them, and anyone, no matter who, can sing them to amuse themselves when the desire to do so comes over them, which furthermore, happens pretty often" (de Angulo and d'Harcourt [1931] 1988:21).

As Nettl ([1965] 1979:211) so astutely remarks, "these recordings are an amazing personal document. Ishi was presumably not an outstanding singer in his tribe – indeed, he did not live in a truly tribal environment. Yet he was able to sing over fifty songs, and to sing them, if the recordings are reliable, in an assured and self-confident manner. How many members of Western civilization, left alone as the only survivors of their cultures, would be able to do the same?"

TRANSCRIPTION AND TRANSLATION

For most anthropologists, especially at the turn of the twentieth century, recording was just the beginning. In order to make the material available to scholars and as the first step in analysis, it was necessary to transcribe the performance in musical and linguistic notations and then translate the texts. Most of Ishi's song recordings were transcribed in musical notation by William Kretschmer shortly before his death in September 1914. They were revised by Kroeber, who added the Yahi words, during that spring and summer, as part of his analysis of the material.[41] From his surviving files, it is clear that Kroeber spent an enormous amount of time on the topic of Ishi's music, both in working with the man and in formal analysis.

Although Alfred Kroeber did not have the thorough musical training that Franz Boas had (Jacknis, forthcoming), he evidently acquired some technical knowledge during his upbringing in the German-American community of New York. There seems to be no clear indication that Kroeber had music lessons, but his analyses of Ishi's music demonstrate that he understood music theory and could read musical notation. One of his biographers notes that young Alfred and his siblings accompanied their parents to operas and concerts, "which remained a major interest and recreational outlet throughout Kroeber's life" (Steward 1973:4, cf. 1961:1040; Kroeber 1970:20). Kroeber's musical interests were undoubtedly encouraged by his first wife, Henriette Rothschild (1877–1913), who was a trained pianist and an active member of the German-Jewish cultural community of San Francisco (Kroeber 1970:77). And in later years, he maintained an active correspondence with Boasian ethnomusicologists such as Helen Roberts and George Herzog as well as with professors of the university's Music Department such as Edward Stricklen and Albert Elkus.

Although he did not finish his analysis of Ishi's songs, Kroeber discussed their musical structure, phrasing, words, concordance of the recordings and transcriptions, and aspects of tonal and rhythmic patterning. For instance, for a girl's adolescence song (cat. no. 14–1824), a song that caused Kretschmer and Kroeber a great deal of trouble and thought, he wrote: "The melody also falls into four bar phrases, in common time. Within the normal phrase, designated by A B C D, A and C are identical except for the suppression in A of the last note of C, corresponding to the words *ainihinowen* and *ainihinowena*." And of a flint song (1688b), he wrote, "The song as obtained in transcription runs: A B C A B C A B C A. Unless this close was occasioned by an interruption, it would indicate that the beginning of the song was more definitely in the singer's mind than the ending – a circumstance of bearing on the question of tonality." This, incidentally, is just one of the many comments as to what Ishi must have intended. Where he could, Kroeber also addressed issues of musical practice. Of a song for the girl's adolescence ceremony (1686a), he noted that it was "sung in the middle of the night."

As the transcriber of the Yahi words, Kroeber was able to investigate the role of textual meaning in California Indian song. As he concluded to a colleague (Kroeber to Donald N. Lehmer, February 4, 1921, DA): "In general there is a surprising scantiness of meaning to the words of the songs from our California Indians. In many cases the words are wholly a meaningless refrain. When there are actual words they are few in number and make no connected sense. I mean by this that the background of significance is in the mind of the singer or perhaps his audience and that he selects a word here and there which will suggest the significance without expressing it intelligibly to anyone else." Most commentators since have agreed with the allusiveness of California Indian lyrics.[42]

Thomas T. Waterman was responsible for transcriptions and subsequent translations for the textual material. Interestingly enough, though, he did not work directly from the wax cylinders. Instead, he "wrote out from the Indian's own repronunciation of a phonograph dictation in the first days he was with us." According to Kroeber, this yielded "some 50 or 100 pages of text of the Duck myth. . . . The text thus is straight Yana, but Batwi's English to it is nonsense" (Kroeber to Sapir, May 29, 1915; cf. Golla 1984:193). Moreover, Waterman did not transcribe and translate all of the Wood Duck recordings. Of the fifty-one cylinders, only the first twenty-four were transcribed, and of these only about eleven were translated.[43] Similarly, only parts of the account of the Fate of the Dead and the girl's adolescence were transcribed and translated. Another six cylinders containing a discussion of earthquakes, gambling songs, and adolescent songs were transcribed and mostly translated (Kroeber and Valory 1967:10).[44]

Although today we are so interested in the sheer sound of Ishi's voice, for Waterman and many of his contemporaries the recordings were more of a means to an end, allowing him to make a transcription and from that a translation. During the early days of cylinder dictation machines, the actual recording had a short life, to be copied over after the information was extracted (Morton 2000:92, 150; cf. Brady 1999:62). Even today, many oral historians hold a similar lack of interest in their recordings, which are often not preserved after their transcription.

Waterman derived his method of textual transcription from Franz Boas, who recommended that the texts be "written out from re-dictation" ([1914] 1940:452; cf. Jacknis 1996b:196). This practice was thus something of a middle ground between transcription from the repeated playing of the sound recording only or from the living informant only.[45] As Sapir carried out the latter method with Ishi in 1915, he proceeded line by line and repeated back both the phonetic transcription and the translation. For the Boasians, if at all possible, it was vital to work from an informant's intuitions, not a merely phenomenal record. This method ensured that the investigator truly comprehended the Native sense (Jacknis 1984:48–50). As Goddard complained, with cylinders one had the "difficulty in breaking up the sounds of a strange language so recorded into words and in connecting these words with their proper meanings" (Goddard 1905:619).

During his final treatment of the cylinder collection, Kroeber (1960) explained their rationale:

> In making tape copies of the speech recordings the materials to be reproduced were selected on the basis that no mechanical reproduction of speech can be fully or accurately heard except by a speaker of the language or by a linguistic expert who has had considerable experience in hearing and analyzing it. The important cylinders to preserve on tape were accordingly those of which a handwritten phonetic transcript had been made, a transcription worked out by the interpreter and the transcriber after they both had listened to the recording. Without this transcription the *content* of the language has been lost although the *sound* is still present.

The question of the translation of these formal language recordings must be set into the context of Ishi's general difficulty in communicating with those around him. Despite the best efforts of his anthropologist friends, he was never able to speak much English, and they were never able to command much Yahi (Chapter 13, this volume). As noted, even Sapir, perhaps the most-skilled linguist of his day, found it difficult to get a translation. Of the six texts, Sapir left the first untitled fragment completely untranslated, and much of the rest is without English glosses (Chapter 13, this volume).[46] As a Central Yana speaker, Sam Batwi's command of Yahi was approximate. These semantic difficulties undoubtedly were a factor in the limitation of the number of stories that Ishi was able to tell and then have translated. That the untranslated cylinders exist is testament to the fact that one can make a recording of a narrative that one does not understand.

THE STORY OF WOOD DUCK

Until the texts of the cylinder recordings are fully transcribed and translated, we are limited to secondary sources, which do not permit a stylistic analysis of linguistic patterning. However, the importance of the Wood Duck story in Ishi's recorded oeuvre demands further comment. This myth revolves around Wood Duck's search for a wife. The protagonist, who lived with his two sisters, wanted to find a wife. His song attracted twenty female creatures. Although accounts differ, they included Waterdog, Waterbug, Bat, Fishhook, Chipmunk, Shikepoke, Flint, Rainbow, Mussel, Abalone, Fox, Skunk, Mountain Quail, Brown Bear, Dentalium, Magnesite, Morningstar, Blue Crane, Beaver, and Turtle Woman.[47] But each time he found something objectionable and rejected each one, sending them away with baskets of food and other presents. Unfortunately, when he finally fell in love with a young (unnamed) woman, she rejected him in favor of Lizard. The two suitors fought, with Lizard cutting Wood Duck in two. Wood Duck's two sisters restored him to life, but in the end he did not find a wife.[48]

The repetition that we find in the plot, a common characteristic of Native Californian oral performance, is an opportunity for inflection and modification. Each instance is distinct, and each telling is a performance: "A skilled storyteller did not simply repeat a story he or she had heard or learned, but would recreate a story by arranging the incidents and plots into unique forms pleasing to the listeners" (Silver and Miller 1997:123). According to Theodora Kroeber, "Turtle Woman fared no better than the others, but she was rather special in that she wore a skirt made of elkhide and came from the *Affiliated Colleges!*" ([1961] 1976:210). This kind of indexical reference would have been traditional in Native Californian story telling. Here Ishi modifies it to account for a new setting – the location of the anthropology museum – and listeners.[49]

What made Ishi choose the Story of Wood Duck in the first place? Theodora Kroeber ([1961] 1976:210) speculates that

> Ishi may have chosen to tell it to amuse his friend Watamany as a tale whose motivation would not tax too heavily the language barrier between them. . . . It is a man's wish-fulfillment tale, the kind to be told to while away a long evening in the men's house when nothing serious was afoot. It would lend itself to adumbration or elaboration and change, accommodating its content to the imagination and mood of the teller and his audience. It retains, through the mutilation of translation, some faint suggestion of Ishi's delight in absurdity and *double entendre*, for, under Yana sex code, Wood Duck's behavior is the height of humorous exaggeration, suggesting perhaps *Innocents Abroad* in our literature.

She stresses the moral of Wood Duck's reiteration of being Yana and his rejection of the others for their inappropriate behavior.

Although all that may be true, Ishi may have had more personal and reflexive reasons for telling this tale. Perhaps significantly, a reporter (*San Francisco Call*, 6 September 1911, in Heizer and Kroeber 1979:100) noted that during the time while Ishi told this story,

> When he is asked anything about his wife, he begins to tell Indian myths or legends; how the coyotes stole the fire; bits of stories of women's work; imitations of

a woman cooking mush, with bubbling sounds of boiling. This is perhaps because aboriginal tribes will never speak of the dead. Waterman said yesterday: "It's as though you asked a man when he got his divorce and he began to tell you the story of 'Cinderella.'"

Like Wood Duck, Ishi did not have a wife (and probably never had the opportunity to seek one). Although Ishi of course had a name, he refused to share it, and perhaps it was not merely a coincidence that Wood Duck's beloved remained unnamed. Wood Duck sings a courting song, which Ishi sang for his friends. As Ishi tells the story, there are repeated scenes of cooking and eating, perhaps a reflection of the difficulty he and his family often had in feeding themselves. Finally, an observer must be moved by the telling conclusion of the death and resurrection of Wood Duck, perhaps not too far removed from Ishi's own experience.

PRESERVATION AND REPRODUCTION

In their introduction to Bruno Nettl's analysis of Ishi's music, Robert Heizer and Theodora Kroeber (1979:203) remarked, "If it took a half-century to finally offer this to the world, that is a small matter because these songs are timeless." Well, not quite. Ishi's songs vanished into the air as he sang them; what remains are the impressions made in a wax surface. Despite the ethnographer's goal to make inherently ephemeral performances into enduring objects, these objects have their own problems of preservation. Although certainly longer lasting than the original performance, they, too, will decay and eventually disappear.

The history of ethnographic field recording has been caught up in a tension between ease of recording and preservation. Early recordings, such as Ishi's, were made on small, portable machines, and, for the recorder to create a sonic image easily, the medium had to be relatively soft.[50] However, this very pliability meant that the recording has a limited life. Each time it is played, it loses some aural information – a problem compounded by the multiple playings needed for transcription and analysis. Yet another problem for this organic material was the growth of mold. Compounding the problem, this technology resulted in unique recordings.

As ethnographic sound archives at the turn of the century struggled to preserve their fragile cylinder recordings, the solution they found was some form of duplication (List 1958–59). Once copied, "they could be played repeatedly for transcription and analysis; they could be placed in other locations as an insurance against loss of the originals through deterioration, fire, water damage, theft, and war; and they could be used in expanding collections through exchange" (Gillis 1984:324, 326).

In these early years duplication meant the creation of a master, from which an almost infinite number of positive copies could be made. Because commercial recordings are stamped from a negative in a factory (after the recording), they can be made of harder materials. In photography, one finds the same issue in the distinction between daguerreotypes or Polaroid prints, which exist in unique copies, and prints made from negatives. That these issues are still with us can be seen in the difference between flexible magnetic tape and commercial LPs or CDs, which (until recently, at least) could not be used for recording. Edison cylinders were unique until the 1890s, when a pantograph system was introduced to replicate a master, but it was limited. During that decade, Emil Berliner developed a system of mastering with a disc format. Although by 1901 Edison had responded with a procedure of electroplating a cylinder in order to make a master, by then the disc format had captured the market (Morton 2000:18).

Despite his development of a mastering process, Edison continued to push the cylinder's ability to make home recordings, which was just what the ethnologists wanted. The "natural habitat" for so much of traditional Native music was – and largely still is – in rural areas, far from the urban studios with their sophisticated recording and duplicating equipment. Ironically, while the University of California Museum did some recordings in San Francisco – notably those by Ishi – they were not able to make use of the more advanced (and expensive) recording equipment.[51]

Whatever the prospects for duplication, museums and archives still maintained their collections of original sound recordings. Following contemporary conservation theory, one may distinguish between preservation (maintenance and delaying decay) and restoration (active repair). Although it usually leaves the original more or less untouched, duplication is a kind of restoration. More recently duplication can actually be restoration, with the electronic manipulation of the sonic signals.

THE UNIVERSITY OF CALIFORNIA'S EFFORTS
IN SOUND PRESERVATION

Around 1916, Charles Seeger, University of California professor of musicology, began his lifelong interest in folk music and comparative musicology by listening to the Anthropology Museum's wax cylinder collection. These were the first field recordings he had ever heard, but he was worried about their preservation. As he reminisced to his daughter, "So I started to listen to one. And I realized that wax was being peeled off the cylinder while I was listening, and I immediately stopped the machine and went to the curator and said, look, I'm ruining the record by playing this. Oh, he said, that's all right, everybody does it. And I said, you're a criminal, you ought to put these things under lock and key and not allow anybody to touch them, until you've made copies of them. I didn't know anything about copying at that time. . . . I think he took my advice" (Pescatello 1992:72–73). Despite Seeger's report, anthropologists at the University of California were well aware that their wax cylinders were vulnerable.[52]

Pliny Goddard took the lead, corresponding in 1907 with the local San Francisco office of the Columbia Phonograph Company. The company suggested using the original cylinder to make a matrix in a harder material, which could then be used to cast new listening copies. As they could not recover their costs with such custom work, they asked for some publicity credit. Although Goddard decided to go ahead with the duplication project, he was never able to come up with the required funds. The university and the phonograph company continued to correspond in an effort to devise improved recording machines and blanks (Walter S. Gray to Pliny Goddard, January 31, March 4, 1907; Goddard to Gray, March 8, 1907; Columbia Phonograph Company, 1904–10, (DA).[53]

The first known duplication project for the museum came just two years later, in 1909, when the university reproduced some of its cylinders for exchange with the American Museum of Natural History. Constance Goddard DuBois had made recordings for both Berkeley and New York, and Kroeber wanted copies for comparative purposes. In exchange for some of her Diegueño and Luiseño cylinders, he sent a small selection of duplicated northern California cylinders. In turn, he instructed his colleague Clark Wissler (Kroeber to Wissler, January 8, 1909, AMNH) how to make his duplicates by placing two machines next to each other.[54] This is a method that Berkeley used from time to time, but the scope is not documented (Kroeber 1960).

By the late 1920s, not finding an American company that was willing to do reproduction work at a reasonable cost, Kroeber and his colleagues turned to the Berlin Phonogramm-Archiv.[55] Begun informally in 1900 and officially in 1905, this institution was the largest European sound archive and specialized in cylinder reproduction (Reinhard [1962] 1971; cf. Gillis 1984:324). After 1906 they used a process called "galvanolysis," a form of mastering in which the original cylinders were cast as copper negatives, allowing an unlimited number of positive copies, although with some loss in sound quality (Inman 1986:1). Between 1926 and 1930, the University of California sent 226 cylinders to Berlin for electroplating (Kroeber 1960). Drawn mostly from the California collections, they included four Ishi recordings.[56] The University received new positive copies, with the Archiv maintaining the master matrices (as property of the University). However, Berkeley was soon forced to end this arrangement due to Depression-induced budget cuts.[57]

The termination of the Berlin collaboration coincided with the shift to a new recording technology, one soon adopted in California. About 1931 portable disc machines became popular. Although discs had been in use for decades, they were now integrated with microphones and electrical amplification. Between 1931 and 1933, the UC anthropologists experimented with aluminum disc recorders owned by the French Department. Doing this work in-house also avoided the continual damage to the cylinders through shipping. They made some new recordings and evidently transferred some of their cylinder collection.[58]

After a lapse owing to the Depression and the Second World War, the University made another attempt to duplicate its cylinder collection. In November 1947, Edward Gifford sent ninety-seven cylinders (mostly Pomo and some Sierra Miwok, recorded between 1902 and 1927) to the Library of Congress so that they could be duplicated on discs (Kroeber 1960; Gray and Schupman 1990:3; correspondence between Edward Gifford and Duncan Emrich, 1947–49, DA).[59] This method also employed a master matrix, but this time producing an acetate-covered aluminum disc. With a collection of over 2000 items and limited laboratory facilities, it was acknowledged that the project would have to proceed in stages (Emrich to Gifford, January 10, 1947, DA). Unlike the Berlin project, the Library was to bear the costs of reproduction, but, as with that effort, the available funding again ran out (Elkus 1949).

By late 1950, when the Berkeley music department obtained a University appropriation to continue the duplication, the parameters had changed: the format was switched from discs to the new medium of magnetic tape, and University of California personnel were to perform the work (Albert Elkus to Theodore McCown, December 15, 1950, and related correspondence, file for UC Dept. of Music, DA). Tape technology actually goes back to the turn of the century, but it was not made practical before German developments during World War II. Recording companies first used the medium during the 1940s, but it came into common home use only in the following decade (Millard 1995:207). Even then, it took several years for the University to shift to the new form of duplication.

Although a handful of the Ishi cylinders had been sent to Berlin, most had to wait until the mid-1950s for reproduction. The first Ishi recordings to be transferred to another format were some songs duplicated onto open-reel tape by the university's music department in 1955.[60] A few years later, in November 1957, some of Ishi's spoken narratives were also transferred. These were included in a larger project to duplicate some of the original California Indian linguistic cylinders onto tape (Kroeber 1960). As the museum then did not have a single working cylinder machine, linguistics student James B. Hatch investigated the subject and put one functioning phonograph together from the parts of several in the museum. He worked with Kroeber to make the transfers, with his professor identifying the languages, tribes, and ceremonies and advising on which of the alternate versions to use. Among these were portions of the Wood Duck myth and accounts dictated by Ishi to Waterman in 1911 (Kroeber [1961] 1976:132–33).[61] The popularization of the new tape technology coincided with the publication of Theodora Kroeber's Ishi book in 1961, which tremendously increased interest in his life and surviving collections. In 1964 a selection of Ishi's songs were again recorded from the cylinders onto tape, this time as a stand-alone project.[62]

Over the years, each project would cover either the music or the speech components of the collection, depending on the sponsoring body. Yet despite this extensive copying (estimated at 90 percent of the cylinders), the museum was unhappy with the quality of the reproduction and in 1967 began experimenting with better methods (Lowie Museum c. 1973). All the Ishi cylinders, along with all the others in playable condition, were transferred onto Mylar tape in 1975, with funding from the National Endowment for the Humanities. At the same time, the entire sound collection was recatalogued, with listings for each song, associated documentation, and tribal indexing, all of which was eventually compiled and published by Richard Keeling (1991). However, the Ishi recordings were not part of two massive Lowie Museum projects, devoted to distributing copies of the sound collection, which followed this housekeeping: the California Indian Music Project, 1983–85, or the California Indian Library Collections, 1988–94. As both projects were devoted primarily to returning recordings to Native communities, the lack of identifiable Yahi descendants may have been a factor.

THE USE AND STUDY OF THE ISHI RECORDINGS

The recordings of Ishi's speech and song have not gotten the scholarly attention they have deserved. Alfred Kroeber spent much of the spring and summer of 1914 preparing an analysis of Ishi's music, but he was not able to finish it before leaving for a sabbatical.[63] Although he returned to the materials at the end of his life, unfortunately he was never able to publish his research before his death.[64] A few years later, ethnomusicologist Bruno Nettl borrowed a set of Ishi tapes from the Lowie Museum in order to prepare a comprehensive essay on Ishi's songs (Nettl [1965] 1979). It is not clear whether he consulted Kroeber's study, to which he does not refer, but his formal analysis is quite similar to his predecessor's in many respects. Since that time, no scholar has investigated Ishi's music, although an important resource is Keeling's published inventory of the Lowie Museum cylinder collection, which included Ishi's recordings.

The textual material has been even more neglected. Waterman never published the Wood Duck story, and Sapir died before finishing his study. Theodora

Kroeber is largely responsible for what we know about this myth, through the summary in her original book ([1961] 1976) and the news accounts reproduced in her anthology (Heizer and Kroeber 1979). Significantly, Ishi's rendition seems to be the only known version of the Story of Wood Duck. Although Leanne Hinton and her student Herbert Luthin (1991, 2002) have analyzed Ishi's Story of Lizard (Chapter 16, this volume), they have based their work on the Sapir text. Other than Theodora Kroeber's summary, the only published response to Ishi's incredible performance of the Wood Duck myth has been Gerald Vizenor's play (1995; cf. Owens 1999, Chapter 20, this volume). No scholar has yet examined the verbal material on the Ishi cylinders.

For sound recordings, commercial distribution is a form of "publication," with some kind of selection and editing. Two samplers of Ishi's recordings have been released in cassette-tape format. About the same time (the mid-1970s) that it produced a series of five cassette tapes drawn from its California Indian song collection, the Lowie Museum released an Ishi sampler (25.5 minutes). A new edition of twelve songs and narrative excerpts was selected, de-noised, engineered, and remastered in 1992 by Bernie Krause of Wild Sanctuary Communications (Krause 1992, 34.5 minutes). These were the first time Ishi's recordings had ever reached an audience wider than a few scholars and museum personnel. The Krause cassette was produced partly in association with Jed Riffe and Pamela Roberts for use in their 1992 film, which includes an account of Ishi's sound recordings. The filmmakers thought it important to use Ishi's own voice, in the best possible sound, partly because the sources were so limited, but more importantly because of the direct physical connection with Ishi – even in Yahi, these were Ishi's own words and not other people speaking for him (Jed Riffe, personal communication).

ISHI'S SOUND LEGACY

Since the invention of the cylinder phonograph, sound recordings have been transferred to each new format: acoustic and then electrical discs (78 RPM), long-playing discs (33 RPM), magnetic tape (open reel, cassette), digital compact disc, and now other kinds of digital files. The impetus has continually been the commercial market, but sound archives have followed along in a more conservative pattern. Allowing for practical problems, the University of California's Anthropology Museum worked continuously to preserve and duplicate appropriately its immense sound collection.[65] The Ishi recordings have been through many of these formats – some of Ishi's cylinders have been copied onto tape at least three times – with plans being made for their migration to a digital format.

Digitization has radical implications for the objectification of sound. After more than a century of sound recordings as discrete physical artifacts, they are on the verge of disappearing (Morton 2000:187). At the Hearst Museum and other archives, the original cylinders remain and will be preserved, but increasingly they can be converted to information, with no unique location, and then endlessly replicated. In a way, this is simply a further extension of the process of mechanical reproduction, which extended from a unique copy and to the multiples produced from a master. Nevertheless, for the foreseeable future the original documents will likely contain information that cannot be fully captured and that we will want to maintain for future uses. As George Herzog noted, "As long as one keeps the original cylinders safely, even after they had been rerecorded on aluminum, they can be always rerecorded again, with a better technic" (Herzog to Kroeber, July 20, 1934, DA).

Yet, as with all our collections, why should we preserve Ishi's recordings?[66] Why are these recordings relevant today? First, there are issues of preservation and invention. The new technologies (or aspects of them) that were destroying Ishi's culture were also serving to preserve it (Brady 1999:2). On the one hand, these mimetic technologies were profoundly conservative. Ideally suited to the Victorian cult of the dead (Brady 1999:48), sound recordings, as well as photographs, worked to preserve memories of past people, places, and times. With their motive of ethnographic salvage, Kroeber and Waterman regarded these recordings as documents of traditional Yahi culture. For his own reasons, Ishi may have wanted to create a personal memorial to his dead family and people, after a period of isolation, even when he could not mention them directly. Like all objects, these ethnographic representations endure beyond their creation. The original participants – Ishi, Waterman, and Kroeber – are now all dead, but their recordings survive to us in the present. To whom do, or should, they now belong?

In their different ways, Ishi, Waterman, and Kroeber were "inventing" Yahi culture (Wagner 1981:27–31). Each began with some conception of what that culture was and then extended it to incorporate changed circumstances and knowledge. Their recordings (like their photographs, texts, and other ethnographic representations) were the product of a joint interaction of singer and ethnographer, each of whom has some claim to them. In fact, they are a strange cultural mixture, merging aspects of both cultures. Yahi songs and stories were traditionally oral; such physical objects as wax cylinders and photographs are Western creations. As Ishi eagerly made innovative use of such materials as glass, metal, cotton string, and glue in order to make traditional-style artifacts, so his music and storytelling changed to reflect his new home at a San Francisco museum. Despite the desires of the anthropologists, they are not simply "Yahi culture."

No one person can control Ishi's representation, and in the years since Theodora Kroeber's book appeared, an almost morbid fascination has grown around him. One person has discovered a cave frequented by Ishi on San Francisco's Parnassus Heights. Here he periodically retreats for communion with Ishi's spirit, lighting candles and playing a cassette recording of Ishi singing (Sulek 2000). Those perhaps with a more direct concern are Native Californians. Although Ishi had no direct descendants and there is no longer a functioning Yahi culture, there are Yana descendants at the Redding Rancheria and the Pit River community. It is important to preserve and study these recordings for them as well. Unlike Ishi's brain, sound recordings can be copied and easily "repatriated," as they have been in the Lowie Museum's projects of the 1980s. But these Native communities will be the ones to decide how they wish to make use of Ishi's recordings.

Finally, we have a moral imperative to study these recordings and their contents. Scholars, of course, will always wish for more. For Kroeber, linguistic texts obtained without an informant to clarify meaning held little value; Nettl regretted that we can no longer go back and discover in what ways Ishi considered two songs to be "the same." This, however, is a problem with all historical knowledge, whether of ancient Egypt or Elizabethan England. We simply must make do with the available sources. Furthermore, as Luthin and Hinton note of the Sapir texts (Chapter 17, this volume), these recordings contain Ishi's autobiography. They are the only words we have from Ishi directly in his own voice, reflecting his personal concerns. Almost all the rest of our meager records are other people speaking for him. In these recordings, Ishi was sending off a personal message to the future, even when he was narrating the journey of the Dead. These recordings teach us that Ishi was not a victim – or, rather, not just a victim. They attest to his survival and his creativity in the face of great personal and cultural loss, which he shares with other Native Californians. We owe it to Ishi to listen to his words, which he narrated with such great effort and sincerity.

NOTES

For assistance in the research and writing of this chapter I would like to thank Grace Buzaljko, Victor Golla, Leanne Hinton, Kathryn Klar, Clifton Kroeber, Karl Kroeber, F. Alexander Long, Jed Riffe, William Roberts, M. Steven Shackley, Barbara Takiguchi, and Gerald Vizenor.

1. As of this writing, no copy of the Phonograph Company's proposal has been found.

2. My treatment of cultural objectification is partly inspired by Roy Wagner's *Invention of Culture*, especially the section entitled "The Wax Museum," which does contain a short discussion of Ishi (Wagner 1981:27–31). Some of the ideas elaborated here were first expressed in the exhibition that I curated, "Ishi and the Invention of Yahi Culture," which

opened at the Hearst Museum of Anthropology, UC Berkeley, in October 1992 and, after several revisions, closed in September 2001.

3. As with the literature on Ishi in general, which consists almost entirely of popular accounts of varying qualities, little scholarly attention has been devoted to Ishi's sound recordings. Theodora Kroeber never claimed to be writing a scholarly treatment but a popular retelling of existing sources. More useful are the original documents and commentary included in Heizer and Kroeber 1979. A contemporary rethinking was generated by the research involved in the making of the Riffe and Roberts film (1992), but the volume of scholarly essays that grew out of this never came to fruition. The film, too, was a popular retelling, without source citations. Among the more important recent scholarship are the studies by Luthin (1991), Buckley (1996), and Shackley 2000; Orin Starn's ongoing research; as well as the comments of Gerald Vizenor (e.g., Vizenor 1992). This chapter is based primarily on surviving original documentation at the University of California, Berkeley, principally in The Bancroft Library (Alfred Kroeber Papers, and Correspondence of the Department and Museum of Anthropology) and the Hearst Museum (Keeling 1991, the original ledgers, a folder titled "Cylinder Recordings" and other notes in the archives for the audio collection).

4. Among the principal histories of sound recording are those by Gelatt (1977), Millard (1995), and Morton (2000).

5. For the early history of American Indian sound recording, see the good reviews by Densmore (1927), Gillis (1984), Seeger and Spear (1987), Lee (1993), and Brady (1999).

6. The Peabody Museum at Harvard acquired the Hemenway collections in 1894.

7. In addition to the University of California Museum (2713 items), the major collections of anthropological wax cylinders were the Smithsonian's Bureau of American Ethnology (3591 cylinders), the American Museum of Natural History (2500), the National Museum of Canada (1530), the Field Museum (1500), and the University of Pennsylvania Museum (cf. Inman 1986:3). Much of the American Museum collection was copied for Columbia University by ethnomusicologist George Herzog between 1936 and 1948 and taken to Indiana University (becoming the nucleus of the Archives of Traditional Music) in 1948, when Herzog was appointed to the faculty. In 1961 the American Museum deposited its entire collection in Indiana.

8. In contrast to those concerned with Native American subjects, folklorists interested in Anglo and other European American traditions at first avoided the use of the phonograph. Although the Library of Congress made some early cylinder recordings, its most active period of sound documentation awaited the development of a field disc machine after the establishment of its Archive of Folk Song in 1928: "In 1931, Robert W. Gordon began his experiments with a portable disc apparatus and made his first foray into the field with a disc machine during the winter of 1931–32. A year and a half later, John and Alan Lomax began a career of disc recording for the Archive of Folk Song . . ." (Hickerson 1982:70).

9. "The first commercial recordings by a Native American were made for Berliner records in the 1890s. In 1904 Ho-Nu-Ses recorded Iroquois Songs for the Victor Talking Machine Company. In the years following, additional recordings of Indian music were made occasionally, sometimes by Indians appearing on the stage, sometimes for ethnographic purposes, such as the Gennett Hopi recordings of 1926. They were obviously intended for sale to people who were not Indians" (Gronow 1982:15; cf. Cohen and Wells 1982:180).

10. The literature on objects and the Boasian ethnographic strategy is huge. I have treated it for Boas and Kroeber (Jacknis 1993,1996a,1996b, and 2002; cf. also Buckley 1996; Cole and Long 1999; Darnell 1999).

11. Anthropologists like Boas and Kroeber were actually leaders in the creation of sound collections. Yet, while ethnographic sound collections have existed almost from the beginning of a practical technology, they consisted principally of unique field recordings. The situation was quite different for commercial recordings, which existed in multiple copies. As with films, each company had its own collection of masters, but preservation of the entire corpus (or sometimes, any) was not necessarily a goal. Most independent museums, libraries, and archives began to acquire recordings actively at a relatively late date (McWilliams 1979:ix).

12. Thomas Talbot Waterman (1885–1936) grew up in the Fresno area. The son of an Episcopalian clergyman, he intended to follow his father's profession, graduating from the University of California in 1907 with a Hebrew major. He entered anthropology after enrolling in a phonetics course taught by Goddard, whom he accompanied on a trip to record Californian Athapaskans. Waterman spent 1909–10 at Columbia, finally earning his doctorate under Boas in 1913. At the University of California he served as museum assistant (1907–9), instructor and assistant curator (1910–14), assistant professor (1914–18), and, after two years at the University of Washington, as associate professor (1920–21).

13. During the first decade, smaller numbers of cylinders were also made by E. O. Campbell, Henriette (Rothschild) Kroeber, Edward Gifford (the most prolific recordist of the following decade), Arthur Warburton, and J. Alden Mason. Among the recordists of this period were two California Natives: Leslie Wilbur (Mohave) and Weitchpec Frank (Yurok), both deputized by Kroeber.

14. Little recording was done in 1901, 1902, 1903, 1905, and 1906; activity was fairly steady from 1907 on.

15. By 1911, in addition to Yana/Yahi, the University of California had documented the following Californian groups: Tolowa; Yurok; Hupa; Nongatl; Whilkut; Chilula; Wailaki; Wintun; Yuki; Maidu; Central, Southeastern, and Northeastern Pomo; Costanoan; Salinan; Northern, Central, and Southern Sierra Miwok; Tule River Yokuts; Luiseño; Diegueño; and Mohave. Outside the state, there were Klamath, Modoc, and Wasco in Oregon; Northern Paiute in Nevada; Bannock and Shoshone in Idaho; Papago in Arizona; Sioux in South Dakota; Thompson River and Chinook Jargon in British Columbia; Eskimo in Alaska. There are also recordings from the Chukchi of Siberia and the Jaluit of

the Marshall Islands, but these were probably recorded from visitors in San Francisco (cf. Keeling 1991).

16. The Yuki Ralph Moore was probably recorded at the museum, and that was certainly the venue for the Warburton recordings of the Eastern Pomo William Benson in August 1909; the collection also contained two Japanese cylinders made from commercial discs.

17. In 1908, when recording Weitchpec Frank reciting a Yurok myth, Kroeber used a speaking tube and a type CB graphophone for the first segment of one cylinder, and a large brass horn and a type C graphophone for the second segment (series 41). From early 1912 (?), there are "recordings made as an experiment to test the phonetic apperception of foreign sounds in words not understood and also intended to test the reproducing ability of the phonograph." There are seven cylinders, spoken by native speakers of Swedish, Urdu, Yiddish, Hungarian, Chinese, and Arabic. In September 1913, Kroeber recorded fifty meaningless words, containing only English sounds, on four cylinders. "These recordings were made in order to test phonetic apperception and the reproducing power of the phonograph" (series 62, 64; Keeling 1991:283,290).

18. The catalog numbers of the Ishi recordings are 14–1591 through 1715 (no recording for no. 1681); 1724 through 1728; and 1814 through 1832. Richard Keeling (1991:269–80,292–94) groups the cylinders into series, evidently based on the date of recording, but his sources are uncertain. Furthermore, he lists them by their tape copies (cat. 24) and not by the original cylinder numbers (cat. 14). By so doing, his publication features individual songs rather than cylinders. He thus lists each song separately, even though several were often on a single cylinder with a single catalog number. A news clipping shown in the film by Riffe and Roberts (1992), along with the narration, claims that Ishi made over 400 recordings on wax cylinders ("Ishi's Speech Preserved on 400 Records"), but this is highly unlikely. There is no indication that any of the collection is missing from the current museum holdings.

19. Although it is possible that the recordings were made during the telling of the Wood Duck story on September 6 and 7, there is no reason to doubt the news account that Ishi repeated it for the phonograph after going through it for hours (cf. Miller 1911b). As Heizer and Kroeber note: "Mary Ashe Miller was a good observer and a good reporter. Her description of Ishi . . . is excellent" (1979:97). However, there is a slight discrepancy in the number of cylinders devoted to the Story of Wood Duck. According to one of her columns, "This tale Ishi repeated into a phonograph yesterday afternoon, and 42 perfect records were obtained" (Miller 1911b). However, fifty-one cylinders survive in the museum.

20. The girls' puberty songs were on cylinders 14–1700, 1687a and b.

21. Kretschmer seems to have made transcriptions of earlier Kroeber recordings, so he may have been working for the university from about 1907, the year he was awarded an honorary doctorate of music. William F. Kretschmer's life and work are poorly docu-

mented; the best summary is in Writer's Program of California 1942 and his obituary, *San Francisco Chronicle*, September 18, 1914.

22. Although Keeling gives this as January, "February" is clearly written on the cylinder containers.

23. Just after this, in May and early June 1914, Ishi and his anthropologist friends traveled to his former homeland in Deer Creek. Shortly after that, Kroeber went east for a sabbatical. The following year, after a summer spent dictating myths to Sapir, Ishi fell ill.

24. Alfred L. Kroeber to Edward Sapir, October 7, 1911 (National Museum of Civilization, Ottawa); cf. Golla 1984:62; the Ishi tracings are in the Kroeber papers.

25. It was impossible to edit acoustically recorded wax cylinders. First made practical with electrical recording, editing became even easier with tape and then digitization. Concerning Western musical notation, as well as other transcription systems, one must deal with the balance between description and prescription. Does the notation indicate what happened or what should happen? Performance practices in Western art music complicate the matter even further.

26. Based on these problems, de Angulo wryly comments: "It seems ridiculous to me to want to calculate the number of vibrations of the intervals in such cases. When I learn that in some laboratory, on the other side of the world, they have reached certain conclusions about Indian music, I cannot help but smile" (de Angulo and d'Harcourt [1931] 1988:25).

27. Batwi, a Central Yana speaker, had extensive experience with anthropologists, having worked as a translator for Jeremiah Curtin in 1884 and 1889, and as a myth narrator for both Roland Dixon in 1900 and Edward Sapir in 1907 (see Chapter 13, this volume). Although perhaps a somewhat difficult old man, he seems to have been a "natural-born storyteller" (Luthin 1994:718).

28. Despite these critical concerns, unfortunately, our only sources on the interpersonal dynamics of the recording session are the several news accounts of Ishi's recitation of the story of Wood Duck (noted above), as none of the anthropologists involved left any relevant commentary. Ironically, we know more about these sessions than any other recorded by the Berkeley anthropologists.

29. While in Oroville, Ishi was taken to his first motion picture, which he called *lopa pikta* or rope picture (Waterman in Heizer and Kroeber 1979:231): "With the greatest interest he looked upon the rapidly passing films. Containing as the pictures do, a tale which does not need an explanation in words, the aborigine was able to gain some idea of the story told. The expression of astonishment at first gave way to interest and amusement. It was only when the picture of a train was shown, that he gave any evidence of fright, and then his fear was most evident" (*Oroville Register* 1911b).

30. Similar reactions were reported a few days later in San Francisco (Heizer and Kroeber 1979:102).

31. One news account claims that he narrated the story for three hours on the after-

noon of September 6, continued for three hours that evening, and intended to finish the next day (Heizer and Kroeber 1979:105).

32. According to Kroeber's note in the ledger, in addition to Ishi's rendition of the song of Wood Duck, cylinder no. 14–1689 contained "two . . . Indian songs but not by Ishi; (a) by Sam Batwi, (b) by T. T. Waterman." Kroeber's singing is noted with the musical transcription for cylinder no. 14–1686a, Kroeber papers; microfilm reel 120, frame 195. Such examples of musical exchange, dubbed "ethnographic anomalies," are not uncommon in cylinder collections (Cassell 1984).

33. This was performed by the Odeon-Streichorcester, presumably conducted by Eduard J. Künneke. More famous was the next recording of Beethoven's Fifth, made in November 1913 by Arthur Nikisch conducting the Berlin Philharmonic (Gelatt 1977:182). Reportedly, there were also several European attempts to record more or less complete operas between 1906 and 1908, but none seems to have lasted more than eighteen sides (about an hour), cf. Gelatt 1977:186–87. In any case, the unprecedented nature of the Ishi recordings still stands.

34. Golla claims that Ishi recorded at least three complete myths (Golla 1995:145), but he appears to be in error. He may have been thinking of the extended narrative accounts.

35. Sapir's Ishi texts are contained in six notebooks, totaling 206 pages, transcribed in Yahi (with partial translations). After Sapir's death in 1939 they were returned to the University of California Anthropology Department and in 1969 were transferred to The Bancroft Library, UC Berkeley, as part of the Ethnological Documents collection.

36. This number differs slightly from that given by Nettl ([1965] 1979:105). From a total of "over sixty songs," Nettl considered only the fifty-two that had been transcribed, yielding forty-four unique songs and eight repetitions. Whether these transcriptions were Kretschmer's or his own is not clear.

37. There is evidence that Ishi knew more songs that went unrecorded. In his files for Ishi's music, Alfred Kroeber left a list of "Ishi songs still to be recorded." Eleven songs are listed, with genre and words. In passing, throughout this file are other notices of songs not yet recorded; Yahi music, Kroeber papers, reel 120, frame 397.

38. Apparently, Ishi's songs represent examples from most, if not all, of the eight genres of northern Californian songs delineated by de Angulo (de Angulo and d'Harcourt [1931] 1988:20–25): curing, gambling, puberty, hunting, war, animal, love, dance. Songs of love and dancing are not plentiful among groups of Northeastern California.

39. The song of Wood Duck is on cylinder no. 14–1689, along with two others. According to Kroeber's note in the ledger: "This is the third song on the cylinder, the first two appearing to be Indian songs but not by Ishi; (a) by Sam Batwi, (b) by T. T. Waterman."

40. "The talk of men and women differed. Men spoke the women's forms when conversing with them; women always spoke female. The differences are not very great, but

sufficient to disconcert one not thoroughly familiar with the tongue. Usually a suffix is clipped by women from the full male form" (Kroeber 1925:337).

41. Nettl ([1965] 1979:210) was mistaken in thinking that Waterman, and not Kroeber, supplied the lyric transcriptions for Ishi's songs. The complete file of musical transcriptions and notes may be found in "Yahi, Notes on Music," three folders, Kroeber Papers.

42. "Few songs were designed to tell a well-rounded story or for that matter to be very informative. Rather, the accompanying word materials tended to be minimal, obscure, and repetitive" (Wallace 1978:642; cf. also de Angulo and d'Harcourt [1931] 1988:21).

43. Waterman notebook 1 (cylinders no. 1591–1602); book 2 (1603–1613), book 3 (1614), Ethnological Documents, Bancroft Library. Although most of notebook 1 has some interlinear translation, the English disappears after the first seven pages or so of book 2.

44. The account of the fate of the dead is in notebook 4 (1643–1646); the adolescence account in notebook 5 (1671–1677; goes with songs on 1685–1687); the discussion of earthquakes (1678) in book 5; gambling songs (two songs and talk; three songs and talk) (1682–1683) in book 5; four girl's adolescent songs (1686–1687) in book 5. Book 5 also contains a discussion of salmon which was not recorded.

45. Although not quite the same, these alternative approaches to the documentation of performance resonated decades later in the varying approaches to the translation of Native American oral literature advocated by Dell Hymes and Dennis Tedlock – emphasizing, respectively, intrinsic grammatical patterning and contextual performance (Fine 1984).

46. Sapir did not provide an interlinear translation of the first, possibly because Ishi dictated it too rapidly (see note 13 in Chapter 17, this volume).

47. Theodora Kroeber ([1961] 1976:209–10), who does not seem to finish the list of prospective brides. Several news accounts give the following ten women: striped skunk, flint, crane, waterbug, turtle, beaver, fishhawk, abalone, bat, rain crow (e.g., Miller in Heizer and Kroeber 1979:104).

48. In addition to the original Waterman notebooks, mostly untranslated, the sources for the Yahi Wood Duck story are limited and mostly secondary: There are four articles in contemporary newspapers (*San Francisco Examiner* [1911] 1979; Miller [1911a] 1979, 1911b; Kinsley 1911) and Theodora Kroeber's retelling ([1961] 1976:209–210).

49. Despite the striking literary impact of the Wood Duck story as summarized by Theodora Kroeber, her source for this account is uncertain. Although she implies that it is taken from one of the Waterman Yahi notebooks in The Bancroft Library, as noted above, these are difficult to interpret, incomplete, and do not, at least, contain the reference to Turtle Woman coming from the Affiliated Colleges. Perhaps she was basing her summary on a secondary account, such as a news article, not relocated, or she may have drawn her story from Alfred Kroeber or some other source no longer available. A possible clue is a note in the Bancroft Library finding guide for the Department of Anthropol-

ogy correspondence (cu-23): "The compiler of this guide [Marie C. Thornton] has been told that prior to this collection coming to the University Archives, Theodora Kroeber borrowed the material relating to Ishi for research on her book. She *did* return the material, but it was not refiled and no one knows where it is" [c. 1973], "Ishi, relating to; 1917–1962."

50. Generally, wax cylinders were not made wholly of wax, but of complex (and secret) mixtures of compounds, resulting from endless experimentation (Millard 1995:46).

51. In a revealing letter to an official of the Victor Talking Machine Company, Kroeber confirmed his awareness of the possibilities, lamenting the museum's inability to obtain suitable machines from phonograph companies (Kroeber to T. Coulson, March 3, 1927, da).

52. For instance, in his summary letter to the Victor Company, Kroeber had concluded that "the cylinders we use are open to three grave defects; first, they are fragile, second, they gradually wear out; and third, they are liable to spoilage by mold. We have therefore for a long time wanted to get duplicates made of our more important records, if possible in permanent form" (Kroeber to T. Coulson, March 3, 1927, da).

53. In 1910 the company offered to sell the university a portable version of their commercial disc phonograph, using wax masters that would then be electroplated (Gray to Kroeber, February 11, 1910, da). This file should be consulted for additional information about the museum's sound recording efforts during those years.

54. Kroeber later cited mold as one motivation for this kind of duplication (Kroeber to Erich von Hornbostel, March 2, 1926, da).

55. When Kroeber met the director, Erich von Hornbostel, in the fall of 1915, he learned about their system of cylinder reproduction. Kroeber renewed his acquaintance in the fall of 1925 (Kroeber to von Hornbostel, October 5, 1925, da). Kroeber's German background (and linguistic ability) made him especially aware of such European scholarship.

56. The Yahi cylinders were 14–1614 (myth of wood duck), 1700 (girl's adolescence song), 1815 (dancing song of dead people in the other world), 1826 (woman doctor's song), sent between 1927 and 1929. Cf. Kroeber to von Hornbostel, February 23, 1926, and George Herzog to Kroeber, December 20, 1926 and April 5, 1933, da; "Reference: Recordings-Matrices. California Ethno-Musical Matrices recorded as 'on deposit in Berlin,'" folder, in Hearst Museum audio-visual archives.

57. The Berlin archive experienced its own problems. In 1933 von Hornbostel was forced to flee Germany because of the Nazis, and the archive was transferred from the national music school to the ethnology museum. The following year it was physically moved. By 1959, when Kroeber returned to the cylinder collection, he was informed that only one of the entire Berkeley set remained in West Berlin, most having been lost in wartime bombing (George List to Kroeber, December 18, 1959; Cylinder Collection, Hearst Museum audio-visual archives; cf. Kroeber 1960).

58. Both the recording and duplicating work was carried out by Philip J. A. Schinhan,

a musicology graduate student (Kroeber to von Hornbostel, April 9, 1931; Edward W. Gifford to George Herzog and Kroeber to Herzog, April 5, 1933, DA).

59. Emrich was chief of the Folk Song Section, Library of Congress. "A number of the 97 original cylinders and 47 duplicate cylinders sent to the Library of Congress were found to be cracked or broken and, as a result, only 78 cylinders were reproduced on thirteen 16-inch double face disks" (Kroeber 1960).

60. The Ishi recordings are on tapes no. 24–262 through 24–266. They were donated back to the anthropology museum in 1964 (Keeling 1991:455). This project copied 1724 cylinders (Kroeber 1960).

61. Listed as 24–92ab, 93ab, 94ab, and 95ab, they consist of excerpts only from the Wood Duck myth, the account of the fate of souls after death, and the ceremony for adolescent girls.

62. Ishi tapes nos. 24–321, 24–322. The material included songs recorded by Waterman in September 1911 and by Kroeber in August 1912 and April 1914.

63. "I have some pretty analyses of music, ms. nearly completed; I may be able to have this sent to N.Y. next winter and finish it up" (Kroeber to Edward Sapir, May 29, 1915, Golla 1984:193; cf. Kroeber to George Herzog, February 25, 1928, DA).

64. Despite his real interest in the subject, Kroeber never wrote much on California Indian music. In explaining his omission of the subject in his comprehensive handbook on California Indians, he commented: "One cultural activity of the profoundest emotional import I have regretfully felt compelled to refrain from considering – music. There is no question that any attempt at a well-rounded description of the culture of a people which omits music from its consideration is imperfect. But in the present case the difficulties were enormous. Primitive music is so thoroughly different from our own as to be practically unintelligible except on long acquaintances. It has been analyzed only imperfectly and usually is even transcribed but inadequately. There is no work which seriously attacks the music of the California Indians. A chapter on this fascinating subject would therefore have had to be either so superficial as to be worthless or so long and detailed as to become disproportionate" (1925:vii-viii).

65. One problem that Kroeber cited was his difficulty in finding qualified and interested people to work on the sound collection (Kroeber to George Herzog, May 4, 1934, DA).

66. The topic of ethnographic sound archives raises many complex issues that can only be touched upon here; see Vennum 1984; Seeger 1986; Chaudhuri 1992.

REFERENCES

AMNH: American Museum of Natural History, Dept. of Anthropology archives.

BP: Franz Boas Papers, American Philosophical Society.

DA: Department and Museum of Anthropology, Correspondence, The Bancroft Library, University of California, Berkeley.

KP: Alfred Kroeber Papers, The Bancroft Library, University of California, Berkeley.

Boas, Franz. [1914] 1940. Mythology and folk-tales of the North American Indians. *Journal of American Folklore* 27:374–410. Reprinted in *Race, language, and culture.* New York: Macmillan, pp. 451–490.

Brady, Erika. 1999. *A spiral way: how the phonograph changed ethnography.* Jackson: University of Mississippi.

Brunner, Lance W. 1986. The orchestra and recorded sound. In *The orchestra: origins and transformations.* Ed. Joan Peyser. New York: Charles Scribner's Sons, pp. 479–532.

Buckley, Thomas. 1996. "The little history of pitiful events": the epistemological and moral concerns of Kroeber's Californian ethnology. In *Volksgeist as method and ethic: essays on Boasian ethnography and the German anthropological tradition.* Ed. George W. Stocking, Jr. History of Anthropology, vol. 8. Madison: University of Wisconsin, pp. 257–297.

Cassell, Nancy A. 1984. Ethnographic anomalies in cylinder recordings. *Record* 3(4): 5–6 (Bloomington: Archives of Traditional Music, Indiana University).

Chaudhuri, Shubha. 1992. Preservation of the world's music. In *Ethnomusicology: an introduction.* Ed. Helen Myers. New York: W. W. Norton, pp. 365–374.

Cohen, Norm, and Paul F. Wells. 1982. Native American traditions: Amerindian. Recorded ethnic music: a guide to resources. In *Ethnic recordings in America: a neglected heritage.* Washington DC: American Folklife Center, Library of Congress, pp. 180–184.

Cole, Douglas, and Alex Long. 1999. Boasian anthropological survey tradition: the role of Franz Boas in North American anthropological surveys. In *Surveying the record: North American scientific exploration to 1930.* Ed. Edward C. Carter II. Memoirs of the American Philosophical Society, Vol. 231, pp. 225–252.

Darnell, Regna. 1999. Theorizing American anthropology: continuities from the B.A.E. to the Boasians. In *Theorizing the Americanist tradition.* Ed. Lisa Philips Valentine and Regna Darnell. Toronto: University of Toronto, pp. 38–51.

de Angulo, Jaime, and M. Béclard d'Harcourt. [1931] 1988. La musique des Indiens de la Californie du Nord. *Journal de la Société des Américanistes,* ns. 23:189–228. Translated in *Jaime de Angulo: the music of the Indians of Northern California.* Ed. Peter Garland. Santa Fe: Soundings, pp. 13–31.

Densmore, Frances. 1927. The study of Indian music in the nineteenth century. *American Anthropologist* 29:77–86.

Elkus, Albert. 1949. Supporting material for state budget request, 1950–51, Dept. of Music special and non-recurrent item: transfer from wax to disks of anthropology collection of American Indian music. 29 July. File for UC Dept. of Music, DA.

Fine, Elizabeth C. 1984. *The folklore text: from performance to print.* Bloomington: Indiana University.

Gelatt, Roland. 1977. *The fabulous phonograph, 1877–1977.* 2nd revised ed. New York: Macmillan.

Gillis, Frank J. 1984. The incunabula of instantaneous ethnomusicological sound recordings, 1890–1910: a preliminary list. In *Problems and solutions: occasional essays in musi-*

cology presented to Alice M. Moyle. Ed. J. Kassler and J. Stubington. Sydney: Hale and Iremonger, pp. 322–355.

Goddard, Pliny E. 1905. Mechanical aids to the study and recording of language. *American Anthropologist* 7:613–619.

Golla, Victor K. 1995. The records of American Indian linguistics. In *Preserving the anthropological record,* 2nd ed. Ed. Sydel Silverman and Nancy J. Parezo. New York: Wenner-Gren Foundation for Anthropological Research, 143–157.

Golla, Victor K., ed. 1984. *The Sapir-Kroeber correspondence, 1905–1925.* Survey of California and Other Indian Languages Report, no. 6. Berkeley: University of California Department of Linguistics.

Gray, Judith A., and Edwin J. Schupman, Jr., ed. 1990. *California Indian catalog, Middle and South American Indian catalog, Southwestern Indian catalog – 1.* The Federal Cylinder Project: A Guide to Field Cylinder Collections in Federal Agencies, vol. 5. Washington DC: American Folklife Center, Library of Congress.

Gronow, Pekka. 1982. Ethnic recordings: an introduction. In *Ethnic recordings in America: a neglected heritage.* Washington DC: American Folklife Center, Library of Congress, pp. 1–49.

Heizer, Robert F., and Theodora Kroeber, eds. 1979. *Ishi, the last Yahi: a documentary history.* Berkeley: University of California.

Hickerson, Joseph C. 1982. Early field recordings of ethnic music. In *Ethnic recordings in America: a neglected heritage.* Washington DC: American Folklife Center, Library of Congress, pp. 67–83.

Hinton, Leanne. 1988. A report on the Yanan Project, University of California, Berkeley: introduction. In *Papers from the 1987 Hokan-Penutian Workshop and Friends of Uto-Aztecan Workshop.* Ed. James E. Redden. Occasional Papers on Linguistics 14. Carbondale: Department of Linguistics, Southern Illinois University.

Inman, Carol F. 1986. George Herzog: struggles of a sound archivist. *Resound, A Quarterly of the Archives of Traditional Music* 5(1): 1–5.

Jacknis, Ira. 1984. Franz Boas and photography. *Studies in Visual Communication* 10(1): 2–60.

———. 1993. Alfred Kroeber as museum anthropologist. *Museum Anthropology* 17(2): 27–33.

———. 1996a. Alfred Kroeber and the photographic representation of California Indians. In *The shadow catcher: the uses of Native American photography,* special issue *of American Indian Culture and Research Journal,* Ira Jacknis and Willow Powers, eds., 20(3): 15–32.

———. 1996b. The ethnographic object and the object of ethnology in the early career of Franz Boas. In *Volksgeist as method and ethic: essays on Boasian ethnography and the German anthropological tradition.* Ed. George W. Stocking, Jr. History of Anthropology, vol. 8. Madison: University of Wisconsin Press, pp. 185–214.

———. 2002. The creation of anthropological archives: a California case study. In *Anthro-*

pology, history, and American Indians: essays in honor of William Curtis Sturtevant. Ed. Ives Goddard and William L. Merrill. Smithsonian Contributions to Anthropology, no. 44. Washington D C: Smithsonian Institution, pp. 211–220.

———. Forthcoming. Franz Boas and the music of the Northwest Coast Indians. In *Constructing cultures then and now: the Jesup North Pacific expedition.* Ed. Laurel Kendall, Margorie Balzer, Igor Krupnik. Anthropological Papers. New York: American Museum of Natural History. Submitted 1998.

Johnson, Jerald Jay. 1978. Yana. In *California.* Ed. Robert F. Heizer. Handbook of North American Indians, vol. 8. Washington D C: Smithsonian Institution, pp. 361–369.

Keeling, Richard. 1991. *A guide to early field recordings (1900–1949) at the Lowie Museum of Anthropology.* Berkeley: University of California.

Kinsley, Philip H. 1911. Primitive man sings lore in phonograph. *San Francisco Examiner,* 8 September.

Krause, Bernie, ed. 1992. *Ishi: the last Yahi.* Music and World Series, mono W S C 1604. San Francisco: Wild Sanctuary Communications.

Kroeber, Alfred L. 1925. *Handbook of the Indians of California.* Bureau of American Ethnology, Bulletin no. 78. Washington D C.

———. 1960. Reproduction of cylinder recordings at the Museum of Anthropology, University of California, Berkeley. *Folklore and Folk Music Archivist* 3(1): 2.

Kroeber, Alfred, and Dale Valory. 1967. Ethnological manuscripts in the Robert H. Lowie Museum of Anthropology. *Kroeber Anthropological Society Papers* 37:1–22.

Kroeber, Theodora. [1961] 1976. *Ishi in two worlds: a biography of the last wild Indian in North America.* Deluxe, illustrated edition. Berkeley: University of California.

———. 1970. *Alfred Kroeber: a personal configuration.* Berkeley: University of California.

Lee, Dorothy Sara. 1993. Native American. In *Ethnomusicology: Historical and Regional Studies.* Ed. Helen Myers. New York: W. W. Norton, pp. 19–36.

List, George. 1958–59. The reproduction of cylinder recordings. *Folklore and Folk Music Archivist* 1(4): 2–3; 2(1): 3; 2(2): 3–4.

Long, Frederick Alexander. 1998. "The kingdom must come soon": the role of A. L. Kroeber and the Hearst Survey in shaping California anthropology, 1901–1920. Master's thesis, Department of History, Simon Fraser University.

Lowie Museum. c. 1973. Preservation and documentation of an ethnographic audio archive. Grant application to National Endowment for the Humanities. Audio-Visual Archives, Hearst Museum.

Luthin, Herbert William. 1991. Restoring the voice in Yanan traditional narrative: prosody, performance and presentational form. Ph.D. dissertation, Linguistics. Berkeley: University of California.

———. 1994. Two stories from the Yana. In *Coming to light: contemporary translations of the native literatures of North America.* Ed. Brian Swann.. New York: Random House, pp. 717–736.

———. 2002. A story of Lizard; Yahi, 1915 (Ishi, narrator; Edward Sapir, collector; Herbert W. Luthin and Leanne Hinton, translators). In *Surviving through the days: translations of Native California stories and songs; a California reader*. Ed. Herbert W. Luthin. Berkeley: University of California, pp. 152–177.

McWilliams, Jerry. 1979. *The Preservation and restoration of sound recordings*. Nashville: American Association of State and Local History.

Millard, Andre. 1995. *America on record: a history of recorded sound*. New York: Cambridge University.

Miller, Mary Ashe. [1911a] 1979. Tribe survivor counts to five, but that's all. *San Francisco Call*, 7 September. Reprinted in Heizer and Kroeber 1979:103–106.

———. 1911b. "Ishi" talks into phonograph: Wood Duck's love tale recorded. *San Francisco Call*, 8 September.

Morton, David. 2000. *Off the record: the technology and culture of sound recording in America*. New Brunswick: Rutgers University.

Nettl, Bruno. [1965] 1979. The songs of Ishi: musical styles of the Yahi Indians. *Musical Quarterly* 51(3): 460–77. Reprinted in Heizer and Kroeber 1979, pp. 203–217.

Oroville Register. 1911a. University savant finds Indian sought for past two years. 1 September.

———. 1911b. President and Senate to make treaty with aborigine. 4 September.

Owens, Louis. 1999. Courting the Stone Age: Native authenticity in Gerald Vizenor's *Ishi and the Wood Ducks*. *Multilingua* 18(2/3): 135–147.

Pescatello, Ann M. 1992. *Charles Seeger: a life in American music*. Pittsburgh: University of Pittsburgh.

Reinhard, Kurt. [1962] 1971. The Berlin Phonogramm-Archiv. *Folklore and Folk Music Archivist* 5(2): 1–4. Reprinted in *Readings in ethnomusicology*. Ed. David P. McAllester. New York: Johnson Reprint Corporation, 17–23.

Riffe, Jed, and Pamela Roberts (producers/directors). 1992. *Ishi, the last Yahi*. 16 mm film/video, color, 57 minutes. Distributed by Center for Media and Learning, University of California Extension, Berkeley.

San Francisco Chronicle. 1911. Ishi in concert attracts crowd. 12 November.

San Francisco Examiner. [1911] 1979. Ishi tells tale of Wood Duck for 6 hours. 7 September. Reprinted in Heizer and Kroeber 1979:105–106.

Sapir, Edward. 1910. Yana texts. Together with Yana myths Collected by Roland B. Dixon. *University of California Publications in American Archaeology and Ethnology* 9(1): 1–235.

Sapir, Edward, and Leslie Spier. 1942. Notes on the culture of the Yana. *Anthropological Records* 3(3): 239–298.

Seeger, Anthony. 1986. The role of sound archives in ethnomusicology today. *Ethnomusicology* 30(2): 261–276.

Seeger, Anthony, and Louise S. Spear. 1987. Ethnographic cylinder recordings: an introduction. In *Early field recordings: a catalogue of cylinder collections at the Indiana University Archives of Traditional Music.* Ed. Anthony Seeger and Louise S. Spear. Bloomington: Indiana University, pp. 1–14.

Shackley, M. Steven. 2000. The stone tool technology of Ishi and the Yana of North Central California: inferences for hunter-gatherer cultural identity in Historic California. *American Anthropologist* 102(4): 693–712; revised as Chapter 11 of this volume.

Shelemay, Kay Kaufman. 1991. Recording technology, the record industry, and ethnomusicological scholarship. In *Comparative musicology and anthropology of music: essays on the history of ethnomusicology.* Ed. Bruno Nettl and Philip V. Bohlman. Chicago: University of Chicago, 277–292.

Silver, Shirley, and Wick R. Miller. 1997. California Indian storytellers and storytelling, A conversation with a California storyteller. In *American Indian languages: cultural and social contexts.* Tucson: University of Arizona, pp. 122–128.

Spottswood, Richard K. 1990. *Ethnic music on records: a discography of ethnic recordings produced in the United States, 1893 to 1942.* Vol. 5, *Mid-East, Far East, Scandinavian, English language, American Indian, international.* Urbana: University of Illinois.

Steward, Julian H. 1961. Alfred Louis Kroeber, 1876–1960. *American Anthropologist* 63:1038–1087.

———, ed. 1973. *Alfred Kroeber.* New York: Columbia University.

Stocking, George W., Jr., ed. 1974. *The shaping of American anthropology, 1883–1911: A Franz Boas reader.* New York: Basic Books.

Sulek, Julia Prodis. 2000. Ishi's final journey. *San Jose Mercury News,* 6 August.

Vennum, Thomas, Jr. 1984. Who should have access to Indian music in archives? In *Sharing a heritage: American Indian arts.* Contempory American Indian Issues, no. 5. Los Angeles: American Indian Studies Center, University of California, Los Angeles, pp. 137–146.

Vizenor, Gerald. 1992. Ishi bares his chest: tribal simulations and survivance. In *Partial recall: photographs of Native North Americans.* Ed. Lucy R. Lippard. New York: The New Press, pp. 65–71.

———. 1995. Ishi and the wood ducks: postindian trickster comedies. In *Native American literature: a brief introduction and anthology.* Ed. Gerald Vizenor. New York: HarperCollins College Publishers, pp. 299–336.

Wagner, Roy. 1981. *The invention of culture.* Revised and expanded ed. Chicago: University of Chicago.

Wallace, William J. 1978. Music and musical instruments. In *California.* Ed. Robert F. Heizer.. Handbook of North American Indians, vol. 8. Washington DC: Smithsonian Institution, pp. 642–648.

Writer's Program of California. 1942. *A handbook of San Francisco composers.* History of Music in San Francisco, vol. 8, pp. 174–175; mimeograph copy in Music Library, UC Berkeley.

15
When the World Was New
Ishi's Stories

JEAN PERRY

When Ishi died in 1916 and made his own journey to the Land of the Dead, he left behind a legacy that is only now coming to light. With great patience he told a number of traditional Yahi stories to various researchers during his time at the museum in San Francisco. Early on, he recorded a variety of texts and songs on wax cylinders for Thomas T. Waterman and Alfred L. Kroeber. Unfortunately, the quality of these recordings is very poor. Waterman made an attempt to transcribe several of these narratives from the wax cylinders and to translate them with the help of Sam Batwi, but the results were disappointing. Waterman, of course, did not know Yahi, and Batwi's Central Yana was a different though closely related language. The relationship among the Yanan languages is similar to that among the Romance languages, with Yahi and Central Yana being as similar as Spanish and Italian (speakers can partially understand each other), and Northern Yana more like French (not mutually intelligible).

During the summer of 1915 Ishi worked with the linguist Edward Sapir. He dictated six stories, five of which include sporadic translations. The longest one is not translated. Sapir transcribed by ear the stories Ishi told him, but they were never mechanically recorded. None of the stories was left in a form that anyone could easily read. It has not been until recently, with the assistance of a computer and further study of Ishi's language, that a reasonably full translation has become possible. Language analysis software developed by Ken Whistler has in large part made this task possible.

The two stories included here suggest the wide range of Ishi's storytelling. In the first, "Journey of the Dead," told to Waterman and Kroeber, Ishi described the journey of the spirit to the afterworld when someone has died. Souls travel, usually underground, toward the south, aided by fires lit for them and food left for them by their relatives in the days immediately following their death. They are conveyed, after some hesitation, into the other world by an unnamed gatekeeper. In telling this story, Ishi has given us a pretty clear description of Yahi funeral practices and the reasons for them, and he does not suggest that the Yahis practiced cremation. The debate about cremation versus burial is one of the unsolved mysteries about Yahi culture; it is possible that some of the confusion around this issue is a result of misunderstanding this text.

The second story, which Ishi called "Long, Long Ago," comes from the time of myths, when the world was new, and is a portion of the Yahi creation cycle. This notion of a mythical time, widespread throughout western North America, provides the temporal and spatial landscape across which many traditional Yahi stories were told. Before Indians came into the world, it was populated by animal people. This race of dwarfish, mythical, supernatural beings brought order to an unfinished world; they established an appropriate way of life for the Indians who came later by doing things for the first time. These activities included subsistence strategies, ceremonies, dress, laws, and customs – essentially everything. One of the multiple purposes of stories in the Indian world is their teaching value. They tell how things should be done, and sometimes why, and are the means by which this knowledge is handed down across generations.

The creation cycle is made up of many, many individual stories, and, in any one telling, the storyteller makes a selection. In relating this story to Edward Sapir in 1915, Ishi wove a handful of stories into a single text. He included the creation of gender roles by Gray Squirrel, Rabbit's putting the sun into the sky, Grizzly Bear's search for fire, and the remaking of things after Coyote burned up the world. Ishi only alluded to the theft of fire, which is yet another story in the cycle.

In many ways the controlling element throughout this text is fire, and Ishi recounts the transformation of a raw and unfinished world in which the sun is not yet in the sky, fire is not yet useful, men and women are not differentiated, and the good and bad things in the world are not sorted out. By the end of the story, all of these transformations have been accomplished.

The Ishi who emerges through the telling of these stories in his own language is very different from the Ishi to whom we have had access in other works through his imperfect English, reconstructed secondhand (although probably not too inaccurately). In his own language he was a sophisticated and subtle storyteller, well educated in the ways of his people. Sections of both stories are told in couplets, or occasionally triplets, but with something changed, so that a reiterated line is not merely repeated but subtly reinterpreted. Often there are one or more intervening lines between iterations, so that the story builds through a series of complex reinterpretations.

Ishi also used a variety of vocal techniques to bring out the nature of the characters. These first people, whom Ishi variously called "little people, but not

children," "story people," "the makers of men," and "*kuwi* (medicine men),"
have definite roles and personalities. There are wonderful ambiguities growing
out of their animal-human status, and sometimes they are wise and powerful,
but they are also fallible and even comical. Ishi gave some characters a special
voice by changing tone of voice or changing various speech sounds. This is preserved, for example, in Sapir's transcription of Coyote's speech. The most
widely known equivalent in English is found in the voices of characters in animated cartoons. In other words, Ishi made Coyote sound something like Bugs
Bunny. Unfortunately, it is not possible to render this effect in the translation.

A fundamental choice guiding this translation has been to leave things alone.
The result is a very literal translation rather than one edited for English speakers' sensibilities. I also do not want to impose European-derived poetic forms on
these texts, nor do I want to impose the traditions of other, very different tribes.
Ishi's stories have a great deal of literary merit in their original form. Decisions
about line breaks were based on evidence internal to the original notebooks,
where Sapir sporadically recorded punctuation to indicate pauses and intonation, mostly using commas and periods. Although he was not consistent in doing so, there is enough there to reveal Ishi's intonation patterns, which relate to
grammatical patterns in clauses and sentences. Decisions about breaks in larger
sections of text were based on my understanding of Yahi narrative transitional
devices, which are radically different from those of English.

Because these translations are very literal, there will be passages that many
readers may find confusing. Stylistically, the emphasis on direction and location, plus the frequent use of repetition, are traditional and integral to the style
and structure of the text and are a necessary part of it. Ishi sometimes included
a short summary of what went before, which might seem like backing up in the
narrative but is all part of how one tells a story in Yahi.

There are also many references to things and people that may seem vague.
The level of presumed knowledge in a Yahi story is much higher than in English
narration because these people lived in a small, face-to-face society, and stories
were told over and over. A native audience would be familiar with the characters
and plot, and therefore much of the emphasis is on detail and technique rather
than plot. Characters are often introduced without being identified by name.
There are also vague references to other stories, which are not clear to us but
would be to a Yahi, even a child.

Perhaps the greatest difficulty in translating these stories lies in reconciling
the profound difference between the Indian and white worlds. These are old stories; there in nothing in any of them that is personal to Ishi or his own history.
There is also very little influence from English narrative style or the white way
of life.

However, there are references to various things that a little explanation may make clear. These first people were magical beings, so they had various modes of rapid travel, mentioned in both stories. These include travel underground, by whirling around in a whirlwind across the landscape, and by swinging from mountain to mountain on ropes (which may be seen in that area today as veins of white quartz running across the dark mountainsides).

When Grizzly Bear tied his hair up in a topknot and "prepared himself," he was changing himself into his most powerful mode by praying and fasting and changing his appearance so that he could go through the hole in the sky. In the Yahi cosmology, the world is seen as a round disk, with the sky like a dome above it coming down and meeting the earth at the edges. Above the sky there is another world parallel to the ordinary one, with a hole in the sky that allows passage between the two. It is this hole that Grizzly Bear went through to look for fire, and it took all his powers to do so. It was the edge of the sky that Rabbit bumped the sun into so that it would go up. It is this parallel but ideal world that the dead go up into on their journey.

The white roots that they roast and eat are various lily family species and other edible roots commonly called "Indian potatoes" in California. They were a staple food, nutritious and tasty, along with acorns, pine nuts, meat, and fish.

There is a wide variety of references to the precontact Indian lifestyle (clothes, cooking methods, camping trips, etc.). Altogether, the entire corpus of Ishi's stories gives us a fairly clear description of the Yahi way of life that his people struggled for so long to preserve. He offers us a short sojourn into the Yahi world, and we have to accept that it is a different world if we are to understand these two stories fully.

I hope that by taking this journey into Ishi's world we may learn to value what remains into the present of California Indian culture. There are other Ishis living among us today, and often they are not treated kindly.

JOURNEY OF THE DEAD

> To tell about the dead, the dead,
> They see, the dead,
> They see a little at a time,
> See in the west, keep going, the dead.
> Seeing, they see.
> They don't hear, the dead, the dead.
> So many dead,
> Dead people, rolled up,
> Their bodies rolled up, flexed, stiff and cold.

They go south,
They jump through the hole (into the other world).
One by one, they come this way and close the door.
Make fire, make firelight . . .
They stop and talk by the fire
Then they go through,
Go right through the door.
The fire is put out.

From the north,
He conveys people from the north.
Go right through the door,
They go through the door in the south,
Go south instantly and shut the door,

He takes one person through at a time.
They shut the door and climb up the sky.
They don't believe it.
They go back down, go down and walk, the dead,
Walk around on the ground.
Then they whirl,
A whirlwind, people say.
They go up through the sky on a rope, the dead.

They go down in the ground in the north,
Through a hole in the ground.
They travel through the ground down to the south,
A place in the south
Yomai it's called.
(Long ago) they came and made it split,
Split open . . .
Down in the ground.

People put food aside for them.
The Wintun in the west,
The west people,
The Hat Creeks in the east . . .
They look north, south, east west.
The people in the north and east look there,
They look through in the middle.

Then they are done.
The people, they are all done.
Look north, look west, look east.

LONG, LONG AGO

Long ago women didn't have any genitals.
Men pounded acorns,
Women went out to hunt deer.
One man was Gray Squirrel, he made fire.
Women did not have any genitals, long ago.

The bow was bent by women,
But they just ran away, the women hunting deer.
They didn't see any deer, just ran back home empty-handed.

"We'll go out to hunt the deer," the men said,
"And you pound the acorns."
They went off and all killed deer, the deer hunters,
The acorn pounders were all busy.
But they were not able to make fire.

The men said, "Go out and hunt deer!"
So the women went off to hunt deer.
They just came back home empty-handed.
They couldn't make the fire blaze up.

Gray Squirrel put rocks in the fire.
Slivers exploded from them,
And that way he made women.
Then he went off to hunt deer and came back.
"It shall be like this," said Gray Squirrel.
He was done with it.

So women began to wear the tasseled apron,
They put aprons on and buckskin skirts.
"It will be like this," said Gray Squirrel.

The women did not have any genitals
Until the rocks splintered apart,
Blown apart, burst from heat.

Now women handle acorns,
They came back home and prepared acorns.
Gray Squirrel went to hunt deer.
The ones who now are women pound acorns,
The men go to hunt deer.
They killed deer, every one.
The fire was not yet blazing.

It was really dark in the mornings then.
Rabbit took the sun on his back,
He went along with the sun to the east.
The sun appeared,
Coming from the east over the earth.
It was no longer dark.

They told Cotton-tailed Rabbit,
"You be the one who packs the sun to the east."
So he took it,
He balled it up with his hands,
He whirled it around,
Dust flew about in the air.
It whirled to the east like a whirlwind.
He whirled it around, all about.
It flew down to the river in the east,
He let it fly all around.
It flew high to the east across the water in the river.
He let it fly from place to place.
He bumped the sun up against the wall in the east where the sky
    comes down.
Then he put it down.
He was done.

"You shall go up
And you shall come up from the east in the sky," he said to it.
He was finished.

"Now I'll go home," he said.
So turning back, he whirled himself up in the air,
and moved ahead like a whirlwind,
coming back from the east river.

He took up the rope (in the rocks in the mountains),
threw it and pulled the mountains together in the west.
He took it and brought down the mountain,
then put it back up.
This way he brought himself down to his house in the west.
He came back home at night.
Rabbit is the one who packed the sun to the east.

Now early in the morning the sun came up,
at midday the sun moved directly overhead.
"The sunrise will always be like this," they said.

Then Grizzly Bear said, "Go get white roots (*Brodea*) to eat,
dry them in the sunlight!"
Now they made roots dried in the sun.
"Eat!" he said.
It was no longer dark.

So the sun was carried.
Now it comes up in the sky from the east, the sun.
Cotton-tailed Rabbit packed the sun to the east.

"Go out to collect roots!" Grizzly Bear said.
So they went out.

Little girls were playing.
They patted their hands down in ashes.
They showed this to their parents.
"This is from fire," they said.
It looked like ashes from fire.

Early the next morning they got up.
"What are we going to do?
What does it mean, cinders shooting up in the air?"
They floated themselves up in the air to look for the fire. But they
    all ended up seeing nothing.

Grizzly Bear tied up his hair in a topknot.
He got himself ready (praying and fasting).
Then he rose up,

floated up in the air.
He swung up to the east, back and forth,
until he came to the hole in the sky.
Grizzly Bear went from side to side, floated up,
he went through the hole in the sky.
Then he sat down on the sky ground,
with his legs drawn up and his arms folded.
He held up his head to look west,
Then he looked back down seeing nothing.
He turned around, looked north, then down.
He looked to the northern regions.
He turned around and looked east.
He didn't see anything.
"He doesn't seem to see anything," said Rabbit, watching from
  below.
Rabbit had good eyes.
Grizzly Bear turned around and looked south,
he looked down, seeing nothing.
The Rabbit looked up.
Grizzly Bear turned around,
he saw fire in the south, streaming up, blazing.
"It is blowing upward, blazing," said Grizzly Bear.
"He's just seen it, it seems," said Rabbit.
"Now he is turning back to show us all is well," he said.

Grizzly Bear let himself loose and turned back from the sky.
He dropped back,
came back down from the sky.
He crashed down and sliced off Rabbit's mouth.
"Wat, wat, wat!" cried the Rabbit.

The people asked, "Is there really any fire?"
"It is burning there in the south," Grizzly Bear said. "Indeed it is
  so," they said.

"Let's not take him along, the Coyote!" they said.
"You just go off into the woods!"
Early the next morning he took his string bag,
He went west, Coyote, early in the morning.
He put down his bow.

He took his soaproot and put it on the ground.
He was really busy, mashing up the roots with a rock.
He pounded them.
He put the soaproot into the water
And poisoned it to get fish.
Then he was done.

So he went off,
He went north to the mountains.
They had told him, "Roots are there to dig,
The black Manzanita berries are ripe!"
He knocked the berries off with a stick.
He picked out the pale ones
And left the ripe ones on the ground.
Then he lay down to sleep in the woods.
At sundown he picked out the pale berries and put them in his bag.

"I must go back," he said,
"They might have gone off somewhere!"
He sorted out his berries
He tied up his two bags as though they were full,
He took them up on his back
And walked along the trail.
He came to the lake to get his poisoned fish.
He wrapped them up in grass,
He took them up too and carried them on his back.
He went along the trail
And arrived home.

Everyone had left the house, taking all the food.
"Where have they gone to?" asked Coyote.
He rushed about all over to find where they were.
He followed all tracks, but came back without finding anything.

Before sunrise, early in the morning,
he asked a piece of wood,
"Where have they all gone to?"
No answer.
"It seems it will not talk," he said.
He asked the rocks and the grass.

No answer.
"It seems they are not talking."
He ran around and rushed back home.
He didn't find anything.
Then after all, suddenly he saw a comb.
He picked it up,
"Maybe it can tell."
"They have all gone down in the ground here," it said.
The acorn mortar rock had been loosened from its hole in the
   ground.
Coyote took it up out of its place.
He ran up, rushed about, ran back home.

He went down into the ground to follow them,
he ran south after them through the earth.

They were all camped at Howimanna.
They were resting on the ground,
Those who had gone away were resting all about.
They had gone down over the mountain to a rocky place,
They came down to water,
They went south up a mountain.
They had climbed up the mountain on its rope.

"Show me the way!" Coyote said.
"Their way is here," said a stone.

Coyote followed in their steps behind them.
He went up the mountain on the rope,
he came south after them.
Suddenly there was their camp,
the women were camped about here and there.
He came up to them,
"Please tell me where they have gone to?"
"They have gone south there."
He turned and rushed off,
he ran south after them.
He looked to the south.

The fire was gleaming white hot.
Coyote met his villagers as they came back.

"He's going to want to look at it too," they said.
"Run! Run north for your lives!" cried the headman
(he knows what Coyote will do).

Coyote came up to meet them.
He begged for fire.
"You can't have it.
You'll burn your hand," they told him.
He took the fire into his hand.
"My hands are all burnt! " said Coyote.
So, in secret, he threw the fire down on the ground.
It broke into pieces.
He let it fall,
he let it fall to the ground and break into pieces.
The fire made a burning sound.
It burned to the west, the east, back to the south,
it burned to the north.

They ran back to get the women,
ran back to the north.
"You go back first," they said to Grizzly Bear and his little people.
Chipmunk.
Woodchuck burrowed into the ground.
They traveled away from the south underground.
"The fire is still far away in the south," said Grizzly Bear.
"It is all right.
Everyone go inside the earth! Go in!"

Coyote got crazy and ran back to the door.
"Let Coyote go back out of the tunnel!" they said.
Coyote rushed out, going back south.
"Please close the door," they said.
He closed the stone slab,
he started to run.
He ran north.
Now he got tired, panting.
Coyote was scorched by the fire, getting near.
He ran to the north.
He asked the things around him to save him.

Stone said, "I will burn."

"I will burn up," said the tree.

The earth said, "I will get hot."

Water said, "I will boil off into steam from the heat."

"Indeed, this is how it is," said Coyote.

And then there was the oak tree, bearing acorns.

Coyote said to it, "Maybe you will burn up too?"

"I will be attacked by the fire.

I'll burn on the outside but not the inside," it said.

"Ah!," said Coyote.

He burrowed out a hole in the tree with a stick,

by scratching with a stick.

"Go inside, try to get in," the tree said.

He scrambled in, but he had to leave his feet sticking out.

Fire came from the south,

and his feet were burnt on the outside.

Early in the morning he got out again.

He looked down.

Sure enough, his feet were cut up and burnt.

"Mmm."

"Look at my Pit River grasshoppers."

He picked up his feet and put them in his mouth,

"They are better than grasshoppers!"

Now he ran back south.

The people there came out of the burrow.

Coyote ran to meet them.

They all went north to pick grasshoppers.

They looked for trees,

But all of them had disappeared.

The people came back to their houses.

"How are we going to make fire?" they asked.

"Let's try this one!"

They scraped off the charred part with a stone.

They twirled for fire.

They dug up roots to eat in the north,

And roasted them in the fire.

The fire burned.

He drilled for fire, Coyote.
"It's all right this way," he said.
It burned, the fire they made.

They made acorn bread,
They ground up acorns for mush,
Eating it together with salmon.
"This is how it is, like this," they said.
They kept drilling for fire, in the south.

"Who is going to be made into deer?"
They tried to roast a pretend deer on the fire.
It was made of wood.
"It's no good."
So they took some pitch
And put it at the end of a stick over the fire.
They put the stick over the fire with pitch.
The deer fat simmered and sizzled.
"This is how it is,
It's good now."
They were done, the ones who made pretend deer meat.
"Who will be the ones to go hunting?"
"Deer are coming from the east.
This is how it is.
When a deer is eaten, other deer are told."
So they said.
"If someone puts deer fat on a stick over the fire, other deer know."
They finished.
"It's good now," they said.
They finished the made-up deer.
"Let it be this way," they said.

"Here is deer. How are we going to make grizzly bear?"
Right away one sprang up as grizzly bear,
he fell on his prey and grabbed it,
but he just let go of it.
"He's no good," people said.
"Let it be panther."
He sprang up.

He pulled down prey
And just let it go.
"What shall we make into grizzly bear?" they said.
"Let it be the one lying there (panther), become grizzly bear," they
   said.
"Cut off his tail with a flint!" they said.
"Open the door to the north!"
They did all this.
He slept face up.
They cut his tail off on the ground.
"Heeey!"
He jumped up from his sleep.
"Haaa!"
He bawled and whooped.
They cut off his tail.
"You look north!"
"He's going north, the grizzly bear," they said.
He went off north and lay down to sleep up against the mountains.
"That's how he does, like that," they said.
"It is right now," they said.
"You shall claw and bite people."
"It seems he was the one to be grizzly bear."

Rattlesnake was also spoken to.
"He is biting, the grizzly bear.
He is killing people," the rattlesnake was told.
"What shall we make be rattlesnake?" they said.
"What will we turn into rattlesnake?"
Then they took a jointed reed by the water (*Equisetum*),
They cut it off and took it up.
And they came back to the house with it.
"It will be like this," they said.
"Ch ch ch ch,
It makes a hissing noise this way."
They were satisfied.
They are two of a kind, the grizzly bear and the rattlesnake.

"Let there be scorpion!"
It came out.

"People will be killed.
It will be like this.
Now it is right," they said.

"Are there ones who kill people?"
"Rattlesnake bites," it was said.
"Grizzly bear bites," they said.
"Scorpion stings, it will be said," they said.
"Now it is right," they said.
"He bites," they said of the rattlesnake.

"People will be sick from poison, it will be said.
They will be doctored by healers, it will be said,
So indeed it shall be," they said.
"Now it shall be this way," they said.
"There's sickness, they will say.
It shall be like this," they said.
"People will get hurt from falling, it will be said of rock.
People will fall down gathering pine nuts, it will be said,
They'll fall down, it will be said.
So indeed it shall be," they said.
"Thus people will do.
They'll swim,
They'll swim in water,
They'll drift away and die, they will say.
They'll fall down a cliff, they will say,
They will fall.
They'll be hit by an arrow point, it will be said.
They'll drink water,
They will be thirsty.
They'll die from drinking too much, it will be said.
It shall be this way," they said.
"They'll be lost, it will be said.
It will be so.
It shall be said.
Someone has fallen down a cliff, it will be said, climbing over the
    edge of a cliff.
He has fallen down, it will be said.
It will be like this," they said.
They were finished with the grizzly bear.

"He falls down, the one climbing up the sugar pine,
So indeed it shall be," they said.
"It will be this way," they said.
"It is right now," they said.
"He'll have a sliver of wood get in his eye,
It will be like this," they said.
"There will be sickness.
People will be healed by doctors, it will be said."
They finished talking.
"People will eat
And be poisoned by a disease arrow shot into food by bad men,"
   they said.
"They will aim, shoot at one another, and be shot.
Poison will be shot into the basket of food and they will be sick,"
   they said.
"They put roots on the fire to roast," they said.
"Someone secretly shoots roasted food with poison.
So it shall be," they said.
"It is right now," they said.
They finished talking.
"It will be this way," they said
"Someone will be blind,
Feeling about with his foot, it will be said," they said.
"He is just helpless wherever he goes, finding his way with his
   hands,
It will be said."
They finished.
"Now it is right," they said.
"He runs back into the house
A sick person runs back into the house,
It will be this way," they said.
"He is sick, and does not go out.
Sicknesses are put into warm water in a cooking basket."
They finished talking.
"His hair will come out, it will be said,
Of a sick man whose hair has come out."
They ate,
They finished talking, the makers of men.
They made fire,
They ate, the story people.

They went out to hunt deer,
They went out to hunt birds,
They went out to catch fish.
"It will be like this," they said.
Now they ate, the story people.
The deer came from the north along the mountains,
And the grizzly bear.
"This is how it will be," they said.
They made sunflower seeds out of sand.
"They will go like this," they said.
"And there will be salt,
Strew sunflower seeds and salt over deer meat,
Like this."
They made grasshoppers out of snow.
"Acorns are called this," they said.
They made acorns out of rain.
"They beat acorns down from a tree with a stick," people will say.
"They will eat in this way now," they said.
Now they went to hunt deer.
Lizard made arrows.
They were taught.

NOTE

These translations are my own, and I take full responsibility for them. I would like to thank those who helped, especially Ken Whistler, without whom this work would not have been possible, and Herb Luthin, Leanne Hinton, and Mike Nichols for their help in the early stages of this project. Special thanks to Ken Whistler, Herb Luthin, and my husband, Merle Olives, for moral support during the hard times; to Florence Shaughnessy, who guided my understanding of Ishi's world; to Ishi, who told these stories; and to the elders who taught him.

16

The Story of Lizard

HERBERT LUTHIN AND LEANNE HINTON

INTRODUCTION BY HERBERT W. LUTHIN

Ishi, the narrator of this story, is something of a legend in the history of post-Contact Native America and is a touchstone figure in California anthropology. His story is well known – it's been told in books, articles, and films – so I won't do much more than summarize it here. But it's only fair to say that the "legend" of Ishi is nothing if not a conflicted one.

The subtitle to Theodora Kroeber's celebrated Ishi source book, *Ishi in Two Worlds*, provides us with a good starting point in this regard: *A Biography of the Last Wild Indian in North America*. Whatever he may have been to himself, for non-Indians Ishi, quite simply, stood as an icon of the natural man, a latter-day remnant of pre-Contact Native America. The irony, of course, is that Ishi lived anything but a natural human life, was anything but a pre-Contact "natural man."

Ishi was the last Yahi. His tribe (the southernmost division of the Yana group), after decades of conflict with settlers and prospectors, skirmishes with the U.S. Army, and what can only be called the wanton "poaching" of white vigilantes who killed for sport, was all but wiped out along with the rest of the Yana in a concerted campaign of genocide carried out by local militia groups. Ishi was born into this shattered world – probably in 1862 – about two years before the "final solution" massacres took place.

Ishi survived because his band survived, decimated but intact, only to be surprised a year later by vigilantes in their Mill Creek camp and decimated once more. Only a handful, perhaps as many as a dozen, escaped – among them the little boy Ishi, his mother, and an older sister. This small group then went into deep hiding, vanishing almost without a trace for forty years. Except for a few scattered incidents, as far as anyone knew, by 1872 the Yahi were functionally extinct. But life went on for Ishi's people in hiding. With no births, though (there were no marriageable children in the group when it slipped "underground"), the old just grew older, and the group gradually dwindled. By the time Ishi reached the age of forty, after nearly four decades of hiding, the last member of his group, his own aged mother, had died.

That year was 1908. On August 29, 1911, naked and starving, hair still singed off in mourning three years after the death of his last human companion, Ishi gave himself up outside a slaughterhouse in Oroville. Until he walked out of hiding and into the history of twentieth-century California, Ishi's entire life, from infancy to middle age, was spent in hiding – a sort of backcountry version of Anne Frank's concealment. The stress of that existence, a life of constant hardship and fear of discovery, is difficult for us even to imagine. Ishi was Yahi, all right – purely, deeply, fully so. But the Yahi life he knew was not the free, self-possessing, traditional existence of his ancestors; and it is a mistake to think that Ishi can represent for us – for anyone – some animistic "free spirit" or serve as a spokesman of untrammeled Native American life and culture.

Upon his discovery, Ishi became an overnight media sensation: a "wild Indian," a living Stone Age man – captured in the backcountry of modern California! When the news hit the stands in San Francisco, Alfred Kroeber, head of anthropology at the University of California, dispatched the linguist-anthropologist T. T. Waterman to Oroville to establish communication and bring him to the university. To protect him from exploitation (though let's not forget that Ishi was also the anthropological "find" of a lifetime), Kroeber gave him light employment as a live-in caretaker at the university's new Museum of Art and Anthropology as a way of providing him with pocket money and safe lodging. His days were often filled with linguistic and ethnographic work, for there was an endless stream of scholars coming to work with him, and other interested visitors seeking audience. And on Sunday afternoons, he appeared as a kind of "living exhibit" in the museum itself, chipping arrowheads, drilling fire, and demonstrating other native Yahi crafts and techniques for the public. Thus did Ishi live out the last five years of his life – in truth, in relative contentment and ease, unlikely though this may seem. Those who knew him and became his friends came to love him. He died of tuberculosis in March of 1916.

Given this extraordinary life, it should come as no surprise to learn that Ishi's stories – which only now, eighty years after their narration, are finally being made available to scholars and the public alike – are strikingly unlike anything else known in California oral literature. In some respects, they are of a piece with known Yana tradition; in others, they are eccentric to an amazing degree. Yet we are extremely fortunate to have them, for they tell us a great deal about Yahi life and custom and even more about Ishi himself.

The story presented here was taken down by the great linguist Edward Sapir, who came to California in the summer of 1915 to work with Ishi in what was to be his last year. Ishi was probably already ill by the time Sapir arrived, but in August, after many weeks of steady work, his illness grew too pronounced to ignore, and he was placed in the hospital, where he died about six months later. Ishi's untimely death was no doubt the main reason Sapir never returned to his notebooks and worked up these texts for publication. And in truth, it would have been a daunting task, for much of the work of translation and verification was not complete at the time Ishi was hospitalized. Sapir called his work with Ishi "the most time-consuming and nerve-wracking that I have ever undertaken," noting that "Ishi's imperturbable good humor alone made the work possible" (Golla 1984:194).

Sapir recorded Ishi's stories the hard way: by hand, in detailed phonetic transcription. All told, he recorded at least six stories, filling five notebooks – more than 200 pages of text. Most of the pages are only sparsely glossed at best (indeed, two entire notebooks contain only unglossed Yahi text), and this is what poses the challenge for linguists of the Yahi Translation Project, who are trying to reconstruct their meaning.[1] For that reason, it is the best-worked, best-glossed text, "A Story of Lizard," that we present here. Even so, there are places (duly marked) where we are simply still not sure exactly what is going on.

Ishi's narrative style is often demanding, at least for those coming from a Western literary tradition. Readers may well find this to be a most difficult selection, thanks to Ishi's stripped-down, elliptical approach to telling a story (even a long one) and the short, bulletlike bursts of his delivery. Compositionally, "A Story of Lizard" is more of a suite than a story. Rather than a single overarching plot, it contains a series of episodes and situations, each with its own interior form, all of which combine to form the larger whole. Some of these episodes and situations recur cyclically a number of times. For instance, the Ya'wi, or "Pine Nutting," episode occurs three times, in parts verbatim; and there are four separate "Arrow Making" episodes, some quite elaborately detailed. The remaining two episodes are unique. One, a "Grizzly Bear" adventure, is essentially a story within a story; the second is a "Night Dance" episode that is not matched by other elements within the tale. Rather than recounting the story sequentially, I will briefly describe the individual episodes, then explain how they are pieced together to comprise the whole.

ARROW MAKING

Ishi opens his tale with a glimpse of Lizard making arrows, an activity that provides the background for the entire story. In some sense it is Lizard's unflagging industry that serves as the story's thematic center. Other adventures – the various alarms and excursions that make up the "plot" – may come and go, but the arrow making is always there.[2] (It is something of a joke among those of us working on these stories that the real reason Lizard always seems to be making arrows is because he keeps losing them all in his fights with the Ya'wi.) Ishi was himself a master arrow maker and reportedly loved to flake arrowheads, experimenting with all sorts of materials. Indeed, the arrowheads he made during his brief tenure at the old Museum of Anthropology in San Francisco are among the finest in the Lowie (now Hearst) Museum's collection of artifacts. One can almost learn how to make arrows from Ishi's descriptions of the process in the four "Arrow Making" episodes.[3]

PINE NUTTING

The "Ya'wi" is what the Yahi called the Wintun people to the west – enemies in ancient times. Lizard ventures into hostile territory to collect pine nuts for his people and is attacked by a band of Ya'wi warriors. He keeps his cool, pretending their war whoops are "nothing but the wind," and shoots his arrows "straight into their faces." In the end, he makes it back home with a fresh supply of pine nuts. The oral-formulaic style of patterned repetitions is very prominent within these sections, based primarily on the variation of Yahi directional elements ('to the west,' 'to the east,' 'across a stream,' 'up a mountain,' and so on.) against a common stem, especially *mooja-* 'to shoot' and *ni-* ~ *ne-* 'to go'. (See the Yahi excerpt in the following section, along with its translation, for illustration of these features.)

GRIZZLY BEAR AND LONG-TAILED LIZARD

This is the most complex episode of the story – a fully developed narrative in its own right. Lizard runs out of *báiwak'i* sticks for making the foreshafts of his arrows. He sends Long Tailed Lizard to collect some more. Long-Tail is surprised by Grizzly Bear, who swallows him up and "grows pregnant." When Long-Tail fails to return, Lizard sets out after him. He finds the *báiwak'i* all scattered around, and Grizzly's tracks, and guesses the rest. Gathering up the sticks, he returns home. As a token of mourning, the sticks are not used, but burned. At daybreak, after cutting off his hair and smearing his face with pitch (further tokens of mourning), Lizard sets out to find the bear.

What happens next is not as clear as we would like it to be, because there are some thorny problems with the interpretation of Sapir's text and glosses throughout this section. But it appears as if Lizard travels to Grizzly Bear's favorite feeding ground and climbs up into a convenient tree toward evening to have a smoke and wait for her. In the morning she comes, as she seems destined to do, to feed on the *k'asna* vines (identified only vaguely as a vine growing near water). Lizard has prepared himself by draping one of the vines around his neck and letting it dangle down, the idea being (we think) that when Grizzly arrives

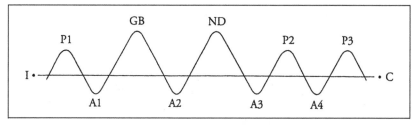

Fig. 16.1. The Architecture of "A Story of Lizard." (I = Introduction; P = Pine nutting; A = Arrow making; GB = Grizzly Bear; ND = Night Dance; C = Conclusion)

and begins to feed, she will tug on the vine and alert him. In the morning she comes and starts to feed. Lizard puts a loop into his bowstring and lets Grizzly pull him down onto her back, whereupon he slips the loop around her neck and lets the strung bow strangle her. After gouging out her eyes (the revenge against a man-eating bear is always harsh), he slits her open and recovers Long-Tailed Lizard. (As Leanne Hinton points out, this is a familiar motif in folklore: Europeans know it from "Little Red Riding Hood.") In the morning it's back to making arrows.

THE NIGHT DANCE

One day, as Lizard is "busy with his arrow making," he breaks a shaft. The break in the shaft foretells a break in the routine: Some neighboring people are having a dance. For the next three days, the domestic rhythms of the camp are inverted, as Lizard's people dance all night and – except for one attempt at gathering food, abandoned the next time around as too much hassle – sleep all day. We simply have no idea what all the "excrement" is about: the way the text reads, at the beginning of the Dance episode, Lizard's people are given some excrement (the stem *wak'i-* 'shit' is unambiguous on this point), which they smear all over themselves. After the last night of dancing, Lizard scolds them for being slug-a-beds, whereupon they all bathe themselves clean and get back to work. Life returns to normal, and Lizard resumes his arrow making.

When you put all these episodes together, paying careful attention to their cycles of repetition, an overall pattern reveals itself: the true architecture of this fascinating tale. If we take the four Arrow Making episodes to be the thematic baseline or rhythmic "pulse" of the narrative, view the Pine Nutting episodes with their Ya'wi attacks as intermittent events that punctuate that baseline, and recognize the unique Grizzly Bear and Night Dance episodes as extraordinary happenings that stand far out against that background "hum," we might represent the narrative structure schematically as shown in Figure 16.1.

What seems at first a hopeless déjà vu of motifs and situations proves now to be quite the opposite: a carefully controlled narration of great balance and dignity.

When I first went to work on this story, some nine years ago now, I felt it to be one of the bleakest accounts of survival I had ever seen – a relentless tale of repetitive drudgery and danger. Now, looking at it anew, I see it in a different light. Like a Beowulf or a Roland in European tradition, Lizard represents the essence of a Yahi culture hero. Lizard provides for his people, unfailingly. Instead of despair, there is reassurance in these unvarying routines, and in Lizard's unflappable reliability in a crisis.

And in truth I think Ishi, as the only able-bodied man among his lost band of survivors for all those long, lean years of hiding, must have been something of a Lizard himself.

A NOTE ON THE TRANSLATION

Because so much has been said for and about Ishi, and so little has ever come forth from Ishi himself, we have felt a special urgency, in dealing with the records he left behind, to let Ishi be heard in his own voice and words at last. Granted, proclamations like this have a hollow ring when the end result is a translation. After all, what Ishi *actually* said in "A Story of Lizard" (as in these lines from the very beginning of the myth) was this:[4]

> Híri',
> > héebil' k híri'mawna . . .
> K'úllil'.
> Niwílji',
> > wísdu' gi iwílc^{hi}.
> Nilóopji'.
> Domjawáldi' k díitel^{la}.
> (Hóok'awdubalgu' gi wéeyump^a;
> dóowayalcidibil' wéeyump^a.)
> Bóot'an' c wís^{hi}.
> Júspja',
> > jóst'al'ⁱ.
> Jewóo c yónbal'ⁱ.
> Jéduwoo' k Busdím' c Yáa'^{wi}!

Since there is no one left alive who can speak or understand this language, the need for translation is unimpeachable. Still, we have wanted to minimize the degree to which the voices of translation mingle with Ishi's own. So where, in most other literary translations, obscure or ambiguous sentences are silently clarified – with the addition of a phrase or transition here, a "she said" there – we have chosen another tack. Though this is still a literary – not a literal – translation, we have nonetheless tried to convey only what is present in the Yahi text, just as Ishi dictated it to Sapir in 1915. That means that we have had to explore other methods of providing readers with the interpretive and textual information they need in order to follow the story. We have settled on two devices, footnotes and sidenotes, to help us "buy" this degree of fidelity.

The sidenotes (set in the right margin, in space fortuitously made available by the broken-line format of the translation) are used mostly to supply key missing information – primarily proper names or specific nouns that are referred to only by pronoun in the original, and which the reader might have trouble intuiting. Less critical information – of a contextual, interpretive, linguistic, or philological nature – has been consigned to footnotes. To illustrate the way the sidenotes work (the footnotes should need no explanation), let's take a look at an excerpt (lines 138–149) from the translation:

He made himself arrows in the morning.
He rubbed them and smoothed them.   the cane shafts of the arrows
He was busy at it all day –
   finished.
As he turned them on the ground,
   he painted on the bands.
He finished putting on the painted bands.
He soaked them in water,   the feathers
   wrapped them on with sinew –
     finished.
He trimmed the feather-vanes –   with a flint blade
   finished.

At line 139, while the reader can certainly deduce that the pronoun "them" refers generally to the arrows of the preceding line, the sidenote allows us to provide a bit more specificity: it's the cane *shafts* of the arrows that Lizard is smoothing, as Sapir's fieldnotes indicate. At line 145, the reader may be forgiven for being puzzled as to the referent for the pronoun "them." But a quick glance to the side supplies that information right when it's needed, and it saves us from having to falsify the text by interpolating the missing referent (either with distracting brackets, or, worse, without them) into the line: that is, "He soaked the feathers in water." Our unembellished translation makes it clear that Ishi himself, to

whom the process of arrow making was second nature, thought the circumstances too obvious to spell out using the concrete noun. Finally, at line 148,
Sapir's own gloss for the Yahi sentence *Dee-wunii-'* (literally, 'cut something-
feather-NARRATIVE TENSE') reads "He cut off vanes with flint," but in fact the
information about the flint blade is not there in the Yahi – it's only implied by
context and cultural knowledge; the sidenote here allows us to provide this information (useful for helping readers visualize the action) without embellishing
the translation itself.[5]

NOTES

This chapter was previously published in Herbert Luthin, *Surviving through the Days:
Translations of Native California Stories and Songs* (Berkeley: University of California,
2002). © 2002 Regents of the University of California. Reproduced by permission.

1. The Yahi Translation Project was constituted at Berkeley in 1986, specifically to prepare Sapir's unpublished Yahi materials for publication. Victor Golla was the project director, and Leanne Hinton coordinated the Berkeley seminar that kicked off the project.
Bruce Nevin and Ken Whistler served as special consultants. Other researchers who have
kept involved in the project over the years include Jean Perry and this author.

2. In others of Ishi's stories, different sets of domestic activities such as leaching acorns
and going for water take the place of arrow making yet serve the same narrative function.

3. In order to determine the complete sequence of steps in arrow making, it is necessary to build a composite sequence based on a collation of steps from the various episodes, because no one episode contains all the steps in the process.

4. This passage is cast in an informal practical orthography devised for the Yanan languages; it balances linguistic needs with the desire to be helpful with regard to pronunciation. Doubled characters represent length, stress is indicated with an acute accent over
the vowel, and superscript letters are voiceless. Certain phonetic processes involved with
prosody (final aspiration, devoicing, secondary and emphatic primary stress) are preserved in the transcription.

5. The text has been parsed into lines primarily on the basis of predication units
(one per line), augmented by reference to prosodic features like final-syllable retention
and Sapir's own field punctuation (see Luthin 1991 for a detailed discussion of these
issues).

FURTHER READING

For an account of Ishi's two lives, Theodora Kroeber's *Ishi in Two Worlds* (University of
California Press 1961) is indispensable as well as good reading; she covers the brutal years
of extermination in great historical detail, as well as what is known of Ishi's life in hiding,
and describes his last years at the museum. For those interested in Ishi's arrow-making,

Saxton Pope's "Yahi Archery" (*University of California Publications in American Archaeology and Ethnology* 1918, 13 [3]) gives a thorough description of the process (Pope was Ishi's doctor and closest friend at the university). The Ishi texts will eventually be published as volume 9 (ed. Victor Golla) of *The Collected Works of Edward Sapir* (Mouton de Gruyter [forthcoming]). Leanne Hinton, with artist Susan Roth, has excerpted this story in a stunningly illustrated children's book called *Ishi's Tale of Lizard* (Farrar, Straus, Giroux 1992). Finally, there have been two recent films made about Ishi: the HBO production, *The Last of His Tribe* (Hook 1992), starring Graham Greene as Ishi, and the Yahi Film Project's excellent documentary, *Ishi, the Last Yahi* (Riffe and Roberts 1994). A fair amount of Ishi collectanea is on more-or-less permanent display at the Hearst (née Lowie) Museum in Berkeley.

A STORY OF LIZARD

He made arrows,
> he was busy with his arrow making . . .

I.   [PINE NUTTING 1]

He wanted to start back.
He went westward across a stream,
> went to gather pine nuts west across a stream.   5

He went westward up a mountain.
He put his quiver down on the ground.
He had just gone and gotten some old deer antlers;   to use as a quiver
he carried the antlers around on his shoulders.)
The one pine-nutting cracked the cones with a rock.   10
He was getting out the nuts,
> got them broken open.

And then he scooped them up in his hands.
He took up his storage basket again.
The Ya'wi shouted their war whoops!   15
He took up his quiver again.
The Ya'wi whooped.
He drew his bow from his quiver.
"The wind is blowing," he said.
> "It is storming," he said.   20

They rushed against him.*

---

*Literally, "He was rushed at."

Now he shot off his arrows,
    hit them straight in the face.
He went back east down the hill.
He shot off arrows to the north,   25
    shot off arrows to the south,
    shot off arrows to the east,
        hit them straight in the face.
He went back into the water at the river,
    went back east across the water,   30
    came out of the water at the river.
The Ya'wi scattered out of sight.

Now he stepped along the trail.
He got back home during the night.
He put his storage baskets away again.   35

II.   [ARROW MAKING 1]
Early in the morning he smooths them down.   the arrow shaft canes
He made arrows,
    rubbed the shafts smooth,
    worked at his arrow making –
        finished.   40
  He fitted the cane shafts tight around the arrow shafts –
    finished.
He socketed the foreshafts.
Turning them on the ground,
    he painted the bands.   45 on the arrow butts

Now he was busy all the day.
He fletched the arrows –
    finished.
And then he trimmed the feathers –
    finished.   50
He charred the feathers black,
    bound the shafts together with sinew –
        finished.

Now he smoothed the foreshafts.   with a scouring rush
He finished and put them aside for the night.   55

III.   [GRIZZLY BEAR EPISODE]

"It seems there aren't enough to eat," he said.

(Enough pine nuts,

    for those coming to him for food.)

The woman shared them out.

"There are no more of my foreshaft sticks," he said.   60

"Let's have Long-Tail* get some for me," he said.

"Let's see you go get *báiwak'i*!"† he said to him.

And then the one getting *báiwak'i*,

    now he went off.

He twisted the *báiwak'i* shoots out of the ground,   65

    broke them off at the roots.

He laid the shafts down on the ground.

"There are plenty of sticks!" said Long-Tail.

Up jumped Grizzly Bear!

And then she eats him!   70

Grizzly Bear swallowed him down and grew pregnant.

She turned around,

    lumbered back down the middle of the trail.

When it was just too dark for gathering *báiwak'i*,

    Lizard took up his quiver.   75 to go find out what happened

Sure enough, there was the *báiwak'i* –

    it was lying on the ground.

Now he looked around all over.

Sure enough, there was the grizzly bear,

    her tracks.   80

"Little one,

    did you get eaten?" he said.

He gathered up the *báiwak'i*,

    carried it back to the house in his arms,

    placed the *báiwak'i* in the fire.‡   85

*Referring to *páat'elwalla*, a long-tailed lizard.

†A type of wood for making foreshaft sticks.

‡Because of the death associated with it, the wood is now tainted and must be destroyed.

In the morning,
　　"What shall I do?" he said.
And then he cut off his hair.　　　　　　　　　　　　in mourning
He took some pitch,
　　finished smearing his face with pitch.　　　　　90

"Now how long will it take before you return?" he said.　　said Lizard, to absent Bear
　　"Don't let it be long," he said.*
　　"Aren't you getting hungry?" he said.

He strung a *k'asna* vine around his neck.†
He smoked, then filled his pipe:　　　　　　　　95
　　"I'm having myself a smoke!"
　　"How long before your return?
　　Don't let it be long," he said.
　　"These are your feeding grounds!" he said.
　　"This is the one, all right!" he said.　　　　　100
He climbed up the *k'asna* tree,
　　settled himself up in the grape vines
　　　　as the sun went down.

When the sun came up,
　　"I want to go back west," she said.　　　　　105 Grizzly Bear
　　"He may be sleeping there," she said.　　　　at the *k'asna* place

Now Grizzly Bear went back west,
　　pregnant with Long-Tail.
Lizard heard her to the east:
　　"It must be her," he said.　　　　　　　　　110

Now she came padding from the east after *k'asna*.
The *k'asna* vine was hanging down from the tree,
　　the one wrapped around his neck.
She pulled down on the vine.
"Pull hard at me, you who bereaved me!　　　　　115
　　It would be good if you would die," he said.
　　"Pull me down on your back!" he said.
He loosened his bowstring.

*This is just a wild guess as to the meaning of this difficult line.
†Sapir identifies *k'asna* as "wild grape."

"Let it be me who gets packed on your back," he said.
The pregnant one started to climb up.   120
He tied his bowstring into a noose,
    looped it back onto itself.
He was pulled back down from above.   onto her back
Grizzly Bear climbed down again,
    tumbled back down to the ground.   125
Grizzly Bear's head fell off,
    strangled in two by the bowstring.
He took his stone knife,
    gouged out her eyes.
He picked up his Long-Tail,   130
    placed him in water,
    bathed him.
He picked up his quiver again –
    put Long-Tail into his quiver.

He got back home.   135
He threw away the makeshift "necklace."
He got back home.

IV.   [ARROW MAKING 2]
He made himself arrows in the morning.
He rubbed them and smoothed them.   the cane shafts of the arrows
He was busy at it all day –   140
    finished.
As he turned them on the ground,*
    he painted on the bands.
He finished putting on the painted bands.
He soaked them in water,   145   the feathers
    wrapped them on with sinew –
        finished.
He trimmed the feather-vanes –   with a flint blade
    finished.

Now he charred the feather-vanes,†   150
    finished putting them away.

---

*That is, while holding the brush stationary, he rotates the arrows to apply the paint bands.
†With a hot stick, to "seal" them.

Now he bound the joins* with sinew –
   finished.
He put the arrows in his quiver.

Early in the morning,   155
   she took up her fire making,
      the woman.

Now he rubbed them –   the arrows
   finished.

Now he was busy with it.   160
He finished socketing the arrow shafts.
And then he painted on the bands.
He put them away finished.
He soaked the feathers in water.

Now he fletched the arrows,   165
   wrapped them on with sinew –   the feathers
      finished.

Now he was busy trimming the feathers –
   finished.
He charred the vanes,   170
   put them away finished.

Now he went ahead with putting on red paint.

Now he worked at it,
   put on the red paint,
   put them away finished.   175

Early in the morning,
   as he turned them on the ground,†
      he flaked arrowheads.   made of obsidian

Now he chipped off flakes.

*Where the foreshaft fits into the main shaft.
†Here, the action seems to refer to pointing arrowheads.

He finished at sundown.   180

Early in the morning,
    as he turned them on the ground,
        he attached the points to the foreshafts –
           finished.
His deer-horn quiver was slung over his shoulder.   185
He finished,
    put the arrows into it.
At night,
    he finished working.

Early in the morning,   190
    he went after more foreshaft sticks.
He packed home the new *báiwak'i* and put it down.

Now he started scraping the bark off: with a stone scraper
    he scraped off the *báiwak'i*.
He finished at sundown.   195

Now he was busy with it –
    he finished working in the dark.

V.   [THE NIGHT DANCE]
Early in the morning,
    he took his arrow shafts,
        spread them out in front of him.   200

Now he rubbed the arrow shafts smooth.
"What's the matter?" he said.
He broke it on the ground,   the arrow he was smoothing
    broke it in two on the ground.

Now he just sat there, waiting.   205

"The women are dancing together," she said.*
"The men are dancing together," he was told.

---

*Unclear; Sapir's notes say, "not girls but 'story' creatures," whatever that means.

"Aaah, and you would spread the news, too," he said.
    "That smoothing work of mine just broke for no
        reason."
"They are going out there to dance," she said.   210
He put away his arrow-making things.

At sundown:
    "Some funny kind of pitch –
        it smells like that," he said.*
    "They must be dancing," he said.   215
And then the pitch –
    it was given to him,
        the pitch.
"What's the matter?
    Aaah, so that's what this is," he said –   220
    "some funny kind of pitch."
"Evidently what it is is excrement," a man said.†
He gave him the excrement.   gave Lizard
Lizard smeared it all over,
    smeared the excrement smoothly over himself –   225
        finished.
"Build a fire!
    I'm going to dance and play!" he said.

Now they danced:
    the young women danced, it is said,   230
    the young women rested, it is said.

Now he sang out,   Lizard did
    he went to sing the lead.
He called out the dance.‡

Now he sang along.   235
They danced.
"I'm just going to let it down, children!" he said.   i.e., 'stop dancing.'

*The smell is coming from where they are dancing.
†It is not clear who is speaking here.
‡Or 'accompanied his dance-song with whispered shouts'.

"Dance and play!" he said.
   "Say it!" he said –
      "your play-dancing song!"   240
The play-dancers sang.*
"Now the women shall dance," he said.

   "Henééyah, paneyáh,   *[singing]*
   Henééyah, henééyah, hiiyaa!"

"Say it!"   245
He called for a dance:
   "Children!
      Say your song!" he said.

Now they were dancing, dancing.
   "Say it!" he said,   250
      "Children!"
They're dancing to the south,
   they're dancing to the north,
      they're dancing to the south,
         they're dancing to the north.   255
"*Hiiyaa!*" he said.
He called for a dance:
   "Say it, children!" he said,
      "your play-dancing song," he said.
"I'm just going to let it down," he said.   260 i.e., 'stop dancing'

Early in the morning:
   "Everybody go off to the woods!" he said;   to gather food
   they all went off and headed into the woods.

At night:
   "Dance, children!   265
   Dance!" he said.
[Then:] "To sleep, all of you!" he said.
   "Children!
   Let it down," he said.

*Or, 'They sang and danced'

Early in the morning,   270
    they got up.
"Guess I'll just stay home."   said Lizard
The young women danced.

At sundown:
    "Dance and play, children!" he said.   275
Again the dancers danced.

Early in the morning,
    they got up.
"All this sleeping is a bad thing," he said,
    "it's not good," said Lizard.   280
The woman went back home.*
They bathed themselves.   Lizard and the woman
He took up his arrow making again.

VI.   [ARROW MAKING 3]
He rubbed the arrows smooth all on his own.
He socketed shafts throughout the day –   285
    finished.

Now he painted on the bands during the day,
    put them away when they were finished.
He soaked them in water.   the feathers

Now he fletched the arrows – †   290
    now, while he was busy at it,
        he fletched the arrows –
            finished.
He turns them on the ground.
He trimmed the vanes –   295
    finished.
He charred the feathers:
    finished.
He put them away when they were finished.

*Sapir's gloss regarding the woman notes "little, but not child."
†By attaching the feathers with strips of sinew.

He carried the deer antlers slung over his shoulder.   300
(That's what made his quiver:
    he just cut deer antlers off at the stump.)
He placed the arrows inside.

"Off to the woods, children!"   for food
He took up his flints,*   305
    chipped off a piece.

Now he flaked away during the day.
He scoops the loose flakes into a basket.

"Eat, children!" he said at night.

Now they began eating their meal: 310
    they ate it,
        they finished eating.

"Off to the woods, children!" he said.   for food
They went off and gathered food.
He inserted the arrowheads –   315 into the foreshafts
    finished.
He put his finished pointed shafts away.

"Eat, children!"

VII.   [PINE NUTTING 2]
Early in the morning,
    he took up his quiver,   320
    he took up his net bag.

Now he went westward,
    he went west across the water.
He put his quiver down on the ground.
He climbed up after pine nuts,   325
    climbed back down.
And then he pounded out the cones.

---

*xaka 'flint' probably represents chert or obsidian.

Now he kept on pounding –
 finished.
He took up his net bag and scooped them in.   330
And he filled one up –   his net bag
 finished.
And then his other bag –
 finished.

Now, as they were spilling,   335 the pine nuts
 he scooped them up from the ground.
They made a sound like the wind there, and the
 sound came down:
  the Ya'wi,
   they howled their war whoops at him.
"I'll presume you're not just the wind blowing," 340
 he said.
He picked up his net bags,
 tied both his net bags together to carry home.
He reached for his bow.

Now he stepped along the trail.
He shot off arrows –   345
 shot to the north,
 shot to the east,
  hit them straight in the face.

Now he stepped along the trail,
 fired his bow down into them.   350
"You are just barely visible,
 scattered all around me," he said.
He shot to the south,
 shot to the east –
  he killed them off, these Ya'wi.   355
He went back home through the water.

Now he stepped along the trail.
He arrived back home at sundown.
"Here is plenty to eat, it seems," he said,
 as he was asked for food.   360

"It looks like it's really raining down out there,
    with the wind," he said.

VIII.   [ARROW MAKING 4]

Early in the morning,*
    "Off to the woods, children!" he said.   to gather food

Now he was busy trimming feathers all day.
At sundown he finished it,   365
    his feather trimming.

Early in the morning:
    "Off to the woods, children!"
He took up his cane shafts,
    spread out the canes.   370

Now he rubbed them smooth –
    finished.
Drilling out the cane shafts,
    he bored into them –
        finished.   375

Now he socketed the foreshafts –
    finished.
He painted on the bands,
    put them away, finished.
He fletched the arrows,   380
    soaked the feathers in water –
        finished.

At sundown,
    he trimmed the feather-vanes.   with a flint knife

Now he was busy with it: 385
    he charred the feathers,
        put them away finished.

"Eat, children!" he said.

*Line inserted by translators.

Early in the morning,
    he took up his sinew-binding,*   390
        put them away finished.
Now he was busy with it:
    he smoothed the foreshafts –   with a scouring rush
        finished.
He slung the quiver over his shoulder: 395
        finished.

At sundown,
    those who had gone to the woods came home.
"Eat, children!" he said.

Now they started eating their meal.   400

Early in the morning,
    as he turns his arrows on the ground,
        he flaked arrowheads.
He finished at sundown.

Now he was busy with it.   405

Early in the morning:
    "Off to the woods, children!" he said.   to gather food
    "I won't be doing like the rest of you,
        as for myself," he said.

And he smoothed the arrow shafts: 410
    early in the morning,
        as he turns them on the ground,
            he smoothed the arrow shafts.

Now he rubbed them smooth.
He finished during the day.   415

Now he was busy,
    he bored holes into the cane shafts –
        finished.

*Binding the juncture of the cane shaft and foreshaft with sinew.

He socketed the foreshafts,
    put them away, finished.   420

Now he was busy with it:
    he finished with the painted bands.
He soaked feathers in water.

Now he was busy with it:
    he finished and trimmed the feathers.   425
He put down his arrows –
    finished.

Now he charred the feathers.

"Eat, children!" he said.

Early in the morning,   430
"Off to the woods, children!" he said.   to gather food
    "I won't be doing like the rest of you,
        as for myself," he said.
He finished his sinew-binding.

Now he was busy inserting the flaked arrowheads.   435
He put them away finished.

IX.   [PINE NUTTING 3]
Early in the morning,
    he took up his net bag.

Now he went westward,
    went west across the water,   440
        went westward up a mountain.

He put his quiver down on the ground.
He climbed up after pine nuts,
    climbed down again.
And then he piled pinecones all around the fire.   445

Now he was busy with it,
    now he started pounding.

He pounded out the nuts –
   finished.
He took up his net bag,   450
   he took up his other net bag.

(Not yet . . .)*

Now, as they were spilling,   the pine nuts
   he scooped them up from the ground.
They made a sound like the wind there, and the   455
    sound came down:
   the Ya'wi,
     they howled their war whoops at him.
"Ho, I'll presume you're not just the wind!" he said.
   "It really looks like it's raining down, now –
    maybe I'll sit and shell some pine nuts," he said.   460
He took up his net bags.
   "I have just seen you, everywhere down on the
     ground," he said.
He slung the bags over his shoulder again.
He took up his bow.

Now he stepped along the trail.   465

Now he shot at them:
   he shot to the east,
    he shot to the south,
     he shot to the north.

Now he stepped along the trail.   470
He fired his bow at them,
   hit them straight in the face.
He went into the water again,
   came back out of the water.
The Ya'wi scattered away.   475

Now he stepped along the trail at sundown.
He came into the clearing.   where his camp was

*Perhaps a foreshadowing device: Lizard (and Ishi) anticipating the Ya'wi rush.

"Here is plenty to eat, it seems," he said.
"It really looks like rain, coming down out there on
    the wind," he said.

[To Sapir:]

"Be gone, now!" as they say.   480
Now he has finished talking . . .

17

The Days of a Life

What Ishi's Stories Can Tell Us About Ishi

HERBERT LUTHIN AND LEANNE HINTON

In the summer of 1915, six months after Ishi showed the first signs of the tuberculosis that would shortly claim his life, Edward Sapir came to California in great urgency to work with him, hoping to record what he could, while he could, of Ishi's Yahi language and oral traditions. He was all but too late. Ishi soon became too ill to continue the work and had to be hospitalized. Sapir returned home to Canada in September. When Ishi died in March 1916, Sapir was left with several notebooks of unfinished and partly finished materials. For one reason or another, he never really managed to return to them.

After Sapir's death, the notebooks came back to California, where they now (after an untimely walkabout in the 1960s, when no one could find them for Morris Swadesh during the preparation of his *Yana Dictionary*) reside in the Bancroft Library. This chapter is based on work from an ongoing group project to translate Ishi's stories as Sapir transcribed them. Because of the great fascination the public has with Ishi, people have long wanted to know what these tales are like and what they tell us about Ishi himself. They are, after all, the only example we have of Ishi's own words.

At the outset, we were full of anticipation, but when we finally started looking over the materials, we were – some of us, even if we admitted it only to ourselves – just a bit disappointed. We had imagined finding all sorts of things in Sapir's old black notebooks. It would have been wonderful, we thought, to find an oral history, an autobiography, an account of his years, especially those he spent in hiding. Instead, the notebooks contained grammatical information, an origins myth, and five traditional tales. We found ourselves wishing we had discovered more than we did. The tales, after all, were just traditional stories being transmitted by and *through* Ishi and had little of personal interest to say about Ishi himself. Or so we thought.

Our first impressions were mistaken. The tales Ishi told truly *are* unique,

318

very different in style from anything else we have ever read or heard. They are not rare or unknown tale-types – indeed, several of the stories are simply Yahi versions of Northern and Central Yana tales published earlier in Sapir's *Yana Texts* (Sapir 1910). (Ishi's language, Yahi, is the southernmost language of the Yanan family, whose three attested languages are somewhat less differentiated from each other than the Romance languages of western Europe.) Rather, they are different because they focus on different aspects of these stories than is usual.

To tip our hand early, Ishi's storytelling takes stock elements that function as background information in other narrative traditions and gives these elements strong – unexpectedly strong – prominence. What we might call the "core story" or tale-type proper comes, in Ishi's performances to Sapir, almost as an afterthought to a hyperdeveloped introductory section. In this chapter we will discuss the notion of *prominence* and explore this peculiar characteristic of Ishi's storytelling, first by looking at this feature as it works – unexceptionally – in a neighboring narrative tradition, then comparing that to what we find in Ishi's. In the final section we will try to interpret what these facts may be telling us about Ishi himself.

EVALUATION IN DISCOURSE

When telling a story, a narrator must be able to highlight important or revealing information in order to make it stand out and be well received and well remembered. This assignation of prominence is, in effect, an act of *evaluation*, because it is up to narrators to decide what the most salient points of their stories are and to highlight them accordingly. Polanyi (1989:22) – inspired, as are we all, by Labov (1972) – describes the process as follows:

> Evaluation, as [the] process of assigning prominence is called, is accomplished by encoding the information to be accorded increased weight in a way which departs from the local norm of the text. In spoken language, speakers signal salience by using any one of a fairly large battery of conventional linguistic and paralinguistic evaluative devices drawn from every level of linguistic structure.

Thus, to highlight those story elements that stand out from others in terms of special content or significance, narrators must be able to frame those elements in language that likewise stand out from the surrounding verbal terrain. Such evaluative devices may be expressed in all or any of the following domains (among others not listed):

> Phonological: repetition of sounds, changes in stress, volume, rhythm, speed, pitch, and enunciation

Lexical: aesthetic choice of words and affixes, which may in turn create effects that
   can surface in other domains, such as the phonological and syntactic

Syntactic: selection of elements such as modifiers, comparators, and adverbials, as
   well as of focusing transformations (clefts and the like)

Discursive: use of parallelism, episodic repetition, and elaboration (the rich clustering of images and events at key passages of a story) being three important
   examples

We will compare here two different versions of the same tale type from sib-
ling traditions. One is a Central Yana text, "Coyote and His Sister," told by Sam
Batwi (Sapir 1910). The other is a Yahi text, Ishi's own "Coyote Rapes His Sister"
(Sapir 1915*ms*). Unfortunately, space does not permit us to present the complete
stories here, since both are quite long. Instead, we will focus the discussion by
exploring a series of illustrative excerpts. In each case we will examine the narrator's individual stylistic use of evaluative devices. To make quantitative comparison possible, both texts have been "parsed" into lines according to the same criteria (essentially establishing an equivalence between independent clause and
line).

The format for most of the excerpts will be as follows: first a two-line interlinear presentation where Sapir's phonetic transcription is accompanied by his
word-by-word glosses; then our own free translation, with line breaks keyed to
the interlinear section.[1]

EVALUATIVE DEVICES IN BATWI'S "COYOTE AND HIS SISTER"

Sam Batwi's version of this widespread Coyote tale begins with a brief introduction of eleven lines, wherein Coyote and his sister are presented to the audience.
These lines set the stage for the story that follows. In them, we learn that Coyote
goes out every day to hunt small game, while his sister stays home preparing
acorn mush for his dinner upon his return in the evening. This short introductory scene is presented below as Excerpt 1.

EXCERPT 1
Yana Texts, *93.1–94.3*

Yaa'nt^h aij mec'i gi Haudulilmauna.   1
he dwelt | the | Coyote | at | Haudulilmauna

Bairigu$^{\prime}$ aij mec'i marii'miyauc'gu.   2
he stayed one | the | Coyote | together with (his) sister

Waawicai' ki marii'miyauna; 3
she pounded acorns | his | sister

juwaac'iru' aij mec'i. 4
he went to hunt small game | the | Coyote

Niiduuan' ai mec'i gi juwaac'iruyauna 5a
he arrived home | the | Coyote | at | going to hunt small game

baawisaki'a. 5b
when it was dark

Jeeri' aigi iiwaltpa jiic'au'i, mari'mi. 6
she soaked acorns | at it | south on ground | creek | woman

Xa'naip'amaki'ᵃ, juwaac'iru' mec'i; 7
when it was morning | he went to hunt small game | Coyote

niiduuantimai' baawisaki mec'i. 8
again he arrived home | when it was dark | Coyote

"Auwi' yuucayh aij!" mari'mi tii'i, 9
take it | acorn mush | this here! | woman | she said

joodunauyau aigi mec'i gi yuucaina. 10
giving him to eat | to him | Coyote | at | acorn mush

Hek'al' ai mec'i gi yuucaina. 11
he ate it with his fingers | he | Coyote | at | acorn mush

~~~

Coyote was living at Haudulilmauna, they say. 1
Coyote stayed alone with his sister. 2
His sister pounded acorns; 3
Coyote hunted for small game. 4
Coyote [would] come back home from small-game hunting 5a
    when it was dark. 5b
She soaked acorns in the ground south of the creek, 6a
    the woman. 6b
When it was barely light, 7a
Coyote went out to hunt small game, 7b

[and] again Coyote came home when it was dark.   8
"Take this acorn mush here!"   9a
   said the woman,   9b
      giving Coyote some mush to eat.   10
Coyote ate the mush with his fingers.   11

This scene-setting passage is then followed by the 309 lines of the core story it-self, where Coyote, having conceived an unnatural lust for his sister, fools her to get what he wants. Pretending to be ill, he tricks her into stepping over his head so that he can see her private parts. Next he sends her off to a dance, then dis-guises himself and follows her to the dance, where she has sex with him thinking he is someone else. But she soon discovers the deception, gives birth to a litter of coyote pups, and throws them into the river in disgust. Coyote rescues them. The sister then leaves forever, abandoning the babies to him. Following the core story, there is a shorter "tag story" of 64 lines involving an encounter Coyote has with Frost, in which Coyote does not fare nearly as well as he did with his sister.

Having laid out the contours of the tale itself, we will proceed to examine Sam Batwi's story and narrative techniques with respect to three key narrative devices: repetition, highlighting, and elaboration.

REPETITION

There are several different types of repetition, of course. Indeed, short as it is, the introductory section of the story (Excerpt 1 above) involves a number of different kinds of repetition. For instance, there are frequent lexically expressed references to Coyote and his sister. This is true throughout the story, naturally enough, but the density of terms referring to these two characters is especially great in the introduction, thereby establishing them both as main characters. Coyote is overtly named as *mec'i* eight times. His sister is referred to four times – twice as *marii'mi* 'woman', and twice as *marii'miyau(na)*, a word that is based on the same root as the word for 'woman' but that translates as 'sister.' These are cases of **lexical repetition.** In addition, there are frequent references to acorns and acorn mush, thus establishing the prominence of acorns within this section. However, the repetition this time is not so much lexical as thematic. The word for acorn mush (*yuucai-*) is indeed repeated three times in three different lines in the introduction. Other lines refer to acorns as well, however. For instance, lines 3 and 6a refer to acorns obliquely, by the lexical choice of verb stems that incorporate (*waawicai-*) or imply (*ceri-*) their reference. Thus this is an example of topical or **thematic repetition,** which includes within it some cases of simple lexical repetition.

In certain situations entire scenes or motifs may be repeated in a story and thus be given prominence. We will call this **episodic repetition.** In Excerpt 1, Batwi twice says that Coyote went out to hunt small game, and twice says he came back when it was dark. Episodic repetition, when applied to the recounting of daily chores and activities, is a standard narrative technique used to mark the passage of time, giving the listener the sense, by dint of the repetition, that this is the domestic routine that is followed every day. In this introduction, it serves to establish a status quo – a rhythm, a repetitive cycle of daily activities wherein everyone is doing what he or she is supposed to do and life is in balance.

As has often been pointed out, stories typically involve a deviation from norms, standard values, and expected states of affairs. Indeed, this deviation is what makes a story "tellable," or newsworthy, in the first place. These first 11 lines of "Coyote and His Sister" serve not only to single out the characters who will become important to the story but also to establish a default pattern of activity, so that we may anticipate its disruption as the tale begins to unfold. In most stories the state of disruption is temporary, and we are returned to a state of equilibrium at the end. Here, the importance of acorn preparation is recalled thematically at the end of the story, when Coyote tells his children that they will have to "spread out in every direction and get food for yourselves" (Sapir 1910:107). The preparation of acorns and the giving of acorn mush to eat can no longer happen, because the woman of the house is gone. The old order has changed, and a new (if less ordered) order takes its place.

The episodic repetition in the introduction is minor, however, and its prominence is largely local. A more important case may be found in the scene where the sister steps over Coyote as he lies in the doorway pretending to be sick – a scene that is portrayed twice. We present Sapir's free translation of this doubled scene, with parts labeled "A" and "B" for reference, in Excerpt 2.

EXCERPT 2

Yana Texts, *p.104*

... [A] The woman came back from the south, having gone to fetch water. She went in by the door, but Coyote was lying there sick. ... "Hey!" said the woman, "go back inside! Move away! Move away from the door! Lie down yonder on the north! You might be hurting your cheek if I step on you." "Enh," groaned Coyote with (pretended) pain. "Step over me, take your water. Step over me, sister." The woman did so, stepped over him. Coyote was lying on his back and yelped (when she stepped over him) (pretendedly with pain, really with lust). "Mh!" said the woman. "You see, why did you do that, not lying away from the door? I told you that your cheek would be hurt." [B] She pounded acorns, and soaked them in a small creek to the south. Coyote Woman came back into the house, fetching water. Coyote was lying at the door. "Lie down away from here!" (she said). "Step over me, sister." "Mh!" said the woman. The woman did as he asked her, stopped over him. Coyote yelped as before. "See now, you hurt your cheek."

On the theory that what is funny once will be funnier twice, the scene is repeated. At the same time, by giving this scene an "instant replay," Batwi lets us linger on the image of this absurd scenario and thereby assigns it a special prominence within the story as a whole. Both its humor and its repetition make it especially salient.

In the same way, a more complex instance of lexical repetition is illustrated in Excerpt 3. At the most dramatic part of the story, where Coyote tricks his sister into grabbing him and later having sex with him, we find a great deal of repetition or near-repetition of words, morphemes, and phrases. In the following passage, repetitive elements (excluding particles and inflectional morphemes) are underlined in their first appearance and double-underlined in subsequent reappearances; in the free translation all repetitive elements are placed in boldface.[2] For the time being, you may ignore the asterisks; we will return to this excerpt later for other purposes.

EXCERPT 3
Yana Texts, 98.1–98.7

Nibil' iitau basiiki.   1
he went about | in middle | when it was night

"Hau-hau, hau-hau!" gaac'an'i mec'i –   2
hau hau, | hau hau! | he shouted as leader | Coyote

tuu' aigija, k buriyauna muujaup'aa.   3
he did | in that way | his | dancing | chief

Mari'mi, hatki'i.   4
woman | she came from east

Mec'i, tuu' aigija, buriyauna,   5
Coyote | he did | in that way | dancing

Mari'mi, tuu' aigija, k jatkiyauna.   6
woman | she did | in that way | her | dancing from east

*   <u>Auwindi</u>ʔ aij <u>mari'mi</u> gi yaa'wi <u>mujaup'aa</u>,   7
    she took hold of him now | the | woman | to | Ya'wi | chief

*   <u>auwindi</u>ʔ k hisii'yauna,   8
    she now took hold of | her | brother

*   <u>j</u>amamc'<u>iriyawand</u>ⁱ,   9
    they now dancing with each other

k <u>jariyauna</u> <u>basiiki</u>ʔ.   10
their | dancing | when it is night

~~~

[Coyote] went about **in the middle of the night.**   1
"Hau-hau, hau-hau!" Coyote shouted, as leader –   2
he **did just like that,**   3a
    dancing like a chief.   3b
The woman [then],   4a
    she came **from the east.**   4b
[Then] **Coyote,**   5a
    he **did like that,**   5b
        dancing.   5c
[Then] **the woman,**   6a
    she **did like that** [too],   6b
        dancing from the east.   6c
*   **Now the woman took hold of** the Ya'wi **chief,**   7
*   **now** she **took hold of** her brother,   8
*   **now** they're **dancing** with each other,   9
    dancing in the night.   10

As can be seen, the degree of resonance here is quite high – much higher than the average levels in the text as a whole.[3] This passage also makes a good illustration of how effects created in one domain (here, lexical) can ripple into others (phonological), since the consequence of all this lexical and morphological repetition is that the *sounds* contained in those morphemes are compounded. This use of repetition is an enhancing device: by making the language echo with itself, the narrator calls a special attention to the scene.

ELABORATION
For any event in a story, a narrator must choose the degree of detail to provide. Where he goes into detail, the event so developed acquires depth and promi-

nence. But repetition alone does not necessarily assign significance to events – it only establishes their repetitiveness, whatever the end. In Batwi's story there is no elaboration in the background episodes of acorn preparation or hunting we examined in Excerpt 1; the events are repeated, but not elaborated. Without other signs of prominence, they are bleached of any larger significance, and that is the point: they establish a background against which the real events of the story can be measured. On the other hand, there is considerable embellishment in the two dressing scenes for the dance, as we shall see in Excerpt 4, given in the authors' free translation:[4]

EXCERPT 4
Yana Texts, *96.17–96.19 / 97.15–98.1*

(A) COYOTE WOMAN DRESSES FOR THE DANCE

Now Coyote Woman dressed herself up nicely.
She brightened her face with red paint,
she slipped her tasseled buckskin skirt over her hips,
she put on her tasseled white-grass apron,
she capped her head with a basket cap.
Ah, but she was a pretty woman!

(B) COYOTE DRESSES FOR THE DANCE

Now he dressed himself up.
He smeared grease on his face,
    suckerfish grease.
"Let there be an otterskin quiver!
Let me become tall!"
He did so:
Coyote became tall.
An otterskin quiver came to him,
    full of arrows.
Coyote was very handsome.

As far as the plot is concerned, Batwi could have handled these scenes tersely, without elaboration, saying merely, "Now Coyote Woman dressed herself up nicely; she was a pretty woman," and "Now Coyote dressed himself up; he was very handsome." But he chose to dwell in the scene, describing the clothes and the dressing ritual in some detail. In the process, he gives us a personal and rather intimate glimpse of these two characters at a key moment of the story. Batwi could have gone into this same kind of detail with small-game hunting and acorn preparation in his introduction, had he wanted to, but he did not. Thus are we led, by his expert narration, to know that acorn preparation, though structurally important to establishing the background scenario, is *not* key to the story proper and that the lavishly embellished scenes in Excerpt 4 (themselves just a build-up to the seduction scene that follows them) is where our attention should – and quite literally does – linger.

GRAMMATICAL DEVICES: HIGHLIGHTING

We will exemplify the use of grammatical processes for assigning prominence with one important suffix, the perfect (so-called "perfective") suffix - $\overset{?}{a}ndi$, usually glossed as "now" by Sapir.[5] According to his description of the suffix, - $\overset{?}{a}ndi$ is a "verb suffix marking point of time, translatable as 'now, then' or as perfective, but not generally capable of adequate rendering" (Sapir 1923: 269). The main reason for its intractability is that its domain is ultimately not local, but belongs to the discourse itself.

In Batwi's text this suffix shows up primarily at points of great drama in the story, where something clearly different and important is happening. Excerpt 5 offers a passage showing this function of the suffix.

EXCERPT 5
Yana Texts, *98.19–99.4*

Murulduwaldi' ai mec'i gi jeeja'lak'iyaumadu.   1
he lay down again on ground | he | Coyote | at | door place

*   Hadoojundi' ai mari'mi, ha'winjamauna.   2
now she came back from west | she | woman | walking fast

Miik'ai' ai mari'mi k juguc'ⁱ.   3
she was angry | she | woman | her | heart

Gimac'xayagu'.   4
she thought to herself

Haduuan' ai mari'mi,   5
she arrived home | she | woman

deewai⁷ai mari'mi hiiduwulyauki gi mec'i.   6
she saw him | she | woman | going back into house | to | Coyote

Mari'mi hiiduwul⁷i.   7
woman | she went back into house

Mec'i murul⁷i.   8
Coyote | he lay.

*   Mari'mi, yooxaiandi⁷.   9
woman | she was pregnant now

"He+!" mari'mi tii⁷i,   10
hey! | woman | she said

"Hi⁷pal⁷, wak'alp'ayauyii!"   11
get up | husband

~~~

Coyote lay back down in the doorway.   1
*   **Now** the woman came back from west,   2a
        walking fast.   2b
The woman was angry in her heart.   3
She thought to herself.   4
The woman arrived back home.   5
The woman saw Coyote,   6a
        going back into her house.   6b
That woman went back into the house.   7
Coyote, he [just] lay there.   8
*   That woman, **now** she was pregnant.   9
"Hey!" the woman said,   10
"Get up, *Husband*!"   11

The two clauses here that are flagged by the -⁷ándi suffix are clearly both pivotal dramatic developments in the story.

There are only 28 verbs containing the suffix -⁷ándi in all of Batwi's text, out of a total of 383 clause-based lines. Thus, the vast majority of narrative lines – about 94 percent – lack the suffix altogether. In Table 17.1 below, we list all 22 lines in the core story of Batwi's narrative that contain occurrences of -⁷ándi. (In our free translations, the presence of the suffix in its discourse role is usually registered by the word "Now" at the beginning of the line. Left-margin indents represent - ăndi chains – sequences of lines that are actually contiguous in the text. Instances marked with "†" represent true perfects.)

TABLE 17.1
Collated instances of - ăndi in Batwi's core story.

#1 T'uuandiʔ mari'mi: / cet'il'iiwagil'i.
    Now the woman did so: / she stepped over him.

#2 C'u'mpaa[ʔ]andiʔ mec'imari'mi.
    Coyote Woman dressed up nicely.

#3 Ham'cindiʔ baigumauna mari'mi.
    Now the woman went west, alone.

#4† Hiiwaldindiʔ ai t'uina
     The sun having gone down,

#5   basiwaldindiʔ.
        now it became night.

#6 C'um'paa[ʔ]andiʔ,
    Now he dressed himself up,

#7 Auwindiʔ aic mari'mi gi Yaa'wi mujaup'aa,
    Now the woman took hold of the Ya'wi chief,

#8   auwindiʔ k hisii'yauna,
     now she took hold of her brother,

#9   jamamc'iriyauandi,
        now they are dancing with each other,

#10 yaup'aiyauandi,
     now [he's] having sex with her,

#11   jeejabilyauandi gi mari'mi.
      now [he's] really moving the woman around.

#12 Badooandiʔ aij mec'i,
     Now Coyote ran back home to the east,

#13 Hadoojundiʔ ai mari'mi,
     Now the woman came back home from the west,

#14   Mari'mi, yooxaiandi'.
       The woman, she was pregnant now.

#15   Wayundi'i,
       Now she gave birth to children,

#16   Juum'cindi' mec'ic'gi gi xana.
       Now the coyote pups were floating west with the water.

#17†   Bac'aum'ciyauandi, / baidimʰci' ai mec'i ki dad'tiwi.
       Having run west along the creek, / Coyote ran west, abandoning his children.

#18†   Hinda' k'iwac'i wagayauandi.
       He made a willow fish-trap, having twined it.

#19   Cuutkiyauandi mec'ic'gi gi xamadu,
       Now the coyote pups [are] floating west from the water place,

#20   waak'cil'auandi',
       now they got up out of water,

#21†   cinaayaa'ayauand i.
            having already grown up.

#22   Niisaa['']and ai mec'i, / niidiyau gi yuwunc'gi.
       Now Coyote went off, / leaving the boys behind.

Notice that, when you abstract only those clauses with verbs containing this suffix from the text, as we have done here, what you get is a rough but service-able synopsis of the plot. Try reading through this list as if all the lines were con-nected: the -ándi suffix picks out for us a skeleton text of the key dramatic events of the story. With few exceptions (for instance, numbers 4, 17, 18, and 21 seem to contain instances of genuine perfect aspect and hence do not really be-long in this list), -ándi flags events as dramatically salient.[6] Remove those true perfects, and the synoptic effect is not disturbed – indeed, it is tightened. In short, this suffix is a stylistic narrative device that assigns special prominence to its clause.[7]

There is a parallel, or perhaps merely extended, stylistic use of -ándi that is worth remarking on. In the story's long seduction scene, where the sister and brother come together to dance and later make love, we find verbs with -ándi chained together in sequences. Excerpt 3, the dancing portion of the seduction scene, which we used to illustrate the device of repetition, happens also to contain a chain of three - ˀándi clauses (lines 7–9, marked with asterisks). Excerpt 6, which contains a short chain of two - ˀándi clauses (lines 12–13, translated "now" and marked with an asterisk), picks up and continues that scene into the seduction itself.

EXCERPT 6
Yana Texts, *98.7–98.16*

Then Coyote drew the woman off toward the east.	1
"Let's go off to the east!" [he said];	2
"Come on!"	3
The woman did:	4
they're going off east into the bushes.	5
They lay down to sleep,	6
sat there on the ground,	7a
talking to each other.	7b
Coyote did this:	8
he tickled the woman.	9
The woman did the same to the man.	10
He lay down with his arms around the woman,	11
* making love to her **now**,	12
* really moving the woman around **now**.	13
The woman's a big one,	14
she's fat and very pretty.	15
Along towards dawn,	16a
Coyote got up,	16b
done with making love.	17
Coyote ran away back home.	18
She stayed behind in the bushes,	19a
the woman.	19b

However outrageous, the seduction scene marks the very heart of the story, and is clearly marked that way: by repetition, by the rich clustering of detail, and by the liberal use of - ˀándi (five instances altogether, when excerpts 3 and 6 are joined), including the - ˀándi chain that occurs at lines 11–12 – patently the climax of the whole story. In this way, the clustering and even chaining together of - ˀándi clauses helps assign high prominence to an entire passage.[8]

To summarize our discussion so far, then, we see that Sam Batwi, an expert narrator, employs (among other devices) repetition, elaboration, and high-lighting elements like the -ándi suffix as evaluation devices for assigning narrative prominence to the most dramatically salient parts of his story.

ISHI'S VERSION: "COYOTE RAPES HIS SISTER"

Ishi's tale is very similar in broad outline to Sam Batwi's version. It begins with an introduction depicting Coyote and his sister engaged in the day-to-day conduct of their lives, he hunting game, she preparing acorns. Once the status quo has been established, the plot takes its "turn," as Coyote pretends to fall ill. In both versions, Coyote puts something in his mouth to make his cheeks look swollen (stones for Batwi, buckeye nuts for Ishi), as part of his deception. Ishi's version lacks the scenes where the sister steps over the brother, but both versions have a dance, dwell on the details of dress, and have the sister and brother dancing together and later having sex in the dark. In Batwi's version, the sister sees him sneaking home and is thus made immediately aware of the betrayal. In Ishi's version it is not until she gives birth to coyote pups that she realizes she has been deceived. The tag stories are different in the two versions (although it is certainly interesting that both versions *have* a tag).

The story lines are very similar, then. What is strikingly different between the versions has to do with two things: (1) proportionality and (2) the fact that Ishi applies his evaluation devices to very different aspects of the narrative. By doing so, he creates a strange and unexpected scale of prominence in his rendition of the story. Specifically, the foregrounding and backgrounding of narrative elements is drastically changed. Applying the same criteria to Yahi that we used to assess the Central Yana story, we would have to conclude that Ishi awards prominence, not – or not only – to the events of the story proper but to the routine details of daily life that we would expect, in any other tradition or style, to be confined in skeletal form largely to the introductory portion of the tale.

REPETITION

A comparison (Table 17.2) of the relative length of narrative sections between Batwi's and Ishi's versions makes this difference very clear. Ishi's introduction is enormously elongated – it's longer even than the core story itself, accounting for more than half of the narrative as a whole: 53.9 percent of the total, as opposed to a mere (and more typical) 2.9 percent for Batwi's version. In terms of sheer length, this proportional prominence places the material and thematic content of the introduction on a par with the events of the story itself; indeed, it threatens to drown it out before the latter even begins. Or perhaps the story is not where we think it is – a notion to which we will return in the final section of the paper.

Table 17.2. Length of Narrative Sections

	BATWI		ISHI	
	Lines	%	Lines	%
Introduction	11	2.9	377	53.9
Core story	309	80.5	299	42.9
Tag story	64	16.7	22	3.2
Total	384	100	698	100

One obvious key to this extraordinary elongation is episodic repetition, a device we discussed earlier for the Central Yana version. (The other key is elaboration, as will be discussed subsequently.) Batwi's introduction, given in Excerpt 1, contains two acorn preparation cycles, two hunting cycles in which Coyote goes out after small game, and one eating scene – all of them very brief. In contrast, Ishi's introduction contains *fourteen* distinct food preparation scenes (the three longest involving acorn preparation, with most of the rest involving rabbit and buckeye preparation), four hunting scenes, four firewood-gathering scenes, and seven eating scenes – not to mention three arrow-making scenes thrown in gratis: thirty-two scenes and 377 lines in all.

ELABORATION

Unlike Batwi, who treats these routine background activities with the utmost brevity, Ishi focuses his most consistent and methodical attention on these daily events, returning to them again and again, varying the details slightly each time, but always articulating them with a thoroughness not reserved for any other aspect of the story. To demonstrate this point, Excerpt 7 presents the second of Ishi's three acorn preparation scenes. (Incidentally, notice how stripped down and bulletlike Ishi's syntactic style is, as compared to Batwi's more varied and ornate constructions.)

EXCERPT 7
Yahi Texts, *Y3.546–778*

Doo'yusjaram$^{?}$,   1
she took acorns in *k'awaala* out of house

jeduwoo$^{?}$k kee'mau^{na},   2
she took | her | acorn pounding hopper

*   baam'ca*ʾandi*ʾ.   3
now she pounded

Jomʰlauʾ –   4
she sifted acorn meal into the *k'awaala*

deeduk'auʾ.   5
she finished

Jeetumariʾ.   6
she put acorns back into hopper

T'ooguk'araʾᵃ-ti.   7
let that be enough![?] she said.

Doxpaʾ.   8
she swept together acorn fragments on rock mortar (and discarded them)

Boibalʾ,   9
she took up (her *maamauna*)

hai'yaubalʾ kʾaunᵃ,   10
she took up (little) fire | her | fire

ha'c'gilʾ gi xanᵃ.   11
she went to creek | at | water

Jeduwooʾ kʰ beeʾaimaunᵃ,   12
she took | her | rocks heated in fire (rocks for heating in fire)

deejayuududamc'iʾ –   13
she put hot rocks together on fire to heat them

deeduk'auʾ.   14
she finished

Yuuyuwawaldiʾ.   15
she made fire-heated rocks (by means of grass and fire taken) [?]

Jewooʾk kui'yaunᵃ,   16
she took | her | sand

boot'at'ai' –   17
she smoothed it down by patting

deeduk'au'.   18
she finished

* Hom'laja a̱ndi'.   19
she put acorns down into sand-pit.

* Doowoo a̱ndi' –   20
She put water on (acorns)

deeduk'au'.   21
she finished

* Booma a̱ndi' –   22
now she heated them with rocks

deeduk'au'.   23
she finished

* Heebil a̱ndi'   24
she was engaged in [it]

kem'laidi',   25
she stopped pouring water

jeduwoo' k maamaun^a.   26
she took | her | cooking basket

* Bam'k'ui a̱ndi' –   27
now she roasted them under the sand [??]

deeduk'au'.   28
she finished

Jewoo' k de'nwalsa' gi k'ain^a,   29
she took | her | put aside | to | rocks

jeduwoo' gi t'aap'al^na;   30
she took | at | leaves

*   ʾoo'laja a̱ndiʾ –   31
she put acorn flour down on leaves

deeduk'auʾ.   32
she finished

*   Jusli a̱ndiʾ.   33
she put layer of leaves over acorn flour

*   De'nli a̱ndiʾ –   34
she put hot rocks on top by means of tongs

deeduk'auʾ.   35
she finished

Jeduwooʾk yuucainᵃ,   36
she took | her | acorn mush

boomaʾ –   37
she put hot rocks in with them to cook

deeduk'auʾ.   38
she finished

Baidici'lawʾ.   39
she took out rocks in *maamauna*

Doo'yusjasaʾ.   40
she ceased to put more water on hardened acorns [?]

*   Juk'wola a̱ndiʾ,   41
she sat

dawooʾk ʾuini'maunᵃ.   42
she sat at | her | roasting

Jeduwooʾc joobaʾ.   43
she took | the | she removed rocks from fire [?]

Peejawaldiʾ k'awaaˡᵃ;   44
she put down | basket

joobaas,   45
she removed them from the fire

meec'imaari',   46
she put *mayauna* (=*joobamauna*) into *k'awala*.

doo'yusjaxaise'.   47
she filled the basket [?]

Jeduwoo' k maamaun^a;   48
she took | her | cooking basket

xaik'aldilau',   49
she cleaned it out (to get dirt out)

peejaduwaldi'.   50
she put it back down

Jeduwoo' yuucain^a,   51
she took | acorn mush

buidubal',   52
she took up load

buiduwul'.   53
she packed it back inside

Haduwoo' k mayaun^a,   54
She went back to | her | food[?]

Boi'idubal',   55
she took up load after first

boi'iduwul'.   56
she packed it back into house

Jeduwoo' k da'namaun^a,   57
she took | her | water taken up for drinking

Boi'iducilau'ⁱ.   58
she took it back out of water

Boidolootpaʾ.   59
she went back South (to cave) with her load

~~~

She took a basket of acorns out of the house,
she took up her acorn-pounding hopper,
*   **now** she pounded them.
She sifted acorn meal into the basket –
        finished.   5
She put more acorns into the hopper.
"That ought to be enough!" she said.
She swept away the acorn fragments [on the rock mortar].
She took up the food,
gathered up a bit of fire,   10
went to the creek for water.
She took out her cooking stones,
put the stones together on the fire to heat –
        finished.
She made the stones hot in the fire.   15
She took up her sand,
patted it smooth –
        finished.
*   **Now** she put the acorns down into the sand-pit.
*   **Now** she poured water on [the acorns] –   20
        finished.
*   **Now** she heated them up with the stones –
        finished.
*   **Now** she was busy with it:
she stopped pouring water,   25
took up her cooking basket.
*   **Now** she roasted them under the sand –
        finished.
She took the stones she set aside,
she took some leaves,   30
*   **now** she put acorn flour down on the leaves –
finished.
*   **Now** she put a layer of leaves over the acorn flour.
*   **Now** she put hot stones on top [with tongs] –
        finished.   35
She took up her acorn mush,
put hot stones in with them to cook –
        finished.

She took the rocks out of the food.
She stopped pouring water on the cooked acorns. [?]   40
* **Now** she sat,
  she sat at her roasting.
She took and removed it from the fire. [?]
She put down the basket;
as she removed them from the fire,   45
she put the food into the basket,
she filled up the basket.
She picked up her cooking basket,
cleaned it out,
put it back down.   50
She picked up the acorn mush.
She took up her load,
packed it back inside.
She went back for her food [?];
she took up a second load,   55
packed it back into the house.
She took up her [water basket],
lifted it back out of the water,
[and] went back home south with her load.

Long as it is, it must be remembered that this is only one of three acorn preparation scenes in the introduction, all of which are nearly as well delineated and
elaborate as this one. In contrast to this high degree of elaboration, the sex scene
that Batwi described in such ribald detail in Excerpt 6 is only starkly covered by
Ishi. Ishi's version of this scene (9 lines to Batwi's 17) is presented below, in its
entirety, as Excerpt 8.

EXCERPT 8
Yahi Texts, Y3.2250–2282

Handulil',   1
they turned back (to sleep)

hantau'.   2
they went to level (?) place

Camduwaldi' gi teemauna.   3
again they lay down to sleep | on | blanket(??)

Dasgaiki, jewoo'k banᵃ,   4
early in morning | he took | his | deer meat

meec'iram'.   5
he got out [of his blanket, his *jigalp'anᵃ*]

Xa'laisginki, pi'nbal' cumk'smic'iis,   6
at dawn | they got up | those who copulated

pi'nbal'ⁱ gi teemauna.   7
they got up | from | blanket[?]
~~~
They turned back (to sleep),                                          1
they went along the trail.                                            2
They lay down to sleep again on the blanket.                         3
Early in the morning,                                               4a
   he took his deer meat,                                            4b
he got out of his blanket.                                           5
At dawn, they got up,                                               6a
   those who had copulated.                                          6b
They got up from the blanket.                                        7

Though it forms the climax in Sam Batwi's version of the tale, in Ishi's telling the
scene is barely even fleshed out – indeed, in terms of elaboration, it is best compared to the coverage of events in the introductory section of Sam Batwi's story.

Instead, Ishi's creative attention is diverted from the sex scene itself to other
parts of the story. The dressing scenes, for instance, where Coyote and his un-
witting sister prepare themselves for the big dance, are quite elaborate. In particular, the special focus on the face painting and sequencing of garments is analogous to Batwi's dressing scenes in Excerpt 4 – though not quite as lavish, they
seem to have the same sort of intimate, lingering weight and feel. We present
this scene below, in our own free translation, for comparison, as Excerpt 9:

EXCERPT 9
*Yahi Texts: Y3.1750–1874*


(A) COYOTE'S SISTER DRESSES FOR THE DANCE

"Now go and [dance]!" [said Coyote to his sister.]
She took her wildcat skin blanket,
the woman clothed herself in [it].

She took up her [ . . . ], her cooking basket.
"Paint your face!" [Coyote said.]
She put red paint in some water,
laid paint in straight lines on her face –
    finished.
"Now it looks good!" [said Coyote.]
"Put [the paint] back on the ground!" [he said.]
She took her string of white shelldisk beads,
took them out of the basket,
put [the rest] back into the basket.
"Now go and [dance]!" [said Coyote.]
The woman went outside.
She went west, across the water to the north.
She followed the trail to the west.


(B) COYOTE DRESSES FOR THE DANCE

Coyote gets up in a hurry.
He threw off his blanket,
got his water,
washed his face.
He picked up his red fungus paint,
rubbed [it] into his palm thoroughly,
dipped in a finger and rubbed paint in lines on his face –
    finished.
He took up his wildcat blanket,
put it on himself.
He took his pine-marten quiver,
took his basket hat,
took a chunk of cut-off deer meat [for lunch],
took his pine-marten quiver.
**Now** he went west after her.


Following this scene comes the dance, and this scene, too, is quite detailed and elaborate. Considerable attention is paid to who sings, who dances, who files in and from what direction – in short, to visualizing the whole night-time spectacle of the dance.

It is at the dance, when Coyote (in disguise) and his sister meet, dance together, and talk, that Coyote's preposterous scheme finally begins to hatch. In Excerpt 10 (authors' free translation), the two ill-crossed lovers-to-be have a conversation about the "sick brother back home" that is really quite deftly funny. (Coyote is exactly the type who would rig his own funeral just so he could eavesdrop on what others said about him, so the scene is rife with comic potential.)[9]

EXCERPT 10
Yahi Texts, *Y3.2118–2246*

She approached to the west,
[and] pulled him away.
He was startled, they say.
He was grabbed by her,
he was grabbed by the woman.
He dragged away,
he was dragged away to the north in the dark.

"Who is this person who [ . . . ]," he said.
"[ . . . ]," he said.
"Who is this person who [ . . . ]," he said.

"Perhaps you don't see,
and perhaps you don't understand me," [she said].

"[Who are you?" asked [Coyote], they say.

"They say it's me," said the woman.

"So it is you," he said,
"and you are all alone," he said,
    "all by yourself."

"[My brother] is sick," she said,
"he lies sick," she said.
"[ . . . ]."
"He got left behind," she said.

"Was he indeed?
[Let's talk about him]," [Coyote] said.
"Would he be the one who did not sing,
the one indeed who is sick?" he said.

"He is too sick to eat," [the woman] said.

"Is he indeed?
It seems he isn't," he said,
   "isn't sing[ing] along with the others," he said.
"He doubtless isn't sick enough to die," [Coyote said].

"So it is with him," she said.

"Is it indeed?" [Coyote said].

They stopped dancing with the others.
[In the morning,] a speech was made [telling them all to go home].

From these last two examples, it is clear that Ishi *is* capable of delivering a story in a recognizably traditional, if sometimes eccentric, manner. In several passages of the core story we find elaborative detail and even humor in plenty. And yet the story remains oddly different. We need to look further, then, if we are to understand this difference and reconcile these conflicting assessments of Ishi's narrative style.

### HIGHLIGHTING DEVICES:
### THE USE OF -ʾANDI

In the acorn preparation scene given as Excerpt 7 above, there are ten occurrences of -ʾandi (flagged in the margin by an asterisk). That number, in this one scene alone, adds up to more than a third of all the occurrences of -ʾandi in Batwi's entire tale. All told, taking the narrative as a whole, Ishi's use of the suffix outpaces Batwi's by a factor of two. A comparison of the distribution of the -ʾandi suffix is given in Table 17.3.

Table 17.3. Distribution of -ʾandi Suffix

|  | BATWI | | ISHI | |
|---|---|---|---|---|
|  | Tokens | Density | Tokens | Density |
| Introduction | 0 | — | 72 | 5.2 |
| Core story | 23 | 13.4 | 35 | 8.5 |
| Tag story | 5 | 12.8 | 3 | 7.3 |
| Whole Narrative | 28 | 13.7 | 108 | 6.5 |

Altogether in this long introductory portion to the tale, there is an average of one - *ȧndi* for every 5.2 lines of text. (In this measurement, a value of 1 – that is, one - *ȧndi* per line – would be the highest possible density.) In the core story itself, there is considerably *less* usage: one for every 8.5 lines. There is no use of - *ȧndi* in the copulation scene at all. (Recall that for Batwi this scene was marked as the evaluative high point of the tale, involving the highest density of - *ȧndi* suffixes.)

Indeed, there are really only a handful of key narrative clauses in Ishi's version of the core story that carry the suffix and seem to work in a fashion analogous to the way they are used in Central Yana. Two of these cases are situated near the end of the tale in the passage where Coyote's sister abandons Coyote and the babies. This passage is given as Excerpt 11.

EXCERPT 11
*Yahi Texts, Y3.2602–2670*

Jebils mec'[i].                                                              1
Coyote is going about

Poojan':                                                                     2
he bathed (children)

jeduwoo' k daa'n[a].                                                         3
he took | his | children

Yaijadubal',                                                                  4
he took them up again

pooja'n[a].                                                                   5
he bathed them

Doitenxba',                                                                   6
[Coyote] was left all alone

baidisah[i].                                                                  7
he was abandoned

*    Hasa ȧndi':                                                             8
she now went away

"Masi ʾiiyau jum <u>daa</u>ti"-ti.      9
I'm going to | curse | your | children – she said

Jo'nbalʾ,      10
he picked (them) up

<u>yaijadubalʾ</u> k <u>daa'n</u>ᵃ,      11
he took back | his | children

<u>yaijaduwulʾ</u>.      12
he took them back into house

\*   <u>Poojan åndiʾ</u>,      13
he now bathed them

ce'nliʾᵃ gi xanᵃ.      14
he washed them with hot water | with | water

<u>Jebils poojanʾ</u> –      15
he goes about | he bathed them

deeduk'auʾ.      16
he finished

<u>Jeduwooʾ</u> k gaaninⁿᵃ.      17
he took | his | blanket

Comwaldiʾ k <u>pooja'namaun</u>ᵃ <u>daa'n</u>ᵃ.      18
he put them down to sleep | his | having been bathed | babies
~~~
Coyote **is going about.**   1
He bathed them: 2
he picked up **his children.**   3
He picked them up again,   4
he bathed them.   5
He was left all alone,   6
he was abandoned.   7

*   **Now** she went away: 8
"I'm going to curse your **children,**" she said.   9

He picked them up,	10
he took back his children,	11
took them back into the house.	12

*	Now he bathed them.	13
	he washed them in hot water.	14
	He goes about having bathed them –	15
	finished.	16
	He took his blanket.	17
	He put his bathed children down to sleep.	18

In this passage the suffix highlights two key events: the sister's departure and curse in line 9, which marks the end of the old order; and the bathing singled out in line 13, which signals (although the chronology is a bit loose here) the beginning of a *new* order, in which Coyote assumes the role of provider and primary caregiver (however brief his tenure).[10] Most instances of the -*ándi* suffix in Ishi's narrative don't seem to work this way, however. To demonstrate this fact, Table 17.4 presents a listing of all twenty-nine narrative lines in Ishi's core story that are flagged by the -*ándi* suffix:

TABLE 17.4
*Collated Instances of -*ándi* in Ishi's Core Story*

#1	*	Now he drank the water.
#2	*	Now he drank all day.
#3	*	Now she gave him [something] to drink.
#4		**Now he lay around as though sick.**
#5		**At sundown, now [Coyote] curled up near the fire.**
#6	*	Now she gave him [something] to drink.
#7		**Now many people came from the east, from up north in the mountains.**
#8		**Now he went west after her.**
#9		Now he looked to the west.
#10		**Now the Eastern People danced.**
#11	*	Now they made fire.
#12		Now they danced.
#13		Now [Coyote] got up.
#14		**Now she looked west [toward Coyote].**
#15		Now sang Owl.
#16		Now [Owl's people] danced.
#17		Now Coyote danced,
#18		**now he danced along with them.**

#19   Now he danced.
#20   Now she turned back.
#21   **Now she reached out her hand to [touch] him.**
#22 * Now she put rocks on the fire.
#23 * Now the deer meat cooked.
#24 * Now he drank.
#25 * Now she made a fire.
#26   **Now she went away.**
#27   **Now he bathed them.**
#28 * Now he pounded acorns.
#29   Now Coyote and his children ate their fill.

Two things are clear from this list. First, the lines Ishi has flagged with - ʾándi do not provide us with anything remotely like an outline or summary of the plot, the way that Batwi's did. Even though *some* key developments (in boldface) do show up here, it is not possible to reconstruct the main events of the story from this list, even the selected list picked out in boldface. Second, even here in the core story, notice how many of the - ʾándi-flagged lines draw attention to the same mundane daily activities – cooking, making fire, fetching or drinking water, pounding acorns – that were the focus of the extended introductory portion of Ishi's narrative, which itself contains fully double the number of - ʾándi's that the core story does. (These lines are marked with an asterisk in the margin.)

At this point it is germane to wonder whether the - ʾándi suffix in Yahi functions in the same way that the Central Yana suffix does, or whether it is an evaluative device at all in Yahi. If not, though, what is it? There are several possible classifications that manage to capture *some* of what is going on with this marker, but none that account for everything; and all admit to extensive exceptions.[11] When a device is employed only sporadically, we are thrown back on the question of what impulse might govern its appearances. So the evidence that - ʾándi has an evaluative function in Yahi – that is, that its suppression or deployment, whatever the rhetorical or grammatical context, constitutes an evaluative act, an expression of choice – is difficult to refute. What we are suggesting, then, is that - ʾándi functions, in a variety of interrelated grammatical and rhetorical contexts, as a highlighting device that flags lines as having some special or particular salience for their narrator during his passage through his story – just as it does in Central Yana.

The passages that are marked by frequent occurrence of - ʾándi are typically the same passages that bear the richest clustering of detail and display the highest degree of episodic repetition. Also, the preponderance of lines so flagged in the story tend to sound a few prevailing themes, with subsistence and domesticity being by far the dominant themes throughout *all* parts of the story – overwhelmingly so in the introduction, but elsewhere in the narrative as well. These observations, taken together, force us to conclude that Ishi is indeed giving prominence to the introductory portion of his tale (the 376 lines that focus on the rhythms of daily life) and that he actually *de*focuses the core story by making it shorter, by using fewer episodic repetitions, and by underusing the highlighting suffix - *ándi*.

DISCUSSION

What can be learned from all this? How can we connect these linguistic and rhetorical patterns to the man who composed them and to the pattern of his life? Some insights are easily drawn. For instance, it is not hard to account for the differences in highlighting and elaboration between Ishi's version of the "sex scene" and Sam Batwi's. Native American cultures traditionally had few if any taboos governing frank or even graphic depictions of sexual activity; it was not a controlled or gendered topic by any stretch of the imagination. So ordinarily, one would not attribute this apparent lack of interest to repression or decorum on the narrator's part. In Ishi's case, though, we *must* entertain embarrassment and self-censorship as a plausible factor in explaining the short shrift he gives to the "payoff" scene in this story. Theodora Kroeber reports that her husband "found that Ishi was reticent about any discussion of sex, blushing furiously if the subject came up" (Kroeber 1967:220). Whether Ishi's embarrassment was the result of postcapture "contamination" by ambient Victorian morality or, also likely, a consequence of having come of age sexually in a social group where the only available sex partners were off limits because of incest constraints, it is impossible to say. Obviously, he heard this story often enough to have remembered it, despite how he may have retailored it for his own performance. In any case, Kroeber's observation is certainly corroborated by the handling of the sex scene in Ishi's narrative.[12]

Other aspects of Ishi's eccentric style are more challenging to explain. For instance, we have discovered that Ishi assigns enormous prominence to a portion of his narrative – his introduction, which we have seen to be highly elaborated, relentlessly iterated, and profusely highlighted – that the rest of us are hard put to find a plot in. So what is Ishi's story really "about," if not how Coyote duped his sister and upset the tranquility of their life together? Perhaps, in this case, we cannot say after all that Ishi's story is really so much about the breaking of norms (although that is a follow-up story), but rather focuses on the rendering of the old norms themselves.

"Coyote Rapes His Sister" was the fourth in a series of six tales that Ishi told to Sapir.[13] All but one contain long passages detailing these routine domestic scenes. There are at least a couple of reasons why Ishi might have told his stories this way. First, perhaps he learned them that way. As the man who was billed during his lifetime as the "last wild Indian," perhaps he was bringing us the most traditional narratives ever collected. Maybe Sam Batwi, who was bilingual and, like all *other* Indians of his time, lived in association with an encroaching white culture, was acculturated to Spanish or Anglo-American storytelling, and so told his tale in a way more attuned to Western traditions. Ishi, in contrast, could have been telling his stories in the way that people told them before the coming of Europeans.

The problem with this hypothesis is that Ishi's style of telling a tale is, so far as we know, all but unique.[14] We would have to view him, therefore, as the *only* truly traditional narrator ever recorded – a doubtful claim at best. Linguists and anthropologists have recorded many stories from monolingual narrators, people who learned their stories before the great changes that were foisted on Native Americans everywhere, and who were *not* in fact very acculturated to Western storytelling traditions. Even in these cases, however, we do not find this astounding and obsessive focus on domestic activities and corresponding de-emphasis of the core story.

Second, perhaps Ishi focused on the details of daily life because that is what he thought the anthropologists wanted him to do. After all, it was his knowledge of traditional life, material culture, subsistence patterns, and manufacturing techniques, that the people with whom he worked – Kroeber, Waterman, Nelson, Pope – were most interested in. For several years before dictating these narratives, Ishi had been telling and showing anthropologists and museum-goers how to make arrows, how to hunt, how to build native houses, how to make a fire, and other traditional practices. Indeed, it was his *job* to do so. Perhaps he thought this was all they were interested in – and so, to oblige them, he dwelled on those details most of all.

However, it seems unlikely to us that this would have been a primary consideration in Ishi's storytelling choices. There is no particular reason why Ishi would think that Sapir – a man who studied language, not custom – really wanted to know about preparing acorns when he asked for Coyote stories. And there is certainly no way for this line of reasoning to explain the *lengths* to which Ishi indulged this stylistic tendency. (Indeed, the first half of this story – and to a lesser degree the others as well – is so looping and repetitious that it's a wonder Sapir did not protest or simply stop recording, as a less punctilious collector might well have done.)

Third, maybe the psychological stress engendered by the cruel and unusual circumstances of Ishi's life and upbringing took its toll. Say that one of the effects of that long-term stress and isolation manifests itself here in a kind of logorrhea, whereby certain story elements get proliferated beyond the reasonable expectation. Against this view, of course, we have the testimony of Kroeber,

Pope, and others who knew him best that Ishi was a remarkably down-to-earth and well-adjusted man, to all appearances quite steady and unhaunted by his ordeal. Yet even if we were to accept this kind of half-baked psychotherapeutic speculation, it still begs the fundamental question: why are *these* scenes – and *only* these scenes – replayed so lovingly and profusely, and not other elements of the tale as well?

None of these explanations is wholly satisfactory. But there is another explanation that comes to mind. Perhaps Ishi dwelled on these images of daily life because the power and passion of his memory forced him to do so. True, we think it actually quite plausible that Ishi was motivated, by the preoccupations of his anthropological work and again by his own ambivalence or inexperience with sex, to distort his native storytelling style, at least to some small degree. In the end, though, these narrative grooves, as they manifested themselves, full-blown, in his work with Sapir, came to satisfy some deep personal need of his own – a mnemonic gratification that carried him back, again and again, to the time before he surrendered his life. Reading the stories, working with them intimately, clause by clause, we came to see that Ishi imbues these scenes from daily life with great passion. All evidence from patterns of repetition, elaboration, and the deployment of evaluative devices suggests this. For all our initial regrets about the content of his stories, they remind us of an autobiography, after all.

We all can name scenes from our lives that we are able to recall with vivid intensity, and in autobiography we can almost always find passages where the author has portrayed such scenes and images – the texture of a carpet, the pattern of curtains or wallpaper, the smells of a kitchen at holidays, the sound and warmth of a voice, the taste of a madeleine – with a wealth of sensory detail. As Ishi chipped arrowheads, leached acorns, dressed game, and built shelters – all activities that must have been second nature to him – on the museum grounds for his crowds of visitors, what was he thinking? Where did his mind transport him? Judging from these stories, the answer seems to be: *back*, into the past, into reverie, and the reassuringly banal routines of the life he once shared with his loved ones. In the end, we get the same impression from the routines replayed in Ishi's tales: that he was reliving these scenes, reveling in them – not just dwelling on them, but in a real sense, dwelling *in* them.

We suggest that, for Ishi, telling these stories was by no means just the simple repetition of a traditional tale, but much, much more. The tales are in there, to be sure; but in his telling, he was guided by the power of his own memories of his own life. He was in fact telling us a good deal about himself and about the way his people, his handful of people, lived. They survived for so long because these life-giving rhythms kept playing, day after day after day.

These stories reveal Ishi to be a storyteller unlike any other known in the traditional oral canon of Native America. We should take time to reflect on this revelation, for it has consequences for our conception of Ishi himself and for the role he plays in American cultural history. After all, was not Ishi made famous – marketed, if you will – for being absolutely "natural," the perfect exemplar of aboriginal man in native North America, uncorrupted by contact with European civilization? Even the anatomical perfection of his never-shod feet was extolled and immortalized in plaster casts. Headlines and obituaries billed him as "the last wild Indian in North America." Even his closest friends in the white world thought of him in these terms. His stature in European American culture at large is, and always was, more as an archetype than an individual.

In the generations since his discovery and death, and until very recently, whites have romantically tried to read in him the text of the primitive that is buried in us all: the "natural" man, and the undilute emblem of what history vanquished without a second thought. Indians, too, have looked to him, equally romantically, in two complementary ways: as an icon of uncompromised and uncontaminated traditional values – in the words of a Sioux performer who met Ishi at a Wild West show, "a very high grade of Indian" (Pope 1920:189); or as the symbolic victim, the living exhibit in the zoo of American conquest. To both he has been a symbol of what was vanquished or lost. Yet his life was anything but natural, anything but normal. He lived in hiding for thirty years with the tattered remnants of his people, in a society so diminished structurally that he could have no prospect of marriage, since there were no women eligible to him. American civilization, far from leaving him untouched by its influence, exerted a constant and unspeakable pressure on his life.

Ishi was a remarkable man, a hero if there ever was one, but he was not a "natural" man, for his life was not a normal life. It may be that the closest analogy we can find is to survivors of the Holocaust. Anne Frank's life comes immediately to mind. In no sense would we dream of saying that Anne Frank had a "natural" childhood; and Ishi lived thirty *years* in hiding. And yet for all the stress and horror of survival in hiding, a clear reverence and love – even, impossibly, a nostalgia – for that life shines through in his stories.

Though he speaks not a word to us directly about his life and times, Ishi, in telling these stories, gives himself away. He is unique as a storyteller in the stylistic choices he makes toward the establishment of narrative prominence, and this very uniqueness leads us to see that Ishi was telling us something about his own life and values, after all. Most of all, we learn of the enduring value and comfort he found in the cyclic rhythms of the life he led, hidden, day after day, in the California wilderness. Wilderness? To Ishi, it was home.

NOTES

1. In Yahi excerpts, since Sapir never completed a full glossing of Ishi's texts, the word-by-word glosses are an amalgam of Sapir's original work and that of the Yahi Translation Project [ms]. Both Yana and Yahi are presented in a modernized practical orthography similar to that used by Swadesh for the *Yana Dictionary*. Vowels are pronounced with their European values (as in Spanish). Doubled vowels are held for a longer duration, and superscript vowels are whispered. Consonants are pronounced more or less like their English counterparts, with these exceptions: <c> represents a "ch" sound; <g> is always given its "hard" pronunciation, as in *gum*; and <x> represents the sound in German *Bach* or Scottish *loch*. The apostrophe <'> indicates that the adjacent consonant is glottalized, while a superscript <ʰ> marks aspiration. The symbol <ˀ> represents a glottal stop.

2. We are defining *words* here as items sharing a common stem, since inflectional endings may vary and subsequent occurrences of a word frequently also exhibit the incremental addition of derivational suffixes. In the excerpt, *bu-* is the stem used for a male dancing; *ja-* is the stem used for a woman dancing.

3. However, keep in mind that the words *mec'i* and *marii'mi* are repeated here more for syntactic-discursive reasons than for those of phonological cohesion. Although their repeat appearances certainly help the passage to resound, their primary function is as a switch-reference or switch-focus device. (Notice that these subjects are always preposed, or topicalized, when there is a change of subject from Coyote to Sister or back.) Even so, regardless of the motivation, the effort to keep these two characters equally in the narrative spotlight has a phonological effect. The extra resonance is a consequence of the extra attention.

4. Excerpt 3 also contains considerable elaboration, in addition to its high degree of repetition.

5. This suffix seems to have originated as a tense-aspect marker (which function it occasionally still reflects), but it has evolved into a discourse marker in the latter-day Yanan languages. The suffix has several allomorphs, depending on a variety of factors, including register, syntactic position, and phonological environment. The forms -*ˀandi*, -*andi*, and -*ndi* are all commonly attested, as are the devoiced variants -(*ˀa*)*ntʰ⁾ⁱ*. (Superscript vowels and consonants are voiceless, pronounced as if whispered.)

6. Alternatively, the flagging of 5 and 21 may not be primarily or solely grammatical, but just a "spreading around" of the feature of prominence to adjacent clauses within that marked passage, as happens quite clearly in the chained sequences 7–8–9 and 10–11.

7. See Grimes' (1972) article for a useful discussion of these and similar narrative patterns.

8. Thus, occurrences 4 and 5 in Table 17.1, while not exactly salient events if taken individually, by being marked may enhance the highlighting of their passage as a whole, rather than being intrinsically prominent in and of themselves.

9. Here, as elsewhere in the Yahi passages, the notation "[...]" indicates a line or phrase that has (so far) proved untranslatable with any degree of confidence. Spotty though the translation is, the tongue-in-cheek humor of the interchange is clear.

10. The bathing act in line 13 may be being highlighted for other reasons as well. The focus of this entire passage is bathing and water imagery. More than any other sample we have looked at in Ishi's core story, this scene approaches the levels of lexical and phonological cohesion that Batwi attains in passages like that in Excerpt 3. To show this, I have applied the same system of markings to the excerpt here: underlining and double underlining for repeated elements, generalized to boldface in the translation. The resonance of this passage is quite high.

11. This is not the occasion for a full-scale linguistic discussion of the phenomenon. For those who are curious, though, here is a quick rundown of the main contenders and the problems that beset them. One possibility, of course, would be to assign the suffix to its historically antecedent role as a perfect, a role and function that - ʾándi retains even in Central Yana, where its acquired discourse functions are uncontroversial. Indeed, this usage seems to be present in Yahi in some contexts. However, these narrowly perfect usages are a minority.

Then again, it might be that - ʾándi marks actions that follow logically on the heels of a prior one – a kind of consecutive marker that might best be translated as "next" or "after that." Plausible examples of this usage are not uncommon; some may be found in Excerpt 7 at lines 20 and 30. This analysis runs into difficulty, though, when we consider all the cases in which a consecutive marker might be expected but *fails* to occur. If present at line 7.20 (excerpt 7, line 20), for instance, then why *not* at lines 7.16 or 7.48?

Yet another hypothesis, that - ʾándi marks actions that logically *conclude* a sequence of steps or events – a resultative or culminative function that might be translated as "finally" or "at last" – falls onto the same rocky ground. Line 7.3 plausibly culminates lines 1–2, as does line 7.19 the sequence begun with line 16. Why, though, is there no such marker on line 7.8, a culminating action if there ever was one, and no markers at all after line 7.40, despite the latent presence of numerous local "culmination" sites?

In the end, none of these explanations solves our problem, since none of them, however good a fit they may make with *some* subset of the data, is consistently and reliably expressed in the data: either it does not account for all the tokens or it fails to occur in cases where the hypothesis predicts it should.

12. Shackley (1996), in a fascinating article examining the question of Ishi's origins, makes the claim that Ishi was not genetically a Yahi at all. This story, together with Kroeber's observation, constitutes potential evidence to counter his claim. On the other hand, if he is right, and Ishi really *was* a Wintu child adopted into a Yahi band, then it is clear that nurture, not nature, was the deciding factor in determining kinship and sexual eligibility – unless, of course, the Yahi adopted *two* children, a brother and his sister!

13. The first was never glossed. Ishi apparently dictated it so rapidly, not yet having

learned to pause long enough between sentences for Sapir to keep up, that Sapir gave up on the idea of translating it.

14. The only example of narrative style we have found that is even remotely like that of Ishi is a single Nongatl narrative, "Coyote and Gopher," collected by Goddard, in the Bancroft Library.

REFERENCES

Grimes, Joseph. 1972. Outlines and overlays. *Language* 48(3): 513–524.

Kroeber, Theodora. 1961. *Ishi in two worlds: a biography of the last wild Indian in North America.* Berkeley: University of California.

Labov, William. 1972. *Language in the inner city: studies in the Black English vernacular.* Philadelphia: University of Pennsylvania.

Polyani, Livia. 1989. *Telling the American story: a structural and cultural analysis of conversational storytelling.* Cambridge: MIT.

Sapir, Edward. 1910. Yana texts. *University of California Publications in American Archaeology and Ethnology* 9.

Shackley, M. Steven. 1996. Ishi Was Not Necessarily the Last Full-Blooded Yahi: some Inferences For Hunter-Gatherer Style and Ethnicity. *Archaeological Research Facility Newsletter* 3.2 (Spring). Berkeley: *http://www.qal.berkeley.edu/arf/newsletter/3.2/_index.html*

Yahi Translation Project. 1989[ms]. Yahi texts: Ishi's narratives. Manuscript in the Archives of the Survey of California and Other Indian Languages. University of California, Berkeley: Department of Linguistics, Dwinelle Hall.

PART FIVE
Ishi as Inspiration

Previous page. Ishi at Mill Creek, 1914.

Introduction to Part Five

Our final section provides evidence of Ishi's inspirational effects – mostly, of course, for Native Americans, although by no means for them alone. Victor Golla has raised the happy possibility of Ishi sparking a revival of the Yana language (Chapter 13), but, as Justice Gary Strankman reminds us in this section's opening essay (Chapter 18), Ishi's power to inspire arises from a dark history of shameful oppression. That history creates the painful ironies that principally constitute Ishi's potency to influence the future, above all perhaps how his "artificial name . . . eclipses the real names of the namers." In 1993 the University of California (despite some objectors) named a courtyard on the Berkeley campus Ishi Court, and Strankman dryly observes that for "every student or visitor who can give some personal history of Wheeler, Boalt, Sproul, or Dwinelle," whose names adorn campus buildings, there are now "a thousand who can tell the story of the nameless one."

This irony of identities is the starting point for Gerald Vizenor's moving yet hilarious account of how the paradoxes of Ishi's life were multiplied as his fame spread and the white civilization that had destroyed his people sought belatedly to do him honor (Chapter 19). Vizenor, one of the most distinguished of Native American creative writers, has already written much on Ishi, but nowhere has he displayed more perceptively than here in "Mister Ishi" how the contemporary world, more multiprofiteering than multicultural, attempting ostentatiously to pay tribute to the quiet dignity of the last Yahi, can produce farcical self-satire by some of our society's most pretentious pretenders. Yet, characteristically, Vizenor includes in his genial but biting exposé of the self-falsifyings of selfish hypocrites (who do have the power, as he discovered, to drag one into court), a thoughtful comparison of Albert Camus and Ishi offering original insight into the complicated uncertainties of spiritual exile.

Demonstrating the reflexive energy of emerging tradition, Louis Owens, the brilliant Native American novelist, analyzes Vizenor's earlier fantasy-drama, "Ishi and the Wood Ducks" (Chapter 20). Owens's commentary displays how Ishi is already shaping contemporary Indian literature and suggests how much farther his influence is likely to extend as more and more of the intricate truth about him becomes available.

Ishi's influence, however, has already been at work for some years in the realm of the visual arts. Rebecca Dobkins's admirable assessment of Frank Day's celebrated painting of Ishi of many years ago (Chapter 21) enables us to understand the role Ishi played in that Northern California Indian's artistic career, and also offers insight into the directions the image of Ishi is likely to carry other Indian artists. In his more recent painting *What Wild Indian?*, a living Northern California artist, Frank Tuttle, demonstrates (Chapter 22) how his fellow Concow Maidu's representation of Ishi functioned as the starting point for an expression of a new personal responsiveness to the last Yahi. Tuttle is surely correct that Ishi will be a continuing but ever-evolving inspiration for those, particularly Californians, who proudly bear the burden of Native American survival into the twenty-first century.

18

The Power of Names

JUSTICE GARY STRANKMAN

Naming – the act of giving a verbal symbol to that which existed before and which will exist after the act – expresses dominance. A symbol or name identifies without description; the complex becomes manageable; individuals become units; Apache and Creek become the generic Indian; Serbs, Croats, and Bosnian Muslims are Yugoslavians or even Eastern Europeans. He is a plumber. She is a lesbian. You are a student. I am a judge. The namer obliterates by the power of his label all differences, all distinctions. The named is left powerless, as a named object to be manipulated, caught in a narrative not of his making. Naming is an act of power. In Genesis, Adam's first recorded act of domination is naming, assigning the symbol, the act of an I-am-he-who-tells-you-what-or-who-you-are. It is the ultimate gesture of paternalism. The infant child is named. Similarly, the first response to the other, to the outsider, is to assign the name. The one who assigns is the insider, the decider, the winner.

In early California there was little question who were the winners, who were the namers and who were the named. In 1854, George W. Hall was named by the California Supreme Court as " ... a free white citizen of this State, [who] was convicted of murder upon the testimony of Chinese witnesses." Notice the naming: the murderer is a citizen, but the innocent Chinese bystanders are labeled witnesses. There was a problem, however. California law provided that "No Black, or Mulatto person, or Indian, shall be allowed to give evidence in favor of, or against a white man." Who, or better what, were the unmentioned Chinese? How were they to be named? I quote from the court's opinion: "When Columbus [an infamous namer] first landed upon the shores of this continent . . . he imagined that he had accomplished the object of his expedition, and that the Island of San Salvador was one of those Islands of the Chinese Sea, . . . near . . . India. . . . Acting upon this hypothesis, and also perhaps from the similarity of features and physical conformation, he gave to the Islanders the name of Indians. . . ." There then follows a several page discussion by the court of dubious anthropological value about the "common opinion" that Indians, Chinese, and virtually all others not white or black were of the Mongolian race. Clearly these Supreme Court justices never went to Sunday school and sang, "Red and yellow, black or white, all are precious in his sight." The sacred Indian four was transformed into an infernal white three. This grouping of three, this naming was necessary, for without it, "The European white man who comes here would not be shielded from the testimony of the degraded and demoralized caste. . . . To argue such a proposition would be an insult to the good sense of the Legislature." The court continues:

> We have carefully considered all the consequences resulting from a different rule of construction, and are satisfied that even in a doubtful case we would be impelled to this decision on grounds of public policy. The same rule which would admit them to testify, would admit them to all the equal rights of citizenship, and we might soon see them at the polls, in the jury box, upon the bench, and in our legislative halls. This is not a speculation which exists in the excited and overheated imagination of the patriot and statesman, but it is an actual and present danger. The anomalous spectacle of a distinct people, living in our community, recognizing no laws of this State except through necessity . . . whose mendacity is proverbial; a race of people whom nature has marked as inferior, and who are incapable of progress or intellectual development beyond a certain point . . . between whom and ourselves nature has placed an impassable difference . . . is claimed, not only the right to swear away the life of a citizen, but the further privilege of participating with us in administering the affairs of our Government.

Needless to add, after this bit of racist naming, the white citizen's conviction was reversed.

Do not think of this overtly racist opinion as an isolated instance of naming. In 1894, the same court, in upholding laws prohibiting the sale of intoxicants to Indians, said, " . . . Indians, as a class, are not refined and civilized in the same degree as persons of the white race; and for that reason are less subject to moral restraint, and, therefore, not only less able to resist the desire for such liquors, but also more liable to be dangerous to themselves or others when under the influence of intoxicating liquors."

This setting, this civilization, this culture was the milieu into which the "wild Indian" was brought and studied and displayed as a living cultural artifact – an object of voyeuristic delight. A maker of arrows; a teller of stories; a singer of songs; these, you say, are certainly not bad labels. He was not held prisoner, nor was he physically a victim. Yet he was a man denied his manhood. He had no native speaker with whom to share his childhood memories; he had no sexual joy; he had no one to perform his burial. He was a tribal man who had lost his tribe but not his traditions, not his honor, and certainly not his soul. He used those tribal traditions to resist the power of the captors who would never learn his name. Thus he held the power of his identity away from those who assumed that they had all power; thus he preserved his dignity in the silence of anonymity.

Yet the namers did what namers do; they named. Thrice they named; thrice they erred. First, they called him Indian; they never corrected the Columbian error. After all he was not Lakota, not Makah, he was Yahi. Understand there is no generic Indian. Second, they named him "wild." This gentle decent human became "wild" only because he was "other." Deer Creek, Antelope Creek, and Mill Creek – his home – were not then and are not now as wild, if that is the preferred term, as Times Square, Union Square, or Telegraph Avenue. He was not wild; he was natural, as natural as rain, or deer, or flowers. The inside names the outside "wild." The artificial names the natural "wild." Third and finally they named, no they labeled him. He had a name, his name, but they could not know it. And with unintended irony they named him "Ishi." That is in Yahi: Man, "one of the people," Adam, Everyman, No Man. To call that name is to call for Godot. Godot, Ishi: no one comes; everyone comes. The tribal man, holding the power of his name to himself, becomes Ishi – one of the people, a people of one, a tribe of one, all others having been destroyed by the namers.

Irony piled on irony; paradox on paradox. The savage is gentle. The outlaw is harmony. The nameless is present and answers, "Here." The teachers are taught. The name, the symbol of domination, is denied the captors. The artificial name of the nameless one eclipses the real names of the namers. His authenticity overwhelms the artificial title, and he does become a unique man. The generic "man" becomes the individual: Ishi.

On May 7, 1993, the University of California dedicated a monument to irony and Ishi. The university named a courtyard on the Berkeley campus Ishi's Court. The act constitutes yet a further irony surrounding this important man. Some factions within the university community opposed the naming of a university location after a Native American, a tribal man. Yet they had no cause for concern. First, Ishi already had a part of the university, perhaps a more fitting place, a place not of concrete but of earth, grass, and sky. Certainly it is a place named in a more tribal fashion – by usage, custom, and tradition. For on the San Francisco campus, behind the old dental school, people still walk the trail known as Ishi's trail. There, with the red-tailed hawks circling overhead, a few short steps take the walker into a world that is the same as when he walked it during his stay at the museum. Second, to call a place Ishi's Court does not give that place his name. Ishi was not his name. The university bestowed on a bit of earth an alias, not a name – alias wild Indian, alias Ishi, alias man. He, in his existential dignity; he, in his brown presence; he is beyond the power to name.

He is the eternal tribal "I am" without a name. Why should he tell his name? To do so would have robbed him of his dignity and given meaningless momentary satisfaction to the voyeuristic namers. Besides, many of those whose correct names adorn the buildings on the university campus are less well known than he. For every student or visitor who can give some personal history of Wheeler, Boalt, Sproul, or Dwinelle, there are a thousand who can tell the story of the nameless one. Without a name he has achieved a fame and a respect that they can only envy. The dominated achieves dominance.

To reflect on Ishi is to reflect on the history of the European invasion of this continent. His life is relevant because his experience parallels that of his people. Yet he lives not as a proclaimed victim but as a nameless survivor. He displays the reality of a dignity born of patience, irony, and pain. He, the Raven, and the Coyote remain tricky mercurial elements of our reality.

REFERENCES

People v. Hall (1854) 4 Cal. 399.
People v. Bray (1894) 105 Cal. 344.

19
Mister Ishi
Analogies of Exile, Deliverance, and Liberty

GERALD VIZENOR

GERALD VIZENOR

ISHI BY ARCHIVES
Ishi was never his Native name.

Ishi was named by chance, not by vision, a lonesome hunter rescued by cultural anthropologists. Native names are the rise of collective memories, but his actual names and sense of presence are obscure; yet his museum nickname, more than any other archive nomination, represents to many readers the tragic victimry of Native American Indians in California.

The spirit of this Native hunter captured almost a century ago has been sustained as cultural property. Ishi was humanely secured in a museum at a time when Natives were denied human and civil rights. By another suit of cultural dominance his remains have been repatriated to an ancestral scene; united by great sorrow, worried hearts, and political penitence, his ashes and brain have been buried at last in a secret place near Mount Lassen.

"He was the last of his tribe," wrote Mary Ashe Miller in the *San Francisco Call*, September 6, 1911. "Probably no more interesting individual could be found today than this nameless Indian."

Sheriff Webber secured a "pathetic figure crouched upon the floor" of a slaughterhouse, the *Oroville Register* reported on August 29, 1911. "The canvas from which his outer shirt was made had been roughly sewed together. His undershirt had evidently been stolen in a raid upon some cabin. His feet were almost as wide as they were long, showing plainly that he had never worn either moccasins or shoes. In his ears were rings made of buckskin thongs." The sheriff "removed the cartridges from his revolver" and "gave the weapon to the Indian. The aborigine showed no evidence that he knew anything regarding its use. A cigarette was offered to him, and while it was very evident that he knew what tobacco was, he had never smoked it in that form, and had to be taught the art."

Alfred Kroeber read the newspaper reports and contacted the sheriff, who "had put the Indian in jail not knowing what else to do with him since no one around town could understand his speech or he theirs," wrote Theodora Kroeber in *Alfred Kroeber: A Personal Configuration*. "Within a few days the Department of Indian Affairs authorized the sheriff to release the wild man to the custody of Kroeber" at the Museum of Anthropology. Ishi was housed in rooms furnished by Phoebe Apperson Hearst.

Ishi was christened the last of the stone agers; overnight he became the decorated orphan of cultural genocide, the curious savage of a vanishing race overcome by modernity. He was alone but never contemptuous, servile, or the romantic end of anything. His stories were never given to victimry. He was a Native humanist in exile and a storier of survivance.

Ishi had endured the unspeakable hate crimes of miners, racial terrorists, bounty hunters, and government scalpers. Many of his family and friends were murdered, the calculated victims of cultural treason and rapacity. Truly, the miners were the savages.

California Natives barely survived the gold rush, the cruelties of colonial missions, partitionists, and poisoned water. Only about fifty thousand Natives, or one in five, were alive in the state at the turn of the twentieth century.

Ishi never revealed his sacred name or any of his nicknames, but he never concealed his humor and humanity. Lively, eager, and generous, he told tricky Wood Duck stories to his new friends. This gentle Native, rescued by culturologists, lived and worked for over four years in the Museum of Anthropology at the University of California.

Ishi "was to be photographed in a garment of skins, and when the dressing for the aboriginal part began he refused to remove his overalls," reported Miller in the *San Francisco Call*. "He say he not see any other people go without them, and he say he never take them off no more," said the Native translator Sam Batwi.

"Ishi was photographed so frequently and so variously that he became expert on matters of lighting, posing, and exposure," wrote Theodora Kroeber. "Photographs of him were bought or made to be treasured as mementos."

Alfred Kroeber, the eminent academic humanist, pointed out that Ishi "has perceptive powers far keener than those of highly educated white men. He reasons well, grasps an idea quickly, has a keen sense of humor, is gentle, thoughtful, and courteous and has a higher type of mentality than most Indians."

Ishi was at "ease with his friends," wrote Theodora Kroeber. He "loved to joke, to be teased amiably and to tease in return. And he loved to talk. In telling a story, if it were long or involved or of considerable effect, he would perspire with the effort, his voice rising toward a falsetto of excitement."

Saxton Pope, the surgeon at the medical school located near the museum, wrote that Ishi "amused the interns and nurses by singing" his songs. "His affability and pleasant disposition made him a universal favorite. He visited the sick in the wards with a gentle and sympathetic look which spoke more clearly than words. He came to the women's wards quite regularly, and with his hands folded before him, he would go from bed to bed like a visiting physician, looking at each patient with quiet concern or with a fleeting smile that was very kindly received and understood."

Thomas Waterman, the linguist at the museum, administered various psychological tests at the time and told a newspaper reporter that "this wild man has a better head on him than a good many college men."

The Bureau of Indian Affairs sent a special agent to advise Ishi that he could return to the mountains or live on a government reservation. Kroeber wrote that Ishi "shook his head" and said through the interpreter that he would "live like the white people from now on. I want to stay where I am. I will grow old here, and die in this house." And by that he meant the museum.

Ishi died of tuberculosis five years later, on March 25, 1916. His brain was removed during an autopsy, and the rest of his cremated remains were stored in cinerary urn at the Mount Olivet Cemetery in Colma, California.

Kroeber was in New York when he learned that Ishi was gravely sick. He wrote that he would consent only to a "strict autopsy" to determine the cause of death. "If there is any talk about the interests of science, say for me that science can go to hell. We propose to stand by our friends." His letter and cautionary advice, however, arrived too late. Ishi had died at the museum and his brain had already been excised as a racial artifact.

Edward Gifford, a curator at the museum, explained why the brain had been removed. "The matter was not entirely in my hands." What "happened amounts to a compromise between science and sentiment with myself on the side of sentiment." Ishi had earned the respect, favor, and sentiments of scientists at the time, but not enough to secure his spirit at the autopsy.

Theodora Kroeber noted that his estate was divided between the state and the hospital. The Dean of the Medical School "received two hundred and sixty half dollars," she wrote in *Ishi in Two Worlds*. His treasure, in this way, "continues to contribute its bit to the science of healing, a science for which Ishi himself had so great a curiosity and concern." Clearly, greater care was taken to fairly disperse his salary savings than to protect his brain and the journey of his spirit in the world.

Orin Starn, professor of anthropology at Duke University, recently discovered a letter in the Bancroft Library written by Alfred Kroeber to Aleš Hrdlička, who was then the curator of physical anthropology at the Smithsonian. "I find that at Ishi's death last spring his brain was removed and preserved," Kroeber wrote to Hrdlička. "There is no one here who can put it to scientific use. If you wish it, I shall be glad to deposit it in the National Museum Collection."

Kroeber was not sentimental enough, and anthropology was not ethical enough at the time, to consider the spiritual presence, the natural unity, and repatriation of his good friend, the Native humanist he had named Ishi.

ISHI BY EXILE

Ishi created a sense of natural presence in his stories, a Native presence that included others. He was a visionary, not a separatist, and his oral stories were scenes of liberty. This Native humanist was amused by the silence of scripture. He was a tricky storier in exile.

Ishi was in exile by name, by racial wars, and by the partisans of cultural dominance. He was a fugitive in his own Native scenes, pursued by feral pioneers and malevolent miners; yet he endured without apparent rancor or mordancy and created stories of Native survivance, the analogies of leave, deliverance, and sovereignty.

The pioneers were separated from animals and natural reason by monotheism and the biblical covenants of human dominion over nature. Ishi was a humanist more at home in nature than in a museum; clearly, he was a man of natural reason, a mature storier and healer, and, unlike the pioneer predators, he seemed to embrace the merits of a democratic and civil society.

Ishi was "remarkably talkative" with those he trusted, and his "temperament was philosophical, analytical, reserved, and cheerful," observed Saxton Pope in his essay, "The Medical History of Ishi." Moreover, he "probably looked upon us as extremely smart. While we knew many things, we had no knowledge of nature."

Ishi weathered his exile without an obscure cause of cultural or national liberty. He lived by the natural right of seasons not museums, but at the end he was evermore alone, his spirit exiled by an autopsy in the city.

Albert Camus, the novelist and philosopher, and Ishi, the Native humanist and storier, both lived in exile. Camus created a literature of separation and exile. Ishi created songs and stories of natural reason, survivance, and liberty. These two storiers were more at ease in nature, the rush of sun and seasons, than in the causes and measures of history.

"Camus lived in the permanent purgatory of exile – physical, moral, intellectual," wrote Tony Judt in *The Burden of Responsibility*. Always "between homes (in metaphor and reality alike) and at ease nowhere."

Ishi was a fugitive of natural, ancestral scenes and an outsider in a museum of manifest manners and cultural history. Evermore he is discovered in the ironic traces of ethnographic archives. Camus was at home in his memories of nature, his ancestors, and in his stories of Algeria. Ishi was at home in natural reason and his stories. Conversely, they were exiles by sound and silence, by oral stories and scripture.

Camus never mentioned Native oral stories in his essays, but he shared an obvious vision of nature with Ishi. They were betrayed by nations, by cultures, but not by nature. These storiers of exile were not weakened by the absence of ancestral scenes; rather, they created by nature a visionary sense of liberty.

Camus, all his life, "remained true to the convictions that man fulfills himself completely, lives a total reality, insofar as he is in communion with the natural world and that the divorce between man and nature mutilates human existence," wrote Mario Vargas Llosa in *Making Waves*. "Perhaps it is this conviction, the experience of someone who grew up at the mercy of the elements, which kept Camus apart from the intellectuals of his generation." Vargas Llosa might have made a similar observation of Ishi. Always, the anthropologists were separated from natural reason by their measures of culture and history.

Ishi and Camus were exiled from distinctive landscapes, and yet their stories consecrate a primordial sense of nature. Camus was moved by nature, and yet he "was a provincial for better or worse, above all for better in many respects," wrote Vargas Llosa. "First, because, unlike the experience of men in large cities, he lived in a world where landscape was the primordial presence, infinitely more attractive and important than cement and asphalt." Nature was solace by memory and metaphor; separation was minded in history.

"History explains neither the natural universe which came before it, nor beauty which stands above it," wrote Camus in "Helen's Exile," an essay in *Lyric and Critical Essays*. "Consequently it has chosen to ignore them." Nature, however, is always there. "Her calm skies and her reason oppose the folly of men."

Ishi was exiled from traces of the seasons, the scent, sound, and vision of a natural presence in the mountains; he was driven from these ancestral scenes by the predators of culture and history. He was an artist secured in a museum, an obscure Native under surveillance, but that was not an absolute separation from natural reason or from his creative stories of survivance and liberty.

"Both the historical mind and the artist seek to remake the world," wrote Camus. "But the artist, through an obligation of his very nature, recognizes limits the historical mind ignores. This is why the latter aims at tyranny while the passion of the artist is liberty."

Ishi was fortunate, in an ironic sense, to have an audience of dedicated and curious listeners for his stories of liberty. He lived by natural reason and the tease of seasons. Today, almost a century later, the audience has increased and the listeners are even more dedicated to understanding, in translation, the survivance of his Wood Duck stories.

ISHI BY LITIGATION

Harken Lucero reached into the niche and seized the black cinerary urn that contained the remains of Ishi. Lucero, a gushy sculptor, raised the urn as a video camera operator moved closer to capture another scene in the eternal stories of a Native exile.

I can feel the spirit of Ishi in my hands, his spirit is moving through my body, said Lucero. His hands trembled, a vulgar pose and pretension, but not enough to lose control of the remains. Lucero anticipated the audience and surely staged an incredible performance in the columbarium at the Olivet Cemetery in Colma, California, near San Francisco.

I was at this kitschy spectacle, along with Caitlin Croughan, an independent fundraiser who had introduced me to the sculptor; Lorna Fernandes, a correspondent for the *San Francisco Chronicle*; the assistant director of the cemetery association; the maintenance man of the niches; and several other spectators. Alas, if a judge and jury had been present that afternoon at the columbarium, they would have observed the ironic presentiments of the sculptor and decided post hoc to set aside a lawsuit against me, the fundraiser, and the University of California, Berkeley.

Lucero is a dedicated sculptor who easily noted his identity as an Indian. He was also determined to convince a jury that he should be awarded fifty thousand dollars for his preliminary work on a monument to honor Ishi.

Lucero removed the black, polished cinerary urn from the niche to make a rubbing of the precise inscription on the curve.

ISHI

THE LAST YAHI INDIAN

1916

His "hands trembled as he held tightly to the urn," wrote Fernandes. Another artist tried to cover the urn with butcher paper to make an impression of the words, but the paper was too thick to leave a charcoal representation. The comic scene was recorded by video and later played in county court as evidence in a lawsuit.

Lucero assumed that he had been commissioned to create a sculpture for Ishi Court in Dwinelle Hall on the campus at Berkeley. And he pretended that the comical butcher paper image would be used to make an engraving on a memorial plaque at the entrance to the courtyard.

The maintenance man at the columbarium watched the artist struggle with the thick paper on the curve of the urn, and then, in almost a whisper, he offered thin rubbing paper, made for that exact purpose. Finally, a charcoal representation was made of the incised words on the pottery.

The assistant director of the cemetery boldly announced to the audience that the pot was thrown and the very words carved by Ishi the last Yahi Indian. Fernandes wrote as much in her notebook, a mundane romantic notion of a Native premonition of death. I leaned closer and evenly told the reporter than the cemetery official was either a sentimentalist, stupid, or misinformed. Fernandes resisted my intervention at first, but later she was convinced that the letters incised on the curve of the urn were in perfect serif type, closer by design to a roman typestyle that to the cursive hand of a Yahi named Ishi. Furthermore, he was a hunter, not a potter. Most of these comic scenes were video-recorded as a documentary.

I proposed in October 1985 that the architectural extension to Dwinelle Hall should be named Ishi Hall. My proposal won wide support from students and faculty and was unanimously endorsed by the student union at the University of California, Berkeley.

Simply, my proposal focused on the significant contributions that Ishi had made to the University of California. Alfred Kroeber noted that "he had mastered the philosophy of patience." Saxton Pope pointed out that Ishi "knew nature, which is always true," and that he had the mind of a philosopher.

Ishi served with distinction the curatorial interests of the new Museum of Anthropology. He endured without rancor a museum nickname and was, after all, vested as the first Native employee of the University of California.

None of this information, however, fairly impressed the faculty committee that first considered my proposal. Ishi, in name and service, was denied a by-word presence on the campus by the Dwinelle Hall Space Subcommittee. The final decision, after a hearty discussion of toilets and closet areas in the building, could not be overturned by any other committee.

Ishi was twice denied a presence by name, but seven years later my direct petition to the chancellor resulted in an acceptable compromise. The actual decision, however, had more to do with the politics of federal funds, criticism of repatriation policies on the campus, and, because of that, an urgent interest to favor Native issues and academic programs.

Chancellor Chang-Lin Tien reminded me that "the process of naming, or renaming, a campus building involves review at several levels on the campus and at the Office of the President." Chancellor Tien received my letter of appeal on June 2, 1992, to "consider the sense of resentment and anger that you might feel if your reasonable initiatives to honor a tribal name and emend institutional racism were consigned to the mundane commerce of a campus space subcommittee." I pointed out that hundreds of Native American Indians had been "invited to 'reclaim' the campus," which was located on stolen Native land, during the Columbus "quincentenary celebrations, a demonstration that would be worthy of academic, public, and media consideration."

Several months later the director of space management on the campus presented a compromise to me: that the central courtyard of Dwinelle Hall could be named Ishi Court. The concessions were honorable, but the original documents that supported the decision were lost; several months later the case was regenerated, and copies were conclusively transmitted to the Regents of the University of California.

Ishi Court was dedicated on May 7, 1993. Gary Strankman, Justice of the First District California Court of Appeal, said the ceremony "concerns naming, the act of giving to that which existed before and which will exist after a verbal symbol." He pointed out an irony of memorial names, that for "every student or visitor who can give you some personal history of Wheeler, Boalt, Sproul, or Dwinelle, I can find a hundred, no a thousand, who can tell you the story of Ishi. Without a name he has achieved a fame and a respect that they can only envy."

Caitlin Croughan, inspired by the dedication, proposed to raise money to create a monument in honor of Ishi. She invited me to meet with a sculptor whose work she admired, and later to observe the spectacle of the niche at the columbarium. That sculptor, of course, was Harken Lucero.

Croughan, an honorable fundraiser, became a casual agent for the sculptor, and, based on that camaraderie, she set out to find money in the name of Ishi. Lucero, meanwhile, assumed that such notice and his documented pose at the niche was an oral commission to create a memorial sculpture. No promise or parole contract had ever been made; rather, the creative representations of his sculpture were not suitable, in my view, as a memorial in Ishi Court.

Lucero alleged in a "complaint for damages for breach of contract," filed on August 2, 1995, that the defendants, Gerald Vizenor, Caitlin Croughan, and the Regents of the University of California, "entered into an oral contract" to design and sculpt a statue of Ishi and that the defendants would pay fifty thousand dollars to Lucero.

The story became a comic epitome of scammers.

Ishi, the Native in exile, was teased by name in an incredible sculptural association with Mahatma Gandhi. Brashly, the manifest scammers arrived in silky suits to propose fundraiser strategies.

Yogesh Gandhi, then the director of the Gandhi Memorial Foundation of Orinda, California, insisted that we meet to discuss Ishi and Native American Studies. He suggested a sculpture giveaway – a fundraising tactic that worked in his foundation. He had commissioned the creation of a miniature bronze sculpture of Mahatma Gandhi. Bronze copies of the spiritual leader were then given to potential contributors. Ishi, likewise, could be cast in bronze and given away to raise money in his name. I resisted his foundation strategies, but not his interest in Native American Studies.

Croughan considered but declined an invitation to work as a fundraiser for the Gandhi Foundation. Lucero, at about the same time, presented a stone sculpture to Gandhi. Later his name was mentioned as the very sculptor who could create a bronze giveaway miniature of Ishi.

Yogesh Gandhi, a few months later, attended a reception on the campus for Vibert de Souza, the Minister for Amerindian Affairs, Republic of Guyana. Gandhi grandly toured Ishi Court and then visited briefly with Chancellor Tien. Gandhi was soon distracted by the presidential election and seemed to lose interest in fundraiser strategies for Native American Studies.

Gandhi, we later learned, had been charged with federal mail fraud as part of a campaign spending investigation conducted by the Justice Department. The *San Francisco Chronicle* reported on March 6, 1998, that Gandhi was arrested "in connection with two American Express credit card applications he allegedly signed with another man's name."

The *New York Times* reported on November 8, 1996, that the Democratic National Committee returned a large contribution solicited by John Huang. The contribution "initially appeared to come from Yogesh K. Gandhi, a great-grandnephew of Mohandas K. Gandhi who runs a California foundation that honors the Indian leader's memory. Yogesh Gandhi made the donation during a fundraising event in May in a Washington hotel at which he and an associate, a Japanese spiritual leader named Hogen Fukunaga, gave President Clinton a peace award." Gandhi, however, a few months later told a court in California "that he had no assets or bank accounts in the United States." Moreover, "relatives more closely related to Mohandas Gandhi have complained that Yogesh Gandhi has improperly exploited his family name and does not represent its true interests."

Lucero lost his case in judicial arbitration, and a month later, on February 27, 1997, after three days of trial, he lost in San Francisco County Superior Court. The jury rendered a verdict in favor of Gerald Vizenor and the University of California. Fred Takemiya, University Counsel, pointed out in a letter to the vice chancellor that the jury "could not reach the necessary consensus for a verdict" in the case of Caitlin Croughan. "Some of the jurors apparently felt that she should have taken more clear, affirmative steps to stop Lucero's efforts at creating a model of his concept of the statue." The court declared a mistrial in her case.

ISHI BY NAMES

"Mammedaty was my grandfather, whom I never knew," wrote N. Scott Momaday in his memoir, *The Names*. "Yet he came to be imagined posthumously in the going on of the blood, having invested the shadow of his presence in an object or a word, in his name above all. He enters into my dreams; he persists in his name."

Ishi is not his Native name, but we imagine his presence by that museum nickname. Ishi is in our visions, and he persists by that name in our memory. We bear his exile as our own, and by his tease and natural reason we create new stories of Native irony, survivance, and liberty. My stories are an expiation of our common exile in this culture of tricky giveaways.

20

Native Sovereignty and the Tricky Mirror
Gerald Vizenor's "Ishi and the Wood Ducks"

LOUIS OWENS

Ishi's photograph stares out from the *Arizona Republic* on August 8, 2000, in a section of the newspaper titled "Arizona and the West." Wearing a dark suit with his tie slightly askew and his eyes direct, his mouth determined, he looks back at the camera from a confident distance. Above the photograph a headline declares, "Indian's brain, body to be reunited." The headline refers, of course, to the placement of Ishi's brain in the Smithsonian Institution and its repatriation, after eighty years, for burial in California. The headline might well refer, however, to European America's half-millennium endeavor to forge the "Indian" body as pure object, severed from intellect and, therefore, anything one might term intellectual sovereignty.

Frantz Fanon has written that "Man is human only to the extent to which he tries to impose his existence on another man in order to be recognized by him." He adds, "In its immediacy, consciousness of self is simple being-for-itself. In order to win the certainty of oneself, the incorporation of the concept of recognition is essential" (Fanon 1967:216, 217). European America has ever held a mirror and a mask up to the Native American. The tricky mirror is that Other presence that reflects the European American consciousness back at itself, but the side of the mirror turned toward the Native is transparent, letting the Native see not his or her own reflection but the face of the European American beyond the mirror. For the dominant culture, the European American controlling this surveillance, the reflection provides merely a self-recognition that results in a kind of being-for-itself and, ultimately, as Fanon suggests, an utter absence of certainty of self. The Native, in turn, finds no reflection directed back from the center, no recognition of "being" from that direction.

The mask is one realized over centuries through European America's construction of the "Indian" Other. In order to be recognized, and thus to have a voice that is heard by those in control, the Native must step into that mask and

373

be the Indian constructed by white America. Paradoxically, of course, like the mirror, the mask merely shows the European American to himself or herself, since the masked Indian arises out of the European consciousness, leaving the Native behind the mask unseen, unrecognized for himself or herself. In short, to be seen and heard at all by the center – to not share the fate of Ralph Ellison's Invisible Man – the Native must pose as the absolute fake, the fabricated "Indian," like the dancing puppets in Ellison's novel.

If a fear of inauthenticity is the burden of postmodernity, as has been suggested by David Harvey (1989) among others, it is particularly the burden not only of the European American seeking merely his or her self-reflection, but even more so that of the indigenous American in the face of this hyperreal "Indian." In *Midnight's Children,* Salman Rushdie's character Saleem Sinai says, "Above all things, I fear absurdity." Quoting Rushdie's character and reflecting on Sinai's predicament, Leela Gandhi writes that "the colonial aftermath is also fraught by anxieties and fears of failure which attend the need to satisfy the burden of expectation" (Gandhi 1998:5). America not only contains no "colonial aftermath"; it also places no burden of expected achievement on the American Indian; the Indian need not "achieve" but only "be" and cease to be. For Native Americans the only burden of expectation is that he or she put on the mask provided by the colonizer, and the mask is not merely a mirror but more crucially a static death mask. He or she who steps behind the mask becomes the Vanishing American, a savage/noble, mystical, pitiable, romantic fabrication of the European American psyche fated to play out the epic role defined by Mikhail Bakhtin: "The epic and tragic hero," Bakhtin writes, "is the hero who by his very nature must perish. . . . Outside his destiny the epic and tragic hero is nothing; he is, therefore, a function of the plot fate assigns him; he cannot become the hero of another destiny or another plot" (Bakhtin 1981:36). For many, Ishi epitomized this perfect epic figure, the Vanishing American. For years, the Anishinaabe writer Gerald Vizenor has worked to unite Ishi's body and brain, to force us all to recognize that the man called Ishi held his sovereign intellectual ground at a distance from the objectifying gaze of the white world, and beyond the role of tragedy and victimage assigned to him in the general imagination.

"Ishi was never his real name." So begins Vizenor's "Ishi Obscura," in *Manifest Manners* (1994). An essay on the last "wild man" of America captured in a museum and photographs, "Ishi Obscura" interrogates the invention of Ishi, the reputed last of the Yahi people in California, as museum artifact and photographic "other." In "Ishi and the Wood Ducks," Vizenor's four-act play, the author invites the Yahi survivor into the courtroom of contemporary "indianness" and, through Ishi, deconstructs the deadly desire of European America for the simulated Indian. "The *indian*," Vizenor writes in *Fugitive Poses,* "is a misnomer, a simulation with no referent and with the absence of natives; *indians* are the other, the names of sacrifice and victimry" (Vizenor 1998:27).[1] Ishi, the actual man who walked out of California's Sierra Nevada range to die in a museum, offers tragic visionaries the quintessential material for "sacrifice and victimry," what Vizenor also terms "the metaphor of the native at the littoral" and a history of "aesthetic sacrifice" (Vizenor 1998:27). However, Vizenor's aim in giving the "last man of the stone age" a storyteller's voice in his play is to contradict the entropic story of the American "*indian.*"

Vizenor has had a long and intense fascination with Ishi, the latest fruit of which is "Ishi and the Wood Ducks," a work that deploys compassion, humor, and the ironies of trickster to dissect European America's invention of Indians at the same time that it pays homage to the man called Ishi. At the heart of the work is what Vizenor defines as "trickster hermeneutics": "the interpretation of simulations in the literature of survivance, the ironies of descent and racialism, transmutation, third gender, and themes of transformation in oral tribal stories and written narratives" (Vizenor 1994:15). As a "postindian" survivor, Vizenor's Ishi steps outside the frame of the nostalgic colonial camera, defies the melancholy and terminal definition called "Indian," and appears on stage as a good-humored signifier of indeterminate human consciousness, a counteragent against the "hyperreal simulation and . . . ironic enactment of a native presence by an absence in a master narrative" (Vizenor 1998:27). In the end, despite European America's desperate attempts to fix Ishi as a phenomenon called a "primitive Indian," Vizenor makes it clear that Ishi exists forever in the moment of his stories, reinventing himself within the oral tradition with each utterance.

Whereas the first line in Vizenor's opening "Historical Introduction" to "Ishi and the Wood Ducks" quotes a description of the newly discovered Ishi as "a pathetic figure crouched upon the floor," Ishi's first words in the play are "Have you ever heard the wood duck stories," a telling contradiction. Within his stories Ishi embodies what Vizenor terms "survivance" and "sovenance": "The native stories of survivance are successive and natural estates; survivance is an active repudiation of dominance, tragedy, and victimry. . . . Native sovenance is that sense of reason in native stories . . . not the romance of an aesthetic absence or victimry" (Vizenor 1998:15). "Ishi and the Wood Ducks" provides Vizenor with yet another opportunity to dissect the pathological impulse that has driven European America for five centuries to discover an aboriginal something commensurate to its own needs, to call that something "Indian," and to obscure the Native in the process. Imagining the Indian as a natural resource to be mined for some kind of catalyst that will make the "American" alloy so much the stronger, the European American metanarrative peels away the man or woman to find the Indian. Vizenor's art strips the artifactual veneer of Indianness to find the Native humanity at the center, to liberate the original American from the deadening servitude of Indianness.

In the writings of Gerald Vizenor, as his readers know well, "real" life permeates fiction, and fiction warps real events and recognizable contemporary and historical figures into trickster's endless and endlessly self-reflexive tropes. Those who know Vizenor's work will also be familiar with the utopian impulse that drives often harsh satires, the same utopian desires that lie at the paradoxical heart of trickster stories. The goal is to illuminate hypocrisies and false positions, to challenge all accepted mores or fixed values, to shock and disturb us, and cause us to reexamine and readjust, moment by moment, our conceptions of and relationships with both self and environment. The purpose of "holotropic" trickster,[2] with his/her indeterminable shape-shifting, contradictions, and assaults upon our rules and values, is to make the world better. "Ishi and the Wood Ducks" has its inception in Vizenor's "real life" challenge to the University of California, a challenge arising out of his desire to readjust history, force the University and the rest of society to recognize its false positions and culpability, and do honor to an exceptional man we erroneously call Ishi.

In the fall of 1985, as a visiting professor in Ethnic Studies at the University of California, Berkeley, Gerald Vizenor formally proposed that the north part of the campus's Dwinelle Hall (which housed and still houses the offices of Native American Studies) be renamed Ishi Hall. The student senate at Berkeley voted unanimously to support Vizenor's proposal, praising in their bill Ishi's "Intellectual contributions to the University of California in the fields of anthropology, linguistics, and Native American studies" (*Daily Californian* 1985:1). When an administrator in the university's splendidly titled Space Assignment and Capital Improvements Group demurred and offered instead to consider naming a proposed addition to Kroeber Hall after Ishi, Vizenor said no: "We're not about to yield to anthropology and a new intellectual colonialism," he declared (*Daily Californian* 1985:1). For seven years – that powerful tribal number – the matter rested there.

Who doesn't know the name of Ishi? "He was the last of his tribe," Mary Ashe Miller, a reporter for the *San Francisco Call*, wrote on September 6, 1911, before going on to declare that "[t]he man is as aboriginal in his mode of life as though he inhabited the heart of an African jungle; all of his methods are those of primitive peoples" (Vizenor 1994:128). Miller, suffering pangs of ethnostalgic despair over a vanishing, generic, and thus entirely invented savagery, obviously saw through Ishi the man to the aesthetic of absence Vizenor describes. Discovered weak and starving in a slaughterhouse in northern California in August of 1911, the prototypical "primitive" and ultimate Yahi was immediately placed in jail by the county sheriff because "no one around town could understand his speech or he theirs" (Vizenor 1994:131). Not the first or last Native to be imprisoned for possessing liminal linguistic identity, the man who would be called Ishi was quickly transferred to the proprietorship of the University of California, Berkeley, Museum of Anthropology and the care of noted anthropologist Alfred Kroeber, as Theodora Kroeber explained with undoubtedly unconscious irony: "Within a few days the Department of Indian Affairs authorized the sheriff to release the wild man to the custody of Kroeber and the museum staff . . ." (Vizenor 1994:131). In a statement that doubles delightfully back upon itself trickster-fashion (the "wild" man "released" into "custody"), Kroeber's words make it clear that the generic "Indian" body was immediately and apparently unselfconsciously recognized as property of a federal agency (the BIA) which could "authorize" his transfer, as property, to the "custody" of another institution. Nowhere in this statement is there room for the possibility of the indigenous person's own individual agency; Ishi was, like all "Indians," a "bankable simulation" (Vizenor 1994:ll).

The last known survivor of the Yahi, a division of the Yana Tribe of California, the Native person called Ishi was the perfect Indian for colonial European America, the end result of five hundred years of attempts to create something called "Indian." With his family and entire tribe slaughtered, starved, and decimated by disease like countless thousands of the original inhabitants of California, he became the quintessential last Vanishing American, a romantic, artifactual savage who represented neither threat nor obstacle but instead a benign natural resource to be mined for what white America could learn about itself. And when, after living for five years in the anthropology museum at San Francisco, he did perish as scripted, on March 25, 1916, of tuberculosis contracted from his white captors and custodians, the *Chico Record*, a little newspaper in a minuscule northern California town, saw through the staged drama with cynical insight (Vizenor 1995:3):

> Ishi, the man primeval, is dead. . . . He furnished amusement and study to the savants at the University of California for a number of years . . . but we do not believe he was the marvel that the professors would have the public believe. He was just a starved-out Indian from the wilds of Deer Creek who, by hiding in its fastnesses, was able to long escape the white man's pursuit. And the white man with his food and clothing and shelter finally killed the Indian just as effectually as he would have killed him with a rifle.

Perhaps most exceptional in this newspaper account is the writer's recognition that the "white man's pursuit" of the Indian is inexorable. Central to the extensive body of Gerald Vizenor's writing is his recognition that the white man's pursuit of the Indian is indeed unending, that it represents an unrelenting desire to capture and inhabit the heart of the Native just as surely as European America has appropriated and occupied the Native landscape. Key to this pursuit is language, the struggle for definition and dominance through authoritative discourse.

The University of California must have thought, with considerable relief, that the irritating matter of Ishi Hall had ended when Visiting Professor Gerald Vizenor left the campus to teach elsewhere. However, in January of 1992, having given up an endowed chair at the University of Oklahoma to return to Berkeley as a senior professor, Vizenor raised the banner of Ishi's cause once more, writing to Chancellor Chang-Lin Tien to say: "This is a proposal to change the name of the north part of Dwinelle Hall to Ishi Hall in honor of the first Native American Indian who served with distinction the University of California." This time, a full seven years after his first proposal had vanished into the bowels of a university committee, Vizenor cleverly made sure that his proposal coincided with the hullaballoo surrounding the quincentenary of Columbus's "discovery" of America. "This is the right moment," he explained to the Chancellor, "the quincentenary is time to honor this tribal man who served with honor and good humor the academic interests of the University of California." (Vizenor to Tien, January 9, 1992, author's personal papers).

Vizenor's proposal was forwarded to a committee once again. Two months later, in March, after hearing nothing, he wrote politely to the Chancellor: "I understand the administrative burdens at this time, even so, my proposal is urgent because it is tied to an unmistakable historical moment." Three months later, in June 1992, he wrote to the Chancellor yet again, this time a bit more heatedly:

> Consider the sense of resentment and anger that you might feel if your reasonable initiatives to honor a tribal name and emend institutional racism were consigned to the mundane commerce of a campus space subcommittee. Sixty-eight years ago today, on June 2, 1924, Native American Indians became citizens for the first time of the United States. Indeed, these historical ironies, and the national sufferance of the quincentenary, could be much too acrimonious to resume; the very institutions and the foundational wealth of this state are based on stolen land and the murder of tribal people.

On August 31, 1992, the Director of the Space Management and Capital Programs Committee on campus circulated a memo informing everyone that "The Naming of Buildings Subcommittee did not approve naming a wing of Dwinelle after Ishi. It suggested instead that the central courtyard of Dwinelle Hall be named *Ishi Court.*"

On May 7, 1993 – almost eight years after Vizenor's initial proposal – Ishi Court was officially dedicated on the Berkeley campus. In his dedication address, Vizenor said, "There is a wretched silence in the histories of this state and nation: the silence of tribal names. The landscapes are overburdened with untrue discoveries. There are no honorable shadows in the names of dominance. The shadows of tribal names and stories persist, and the shadows are our natural survivance." He concluded his speech by declaring, "Ishi Court, you must remember, is the everlasting center of Almost Ishi Hall."

"Ishi was never his real name," Vizenor writes in "Ishi Obscura." "Ishi is a simulation, the absence of his tribal names. . . . Ishi the obscura is discovered with a bare chest in photographs; the tribal man named in that simulation stared over the camera, into the distance" (Vizenor 1994:126). A Yahi word meaning "one of the people," the name Ishi masked the Native survivor's sacred name, which he never told to anyone.[3] Ishi became the simulation. "The notion of the aboriginal and the primitive combined both racialism and postmodern speciesism," Vizenor writes in "Ishi Obscura," "a linear consideration that was based on the absence of monotheism, material evidence of civilization, institutional violence, and written words more than on the presence of imagination, oral stories, the humor in trickster stories, and the observation of actual behavior and experience" (Vizenor 1994:128).

For European America, the Indian is defined by absence, not presence. The determination is to know the "other" as not-European and to thus delineate the European, while paradoxically to find and extract some aboriginal distillation that, like the single drop of black in the white paint of Ralph Ellison's *Invisible Man*, will somehow make white America greater. The goal is, as Vizenor stresses, never to *know* the "other." "The word Indian," Vizenor writes, "is a colonial enactment, not a loan word, and the dominance is sustained by the simulation that has superseded the real tribal names. The Indian was an occidental invention that became a bankable simulation; the word has no referent in tribal languages or cultures. The postindian is the absence of the invention, and the end of representation in literature; the closure of that evasive melancholy of dominance. Manifest manners are the simulations of bourgeois decadence and melancholy" (Vizenor 1994:11). Finally, once the Native is fully defined as the "absent other," the aboriginal space has been figuratively (and, of course, often quite literally through concerted programs of genocide) emptied so that it may be reoccupied by the colonizer, realizing the invader's wistful dream of achieving an "original" relationship with the invaded space.

For indigenous Americans, the paradox that arises from the ironies of invention is that it seems the Native person must pose as the absent other – the *indian*, as Vizenor writes – in order to be seen or heard, must actually become the simulation at the border. Simply put, the central paradox of Indian identity is that Indians must pose as simulations in order to be seen as "real." Vizenor quotes Umberto Eco on this point: "This is the reason for this journey into hyperreality, in search of instances where the American imagination demands the real thing and, to attain it, must fabricate the absolute fake." Vizenor adds that "Indians, in this sense, must be the simulations of the 'absolute fakes' in the ruins of representation, or the victims in literary annihilation" (Vizenor 1994:9). "Ishi," he writes, "has become one of the most discoverable tribal names in the world; even so, he has seldom been heard as a real person" (Vizenor 1994:137). In "Ishi and the Wood Ducks," the patient Yahi survivor becomes the "postindian," one of the original people of America freed from the humorless "melancholy of dominance" that requires the invented Indian.

Vizenor's play opens with an introduction that sketches the history of Ishi's discovery in northern California and his transfer from jail to museum. The introduction quotes a number of statements by those who surrounded Ishi in the museum, including Kroeber's declaration that Ishi "has perceptive powers far keener than those of highly educated white men. He reasons well, grasps an idea quickly, has a keen sense of humor, is gentle, thoughtful, and courteous and has a higher type of mentality than most Indians" and Thomas Waterman the museum linguist's observation that "this wild man has a better head on him than a good many college men." Following the introduction, a Prologue opens with the characters of Ishi and an "old woman" named Boots Story, both waiting on a bench outside a federal courthouse, Ishi dressed in "an oversized suit and tie" and carrying a leather briefcase. Boots, a Gypsy, informs Ishi that she must appear in federal court in order to get a "real name." Otherwise she will be deported, or sent "home."

The cast is drawn from the same ten characters in each of the play's four acts, but, with the exception of Ishi himself and his choral accomplice Boots, the roles and identities of the characters change in each act, a strategy the author explains: "The actors are the same but the names of characters are repeated in the prologue and four acts of the play. The sense of time, manifest manners, and historical contradictions are redoubled and enhanced by the mutations of identities in the same characters."

As noted above, Ishi's first words in the Prologue, addressed to Boots, are "Have you ever heard the wood duck stories?" A few lines later he says, "Ishi is my museum name, not my real name." Turning to the audience, he explains with nice irony, "Kroeber was an anthropologist and got me out of jail to live in a museum (*pause*), he was one of my very first friends." He adds: "Kroeber named me (*pause*), in my own language, he named me the last man of the stone age."

This Prologue foregrounds the archival contradictions and values of names, museums, and stories: "How about a museum of stories?" Ishi asks Boots, invoking "that trace of creation and natural reason in native stories." When Boots says, "Who can remember stories anymore?" Ishi replies, "That's why you need your own museum." "Names without stories are the end," Ishi says with finality. *Ishi and the Wood Ducks* discovers the dead end of the name "Indian," which arises out of a static, monologic story of cultural dominance (and ethnocide) central to the European American metanarrative but has no story at all within the hundreds of cultures it supposedly comprehends, or, as Vizenor explains above, "has no referent in tribal languages or cultures."

The first act of the play takes place in the Museum of Anthropology at Berkeley, where Ishi is first seen flaking arrowheads (including one out of a piece of broken glass) in front of a "wickiup." Boots Story, silenced on stage, has mutated into a custodial worker who pushes her duster around the room and offers silent facial responses to the words and events of the act. The act centers on a visit to Ishi by characters associated with the museum and attempts by Ashe Miller, the newspaper reporter, to interview Ishi while Prince Chamber, a photographer accompanying her, tries unsuccessfully to take Ishi's photograph. In the opening lines of the act, Saxton Pope, "the medical doctor," praises Ishi as a natural healer and asks Ishi to "show us your home in the mountains" and to teach Pope's son "how to hunt and fish with a bow and arrow, and how to make arrowheads out of broken bottles." Ishi turns to the audience to say, "The mountains are dangerous." When pressed by Pope, he explains that the danger comes from the "savages": the gold miners who "have no stories" and "no culture." Informed of the photographer's visit, Ishi says, "Pictures are never me," and "My stories are lost in pictures." Ishi's words here echo Vizenor's insistence in "Ishi Obscura" that "The miners were the real savages; they had no written language, no books, no manners . . . no stories in the blood. They were the agents of civilization," and "The gaze of those behind the camera haunts the unseen margins of time and scene in the photograph; the obscure presence of witnesses at the simulation of savagism could become the last epiphanies of a chemical civilization" (Vizenor 1994:127). "Savages land in your pictures," Ishi tells the anthropologist Kroeber. (Roland Barthes [1981:57] wrote that "essentially the camera makes everyone a tourist in other people's reality, and eventually in one's own.")

When Ashe Miller says, "Big Chiep [Ishi's nickname for Kroeber] said you come from a 'puny civilization' and that you are 'uspeakably ignorant' (*pause*). Do you know anything?" Ishi's response is "Too much pina." "Pina," we are quickly told, means "pain," an explanation that embarrasses Kroeber. Act one ends with the photographer's request that Ishi engage in what Vizenor has called "cultural striptease": "Ishi, bare your chest, the light is good." Ishi, content to remain unseen and unheard as a "primitive," and refusing to simulate European America's fake Indian, whispers to Kroeber, who explains (in an instance drawn from Ishi's "real life" in the museum): "Ishi say he not see any other people go without them, without clothes (*pause*), and he say he never take them off no more." Ishi repudiates aesthetic absence and victimry, refuses to stop the clock. Obsessed with the way his mother is dressed in a photograph, Barthes declares that "clothing is perishable, it makes a second grave for the loved being" (Barthes 1981:64). Costumes are not perishable, however. Early ethnographic photographers clearly understood this when they carted generic "Indian" dress around for those Native subjects who might not possess such essential accoutrements (see Hoobler and Hoobler 1980:117; Vizenor 1998:163). Ishi perceptively refuses to costume himself in essential savagery for the camera.

Act Two is set in the Mount Olivet Cemetery columbarium, where Zero Larkin, a "native sculptor with a vision," has come seventy years after Ishi's death in order to receive inspiration from Ishi's ashes. He is accompanied by Ashe Miller, the reporter from Act One, and Prince Chamber, the photographer who asked Ishi to bare his chest in that act. Trope Browne, undoubtedly one of the enormous mixed-blooded Browne dynasty that populates Vizenor's *The Trickster of Liberty* (1988), in which Ishi graduates with Tune Browne from the University of California, serves as attendant at the columbarium. When Zero asks Trope, "Are you a brother?" Trope responds that his answer depends on "how much money you want." Observing and commenting upon the scene, unseen by the others, are Ishi and Boots Story.

Act Two targets both invented Indians and those who would pose as experts on such inventions. When Ishi denies to Boots that he was ever a shaman or that he made the pot in which his ashes are held – both of which "facts" are maintained by the manager of the cemetery, Angel Day – Boots says, "Angel lied then." Ishi replies, "Not really, she's an expert on Indians. . . . Indians are inventions, so what's there to lie about?"

Zero Larkin, the posturing, scathingly satirized native sculptor, intones, "Ishi is with me, our spirit is one in his sacred name," before adding, "I'm going to blast his sacred signature . . . at the bottom of my stone sculpture, my tribute to his power as an Indian." When asked if he's finished the sculpture, Zero says, "Not yet, but with the inspiration of his name it won't take long." Ashe Miller, the penetrating journalist from Act One, asks, "Zero, does it make a difference to anyone that you are not from the same tribe as Ishi?" and Zero, the Vizenoresque "*varionative*,"[4] replies, "We are both tribal artists, and that's our identity." Not aware of the fact that Ishi names not a person but a constructed museum artifact, Zero himself embraces his identity as generic invented Indian – what Vizenor called a "colonial enactment" in "Ishi Obscura." When he touches the false burial urn, Zero chants, "Ishi is with me, his spirit is coming through my fingers." "What does it feel like?" the reporter queries, to which Zero answers,

"The greatest power of my life, the spirit of my people." After Ashe asks if Zero means that his "people" are indigenous Northern Californians like Ishi's, the dialogue continues to the detriment of the "native" sculptor:

ZERO: We are one as tribal people.

Zero trembles, and he smiles as the camera comes closer. Trope moves closer to
be sure he does not drop the pot.

ASHE: Which one?

ANGEL: He means a universal tribal spirit.

ASHE (ironically): That explains it.

Act Two ends with Boots chanting, "Zero, zero and the cemetery liars," and Ishi asking, "Do you think they could hear my duck stories?"

The third act of "Ishi and the Wood Ducks" features a meeting of the Committee on Names and Spaces in Kroeber Hall at the University of California. We are told that "The faculty is seated at a conference table to consider a proposal to rename the building Ishi Hall." In this act, Angel Day has mutated into a professor of anthropology, Trope Browne a history professor, Ashe Miller appropriately a professor in mass communication, and Prince Chamber in visual arts. Professor Alfred Kroeber, the distinguished anthropologist, is present as sponsor of the proposal to rename his own hall in honor of Ishi.

"Why would he want to change his own name?" Trope Browne asks just before Kroeber appears on stage. When questioned, Kroeber says simply, "Ishi made my name . . . ." and adds, "Ishi's name is not genuine." Angel Day says, "Several years ago, as you know, we received a proposal from an errant faculty member to change the name of Kroeber Hall to Big Chiep Hall (*pause*). Naturally, and in honor of your distinction as an anthropologist, we chose not to discuss the proposal." Kroeber replies, "I supported that proposal." Kroeber goes on to explain that "The Big Chiep is one of his [Ishi's] name stories. . . . Ishi honored me with a nickname, in the same sense that we gave him his name (*pause*); the contradiction, of course, is that our name for him is romantic, while his name for me is a story."

Throughout this act, Ishi and Boots stand at the edge of the stage and comment upon the proceedings. "Kroeber said it," Boots tells Ishi, "you are his anthropologist." "Not a chance," Ishi replies, "he's the subject not the object." When Boots says, "Who are you then?" Ishi's answer is "The last object of their stone age." When the committee, just like the "real" committee that buried Vizenor's proposals for Ishi Hall in 1985 and 1992, decides that Kroeber's proposal is a "sad romantic visitation" and denies the request, Ishi and Boots – still invisible – begin to address the faculty members directly, with Ishi saying, "Doctor Ishi Hearst[5] proposes that no building on campus would bear the same name for more than two years at a time." The buildings, Ishi suggests, "would be known by their nicknames and stories, and no building would hold even a nickname for more than two years."

"Ishi and the Wood Ducks" concludes with Act Four set in the Federal Courtroom outside of which Ishi and Boots waited in the Prologue. Ishi, it turns out, has been brought to court on charges of violating the Indian Arts and Crafts Act of 1990, the charge being that "He sold objects as tribal made, and could not prove that he was in fact a member of a tribe or recognized by a reservation government." In this final act, Kroeber is the presiding federal judge, Ashe Miller the prosecutor, Saxton Pope the defense attorney. Other characters from the first three acts are court functionaries or witnesses (and a kind of chorus), including Boots Story. The act opens with Ishi placing "several bows, arrows, arrowheads, and fire sticks on the defense table."

Ishi, we learn, has been arrested at the Santa Fe Indian Market because "other artists complained that he was not a real Indian." Ishi's dilemma is twofold: on the one hand, like many contemporary Native Americans, Ishi belongs to a tribe that is not federally recognized (in his case because his tribe has been ruled extinct, though a number of extant California tribes are not recognized today); at the same time, Ishi cannot be a real Indian because "the *indian* is a simulation, the absence of natives; the *indian* transposes the real, and the simulation of the real has no referent, memories, or native stories" (Vizenor 1998:15). Clearly, other "real" Indian artists saw greater profit for themselves in barring Ishi from the lucrative native arts and crafts market and are exploiting the colonial definition of Indian identity to their advantage. The Indian Arts and Crafts Act of 1990 decrees that it is "unlawful to offer or display for sale any good, with or without a Government trademark, in a manner that falsely suggests it is Indian produced, an Indian product, or the product of a particular Indian or Indian tribe or Indian arts and crafts organization, resident within the United States." The Act stipulates that "[f]or a first criminal offense, an individual is fined not more than $250,000 and/or jailed not more than 5 years; subsequent violations are not more than $1,000,000 and/or 15 years."[6]

Clearly, as Vizenor has pointed out, the "occidental invention" of Indianness has become a very lucrative "bankable simulation" in essentialist and ethnostalgic America. Were Judge Kroeber to find him guilty of criminal offense, Ishi would be in serious trouble indeed. Not only has Ishi violated the Indian Arts and Crafts Act, he is also charged with purchasing a false certificate of Indianness, an enrollment form from the "Dedicednu Indians of California" based in Laguna Beach, a charge that brings great laughter from the courtroom.

Judge Kroeber declares that "Ishi names a very remote tribe with no immediate evidence of his descent and that, clearly, is a burden under the provisions of the new law." In Ishi's defense, Saxton Pope argues that "my client is more tribal than anyone in the country" despite the fact that Ishi makes arrowheads out of broken bottles. For support, Pope points out the spurious (and romantically racist) evidence that Ishi has wide feet, "would rather not wear shoes," and has leather thongs in his ears, none of which counts for much in court. In desperation, Pope then adds, "Ishi never heard of Christmas," but Ashe as prosecutor replies in Vizenoresque language that "The absence is not a presence of character." Finally, Pope introduces Ishi's wood duck stories as the ultimate evidence of his client's tribal identity, arguing " . . . oral stories are none other than a real character, the character of tribal remembrance, the character that heard and remembered the wood duck stories." As Ishi sings "Winotay, winotay, winotay," Pope begins the wood duck stories that (the actual) Ishi liked to tell in his museum home, stories that could take seven hours in the telling and be told only after dark.

Clearly, Judge Kroeber has a humanitarian and philosophical bent. This Kroeber is the man who, at the time of Ishi's death, wrote, "As to disposal of the body, I must ask you . . . to yield nothing at all under any circumstances. If there is any talk about the interests of science, say for me that science can go to hell. We propose to stand by our friends . . . ." This philosophical judge, who bears the name of the anthropologist whom some might consider "Ishi's" inventor, asks rhetorically, "What is criminal in the imagination of a tribal artist?" before adding, "Colonial inventions are criminal, not tribal survivance." A few lines later, the judge ponders, "Consumer fraud? Or is this a case of cultural romance?" to which the court clerk Prince Chambers replies, "Who knows the difference in Santa Fe?" When the prosecutor says, "The government protects the true Indian," Kroeber responds with, "Then the Indian, not the buyer, must beware."

Forced to make a ruling, Judge Kroeber finds that "Clearly the performance of wood duck stories, no matter how great the audience response, does not establish tribal character or identity under the provisions of the Indian Arts and Crafts Act of 1990." He then turns directly to the audience to ask, "What would you do under the circumstances?"

Act Four and the play both end with Kroeber ruling that "Ishi is real and the law is not. Therefore, my decision is to declare that the accused is his own tribe. Ishi is his own sovereign tribal nation. . . . Ishi, the man so named, has established a tribal character in a museum and in his endless wood duck stories. . . . Ishi is an artist, he is our remembrance of justice, and that is his natural character." Ishi becomes "a native presence" in the play, "not the romance of an aesthetic absence or victimry" (Vizenor 1998:15).

"Ishi and the Wood Ducks" manages in brief compass to suggest nearly all of the major issues found in Vizenor's significant body of published work. Among these are the colonial invention of Indianness; the "word wars" that characterize the five-hundred-year-old Euramerican program to fix the Indian within what, in *Bearheart*, Vizenor calls a "terminal creed"; the posturing of those "variona-tives" who (like Zero Larkin) would pose within the dominant culture's con-structed definition of universal Indianness; the "archival" erasure of the Native in photographs of the *indian*; and the "survivance" of the "postindian" within oral stories. In foregrounding the issue of Ishi's undocumentable identity, Vizenor illustrates sharply his contention in *Manifest Manners* that "The Indian is the simulation of the absence, an unreal name; however, the misnomer has a curious sense of legal standing. Some of the definitions are ethnological, racial, literary, and juristic sanctions." Vizenor concludes this discussion of Indian identity in *Manifest Manners* with the observations, "Clearly, the simulations of tribal names, the absence of a presence in a mere tribal misnomer, cannot be sustained by legislation or legal maneuvers" (Vizenor 1994:14).

In Ishi's defense counsel's argument that "oral stories are none other than a real character, the character of tribal remembrance," Vizenor echoes his posi-tion in "Ishi Obscura" that "The natural development of the oral tradition is not a written language. The notion, in the literature of dominance, that the oral ad-vances to the written, is a colonial reduction of natural sound, heard stories, and the tease of shadows in tribal remembrance" (Vizenor 1994:72). In "Ishi and the Wood Ducks," the written advances to the oral, and the co-constructive audience – brought immediately onto the stage by both Ishi and Judge Kroe-ber – become the active jury challenged to deconstruct the *indian* to find the lonesome survivor who, in good humor, honored his sacred name and pre-sented himself in a museum as "one of the people" (see note 3). In Vizenor's play, in short, Ishi the man is made complete, both in and out of the drama di-rected by America and, at long last, restored to himself.

NOTES

1. For a definition of "*indian*" vs. Indian, see Vizenor 1988, especially pp. 14–16.

2. Vizenor (1988:x) defines trickster as a "comic holotrope: the whole figuration; an unbroken interior landscape that beams various points of view in temporal reveries."

3. [Sapir's *Yana Texts* indicates that "one of the people" in Yana would be *yaahi*, whereas *ishi* means "a man." *Eds.*]

4. "The *varionative* is an uncertain curve of native antecedence; obscure notions of native sovenance and presence" (Vizenor 1998:15).

5. In "Ishi Obscura," Vizenor describes Phoebe Apperson Hearst as the creator of the Department and Museum of Anthropology at the University of California (Vizenor 1994:131).

6. U.S. Department of the Interior – Indian Arts and Crafts Board, "Summary and Text of Title I, Public Law 101–644 [104 Stat. 4662], Act of 11,29/90."

REFERENCES

Bakhtin, Mikhail. 1981. *The dialogic imagination: four essays by M. M. Bakhtin.* Ed. Michael Holquist. Tr. Caryl Emerson and Michael Holquist. Austin: University of Texas.

Barthes, Roland. 1981. *Camera lucida: reflections on photography.* New York: Hill and Wang.

Daily Californian. 1985. October 25, p. 1.

Fanon, Frantz. 1967. *Black skin, white masks.* New York: Grove.

Gandhi, Leela. 1998. *Postcolonial theory: a critical introduction.* New York: Columbia University.

Harvey, David. 1989. *The condition of postmodernity: an enquiry into the origins of cultural change.* Oxford: Basil Blackwell.

Hoobler, Dorothy, and Thomas Hoobler. 1980. *Photographing on the frontier.* New York: G. P. Putnam's Sons.

Vizenor, Gerald. 1988. *The trickster of liberty: tribal heirs to a wild baronage.* Minneapolis: University of Minnesota.

———. 1994. *Manifest manners: Postindian warriors of survivance.* Hanover: Wesleyan University/University Press of New England.

———. 1995. Ishi and the wood ducks. In *Native American literature: a brief introduction and anthology.* Ed. Gerald Vizenor. New York: HarperCollins, pp. 299–336.

———. 1998. *Fugitive poses: Native American Indian scenes of absence and presence.* Lincoln: University of Nebraska.

21

The Healer

Maidu Artist Frank Day's Vision of Ishi

REBECCA J. DOBKINS

The early images of Ishi at the time of his 1911 appearance in Oroville depict a shorn, hungry, apparently weak man, desperately alone. Maidu Indian artist Frank Day (1902–1976) portrays an encounter with Ishi just days before his capture in his 1973 painting, *Ishi and Companion at Iamin Mool* (Figure 21.1). In the scene Ishi is a healer, not a victim, attempting to save his Yahi companion. Day's account of this scene from his childhood is a telling of the Ishi story that profoundly differs from the popular version.

Frank Day was born in 1902 at Berry Creek, California, near Oroville, where Ishi was later captured. Frank Day's father, Billy Day, was one of the last headmen of the Konkow Maidu, whose aboriginal territory was adjacent to that of the Yahi. The elder Day lived until 1922, passing on his traditional knowledge to his son. Drawing from this knowledge, Frank Day began in the 1950s to paint narrative images of Konkow Maidu culture and continued until his death in 1976. Day's nearly two hundred paintings, many of which are accompanied by audiotaped narratives, are at once expressions of Maidu folklore and the artist's creative interpretations of these traditions.[1]

Much of Frank Day's work comes from his artistic imagination, and few of his depictions, including this portrayal of Ishi, can be corroborated by the historian's conventional tools. Yet I suggest that the verification of the story is less important than its message: another way of *seeing* Ishi exists. Of course it is possible, even probable, that the events of Day's childhood took place as he told them, but more crucially, Day as artist gives us a vision of Ishi in a powerful role as healer.

Frank Day told the story of the encounter in a 1973 interview with Herb Puffer of Folsom, California, an art trader who promoted Day's work in the latter part of the artist's life. According to Day, on August 2, 1911, he and his father

Fig. 21.1. *Ishi and Companion at Iamin Mool* by Frank Day, 1973. Oil on canvas, 24 × 36 in. Reproduced with permission from the private collection of Herb and Peggy Puffer. Photographer: M. Lee Fatherree.

were walking along the Feather River, a few miles outside of Oroville, at a place called Iamin Mool (Day's spelling of the Konkow Maidu term). The father and son came upon two strangers, one of whom was later known as Ishi. Because this river, like so many others through Indian lands, has been dammed, the scene of the encounter is now under water, but at the time it marked the confluence of the middle and south forks of the Feather. The fact that Iamin Mool is now under water is deeply ironic: the scene is both literally and metaphorically submerged and inaccessible. We know of it only through Day's oral and visual narration; similarly, Ishi's past and that of the Yahi is submerged, accessible primarily through Ishi's stories and artifacts.

Ishi and Companion at Iamin Mool reconstructs Day's childhood memory and envisions Ishi (in Day's words) as a "small-like" but "powerful" healer. Ishi kneels at left over his companion, who appears to be a fellow Yahi because of his similar hairstyle, clothing, and earrings. The wounded companion, with a gash or gunshot in his abdomen, assists Ishi in an elaborate healing procedure by holding a heated stone against the wound. Ishi grasps a rope made of twisted grass and, according to Day, is about to dip the stone in a lava rock basket full of heated water. When startled, he looks up squarely at the observers, Billy and then nine-year-old Frank. At the left of the painting, a small disk of silica stone catches the sun's rays and directs them into the lava basket for heating the water. In the background, the Sierra Nevada foothills situate us outside Oroville.

Frank Day's August 1911 encounter with Ishi and his companion suggests a possible answer to one of the mysteries surrounding Ishi's circumstances just before his capture. Ishi may have had a Yahi companion up until the time of his appearance, rather than being on his own for years as has been asserted. If the companion was indeed mortally wounded and subsequently died, Ishi very well could have gone into mourning and allowed himself to be discovered.

Yet Day's narrative explanation of the painting raises other questions. Excerpts from Herb Puffer's interview with Frank Day in 1973 follow.[2]

FRANK DAY: I was coming down with my father on the date August second, 1911. And we came to the junction, a place where the Feather River and the Middle Fork and the South Fork combine stream[s]. It's based about seven miles out of Oroville. It's under water at the present time.

Now, [at] this particular spot was this man and this buddy of his. They were resting under a large live oak tree that was on a UC, Utah and Company, roadway, a mule trail where they haul supplies in to the railroad tracks for blasting powder.

It was on this bend, there right underneath where the lookout station is now at Oroville Dam. A little north of it, and down underneath the water, about 300 feet down, this live oak grew. That's Kelly Ridge there.

HERB PUFFER: Would that tree still be there?

DAY: No, it's all under water.

He [Ishi] stood up but his hair was not brushed. His hair is supposed to be loose. You know, like that [pointing to the painting]. Instead of down, like you see most painters paint. His hair was like that all the way around. It made him look large, or made his face look round. But he actually had a nice shaped face, but it was kinda long. I saw him in jail after that, too; but that was after they shorn him, you know, with scissors. He looked a little different then. He was the first man [of the two] that saw me. I saw him before he saw me.

PUFFER: Now, this was just pure accident? You and your father were out for a walk –

DAY: [Interrupts] My father and I were walking down [the road], August the second. That was nine days before he was captured. So, underneath this tree, on this UC road, this man was suffering, he couldn't get up. All he could do was turn over like that and look at me.

He was shot. And his hair was exactly the same [as Ishi's]. What he then wanted was to try to heal that wound. This was August, summer, it was very hot. We was on the track, we could see each other, I could see all the whites of his eyes. He could see mine. And he stood like a bear, looking right down. He stood up. He said something to Ishi and Ishi said something to him. And then right away, he laid straight out like that and long. And this strap from a dry limb was sticking out here, with a twisted grass rope. He had on that, tied two rocks, two stones. Because they didn't have fire, [he] caught that morning sun and placed silica stone over here. There's a lot of silica stone in that country. The sun shone on that silica stone, a large one like that, a fifty pound one. Well, you could pick one out, not just any. And placed it there, and place the basket over here. The sun rose up for an hour and a half, that sun shone on that silica stone, and in the basket was water. This basket is a basket that was formed by volcanic eruption.

PUFFER: This is something they would have been carrying with them?

DAY: Oh yes, it's not heavy. See those lava stones are light. They carried that for water. And in this particular place, this basket had that water and of course the sun was a constant stream of light going in with heat. It warmed the body of the basket, [and] the water inside. And he would dip that stone in there, and pull the [cord] over and prop that wound with another stone. And he was just able to hold the stone like that.

PUFFER: So he would use the stones alternatively, and keep one hot, is that it?

DAY: That's right. While this [one] was being used, this [other one] was in the water. So that happened. We didn't see this man no more. We never did see him no more.

PUFFER: Did you ever hear anything more about him?

DAY: I looked for that man, I walked that [road] many times, looked for their bones. I never did find any of it.

PUFFER: And you never heard any story about what happened to him?

DAY: Nothing, no. This is the last place I ever did hear of this man no more. It could be a woman.

PUFFER: That could've been a woman?

DAY: That could've been a woman.

PUFFER: And the person was dressed . . . in what?

DAY: There were no clothes on, with just that garment on. Just that coat. Their coats was identical. There were, these coats were made with, by muletail deer. They were green, yellow-green, brownish.

PUFFER: Were there any words spoken between you or your father and . . . ? Or did you just observe what he was doing?

DAY: No, and we left them. They didn't bother us and we didn't bother them. So we walked into Oroville, about three miles from there, in August.

We harvested at the Hazelbush Ranch, that's Henry Hazelbush ranch. That's thirteen miles south of Oroville, going down the river. We worked there and in September, I think, 11th, 12th, somewhere right along, I don't remember the date because I was with a lot of children and you don't remember too good. Anyhow, the peaches and the prunes were done. And when we came back up there Bill Fitch, he was the city marshal of Oroville at that time, 1911. He met my father and me on the street, in Oroville. He said to my father – oh, they knew one another – he said, he says, "We have an Indian over here that we'd like to find someone who could talk to him." And my father could speak several languages. So my father said, "Well, I'll go and see."

So when we went in there, this man, Ishi – I come aside of my father. You know, Indians don't, we don't, when we walk, we don't walk behind, we don't hide, you know. We want everybody to see us. So I walked aside of my father. He didn't look at my father; he looked at me, he recognized me. And I recognized him.

And I looked over every bit of his face: from his eyes, all of his face, clear on down. He had this same jacket on, but now it was clean. And he had an overall that the county issue[d]. And he had no shoes on. He still had the little buttons on.

PUFFER: The earrings?

DAY: Yeah, that jade, he had two on there. Still had that. He was a small-like man, but powerful, you know, strength. He was healthy and smiling, then.

Well, [my father] did talk to him, but they didn't understand one another. He tried to give him some sign language but [Ishi gave] no answer. Maybe because well, I know your son, your son know me. You didn't see me, or something like this. But my father saw.

My father told me a few days later, after we had this session at the big county jail with the sheriff and others, he said the reason I told you not to look at these people because there was lots of people with a pack on the back, cooking up all on that river, looking for gold. So he thought these people were looking for gold, too. But I knew they were not. They were Indians, because they showed the Indian face to you when they were looking at you.

That was in 1911, just about nine o'clock. Sun was coming out. We know that he went to San Francisco then. That was that day.

In this Frank Day narrative and painting, as in many others, there is a creative tension between documentary and visionary qualities. It does seem likely, for example, that Billy Day, as a speaker of Konkow Maidu and other north central California languages, was called in to try to communicate with Ishi. As far as the likeness of Ishi is concerned, Frank Day had access to photographs of Ishi and in fact painted another portrait of Ishi directly from a photograph. It is possible that, after the death of his companion and according to custom, Ishi singed off the long hair Day remembered and portrayed in the painting.

Other details remain puzzling. The healing procedure, as described by Day, is fantastical. Day's uncertainty about the gender of the companion is confusing. Clothing would perhaps provide a clue to gender, but oddly Day's narrative description of "coats made with . . . muletail deer" doesn't match the painting's visual depiction of garments that resemble the kind of coveralls Ishi was given to wear by those who found him. The Yahi did wear earrings, although certainly not "jade" ones as Day describes.

Ultimately, these questions of veracity give way to more central ones: Who tells Ishi's story? Who controls his images? The significance of *Ishi and Companion at Iamin Mool* is that it is the first known visual representation of Ishi by a California Indian, one that portrays him as an acting subject, not object, of history. Frank Day asks us to imagine Ishi's last days before his capture, as a small, powerful man working to save his last tribesman. The image highlights Ishi's status as a survivor and encourages a subtle yet critical shift in emphasis away from a story of victimization and toward the question of cultural survival. Day has given us another way of seeing Ishi.

NOTES

I would like to thank Herb Puffer of Pacific Western Traders in Folsom, CA, who generously encouraged not only Frank Day, but many other California Indian artists. He, along with Carla Hills, Frank LaPena, and Frank Tuttle have shared valuable information with me about Frank Day and the painting here discussed. I alone, however, am responsible for the interpretations presented.

1. Anthropologist Donald Jewell and his student Lyle Scott in the 1960s and art trader Herbert Puffer in the 1970s had the foresight to record Frank Day's interpretations of his paintings. Without their efforts, Day's images would be difficult to decode. A more complete account of Frank Day's life and art can be found in Rebecca J. Dobkins, *Memory and Imagination: The Legacy of Maidu Indian Artist Frank Day* (Oakland: Oakland Museum of California, 1997).

2. The interview was conducted by Herb Puffer at Pacific Western Traders in Folsom, California, on August 22, 1973. I transcribed the interview, and it is here published for the first time, with Herb Puffer's permission. Some material I judged to be repetitious or extraneous has been omitted, and clarifications are in brackets.

22

What Wild Indian?

FRANK TUTTLE

My images here are made to confront people, as a reminder that Native California people are survivors. Survival, I think, has its basis in the preservation of self – that who you are and what you are is unique and of value. Sacred, or treasured, or alarming symbols of our ancestral legacy and survival as tribal people are ever present for us. Although they may evoke uplifting memory or melancholic misery, these symbols remain ours to share.

With this image (Figure 22.1), I have concerned myself with Ishi in three ways. The framed central panel depicts the visage of Ishi as he was photographed soon after his appearance in Oroville, California, in 1911. I have always seen in this representation a survivor, a man who has seen his world fall away into madness and chaos, tribal geography and cosmology seemingly inert and hopelessly without meaning.

The image of Ishi as depicted by Concow painter Frank Day occupies the top central portion of my painting. This version of Ishi derives from Day's painting *Ishi at Iamin Mool,* which, I understand, conveys a moment from Day's youth as he and his father had a brief encounter with an Indian man (who, they later inferred, was Ishi), attempting to assist another, wounded Indian man. This encounter occurred several days prior to Ishi's Oroville appearance.

The third manner in which I concern myself with Ishi is through the rose bush Ishi is holding in one hand and the small fire he holds in the other. Both of these motifs represent me. In what way? In the sense of rebirth and continuity. From my very first encounter with Ishi, I felt a connection, and I have continually found his life path inspiring. I have chosen to find the beauty in that and to acknowledge it.

Ancestral memories need not be dredged from a fluid, murky past like water from a deep well. Experiences need only to pass and have a reason to remain to nurture memory.

Fig. 22.1. *What Wild Indian?* by Frank Tuttle. Oil, wood, mixed media. 18 × 20 in.
Collection of Ian and Patricia McGreal.

Of his pleasure at having What Wild Indian? *reproduced in this volume, Frank
Tuttle wrote:*

Initially, I like the thought of my question about Ishi continuing to confront viewers. The question asking "What Wild Indian?" may ignite viewers momentarily to
ask themselves this question and momentarily make note of their gut reaction.

Secondly, as a Native American I welcome occasions to speak to the perceptions of Native Americans over time and space. Ishi certainly represents such an
occasion for a variety of academic disciplines – disciplines which, when we seek
commonalty, can contribute to a larger appreciative picture of our humanity.

And, as a Concow Maidu artist, as a surviving descendant of Concow people, I
present Ishi as a nondescript icon, thereby bearing a burden for many California
Native Americans in the twenty-first century, a dreadful physical, spiritual, and
psychological burden, at times eased by self-resiliency and self-affirmation--qual-
ities that remind us as Native Americans what it means that we are the original
people of this land.

Appendix
The Condition of California Indians, 1906

An Act of Congress, June 30, 1905, authorized the Secretary of the Interior to investigate the condition of California Indians and report some plan for improving those conditions. Pursuant to this Act, Bureau of Indian Affairs Special Agent C. E. Kelsey "visited and personally inspected almost every Indian settlement between the Oregon line and the Mexican border." This appendix is excerpted from Kelsey's report to the Commissioner of Indian Affairs in 1906.

Your special agent finds an Indian population in California of a little more than 17,000, of which 5200 are reported as living upon reservations . . . Your special agent has examined their situation and cannot see that their condition is such as to be a matter of satisfaction either to the Government of the United States or to the people of California. The Indian population of California a century ago [is best estimated at] 260,000. . . . A decrease in the Indian population of 94 percent in a single century, and mostly within forty or fifty years, is certainly exceptional and would seem to be a fact in which we can neither take pride nor escape responsibility . . . .

The Act of Congress which provided for the settlement of the titles to Spanish and Mexican grants (in accord with the Treaty of Guadalupe Hidalgo which ceded California to the United States) imposed upon the commission appointed to make the settlement the duty of first setting apart for Indian use all lands occupied by them. It was the duty of the commission to investigate and confirm the Indian title wherever Indians occupied lands within . . . a Spanish or Mexican grant . . . [I have] found but two cases out of several hundred grants where this was done. . . .

The United States has always recognized, and the Supreme Court has held, that the Indians have a right to occupy the land, . . . a right which can be canceled only by mutual agreement. . . . no reason has been advanced why the California Indians alone, of all the Indians in America, should receive no compensation for their lands. . . .

In 1849 the great gold rush began. Within a year or two a considerable portion of the State was overrun by probably two hundred thousand miners. . . . A majority of them had inherited the prejudices and the stories of two hundred years of border warfare with the Indians . . . Opposed to the miners was a practically defenseless people (they had no firearms) . . . Under the circumstances, it is not strange that one of the most shameful chapters in American history ensued . . . The modus operandi of these affairs [slaughters of Indians] was much the same. The Indian camp would be surrounded and rushed, usually at dawn, men in ambush would shoot every Indian who appeared. At first few were spared, but as no one wished to kill the children, they were usually sold into slavery.

But neither the open slaughter of the California Indians . . . nor the ravages of disease, nor the effects of drunkenness . . . can explain the decrease of 94 percent in the number of California Indians in little more than one generation. We are so familiar with the idea that the Indian race is fading away before our own that inquiry is seldom made into the details of the process by which we fade them. In the case of the California Indians, the most potent factor has been . . . the progressive absorption of the Indians' every means of existence. In aboriginal days . . . each tribe was restricted within narrow limits. Game was abundant, but did not hold a very great part in this bill of fare . . . Fish formed a much greater share of their diet . . . the Indians also made a large use of edible roots . . . The largest single item in their menu was composed of acorns and other nuts. The Indians grind the acorns, leach out the bitter principle and make various forms of mush and bread, both nutritious and palatable . . . The first effect of the occupation of the land by the miners was the muddying of the streams by mining operations and the killing or frightening away of the game. The mining population soon needed gardens, and about the only land suitable was that where the edible roots grew. The stock industry followed very soon, and even the oak trees were fenced in and forbidden to the Indians, as the acorns were needed for hogs. Later the era of wheat came and arable lands passed into private ownership. The Indians were thus reduced from a state of comparative comfort to one of destitution. The Indian Bureau did attempt for a time to protect the Indians and several small reservations were set aside by Executive Order. [But] only four reservations in Northern California were finally saved to the Indians [with a total population of 1,720]. The rest of the Northern California Indians who have kept the peace and killed nobody have received nothing but writs of eviction.

At first the Indians occupied pretty fair land and had usually neat little gardens and orchards, especially peach trees. These tidy little places would attract the attention of some frontiersman who would then file on the place and summarily kick the Indian out . . . It is not strange that the Northern California Indians have ceased to try to have gardens, when any appearance of thrift is warrant for their ejection . . . Most of the Indians have now been crowded out of anything like good soil and are found in waste places not having value enough to attract any one else. Many cases are known . . . where white men have deliberately diverted a stream of water from the Indian who could do nothing but watch his trees die and his garden dry up, and be forced to abandon his holding.[1]

Some Indians are settled in little villages called in California rancherias. The sanitary condition of the Indian rancherias is bad, but the feeling of helplessness and despair is worse. Most of the Indians seem to have lost all hope of escape from their present situation and have become familiar with the idea that they will all die off soon. I estimate that 1,700 families with nearly 6,000 souls are dangerously near the famine line . . . The healthy and able-bodied can survive a period of starvation but[, in] the weakened state caused by insufficient nutrition, almost any disease, even common colds, will carry off most of the children in the settlement . . . the proportion of children is small, although births are numerous.

The responsibility of the National Government for the present condition of the non-reservation Indians of California seems clear. Had the Government given these Indians the same treatment as it did other Indians in the United States, their condition today would be very different. No amount of money can repay these Indians for the years of misery, despair, and death which the Governmental policy has inflicted upon them . . . the Northern California Indians have not had a "square deal," . . . It is not too late to do belated justice . . . The Indian Appropriation Bill for the fiscal year 1906 contained an item providing for this investigation and appropriating the sum of $10,000 to cover the expenses, and for the support and civilization of the Northern Indians of California, for 1906. Your special agent would recommend that the unexpended portion of the appropriation be re-appropriated in such form that it can be applied to the purchase of land but not to establishing more reservations. Some of the past reservation experience in California has been so harrowing that the Indians fear reservations above all things.

NOTES

1. As Kelsey wrote to President Theodore Roosevelt on April 10, 1905, "If any tract has escaped the Anglo-Saxon hunger for land, if any quarter section has not been included in any Spanish or Mexican grant, homestead, preemption, railway-land grant, mining claim, stone claim, desert land claim . . . you may be perfectly sure that is because the land is supposed to be valueless for any purpose" [at page 119 of Robert F. Heizer, ed., *Federal Concern About the Conditions of California Indians, 1853 to 1913: Eight Documents* (Socorro NM: Ballena, 1979)].

Suggested Readings

The following bibliography is intended to assist nonspecialists to pursue matters related to Ishi raised by contributions to this volume. The writers most often cited in the foregoing pages are, of course, Alfred and Theodora Kroeber. In addition to those already cited, there are many other items from Alfred Kroeber's immense bibliography relevant to his experiences with Ishi. Among some of the often overlooked of these is "The Anthropology of California" (1908), revealing Kroeber's early view of his professional functions, which in some essentials changed little over the years. But later studies reveal a steady development and refinement of his understanding of ethnographic possibilities and problems. His views seem to have been significantly influenced by his three-decade association with a remarkable Yurok man, Robert Spott, who collaborated with him in some important publications, such as "Yurok Narratives" (1942). "Indians of California" (1914) focuses on postcontact relations between California Indians and Europeans. A 532-item bibliography (Gibson and Rowe 1961) was published in the *American Anthropologist*, although there are numerous subsequent posthumous publications, such as the monumental *Yurok Myths* (1976) and, as late as 1998, the handsome volume *The Archaeology and Pottery of Nazca, Peru*.

Theodora Kroeber's *Ishi in Two Worlds* (1961) was her first attempt (at the age of 60) at biography and history; the latest edition (University of California Press, 2002) contains a new foreword by Karl Kroeber that includes details of the circumstances, especially the decisive role played by Robert Heizer, that led Theodora Kroeber to write the book. In "The Hunter, Ishi" (1962), she contrasts Ishi's manner of hunting as contrary to modern hunting practices with the essential similarity between his modes of fishing and those of contemporary anglers to highlight her interest in what makes adapting to an alien culture possible or very difficult. In "About History" (1963), she describes the historical method she adopted for *Ishi in Two Worlds* and details her difficulties in writing the book. Particularly interesting is her attention to imagination in historical reconstruction. Imagination is important in her *Alfred Kroeber: A Personal Configuration* (1970), which, as the title warns, is not conventional biography – as is apparent in the slipperiness of her datings. She wanted her editorial collaboration with Robert Heizer (Heizer and Kroeber 1979) to encourage new research into all phases of Ishi's experience. This book was an outgrowth of an earlier successful editorial collaboration with Heizer and Albert S. Elsasser, *Drawn From Life* (Kroeber et al. 1977), which reproduces (with superb clarity) virtually all surviving representation by whites of California Indians from 1599 to the mid-1880s, accompanied by commentaries perceptive and sensitive to both the artists and photographers and their subjects.

Burrill, Richard. 2001. *Ishi rediscovered.* Sacramento: The Anthro Company. This sustained effort in local historical research raises pertinent questions as to contacts between local whites and Yahi/Yana in the early twentieth century.

Cook, Sherburne. 1976. *Conflict between the California Indians and white civilization.* Berkeley: University of California. This detailed history is the fruit of research by a distinguished biologist-historian.

Curtin, Jeremiah. [1898] 2002. *Creation myths of primitive America.* Introduction by Karl Kroeber. Santa Barbara: ABC-CLIO. The largest collection of translations of Yana myths outside of Sapir's, collected in the 1880s, it includes an accurate description of the wanton killing of Yana in the 1860s.

Darnell, Regna. 1998. *And along came Boas: continuity and revolution in Americanist anthropology.* Amsterdam: J. Benjamin. This work traces confluences and oppositions in methods and theoretical debates among American anthropologists and linguists in the late-nineteenth and early-twentieth centuries.

Deacon, Delsey. 1997. *Elsie Clews Parsons: inventing modern life.* Chicago: University of Chicago Press. This work gives a good account of the relations, personal and professional, between Parsons and Alfred Kroeber in the years following Ishi's death.

de Laguna, Frederica, ed. [1960] 2002. *American Anthropology, 1888–1920: papers from the "American Anthropologist."* Lincoln: University of Nebraska Press. This is an excellent source for tracing development of anthropological methods and theories.

Gibson, Ann J., and John H. Rowe. 1961. A bibliography of the publications of Alfred Louis Kroeber. *American Anthropologist* 63(5): 1060–1087.

Golla, Victor, ed. 1984. *The Sapir-Kroeber correspondence: letters between Edward Sapir and A. L. Kroeber, 1905–1925.* Berkeley: University of California, Department of Anthropology. This volume contains few specific references to Ishi and Yahi culture, but it offers profound insight into the intellectual and emotional life of both men, especially the period 1916–25. Golla's thumbnail biographies of people referred to and summaries of issues and ideas under discussion are invariably accurate, cogent, and vivid.

Heizer, Robert F., ed. 1978. *California*. Handbook of North American Indians (William C. Sturtevant, general editor), Vol. 8. Washington DC: Smithsonian Institution. This book is comprehensive – an indispensable resource.

———, ed. 1993. *Destruction of California Indians: a collection of documents from the period 1847–1865*. Lincoln: University of Nebraska . This is a valuable if sickening collection of documents, many from the National Archives, detailing slavery, massacre, scalping, indenture, and sexual crimes against Indians.

Heizer, Robert F., and Alan F. Almquist, eds. 1971. *The other Californians: prejudice and discrimination under Spain, Mexico, and the United States to 1920*. Berkeley: University of California. This work is especially useful for documenting early history, often ignored.

Heizer, Robert F., and Theodora Kroeber. 1979. *Ishi, the last Yahi: a documentary history.* Berkeley: University of California.

Hoxie, Frederick E. 1984. *A final promise: the campaign to assimilate the Indian, 1880–1920*. Lincoln: University of Nebraska. This careful and thorough account makes brief reference to Ishi.

Jacobsen, Bruce, and Edward D. Ives, eds. 1996. *The world observed.* Urbana: University of Illinois. This volume comprises self-analyses of recent fieldworks by distinguished ethnographers and folklorists. Especially relevant to Ishi is Barre Toelken's "From Enlightenment to Realization in Navajo Fieldwork," pp. 6–17.

Kroeber, Alfred. 1908. The anthropology of California. *Science* n.s. 17: 281–290. February.

———. 1914. Indians of California. In *History of California*, Vol 5. Ed. Zoeth Skinner Eldredge. New York: Century, 119–138.

———. 1942. Yurok narratives. *University of California Publications in American Archaeology and Ethnology* 35(9): 143–256.

———. 1976. *Yurok myths.* Berkeley: University of California.

———. 1998. *The archaeology and pottery of Nazca, Peru: the final report of Kroeber's 1926 expedition.* Ed. Patrick H. Carmichael. Walnut Creek CA: Altamira Press, for the Field Museum of Chicago.

Kroeber, Theodora. 1961. *Ishi in two worlds.* Berkeley: University of California.

———. 1962. The hunter, Ishi. *The American Scholar* 31(3): 408–418.

———. 1963. About history. *Pacific Historical Review* 32(1): 1–6.

———. 1970. *Alfred Kroeber: a personal configuration.* Berkeley: University of California.

Kroeber, Theodora, Robert F. Heizer, and Albert S. Elsasser. 1977. *Drawn from life: California Indians in pen and brush.* Socorro NM: Ballena.

Merton, Thomas. 1976. *Ishi means man.* Greensboro NC: Unicorn Press. The essays on American Indians in this volume include, notably, "Ishi: A Meditation" (first published in 1968 in *The Catholic Worker*), a response to *Ishi in Two Worlds* – a book Merton says "that *must* be read, and perhaps more than once," because it offers insight into causes of spiritual impoverishment of modern American life.

Mihesuah, Devon A., ed. 2000. *Repatriation reader: Who owns American Indian remains?* Lincoln: University of Nebraska. This work presents a clear discussion of central issues, with attention to a number of important cases, and a fair hearing is given to all viewpoints.

Pope, Saxton T. 1920. The medical history of Ishi. *University of California Publications in American Archaeology and Ethnology* 13(5): 175–213. This is a detailed report by Pope and half a dozen other doctors who attended Ishi.

Rawls, James J. 1984. *Indians of California: the changing image.* Norman: University of Oklahoma. This is a sensitive and well-informed history from the mid-nineteenth century well into the 1920s.

Ridge, John Rollin (Yellowbird). [1854] 1955. *The life and adventures of Joaquin Murietta, the celebrated California bandit.* Republished with an introduction by Joseph Henry Jackson. Norman: University of Oklahoma. This was the first novel by an American Indian. Jackson's excellent introduction explores the probability of Murietta having been not purely fictional and then describes how Ridge's fiction has affected California history.

Rolle, Andrew F. 1998. *California: a history,* 5th ed. Wheeling: Harlan Davidson. This work is an inclusive, balanced history.

Sapir, Edward. 1910. Yana texts. *University of California Publications in American Archaeology and Ethnology* 9(1): 1–235. This is the largest collection of Yana texts (obtained in 1907) with both interlinear and free translations, including the complete Batwi version of "Coyote and His Sister," analyzed in contrast to Ishi's telling in Chapter 17 of this volume.

Thoresen, T. H. 1975. Paying the piper and calling the tune: the beginnings of academic anthropology in California. *Journal of the History of the Behavioral Sciences* 11:257–275. This valuable pioneering study has been significantly deepened by Grace Buzaljko's research.

Waterman, Thomas Talbot. 1918. The Yana Indians. *University of California Publications in American Archaeology and Ethnology* 13(2): 35–102. A brief, personally informed remembrance of Ishi is included in this longest study of Yana culture (reprinted in the indispensable Heizer and Kroeber 1979).

Washburn, Wilcomb E., ed. 1988. *History of Indian-white relations.* Handbook of North American Indians (William C. Sturtevant, general editor), Vol. 4. Washington DC: Smithsonian Institution. This volume contains well-informed essays and extensive bibliographies on all aspects of the subject.

Contributors

RACHEL ADAMS is assistant professor of English at Columbia University. Her book *Sideshow USA: Freaks and the American Cultural Imagination* was published by the University of Chicago Press in 2001.

KAREN BIESTMAN, of Cherokee descent, earned her law degree from the University of California, Berkeley, and has served as dean of students at Stanford's Law School. She is currently Lecturer in American Studies at the University of California, Berkeley, and also director of the California Indian Museum and Cultural Center in San Francisco.

STANLEY H. BRANDES is professor and former chairman of the Anthropology Department at the University of California, Berkeley.

GRACE WILSON BUZALJKO was editor of the Department of Anthropology at the University of California, Berkeley, for a decade and a half and is currently completing a history of the Berkeley Department.

REBECCA J. DOBKINS is assistant professor of anthropology and curator of Native American Art at Willamette University, Salem, Oregon. She curated the exhibition *Memory and Imagination: The Legacy of Maidu Indian Artist Frank Day* for the Oakland Museum of California in 1997 and is the author of the accompanying exhibition catalog. Her research has enabled her to mount several exhibitions featuring Native American artists.

GEORGE M. FOSTER is now retired after distinguished service in the Smithsonian Institution and the Anthropology Department at the University of California, Berkeley, where he served as chairman. In addition to his pioneering work in medical and applied anthropology and his research with peasant communities and studies in the historical dimensions of social change, he has devoted much time to consulting on foreign aid projects aimed at social and economic development.

VICTOR GOLLA is professor of Native American studies at Humboldt State University in California and is editor of the important *Newsletter of the Society for the Study of Indigenous Languages of the Americas*. He was responsible for founding the project to edit and publish material collected from Ishi by Edward Sapir.

LEANNE HINTON is professor and chair of the Department of Linguistics at the University of California, Berkeley. She has worked on texts of Ishi for more than a decade and was a founder of Advocates for Indigenous California Languages Survival, an effective organization devoted to preserving and reclaiming Native California languages.

IRA JACKNIS is associate research anthropologist at the Phoebe Hearst Museum of Anthropology at the University of California, Berkeley. The primary focus of his continuing research is on the history of ethnographic representation, including artifact collecting, photography, and sound recording.

CLIFTON KROEBER is Norman Bridge Professor of History emeritus at Occidental College in Los Angeles. He has published studies of the history of colonial Peru, of the Río De Plata region, of independent Mexico, and of Native Americans of the Colorado region.

KARL KROEBER is Mellon Professor in the Humanities at Columbia University and emeritus editor of *Studies in American Indian Literatures*. His recent publications include *Artistry in Native American Myths* and a new edition of Jeremiah Curtin's *Creation Myths of Primitive America*, a collection of Yana and Wintu myths.

HERBERT LUTHIN teaches in the English Department at Clarion University of Pennsylvania. He has been working on Yana and Yahi language since he was a graduate student in linguistics at the University of California, Berkeley. He recently edited *Surviving through the Days*, a critical anthology of Native California oral literature.

LOUIS OWENS (Choctaw-Cherokee) was a distinguished novelist and professor of English and Native American studies at the University of California, Davis.

JEAN PERRY, professor of Native American studies at Humboldt State University, has been analyzing and translating Ishi texts for more than fifteen years.

NANCY SCHEPER-HUGHES is professor of anthropology at the University of California, Berkeley. Her publications include *Saints, Scholars and Schizophrenics: Mental Illness in Rural Ireland* and *Death without Weeping: The Violence of Everyday Life in Brazil.*

M. STEVEN SHACKLEY is research archaeologist and director of the Archaeological XRF Laboratory at the Phoebe A. Hearst Museum of Anthropology at the University of California, Berkeley.

STUART SPEAKER is an officer in the Repatriation Office of the Department of Anthropology in the National Museum of Natural History of the Smithsonian Institution in Washington DC.

ORIN STARN is associate professor in the Department of Cultural Anthropology at Duke University. His research has focused on Native North America and Latin America, and his publications include *Nightwatch: The Politics of Protest in the Andes.*

GARY STRANKMAN recently retired as Presiding Justice, First District Court of Appeal, San Francisco, California. Justice Strankman is a crossblood raised on the Makah Reservation, Neah Bay, Washington.

FRANK TUTTLE (Concow-Maidu) is a widely exhibited Native California artist currently living and painting in Ukiah, California.

GERALD VIZENOR (Anishinaabe) is the Richard and Rhoda Goldman Distinguished Professor of American Studies at the University of California, Berkeley. He has published more than twenty books about Native American literature and history. His most recent books are *Fugitive Poses: Native American Indian Scenes of Absence and Presence* and *Chancers*, a novel of native repatriation at the University of California.

JACE WEAVER (Cherokee) is an associate professor of religion at the University of Georgia. He is the author or editor of many books in Native American studies, most recently *Turtle Goes to War: Of Military Commissions, the Constitution, and American Indian Memory.*

Index